Nigel Nicolson was the youngest son of Vita Sackville-West and Harold Nicolson. He lived until his death in 2004 at Sissinghurst Castle in Kent, where his parents made their world-famous garden. He was a publisher, a Member of Parliament, an editor and the author of many books on history, politics, architecture and literature.

Portrait of a Marriage

NIGEL NICOLSON

WEIDENFELD & NICOLSON

A W&N PAPERBACK

First published in Great Britain in 1973
by George Weidenfeld & Nicolson Ltd
This paperback edition published in 1992
by Weidenfeld & Nicolson,
an imprint of Orion Books Ltd,
Carmelite House, 50 Victoria Embankment,
London EC4Y 0DZ

An Hachette UK company

19 20

A CIP catalogue record for this book
is available from the British Library.

ISBN 978-1-8579-9000-7

Filmset in Bembo by
Selwood Systems, Midsomer Norton

Printed and bound in Great Britain by Clays Ltd, Elcograf S.p.A.

www.orionbooks.co.uk

To S.A.

CONTENTS

ILLUSTRATIONS

1   Pepita at the height of her dancing career

2   Knole, seen from the air *Aerofilms*

3   Victoria Sackville-West [Vita's mother] in 1897

4   Sir John Murray Scott ['Seery']

5   Vita and her mother in 1900

6   A bust of Lady Sackville by Auguste Rodin *Musée Rodin*

7   Portrait of Vita in 1910 by Laszlo *Sissinghurst Castle*

8   Harold Nicolson, Vita, Rosamund Grosvenor and Lord Sackville in July 1913

9   The wedding of Vita and Harold in the chapel at Knole 1 October 1913

10 Violet Trefusis in the early 1920s

11 Violet Trefusis, a portrait by Jacques-Emile Blanche *National Portrait Gallery*

12 Harold in 1919

13 Vita in 1919

14 Harold dictates to a secretary at the Paris Peace Conference

15 Long Barn, near Sevenoaks

16 Geoffrey Scott at the Villa Medici, Florence

FOREWORD TO THE ORIGINAL EDITION

When my mother, Vita Sackville-West, died in 1962, it was my duty as her executor to go through her personal papers. She was careful about such things, and had filed everything of importance, including all her letters to and from Harold Nicolson during the fifty years of their engagement and marriage, and all her own diaries and the diaries of her mother, Lady Sackville. In the forty pinewood drawers of a large Italian cupboard I found hundreds of letters from the friends who had meant most to her since her childhood. At the time I read very little, making a mental note that while all the material existed for a full record of her life, it should be allowed to simmer.

I took a final look round her sitting-room in the tower at Sissinghurst (a room which I had entered only half a dozen times in the previous thirty years), and came upon a locked Gladstone bag lying in the corner of the little turret-room which opens off it. The bag contained something – a tiara in its case, for all I knew. Having no key, I cut the leather from around its lock to open it. Inside was a large notebook in a flexible cover, page after page filled by her neat pencilled manuscript. I carried it to her writing-table and began to read. The first few pages were abortive drafts of a couple of short stories. The sixth page was headed '23 July 1920', followed by a narrative in the first person which continued for eighty more. I read it through to the end without stirring from her table. It was an autobiography written when she was aged twenty-eight, a confession, an attempt to purge her mind and heart of a love which had possessed her, a love for another woman, Violet Trefusis.

The simplicity of it, its candour, the extraordinary sequence of events which it unfolded, her implicit plea for forgiveness and compassion, for the strength to resist further temptation, stirred me deeply. I had long known the barest outlines of the story (but not from her) and here was every detail of it, written with scarcely an erasure or correction at a moment when the wound was still fresh and painful. Although her narrative began uncertainly with a rambling account of her childhood, when she came to the heart of her problem it grew in power and intensity, sharpened by a novelist's instinctive variation of mood and speed, almost as if it were not her own experience that she was describing but another's.

I never showed it to my father, although in the first paragraph she wrote that he was the only person whom she could then trust to read it with understanding. My mother's death had shaken him so dreadfully that this reminder of the crisis of their marriage might have increased his misery intolerably, and I feared that he might destroy it, or it him. When I quoted in the Introduction to his published Diaries a few innocuous passages from the auto-biography describing her childhood at Knole and their early married life, he never asked to see the rest of it. Now I think that I should have shown it to him when the agony of her loss had been transmuted into numb acceptance of it. He might well have agreed with me that this was a document unique in the vast literature of love, and among the most moving pieces that she ever wrote; that far from tarnishing the memory of her, it burnished it; and that one day, perhaps, it should be published.

Let not the reader condemn in ten minutes a decision which I have pondered for ten years. In Harold Nicolson's lifetime, and in Violet's, no question of publication could arise. He died in 1968; Violet in 1972. I consulted several people, above all my brother Benedict, and Violet's close friend and literary executor, John N. Phillips, to whom I acknowledge my debt for his sympathetic attitude and for copies of certain letters. Both agreed to publication in the form which I suggested. A few of my parents' friends expressed misgivings, but most confirmed my growing conviction that in the 1970s an experience of this kind need no longer be regarded as shameful or unmentionable, for the autobiography was written with profound emotion, and has an integrity and validity of universal significance.

It is the story of two people who married for love and whose love deepened with every passing year, although each was constantly and by mutual consent unfaithful to the other. Both loved people of their own sex, but not exclusively. Their marriage not only survived infidelity, sexual incompatibilty and long absences, but became stronger and finer as a result. Each came to give the other full liberty without enquiry or reproach. Honour was rooted in dishonour. Their marriage succeeded because each found permanent and undiluted happiness only in the company of the other. If their marriage is seen as a harbour, their love-affairs were mere ports-of-call. It was to the harbour that each returned; it was there that both were based.

This book is therefore a panegyric of marriage, although it describes a marriage which was superficially a failure because it was incomplete. They achieved their ideal companionship only after a long struggle which was still not ended when Vita Sackville-West wrote the last words of her confession, but once achieved it was unalterable and life-long, and they made of it (as I wrote in the Introduction to my father's Diaries, without revealing the extent of their difficulties) one of the strangest and most successful unions that two gifted people have ever enjoyed.

Although Vita Sackville-West left no instructions about her autobiography, and as far as I know had never shown it to anybody, I believe that she wrote it with eventual publication in mind. It assumed an audience. She knew that I would find it after her death, but did not destroy it. She wrote it as a conscious work of art, in such a way that it would be intelligible to an outsider, and her use of pseudonyms is itself an indication that she expected, even hoped, that other eyes might one day read it, by this device safeguarding the reputation of her friends while risking her own. There are passages in the manuscript which suggest that the writing of it was for her much more than an act of catharis. She refers to 'possible readers' of it. She believes that 'the psychology of people like myself will be a matter of interest' when hypocrisy gives place to 'a spirit of candour which one hopes will spread with the progress of the world'. That time has come now, more than fifty years after she wrote those prophetic words, and I do not believe that she would deplore the revelation of her secret, knowing that it could help and encourage those similarly placed today.

However, to present the autobiography unexplained and without its sequel would do my parents less than justice, for it was written in the eighth year of a marriage which lasted forty-nine. I came to two conclusions: that it should be published as the first, though main, section of the complete story; and that because it is a story so exceptional, it needed confirmation and amplification, for which all material existed in the Italian cupboard and the files. The events which V. Sackville-West recounted could be retold as they appeared to other main actors in the drama – Harold Nicolson, Violet Trefusis, Lady Sackville – and to secondary characters like Rosamund Grosvenor, Denys Trefusis and Orazio Pucci, and in retrospect to myself, her son, who was only three years old when the climax was reached in a hotel at Amiens in February 1920. The contemporary letters and diaries throw a new light upon certain incidents and reveal others of which she was ignorant, but they utterly substantiate the truth of what she wrote. Her memory of these cataclysmic events was exact.

The story is told in five parts, two by her, three by myself. Parts 1 and 3 are her autobiography verbatim, altered only by its division into two separated sections (for reasons of balance and intelligibility), and by the substitution of real names for pseudonyms, which are given only when they first occur. Parts 2 and 4 are my commentaries upon it, to which I add essential new facts and quotations from letters and diaries. Part 5 is the justification of the whole book and of its title, for it summarizes the remaining years of her marriage, and shows, particularly in the context of my mother's brief love-affairs with Geoffrey Scott and Virginia Woolf, how my parents' love for each other survived all further threats to it, and made out of a non-marriage a marriage which succeeded beyond their dreams. If it does not show that, the book is a betrayal.

Nigel Nicolson
Sissinghurst Castle, Kent
April 1973

Portrait of a Marriage is a story of how love triumphed over infatuation. That was how I saw it when in 1962 I first read my mother's astonishing autobiography, and that was why, after ten years of self-questioning and questioning a few others, I decided to publish it. It is a love story, not the love between Vita Sackville-West and Violet Trefusis, as many people assumed, but between Vita and my father Harold. Her affair with Violet occupied three years, 1918–20, her marriage nearly fifty. The affair was the test of the marriage, and Vita, in writing about it when she was only twenty-eight, was celebrating the triumph that her marriage had survived the test. Harold, for his part, never exulted in it, because he never considered it a triumph. It was inevitable, like a young person's recovery from a dose of 'flu.

The story seemed to me noble in its conclusion, but I was well aware in 1973 that others might think its publication a new form of matricide. One reviewer, an American academic, criticized me for not confessing more openly how much I hated my mother: clearly the book was written in revenge. Let the reader assess the truth of that accusation from the pages that follow. That was not my problem. It was whether Vita would have wanted it published. In the Foreword I gave some of my reasons for deciding that she would have wanted it and since 1973 I have heard from one of her closest friends that she talked about her manuscript shortly before her death, saying that I would find it in her cupboard and she would trust my judgement about publication. I was comforted by this information, but did not trust it absolutely. More convincing to me was a closer examination of the text. She explains things that she would not need to explain to herself, her family or intimates: like 'We bought a country cottage where we spent the summer and Harold went up to London every day'; or, 'Edward, who was my cousin ten years younger than I'. Why tell us this, unless total strangers were expected to read it? Besides, I considered, it was probable that biographies would one day be written of Vita or Harold, or both, and both were. Victoria Glendinning and James Lees-Milne would know from many other sources, particularly Vita's and Harold's letters to each other, that the crisis of their marriage had culminated in Vita's elopement with Violet. It had been common gossip at the time, and had been rumoured many times since. The biographers could hardly ignore it. How much better, then, that they should learn the truth from Vita's own confession, her *De Profundis*, than from the speculations of other people, and that I should put the affair into the context of their whole marriage. It is not a salacious story. It bares the human heart but not the human body. But it is undeniably shocking.

There were critics who wrote that I should have suppressed it. The *Daily Express* declared that my treachery to my mother was repulsive, and Rebecca West that I should have stuffed her manuscript back into its Gladstone bag. Bernard Levin went further. He called the story 'ludicrous'; to him Vita's confession was 'the mooning of a schoolgirl who has a crush on the hockey mistress'. I should have burned it, he wrote. One remembers hostile criticism more vividly than praise. Looking through the reviews twenty years later, I find to my surprise that most were favourable, but I will quote only one, because it expresses exactly what I had intended, the verdict of Desmond Shawe-Taylor who knew Vita and Harold well: 'Let others mock', he wrote. 'The wild passion on the one side, the infinite patience on the other, coupled with the long, loving, creative union that ensued, seems to me moving and wonderful.' In the United States the book received an accolade from every critic except one, John Richardson, an Englishman. Distance, and unfamiliarity with the social scene in England seventy years ago, gave the book the quality of a novel. This couldn't be the story of real people. But it was.

When it was fictionalized by the BBC in 1990 as a four-part dramatization for television, I was not invited to draft the screenplay, rightly, as I had no experience of script-writing. The task was given to an elderly novelist, Penelope Mortimer, the mother-in-law of one of the producers. She had little sympathy with the main characters. To her, Vita, who won several major literary prizes and created the most famous garden in England, and Harold, who in his youth was the confidant of world statesmen, the author of forty books and the leading literary critic of his day, were 'silly people'. When I implored her to give the public some idea of their happiness before and after the brief Violet affair (which was the whole point and moral of the book), she thought it irrelevant. It should end, she thought, except for a misleading tailpiece, with Amiens. Her version was not so much the portrait of a marriage as the portrait of an affair. There was nothing in the film to indicate Vita's contrition, how she spent the rest of her life making up to Harold for the cruelty of those three years. Frank Kermode was right to sum it up as 'an ugly story with a happy ending'. Without the ending it was simply ugly.

I have never denied that Vita was cruel to my father, and it is no excuse that Violet was even crueller. There was nothing in Vita's behaviour to equal Violet's contemptuous treatment of her husband Denys, nor Violet's cynical attempt to destroy the marriage of her most intimate friend. Vita's ruthlessness was always qualified by guilt: Violet's never was. But what worried some readers more than their savagery was the two women's snobbishness. At their very first meeting, aged thirteen and eleven, they talked of nothing but their ancestry, a contest that Vita was bound to win as the daughter of Knole and the Sackvilles' only child. As she grew older, her indifference to people of humbler birth turned to tolerance, and tolerance to a slightly shamefaced awareness of her own advantages. All through her life Vita clung to her belief in a social hierarchy that shouldn't be disturbed. So liberated a woman could be very conservative. But in judging her snobbishness during the Violet period, one must avoid anachronism. What today would be regarded as insufferable (like the Sackville term 'bedint' for middle-class people, or stepping over a pail of soapy water without a word of greeting to the poor girl scrubbing the pavement) was then unremarkable. Vita and Violet were by upbringing class-conscious, but audacity, recklessness, improvidence and selfishness, their dominant traits during those years, were not exclusively upper-class. They acted out of perversity and unquenchable zest and lust, not from any assumption of caste superiority. One indication is that they were often desperately short of money. During the first of their Monte Carlo escapades they were reduced to fifty centimes between them.

I firmly believe that Vita wanted to be rescued from her infatuation, and that its climax in the hotel at Amiens came to her as a relief. As Victoria Glendinning has commented, it simultaneously saved her marriage and her face. It gave her the excuse to abandon Violet and return to Harold. Nothing could ever again be so great a threat to their married happiness, and having survived it, they could both experiment with love-affairs, leaving their love intact. My father advised me when I was about to be married, that 'to sleep with only one person throughout your life would be like saying, "*Wuthering Heights* is the greatest novel in the English language, therefore I shall never read another".' Infidelity, he thought, and so did Vita, need never break up a marriage unless there were other, weightier, causes too. Often it will enrich it. This was not quite so novel a doctrine in the 1920s as one might imagine. It was practised, but never preached. In the 1970s *Portrait of a Marriage* preached it. It argued that mutual support in times of trouble, common tastes and interests, and a shared desire occasionally to be apart, were stronger bonds than sexual compatibility. One has heard of sex between people without love: here was love without sex.

The book, moreover, pleaded the legitimacy of homosexual love between couples who desired it. While by no means the first statement of these doctrines nor the most persuasive, it did propose them, and illustrate their pitfalls. It suggested that in the twenty-first century we may come to accept that most marriages require the stimulus of emotional, and probably sexual, relationships

4

outside them, without weakening the marriage itself. This is the justification for publishing this book, and constantly reissuing it. It represents an increase in human understanding, not a decline in delicacy. I agree with Michael Ratcliffe, whose review in *The Times* was the first I read, with enormous gratitude, that 'Vita wrote with posterity in mind. Publication can only honour the memory of her honesty and passion.'

Nigel Nicolson

PART ONE
BY V. SACKVILLE-WEST

23 JULY 1920

OF COURSE I have no right whatsoever to write down the truth about my life, involving as it naturally does the lives of so many other people, but I do so urged by a necessity of truth-telling, because there is no living soul who knows the complete truth; here, may be one who knows a section; and there, one who knows another section: but to the whole picture not one is initiated. Having written it down I shall be able to trust no one to read it; there is only one person in whom I have such utter confidence that I would give every line of this confession into his hands, knowing that after wading through this morass – for it is a morass, my life, a bog, a swamp, a deceitful country, with one bright patch in the middle, the patch that is unalterably his – I know that after wading through it all he would emerge holding his estimate of me steadfast. This would be the test of my confidence, from which I would not shrink. I would not give it to *her* – perilous touchstone!, who even in these first score of lines should teach me where truth lies. I *do* know where it lies, but have no strength to grasp it; here am I already in the middle of my infirmities.

I start writing, having spent no consideration upon this task. Shall I ever complete it? and under what circumstances?, begun as it is, in the margin between a wood and a ripe cornfield, with the faint shadows of grasses and ears of corn falling across my page. Unkernelled nuts hang behind me, along the fringe of the wood; I lie on green bracken, amongst little yellow and magenta wild-flowers whose names I don't know. I lie so close to the ground that my only view is of tall corn, so crisp that in the breeze it stirs with a noise like the rustle of silk. All day I have been in a black temper, but that is soothed away. There is no place, out here, for temper or personality. There is only one personality present: Demeter.

Yesterday I was on the sea in a sailing-boat; it was very rough, and at moments I was extremely frightened, but I wished I wasn't frightened, because theoretically I enjoyed seeing the ship put her nose down into the waves, seeing the spray break over the deck, and then feeling my face all wet and tasting the salt water on my lips. The world of the sea is quite a different world. There is a whole different set of noises – the wash of the waves, the wind in the rigging, the banging of the blocks, the shouts of the crew – and one has a whole different set of wishes and preoccupations – the wish that the boat would keep still, if only for five minutes, as a rest from the perpetual balancing, the preoccupation as to whether the wind will get up, or go down, whichever it is; the immense, the overwhelming importance of weather, both as regards one's comfort and one's progress.

I realize that this confession, autobiography, whatever I may call it, must necessarily have for its outstanding fault a lack of all proportion. I have got to trust to a very uncertain memory, and whereas the present bulks enormous, the past is misty. I can't remember much about my childhood, except that I had very long legs and very straight hair, over which Mother used to hurt my feelings and say she couldn't bear to look at me because I was so ugly. I know that I wasn't a physical coward in those days, because I can remember doing dangerous things on a bicycle and climbing high trees – and yet, stop, I do believe I must have been a coward already, because I can remember thinking a great deal about whether I should be brave the next day when I went out riding, and I was too much fascinated by seeing other people do things which I knew I shouldn't dare to do myself. I never realized this until this moment. Anyway, I wasn't so much of a coward, and

I kept my nerves under control, and made a great ideal of being hardy, and as like a boy as possible. I know I was cruel to other children, because I remember stuffing their nostrils with putty and beating a little boy with stinging-nettles, and I lost nearly all my friends in that kind of way, until none of the local children would come to tea with me except those who had acted as my allies and lieutenants.

I don't remember much more about myself as a child than that. I remember more about outside things. I don't remember either my father or mother very vividly at that time, except that Dada used to take me for terribly long walks and talk to me about science, principally Darwin, and I liked him a great deal better than Mother, of whose quick temper I was frightened. I don't even remember thinking her pretty, which she must have been – lovely, even. My impression of her was that I couldn't be rough when she was there, or naughty, and so it was really a great relief when she went away. I remember very vividly terrible scenes between her and Dada – at least, she made the scene, he usually said nothing at all, or very mildly, 'Oh, come, dear, is that quite accurate?' Her statements rarely *were* accurate; I realized this, very, very slowly, but was incredibly obtuse over it; in fact I didn't really grasp it until a comparatively short time ago. (Evening is coming on, and I shall soon have to stop writing; thank God I am alone tonight.)

When she and Dada went away, I was left alone with Grand-papa. He was very old, and queer, and silent. He hated people, and never spoke to the people who came to the house [Knole]; in fact, if he got the chance he used to go to London for the day when he knew people were coming, and I used to be left alone to entertain them. It amused me later on, when sometimes I was had downstairs to make fourteen, to see him sitting quite mute between two wretched women who were trying to make con-versation to him, or else crushing them into silence: 'You have lovely gardens here, Lord Northwood [Sackville].' 'What do you know about gardens?', he would snap at them. But at the same time he was always shrewd in his estimate of people, and never liked those who were not worthy of liking, or disliked those that were. Mother used to get furious when in about six words he demolished her friends, but Dada used to laugh, and then she turned on *him*. But I suppose she was really very devoted to Grandpapa, in her own way, because underneath everything her ideas of duty are sound, and although the most incomprehensible, she is certainly the most charming, person upon earth, whom I adore.

Grandpapa liked children and believed in fairies. Every night after dinner he used to fill a plate with fruit and put it ready for me to fetch early next morning; he used to put it in a drawer in his sitting-room, labelled Diana's [Vita's] Drawer, in very elaborate lettering in coloured chalks that he had done himself. He always amused himself in shy, secret ways like that; he used to spend hours whittling little bits of wood into queer shapes, and polishing them with sandpaper till the surface was like velvet, and he had a set of little remarks that he invariably made when the occasion turned up: 'Nice fresh taste', he used to say over the first asparagus; and 'Poor old Cox', whenever anything went wrong with anybody; but I never discovered the origin of that. To go back to the fruit, it was a regular ritual, which nothing would have induced him to forgo, and which I never knew him to forget, even, poor old man, at the beginning of his last illness, while he was still downstairs; even if there were twenty people to dinner he heaped the plate for me just the same and carried it to the drawer, and if ever I forgot to fetch it in the morning he would make a grievance that lasted until it turned into a joke, and so became mellow instead of bitter.

In the same way he minded very much if I didn't go down to his room after tea and play draughts with him. It upset his habits, and also I think he must have been fond of me; he liked having children in the house, and later on he liked Charles [Edward Sackville-West], who was my cousin ten years younger than I, and was a genius, and could play Wagner when he was four. (He was very delicate, always passing from critical illness to critical illness, so that he was always brought downstairs wrapped in an enormous white Shetland shawl, in which he sat at the piano, with his puny little legs dangling, as unable to touch the pedals as his tiny hands were to span an octave.) Grandpapa liked children and he liked flowers, but he didn't care a rap about the house, and when people asked him questions about it, or about the pictures or silver or furniture, he used to refer them to Mother.

Mother made all the capital she could out of the house; to hear her talk about it you would have thought she had built it, but she had no real sense of its dignity, as Dada had, who worshipped it in his bones, but would sooner die than say so. I think it must have been very hard for him then, living in the house as Grandpapa's heir, but being only the nephew, not the son, and having no word to say in the management either of the house, the gardens, or the estate, and hearing Mother make up legends about the place, quite unwarrantable and unnecessary – the place was quite good enough to stand without legends, heaven knows! – and hearing her get all the credit for everything, because she was the kind of person who always came in for a lot of flattery from everyone. That was what came of her being ruthless and completely unanalytical, and having a charm that exacted flattery; and of his being so sensitive and modest. There certainly *was* something ruthless about Mother, and one of the things that has left the strongest and cruellest impression upon me was a horrible little dialogue I overheard once in London, as I lay in bed in the dark next door. She was alone with Grandpapa, and was evidently very much annoyed over something, for I heard her telling him how much in the way he was, with that sort of *flick* in her voice that to this day makes me shudder; and he was moved to protest – he, who never said a word! – and I heard his old voice saying piteously, 'But what do I do? I never even ring a bell.' I wish I could forget that little dialogue, but I can't; it burnt. Mother didn't soften, any more than she would soften towards me when I cried; yet she can soften marvellously if you only touch the right chord – I have noticed this in other people. It is really a sort of sentimentality that is moved emotionally, whether by something real or something unreal – usually the latter.

That was Grandpapa, with his odd little tricks, of always flinging his cap down with extreme violence in exactly the same place, of balancing himself endlessly and maddeningly from one foot to the other; with his dislike of people, his shyness of servants (he spoke the truth when he said he never rang a bell!), his funny jerks and phrases, that sometimes made him seem rather like an old goblin – that, at any rate, was Grandpapa on the surface, though what he was like underneath heaven alone knows. Of all human beings, he was surely the most inscrutable. I lived with him for sixteen years, and had I lived with him for yet another sixteen I have no doubt that he would have remained just as much of an enigma. One might have ended by putting him down as truly insensible, but in contradiction of that theory comes the most surprising fact about him, which I have kept for the end: during his middle youth he lived illicitly with a very beautiful Spanish dancer, by whom he had seven children in, I think, as many years.

This old story, this 'Romance of the Peerage' (*vide Daily Mail*), is so well known that in talking about it I feel as though I were talking about something which happened to some other family than my own. The 'Romance of the Peerage' label is enough to make me feel that. 'Who's who in the story', and then the personages: Asuncion Ramon [Pepita], a beautiful Spanish gipsy, living with Lord Sackville, then Lionel Strangways [Sackville-West], as his wife, calling herself Countess West (poor thing, isn't it pitiful, that title?), Gloria [Victoria] (my mother), their beautiful daughter, now married to the present Lord Sackville, Baptiste [Henry], their son, now claiming the title of Sackville and estates of Knole, and then the leading article on Knole, concluding in triumphant journalese, 'Too homely to be called a palace, too palatial to be called a home'. (Oh my lovely Knole, how right he was, that nameless journalist in his horrible jargon! I stand at the corner of the wall, and look down on you in the hollow, your grey walls and red-brown roofs, and hear myself saying the well-worn phrase, 'You get rather a good view of the house from here....')

The only time I remember Grandpapa breaking out through his reserve was one morning when I followed Mother into his sitting-room holding on to the end of her long, long plait. I can remember him jumping up and saying, 'Never let me see that child doing that again, Victoria.' It sounds an improbably melodramatic phrase, written down like that, but that was precisely what he said. It appears that Mother was in the habit, when a little girl, of walking about holding on to her mother's hair in such a fashion. I have got two photographs of my grandmother, which show clearly how beautiful she must have been; truly beautiful of feature and expression, not merely pretty, although they are ugly faded photographs taken at Arcachon about 1870. She was the illegitimate daughter of a gipsy and a Spanish duke; the gipsy, her mother, had been a circus acrobat, and was no doubt descended from a line of such, and the duke descended from Lucrezia Borgia. I think my maternal ancestry is hard to beat for sheer picturesqueness. It accounts for much in Mother, who at times is pure undiluted peasant.

But Grandpapa! *Qu'allait-il faire dans cette galère?* How did he, the man of silence, set about absconding with the dancer, who was at that time quite respectably married to someone else? I would give my very soul for a fly-on-the-wall peep backwards into one of the scenes between them. And think of their establishment – singing, happy-go-lucky, in the midst of a puddle of tiny children, he, an English diplomat, scion of the most correct old English family, heir to Knole, and given his own elusive character! Of course I knew nothing about this when I was small. My first inkling of anything wrong in my mother's birth was one whose snobbishness I am ashamed to record: some people used to address her letters as the Honble. Mrs Sackville-West, and others didn't; I, from some obscure instinct that resented any aspersions being cast upon my mother, always did.

Pepita died when my mother was nine, leaving Grandpapa with five small children (two of the others had mercifully died), three girls and two boys. He stuck the girls into a convent [in Paris]; I don't know what happened to the boys; I suppose they went to school. My mother was heartbroken, and to this day can hardly talk about her mother's death without tears; also from being the spoilt favourite, she now led a harsh convent life, seeing her father two or three times a year, and spending even her holidays in the convent. Here she remained until she was seventeen, when she was sent to another convent in England to learn English. When she was eighteen a great family clamour arose: should she and her sisters be sent out to join their father, who was now British Minister in Washington? (Washington having since then been made into an Embassy, Mother now always speaks of him as British Ambassador, as she thinks that sounds more impressive.) It was finally decided that they should go, so Mother – eighteen, a vision of loveliness, imperious, capricious, and speaking broken English with a strong French accent – was sent over to America with her two younger sisters.

I reconstruct all this from the unvarying evidence of eyewitnesses. Released from convent rule, she seems to have bounded upright at once like a sapling that had been bent down, to have taken Washington by storm, and left her sisters nowhere in the background. I expect strong seeds of resentment were sown in their minds, that sprouted later in the succession case.

I am getting tired, and all this does not really concern my own lamentable muddle. But it was all there for me, in the background, and as a child I realized dimly that a vinegary spinster aunt [Amalia] lived with us for some years at Knole, and annoyed Mother by giving me preserved cherries when Mother asked her not to, also that there was a person called Henry who from time to time came to the entrance and demanded to see Grandpapa, but was not allowed to. I suppose I overheard servants' gossip. It is a little difficult to disentangle what I actually knew at the time from what I have learnt since. But there certainly was always something, some mystery in the background.

Evening has nearly fallen; sunset-light on the hill opposite has turned the yellow corn-fields rose-pink. I have dined out on the terrace, writing this all the while on my knee. I do love the summer and always dread Midsummer Day as the watershed of the year. Midsummer Day used to be one of Grandpapa's jokes; after it was past he used to say regularly, 'Days drawing in now', and now it has for me yet another significance. I have heard from Robin [Harold Nicolson] this evening that he will not return from Paris for another five days; I had expected him tomorrow. Shall I, by then, have brought this recital up to the lamentable present, I wonder? I am dreadfully tired. Everything is so hushed, and I feel secluded and serene — not melancholy tonight. The country is too lovely for that. How lucky for me that I live in this fruitful and tender country: it *soaks* its serenity into one. Moors and crags would kill me, I think. The Weald is an antidote — alkali on acid, or whatever it is. I must go to bed.

LATER

I have had a bath, and am in bed, and feel less tired. My head swirls with this writing. (I am an incredible egoist, that's the long and short of it.) I keep on thinking of tales, and personages, and places: my old Nannie, whom my Mother sent away after fifteen years because she took it into her head that Nannie had eaten the quails; Lilian [Rosamund Grosvenor], four years older than I, who was brought over to Knole for three days to console me when Dada went to the South African war, and who even in those early days (I was six and she was ten) was always clean and neat whereas I was always grubby and in tatters; my dogs, absorbingly adored; my rabbits, who used to 'course' in secret with my dogs, and whose offspring I used to throw over the garden wall when they became too numerous; the trenches I dug in the garden during the war; the 'army' I raised and commanded amongst the terrorized children of the neighbourhood; my khaki suit, and the tears of rage I shed because I was not allowed to have it made with trousers — no, not so much as a proper kilt; my first play, whose rehearsal was remorselessly scattered by Mother after all my pocket-money had gone in art-muslin: all these, I suppose, made my childhood very much like that of other children, but to me it stands out now, so vivid, that I see myself in the garden, feel the familiar cut of my pocket-knife into the wooden table in the summer-house where I did my lessons, see the little cart into which I used to harness three ill-assorted dogs, see myself, plain, lean, dark, unsociable, unattractive — horribly unattractive! — rough, and secret. Secrecy was my passion; I dare say that was why I hated companions. Anyhow, it's a trait I inherit from my family. So I won't blame myself excessively for it. I forgot to say that two or three times I tried to run away, but was always brought back, and once Mother made me kneel down while she prayed over me.

25 JULY 1920

I was happy last night. I lay awake thinking about this writing, and watching the patterns that the moonlight, shining through branches and lattices, made upon my bed. This morning I woke up to wonder whether it was worth while going on with a bald egotistical statement; it keeps me from *Soap* [*The Dragon in Shallow Waters*] which I ought to finish. I got a rather sad letter from Harold this morning. As a rule he does not allow me to see when he is depressed. His sadness never fails to touch me to the quick. He is the only person of whom I think with consistent tenderness. I can say with truth that I have never, never cherished a harsh thought about him; at the most I have been irritated, but then he has always known it. I would not allow myself to be irritated against him while he remained unconscious, or when he was not there. I can say this with absolute truth. He has complete power over my heart, though not over my spirit. It is real tenderness I feel for him, it is a constant sense of 'Tread gently, for you tread upon my dreams'. I think with tenderness of Dan [Benedict] sometimes, of Basil [Nigel] very rarely, of Chloe [Violet Trefusis] never. I am so harsh to her that I could put almost any strain of suffering upon her without feeling a qualm of pity – could, and have. All this makes the whole thing so agonizing and so puzzling.

I had got to where Mother went out to Washington and captivated everybody in the place, including a Red Indian chief and the President of the United States. She was more or less the queen of Washington, I gather, and it must have been a gratifying alternative for a girl who had been destined to be a governess. (She had got her diploma as a qualified governess from the convent, but I can't believe that she would have remained a governess long! I have seen the diploma. It describes her as José Sackville-West, by which name she had up till then been known, but now that she figured as the Minister's daughter it was changed to her first name of Gloria [Victoria] – a name which suits her so admirably well. Glorious Gloria [Victorious Victoria] as somebody named her.) She didn't marry in America. When Grandpapa succeeded to Knole and, simultaneously, got turned out of the diplomatic service for indiscretion, she and her two sisters came back with him and lived at Knole. The second sister didn't stay there long; she married a Frenchman, and later got divorced and went on the music-hall stage as a dancer. They were very poor at Knole, but Mother, although wildly extravagant in bouts (fairly continuous bouts, I must say), is a good manager in everyday life. I don't know how long she lived there unmarried, but sooner or later she met Grandpapa's nephew, the heir, and married him, and I was born two years later [1892]. She says she would have drowned herself sooner than have another child, so I suppose her love of self-indulgence was rampant already.

She loved me when I was a baby, but I don't think she cared much for me as a child, nor do I blame her. My principal recollection of her then is that I used to be taken to her room to be 'passed' before going down to luncheon on party days, when I had had my hair crimped; and I was always wrong and miserable, so that parties used to blacken my summer. Our common hatred of them was a great link between me and Grandpapa, and we used to have secret jokes about the people while luncheon was going on. I don't mean to imply that Mother neglected me, or wasn't good to me, but simply that she figured more as a restraint than anything else in my existence.

I believe she and Dada were very happy at first, especially after the spinster aunt had finally departed in hostility, but I know nothing of their relations except what she herself has told me, and that isn't in the least reliable. She says he began to flirt with other women, and I know that she herself imported a new personage into Knole when I was six or seven; this was a person we all called Seery, a nickname invented by me in early stages. Seery [Sir John Murray Scott] stood six-foot-four, and weighed twenty-five stone. Once I measured him round where his waist ought to have been, and it was five feet. He had a round pink face like a baby, and white mutton-chop whiskers, and soft fluffy grey-white hair which Mother used to rumple. He was the best humoured, most lovable, genial and generous man imaginable; everybody loved him, even Grandpapa, who behind his back would say, 'Good fellow, Johnny', although they never called each other anything but 'Sir John' and 'Lord Sackville' most punctiliously. Seery was always laughing, when he wasn't asleep – laughing, and saying 'Shoo! pshoo!' to the swarm of flies that was for ever buzzing round his fat face in summer, and at which he used to flick perpetually with an enormous silk pocket-handkerchief. He prided himself on being a very good organizer, and very methodical, but as a matter of fact he muddled every arrangement, and mislaid all his possessions, in spite of the innumerable drawers and leather cases in which he used to put things away. When I think of Seery I see him sitting before an immense writing-table, rattling a bunch of keys and trying every key in every lock in turn, with his spectacles pushed up on to his forehead, and stopping to say 'shoo' to the flies. Then when he had got a drawer open, Mother would come and make a pounce at his stamps, and he would cry, 'Go away, you little beggar', or 'you little Spanish beggar', but of course he worshipped her and let her have whatever she wanted. (At times she wanted a good deal.) I see him like that, or else I see him dropping asleep in his chair after lunch, till the lighted tip of his cigar touched the tablecloth and Mother woke him up crying, '*Voyons, voyons, Seery!*', when he always started up and said, 'I wasn't asleep – I was thinking.' He used to go to sleep too on his shooting-stick out in the turnip-fields, while the birds streamed over his head, for he was very gallant about being so fat, and would always go out shooting or fishing with Dada and the younger men, sometimes riding a pony like a young carthorse that ended by having a permanent curve in its back.

Mother became absolutely the light and air of his life. She bullied and charmed him, fought with him, bewitched him, until he simply could not exist without her. If he had lost her, I really believe he would have pined away and died – or at any rate got thin, which seems even more difficult to believe. I don't know whether one ought to call that being in love. Somehow it seems too grotesque, the idea of anyone so fat being in love in the ordinary sense of the word. She was just life to him, that's all. She used to tell me that he was in love with her, and came whenever possible to importune her at her bedroom door at night; and she arranged with me that, in the event of his falling into a fit outside her bedroom, which might be compromising, she would come to wake me and between us we would bump him downstairs to his own bedroom, she would take his shoulders and I his feet, and she thought that by slipping him from step to step we would manage to shift that enormous mass without waking anybody. I was so accustomed to Mother that it never occurred to me that there was anything odd about this arrangement – on the contrary, I thought she was very clever to have so much foresight. She used to tell me this, I say, but I rather doubt whether there was much truth in it, as during all the years I spent with them (and during the later years I wasn't particularly unobservant, although not particularly sharp either) I never saw anything to corroborate it.

Poor Seery! she *did* lead him a life. But at least it wasn't the deadly stagnation of the life he had led up to then, between two old sisters and a crew of harpy brothers, one more middle-class than the other. Seery wasn't middle-class by nature, although he was by birth. I never knew anyone so grand, or so openhanded. He was very rich. He had been the secretary and adopted son of a famous collector [Sir Richard Wallace], who had died leaving him his whole fortune, much of his collection, and quite a lot of houses. Two of these houses were in Paris. We used to stay with him there every year after I was eight. Most of the house [2 rue Lafitte] was let, and we lived in an apartment on the first floor; it was lovely, in its own way as lovely as Knole, so that I never knew what it was to live in ugly rooms. One could stand at one end of the apartment and look down a long vista of rooms opening into one another, with an unbroken stretch of shining parquet floor, and all the rooms were panelled with cream-white and gilt Louis xv *boiserie*, or else with faded old green silk. All the furniture was French, with rich ormolu mounts, and there were hanging chandeliers in every room, and sconces on the walls, and, in the big gallery, priceless Boucher tapestries. The big gallery was in a hopeless confusion when we first went there, but Mother soon rearranged that. All the servants were very old and very magnificent; the butler had long white whiskers, and there were about six other old footmen, who all wore white gloves. There were endless fat horses and carriages, all equally antediluvian; there were no women, except the cook, who was the butler's old wife and a regular *cordon bleu*, and the *lingère*, who did nothing but look after the linen, and very necessary she must have been, for every sheet was like the finest cambric pocket-handkerchief. Seery kept up a tremendous *train de maison* there; every flower, fruit and vegetable seemed to be out of season, and larger than they would have been anywhere else *in* season. But it wasn't in the least ostentatious; it all seemed perfectly fitting and natural. I loved being there; that is to say, I loved the apartment, where I could wheel myself from room to room in an invalid's chair that I had discovered in a corner of the gallery, but I didn't enjoy the shops much, where I had to sit on a high stool for hours while Mother bought fiddling things that didn't seem to me to matter.

In the evenings they sometimes went to plays, and I was left alone, unless Grandpapa was there, and then he and I used to play a game at the window, of who could see the funniest sight down on the boulevard. When Grandpapa wasn't there I used to light all the candles in all the rooms and prowl about by myself; I liked that. Sometimes I used to go into the big gallery and cry bitterly over a stuffed spaniel in a glass case that I imagined was like a spaniel of mine that had died. I had orgies of sorrow over that spaniel. When Mother rearranged the gallery she did away with it, and I hid it in a cupboard where I could get at it whenever I wanted an excuse for tears, and I remember writing out my prayers and putting them under the spaniel. I must have been very sentimental, but, as I never let anybody know, it didn't matter.

Seery had another place near Paris [Bagatelle], in the Bois. That was a gem of a place, built for Marie Antoinette, and standing in a big garden of the *jardin anglais* sort. The house was empty, but we went there for picnics. There was the statue of a nymph in a grotto, bathing her foot in the water, and I used to deck her with leaves. Years later Seery sold this statue, and one day when I was with Mother in a big dealer's shop in London I saw it there, and not being very old burst into floods of tears; they hadn't dared tell me it had been sold. This episode and the spaniel sound as though I was always crying then, but as a matter of fact I wasn't. I was really rather defiant; only I had loved the nymph so much. I wish Seery could have left her to me in his Will instead of the diamond necklace he did leave me.

Besides going to Paris we went to Scotland with Seery every year. He was nearly always with us, or we with him, which his family didn't relish at all. We had a place in Aberdeenshire, and I have a diary which I was made to keep there in French as a punishment for wrestling with the hall-boy. Next year we had a nicer, wilder place [Sluie], where I ran wild for three months; it was on the Dee, among lovely heather hills and little trout-lochs. I knew really every inch of the hills, and was exactly like the Scotch farm-children with whom I used to play. I was eleven then. The farmer's son was a year older than me, and in the course of long days spent by the river or on the moors he told me a great many things he oughtn't to have told me; but I honestly hadn't got a mind like some children, and as I had always lived in the country I took most things for granted, and was neither excited nor interested by them. I practically lived at the farm, where I built myself a shanty. I was happy there. Mother was sensible about me. I was always out, either with the guns, or with the farmer's boys, or by myself with the dogs (I had an Irish terrier then who could jump like a greyhound). Oh God, oh God, I wish I was back there — those lovely, lovely hills, those blazing sunsets, those runnels of icy water where I used to make water-wheels, those lovely summer evenings fishing on the loch, those long days when I often walked fifteen miles or more with the guns and gillies, I *was* young, I *was* healthy, I *was* simple, my eyes smart with tears to remember it. I had a kilt and a blue jersey, and I don't suppose I was ever tidy once, even on Sundays. Mother was happy too; she used to pound up and down the same level bit of road, singing to herself, and she started an open-air craze which has never abated since, but which has provided every door in every room at Knole with a door-stopper.

I said I was eleven then. We went there every autumn until I was fifteen or sixteen, from early August till late October. When I was about twelve I started to write. (It was *Cyrano de Bergerac* that first initiated me to the possibilities of literature!) I never stopped writing after that – historical novels, pretentious, quite uninteresting, pedantic, and all written at unflagging speed: the day after one was finished another would be begun. I think that between the ages of thirteen and nineteen I must have been quite dreadful. I was plain, priggish, studious (oh, very!), totally uninspired, unmanageably and lankily tall, in fact the only good thing that could be said of me was that I wouldn't have anything to do with my kind. Seeing that I was unpopular (and small wonder, for a saturnine prig), I wouldn't court popularity. I minded rather, and used to cry when I went to bed after coming home from a party, but I made myself defiant about it. I don't mean this to sound in the least pathetic; I wasn't unhappy, only solitary, but I don't pretend that I minded solitude, I rather chose it. (Looking back, I think I maligned myself rather by calling myself totally uninspired: I had flaring days, oh yes, I did!, when I thought I was going to electrify the world; it was like being drunk, and I can find traces of it now in the margins of all those ponderous, interminable books I wrote – two little letters, v.e., which stood for 'very easy', and I look at them now, and re-read the leaden stuff which they are supposed to qualify, and take upon trust that I found those now forgotten moments full of splendour.)

These years are tedious to write about – tedious, and very uncertain. I mean the years from thirteen to nineteen. Things happened, of course, things that made an impression and changed me – not that I changed much, or grew any more sophisticated. What happened? Let me try to remember: there is writing, always writing, and moroseness, and periods of real hard work and proficiency at the daily school to which I went every autumn and winter term in London. I set myself to triumph at that school, and I did triumph – I beat everybody there, sooner or later, and at the end-of-term exams I thought I had done badly if I didn't carry off at least six out of eight first prizes. I think I was quite self-conscious over this: if I couldn't be popular, I would be clever; and I did succeed in getting a reputation of being clever, which was quite unmerited, for I am distinctly *not* clever, but which like all reputations has died hard. I don't believe it is quite dead yet — people say, 'Oh yes, she writes doesn't she?', implying that one must be clever in order to write. I wasn't hated at that school, at least I don't think so; I think they quite liked me. But I really cared not a scrap whether they liked me or not. Those were my most savage years! I worked very hard, and became more pedantic than ever. I've got a scholarly turn of mind, let me face that damning truth.

Other things happened too. I acquired a friend — I, who was the worst person in the world at making friends, closed instantaneously in friendship, or almost instantaneously (to be exact, the second time we saw each other), with Violet [Keppel, later Trefusis]. I was thirteen, she was two years younger, but in every instinct she might have been six years my senior. It seems to me so significant now that I should remember with such distinctness my first sight of her; we met at a tea-party by the bedside of a mutual friend with a broken leg, and she made to me some little remark about the flowers in the room. I wasn't listening; and so didn't answer. This piqued her — she was already spoilt. She got her mother to ask mine to send me to tea. I went. We sat in a darkened room, and talked — about our ancestors, of all strange topics — and in the hall as I left she kissed me. I made up a little song that evening, 'I've got a friend!'. I remember so well. I sang it in my bath.

I long to stop over Violet — to tell how much I secretly admired her, and how proud I was of the friendship of this brilliant, this extraordinary, this almost unearthly creature, but how I treated her with unvarying scorn, my one piece of really able handling; which kept her to me as no proof of devotion would have kept her — but I am going to tell other things first, because all the present is filled with Violet, and during the past she appears constantly too. I will stop only to say that from the beginning I was utterly sure of her; she might be elusive, she might be baffling, she might even be faithless, but under everything I had the rather insolent (but justified) certainty of her keeping to me. I listened to stories about her with a superior and proprietary smile. I would have remained for ten years without hearing a word from her, and at the end of those ten years I would have held the same undamaged confidence that we must inevitably re-unite. There isn't a word of exaggeration in these statements – nothing, for that matter, in the whole of this writing is to be exaggerated or 'arranged'; its only merit will be truth, but truth as bleak as I can make it.

(My writing has been broken here by Violet telephoning to me; I scarcely knew whether it was the Violet of fifteen years ago, or my passionate, stormy Violet of today, speaking to me in that same lovely voice.)

There were other happenings in those years. I went to Italy, to Florence. Violet was there, in fact I went to join her. (See how she comes in again immediately!) That was the first time I had been anywhere except to Paris, and it opened my eyes thoroughly. And Violet – how well did I know her then? My dates are so uncertain and I have no papers to guide me. I must have known her very well – it is coming back to me by degrees – for I had learnt Italian with her in London, and we had been together in Paris, and had acted part of a play I wrote in French in five Alexandrine acts, about the Man in the Iron Mask, and in those days we rather ostentatiously talked to one another in French in order to *tutoyer* one another and so show what great friends we were. It all comes back to me. Her mother [Alice Keppel] was the King's mistress (which added a touch of romance to Violet), and often when I went to their house I used to see a discreet little one-horse brougham waiting outside and the butler would slip me into a dark corner of the hall with a murmured, 'One minute, miss, a gentleman is coming downstairs', so that I might take my choice whether it was the King or the doctor. Often Violet would be sent for to come down to the drawing-room, when we said, 'Oh bother!', much as we did when I was sent for in my own house to see Seery. I took one as much for granted as the other.

Before she went away to Florence, she told me she loved me, and I, finding myself expected to rise to the occasion, stumbled out an unfamiliar 'darling'. Oh God, to remember that first avowal, that first endearment! Then we didn't meet till Florence, and she gave me a ring there — I have it now, of course I have it, just as I have *her*, and I should bury my face in my hands with shame to remember our childish passion for each other (which was too fierce, even then, to be sentimental), were it not for the justification of the present.

I feel I am doing all this part very badly, very confusedly; it is very difficult to do, because I am afraid of taking too seriously what would, normally, have begun and ended as the kind of rather hysterical friendship one conceives in adolescence, but which had in it, I protest, far stronger elements than mere unwholesome hysteria. There *is* a bond which unites me to Violet, Violet to me; it united us no less than it unites us now, but what that bond is God alone knows; sometimes I feel it is as something legendary. Violet is *mine*, she always has been, it is inescapable. I knew it then, albeit only through my obscurely but quite obstinantly proprietary attitude; she knew it too, less obscurely, and took all the active measures to make me realize it. That I left them unseconded, yet without any fear of losing her, proud and mettle-some as she was, only goes to prove how certain I was of my hold upon her. She was *mine* — I can't express it more emphatically or more accurately than that, nor do I want to dress up an elemental fact in any circumlocution of words.

That autumn [1908] I stayed with her in Scotland. I was sent to Scotland to stay with Seery and his sisters because Grandpapa was ill, and I suppose Mother and Dada knew he would die and wanted me out of the way. My parting with him makes me sad to remember now. He got me into his little sitting-room and asked me to kiss him. I said I hoped he would be better when I came back, but he only shook his head. He died while I was staying with Seery. One of Seery's sisters — the big one, whom her family called the Duchess — came to my room before breakfast with the telegram; she had on a pink flannelette dressing-gown, and no false hair, and I remember noticing how odd she looked. She kissed me in a conscientious sort of way, but I wasn't very much moved over Grandpapa's death just then; it only sank in afterwards. I changed my red tie for a grey one, and tried to pray for Grandpapa, but couldn't think what to say. Then I went downstairs to Seery's room, and never to my last moment shall I forget the sight he presented, sitting at his dressing-table perfectly oblivious, the twenty-five stone of him, dressed only in skin-tight Jaegar combinations, and, dear warm-hearted old Seery, crying quite openly over the telegram. I felt I ought to be crying too, if Seery, who was about sixty to my sixteen, could cry, but I was too much overwhelmed by Seery's appearance.

I went to stay with Violet after that, rather proud of my new mourning, and I am afraid I forgot to sorrow much while I was there. I remember various details about that visit: how Violet had filled my room with tuberoses, how we dressed up, how she chased me with a dagger down the long passage of that very ancient Scotch castle [Duntreath], and concluded the day by spending the night in my room. It was the first time in my life I ever spent the night with anyone, though goodness knows it was decorous enough: we never went to sleep, but talked throughout the night, while little owls hooted outside. I can't hear owls now without recalling her soft troubling presence in my room in the dark.

Then I went to London, where I found Mother in deep black, and for the first time I realized Grandpapa's death when Mother told me how much he had suffered and had died saying my name. (I was gratified by that.) We couldn't go to Knole except unofficially, because Mother's brother was bringing a lawsuit against Dada, claiming succession. We were very poor then, because all the money was kept in Chancery. I was taken to the law-courts for a minute while the case was going on, and saw all Mother's Spanish relations sitting there in the well of the court; the case collapsed, and Dada, Mother, and I had a triumphant return to Knole, pulled up in the carriage by the fire-brigade with ropes, under welcoming arches.

I saved up my pocket money to go back to Florence next spring [1909]. I was seventeen then, and less plain (still very plain, though), and an Italian [Orazio Pucci] fell in love with me and wanted me to marry him, which made me feel very grown-up. He followed me to Rome, and then to Paris, where I refused to see him, but I found him waiting for me on the quay at Calais when I crossed to England. In the autumn of that year I went with Mother and Seery to Russia. Oh how I loved it! I don't know whether to give an account of it, or to pass it by. We stayed with a Pole owning an estate 100 miles square between Warsaw and Kieff. At the frontier between Austria and Russia Mother refused to get out of the train to go to the Customs, till they sent two soldiers with rifles to fetch her, and in the grey dawn she was marched between them down the platform, saying to everyone she met, by way of protest, '*Ich bin eine grosse Dame in England*', the only German phrase she could evolve. We finally got to the local station, where we were met by an immense yellow motor and taken in it for fifty miles across atrocious country (no road, nothing but pits and bumps – Seery kept on saying between his bumps, which were more considerable than anybody else's, that Napoleon ought to have made decent roads across Russia, and Mother and I laughed so much we were nearly ill, what with bumps and laughter), until we came to a very elaborate French Château [Antoniny] looking very incongruous in the middle of the steppes. Here we found, besides our host and hostess, about twenty Poles we had never seen or heard of before, but they were all very friendly, and the life there was magnificent. There were eighty saddle-horses, a private pack of hounds, carriages-and-four, Cossacks attached to one's particular service and sleeping across the threshold of one's door, hereditary dwarfs to hand cigarettes, a giant, and Tokay of 1740. Not the least part of it was the host, who had a European reputation as a gambler before he forswore cards; he had teeth like a wolf (in fact he was not unlike a wolf altogether), and when he danced the Mazurka, as he did invariably after the 1740 Tokay, they snapped, and seemed to increase in size, number and prominence.

I found a sort of rhapsody I wrote after that; it is written in Italian (for secrecy), but I translate: 'How much I loved Russia! those vast fields, that feudal life, that illimitable horizon – oh how shall I ever be able to live in this restricted island! I want expanse.' It goes on: 'I am happier this winter. I hope the terrible times of sadness are over. At heart I am still sad, and always shall be.' There is more of it, but that suffices. I must have been suffering from a bad attack of *Weltschmerz*, and indeed I had just finished a play on Chatterton of quite unequalled gloom.

Florence again in the spring, with the Italian still faithful. I saw very little of Violet at this time; the two years between us were a barrier. I 'came out' – a distasteful and unsuccessful process – but the death of the King [Edward VII) saved me many festivities. Thus can the tragedies of great Kings be turned to the uses of little people.

26 JULY [1920]

It was just then, however, that I first met Harold. He arrived late at a small dinner-party before a play, very young and alive and charming, and the first remark I ever heard him make was, 'What fun', when he was asked by his hostess to act as host. Everything was fun to his energy, vitality, and buoyancy. I liked his irrepressable brown curls, his laughing eyes, his charming smile, and his boyishness. But we didn't become particular friends. I think he looked on me as more of a child than I actually was, and as for myself I never thought about people, especially men, under a very personal aspect unless they made quite definite friendly advances to me first; even then I think one wonders sometimes what people are driving at.

I was eighteen then and he was twenty-three.

That summer [1910] I caught a heaven-sent attack of pneumonia, and as a consequence of my being ordered abroad we spent the whole winter from November till April in the South of France near Monte Carlo. My illness revived my intimacy with Violet – I have the panic-stricken letter she wrote me, after hearing an exaggerated account of my being ill – and I suppose I saw something of her that autumn, because I can remember driving round and round Hyde Park with her one night after going to a play, a day or two before she left for Ceylon, and the end of that motor-drive was one of the very rare but extremely disturbing occasions when she kissed me. If I had gone to Ceylon with her, my life would probably have turned out very differently. But oh Lord! What's my miserable life? It only bulks large because these pages covered with pencil happen to be a history of it.

Well, we had an enormous white villa at Monte Carlo [Château Malet], where I lived in a perfection of happiness for those six months. Harold came to stay, and he and I fell into a rather childlike companionship, and I was rather hurt when he said goodbye to me without any apparent regret. I missed him − he was the best actual *playmate* I had ever known, and his exuberant youth combined with his brilliant cleverness attracted the rather saturnine me that scarcely understood the meaning of being young. Later I used to call him 'the merry guide', which name best describes him:

> And in the dews beside me
> Behold a youth that trod
> With feathered cap on forehead,
> And poised a golden rod,
> With mien to match the morning,
> And gay delightful guise ...

That was Harold to the life. 'Gay delightful guise ...' I cannot, *cannot*, bring sorrow into those eyes.

Violet returned from Ceylon in the spring, bringing me rubies, and we spent a day or two at San Remo. She also came to see me at our villa. How little we thought, as we stood under the olive-trees in the wild part of the garden (I remember admiring to myself the thick plait of her really beautiful hair), how little we thought of the next time we were to be together in that same place! When I went to her at San Remo, we saw an acrobat with no arms or legs. We had written to each other copiously during the whole winter, and now when she went to live in Munich, we continued to write, and she kept urging me to go and stay with her there, but I never did.

Harold meanwhile was in Madrid, and, but for an interlude when I dragged a plaintive but self-sacrificing Mother to Florence in the spring, the rest of the year was a repetition of the experience of being 'out'. But now something else happens − something which, I would like to emphasize, started in complete innocence on my part. I want to be frank. I have implied, I think, that men didn't attract me, that I didn't think of them in what is called 'that way'. Women did. Rosamund did. I have mentioned Rosamund as being the neat little girl who came to play with me when Dada went to South Africa. She had come out to stay at Monte Carlo – invited by Mother, not by me; I would never have dreamt of asking anyone to stay with me; even Violet had never spent more than a week at Knole: I resented invasion. Still, as Rosamund came, once she was there, I naturally spent most of the day with her, and after I had got back to England, I suppose it was resumed. I don't remember very clearly, but the fact remains that by the middle of that summer we were inseparable, and moreover were living on terms of the greatest possible intimacy. But I want to say again that the thing did start in comparative innocence. Oh, I dare say I realized vaguely that I had no business to sleep with Rosamund, and I should certainly never have allowed anyone to find out, but my sense of guilt went no further than that.

Anyway I was very much in love with Rosamund.

Harold came back from Madrid at the end of that summer [1911]. He had been very ill out there, and I remember him as rather a pathetic figure wrapped up in an Ulster on a warm summer day, who was able to walk slowly round the garden with me. All that time while I was 'out' is extremely dim to me, very largely I think, owing to the fact that I was living a kind of false life that left no impression upon me. Even my liasion with Rosamund was, in a sense, superficial. I mean that it was almost exclusively physical, as, to be frank, she always bored me as a companion. I was very fond of her, however; she had a sweet nature. But she was quite stupid.

Harold wasn't. He was as gay and clever as ever, and I loved his brain and his youth, and was flattered at his liking for me. He came to Knole a good deal that autumn and winter, and people began to tell me he was in love with me, which I didn't believe was true, but wished that I could believe it. I wasn't in love with him then – there was Rosamund – but I did like him better than anyone, as a companion and playfellow, and for his brain and his delicious disposition. I hoped that he would propose to me before he went away to Constantinople, but felt diffident and sceptical about it.

In January [1912] I went away with Dada to stay in a large country house [Burghley] for a hunt-ball, and when I woke up on the morning after the ball, in a great barn of a room, with the piercing cold freezing my nose and knees, I read with a shock a letter from Mother beginning thus: 'Darling child, I did not wire to you the very upsetting news of poor Seery's death ...'. I was horrified, and very, very sorry. It was difficult to think of that mass of good-humour and kindliness as being dead. I was dreadfully sorry — and also rather doubtful as to whether Harold and I would be allowed to go away next day to another country ball [at Hatfield] as we had intended. This sounds a selfish thing to have thought of then, but he was leaving for Turkey for at least six months directly after, and I wanted to know.

Well, I went downstairs as soon as I was dressed, and found Dada helping himself to kidneys in the dining-room, and I seemed to stand between two contrary factors — poor Seery lying dead, so much of him too — and the burning question of Harold. I didn't dare to ask Dada whether I would be allowed to go or not. It seemed too ironical that the two things should coincide in that way. After breakfast Dada and I went back to London by train through the snow, and all the time I sat staring out of the window wondering whether I would be allowed to go with Harold. When we got to London we drove straight to the hotel (we lived in a hotel that winter, for the sake of economy), and found Mother there, who had on a thick black veil and had evidently been crying. Quite soon afterwards Lady Blanche [Lady Constance Hatch], a stringy, wispy, French-music-hall-Englishwoman, with whom Dada had been for years most inexplicably in love, arrived and immediately burst into tears, which seemed to me silly, because although she had known Seery very well and had stayed with him and us a lot, both in Paris and in Scotland, she couldn't really have minded his death to that excessive extent. Mother went away then into her own bedroom. I kept struggling to make myself feel things as being real, and not as though we were all on the stage. Harold came next; he was very grave. I felt rather important, being the only person having access to Mother's bedroom, and I liked being asked by the others how she was. Mother did not cry; she always tries not to cry, because it gives her a headache. Then we went down to luncheon, Dada, and Mother, and Harold, and I, and I was all the time dreadfully afraid that Mother would break down in the restaurant; however she didn't. It had been settled by then that Dada and Harold and I were to go to the country after luncheon as arranged. I was glad, but rather apprehensive, because by then I was sure that Harold meant to propose to me and I knew I should say yes. He had never kissed me, and I wondered whether he would.

1 AUGUST [1920]

He had never even made love to me – not by a single word – and I only knew he liked me because he always tried to be with me, and wrote to me whenever he had to go away. Besides, people had put it into my head. I had always thought they were wrong, but they weren't, and that night at the [Hatfield] ball he asked me to marry him, and I said I would. He was very shy, and pulled all the buttons one by one off his gloves; and I was frightened, and tried to prevent him from coming to the point.

He didn't kiss me, but we sat rather bewildered over supper afterwards, and talked excitedly though vaguely about the flat we would have in Rome. I had on a new dress.

Only two or three days remained before he had to go away to Constantinople. I went up to London next day and told Mother I was engaged to him, but we were forbidden to write to one another except as ordinary friends, because we were too young, and also there was the question of money. We spent those two or three days together at Knole, and my impression is that we walked the whole time at a great speed through wet grass. Then he went away, and I got ill and was very depressed and miserable. Mother used to come to my room once or twice a day holding a little green bottle of disinfectant to her nose, and saying that there were three hundred steps between her room and mine, and what a bore it was feeling one had to go and see someone who was ill and waiting for one, so that after she had gone away again I used to sob with depression.

When I got better I also got more cheerful, and the Rosamund affair deepened. It was rather ironical that that affair should have started in the same house [The Grove, Watford] as where I spent the night of Harold's proposal. I went to Florence with her that spring, where, with an absurd old governess who had a mump on one side of her face and was always saying, 'Oh my dears, do consider your illustrious names', we shared a three-roomed cottage. I really was innocent over the Rosamund affair. It never struck me as wrong that I should be more or less engaged to Harold, and at the same time much in love with Rosamund. The fact is that I regarded Harold far more as a playfellow than in any other light. Our relationship was so fresh, so intellectual, so unphysical, that I never thought of him in that aspect at all. It was rather his own fault, after all, from the over-respectful way in which he had always treated me. I can best express what I mean about him by saying that he stood at the absolutely opposite pole from the lover-type of man. Some men seem to be born to be lovers, others to be husbands; he belongs to the latter category. Rosamund wasn't exactly jealous of him then; he was too far away, and our engagement was too vague, and she knew that although I was very fond of him I was passionately in love with herself – I use the word 'passionately' on purpose. It was passion that used to make my head swim sometimes, even in the daytime, but we never made love.

Harold came back on leave in August, and we spent most of the next two months together at Knole, but our engagement was still kept a secret and our behaviour was irreproachable. Rosamund was jealous of him then. I wish I could remember things better. All that year Seery's Will remained unproven, but it was known that he had left Mother all the contents of the Paris house and £150,000 as well, but that his family were furious and meant to dispute the Will, so there could be nothing definite about Harold and me. I wasn't particularly anxious to have it settled; I was quite happy as I was. One evening when we were out in the wet garden after a rainy day, he kissed me for the first time, and rather characteristically called me his wife. Looking back, I see how characteristic it is that he should always have thought of me in that way, but I must say I was thrilled then. After that we made a fuss and obtained that we might write to one another as though we were engaged. Rosamund minded dreadfully – as much from envy as from jealousy, I think. In October she, Harold and I, all three, went to Italy, travelling as far as Bologna together, and there Harold left us to go on to Constantinople by the Orient Express, while Rosamund and I went on to Florence.

I hate writing this, but I must, I must. When I began this I swore I would shirk nothing, and no more I will. So here is the truth: I was never so much in love with Rosamund as during those weeks in Italy and the months that followed. It may seem that I should have missed Harold more. I admit everything, to my shame, but I have never pretended to have anything other than a base and despicable character. I seem to be incapable of fidelity, as much then as now. But, as a sole justification, I separate my loves into two halves: Harold, who is unalterable, perennial, and *best*; there has never been anything but absolute purity in my love for Harold, just as there has never been anything but absolute purity in his nature. And on the other hand stands my perverted nature, which loved and tyrannized over Rosamund and ended by deserting her without one heart-pang, and which now is linked irremediably with Violet. I have here a scrap of paper on which Violet, intuitive psychologist, has scribbled, 'The upper half of your face is so pure and grave – almost childlike. And the lower half is so domineering, sensual, almost brutal – it is the most absurd contrast, and extraordinarily symbolical of your Dr Jekyll and Mr Hyde personality.' That is the whole crux of the matter, and I see now that my whole curse has been a duality with which I was too weak and too self-indulgent to struggle.

I really worshipped Rosamund then. We motored all over Italy, and I think it was our happiest time. Meanwhile the growl of the [Scott] lawsuit came closer and closer, and the date was finally fixed for June [1913]. I didn't go to Italy that spring, I went instead to Spain, which I looked on as partially my own country, and where in three weeks I picked up Spanish with comparative fluency. I loved Spain. I would give my soul to go there with Violet – Violet! Violet! How bloodless the Rosamund affair appears now under the glare of my affinity with Violet; how seraphic and childlike my years of marriage with Harold, when that side of me was completely submerged! I am so frightened of that side sometimes – it's so brutal and hard and savage, and Harold knows nothing of it; it would drive over his soul like an armoured chariot. He has blundered upon it once or twice, but he doesn't understand – he could no more understand it than Ben could understand algebra.

Things began to rush, after I came back from Spain. The delay over my engagement began to irritate me, and one day I wrote to Harold saying we had perhaps better give up the idea. He sent me a despairing telegram in reply, and then I scarcely know what happened inside my heart: something snapped, and I loved Harold from that day on; I think his energy in sending me a telegram impressed me, just as I was impressed when he came after me in an aeroplane when I ran away. Anyway, I wired back that everything was as before, and the letter which followed the telegram touched me greatly, for I saw by it how much he truly cared. But I continued my liaison with Rosamund. I say this with deep shame.

The lawsuit was the next thing. It lasted for a fortnight, and had for immediate result a new worship for Mother, which had been incipient for several years. I couldn't bear her to be attacked, and I adored her for looking so lovely in the witness-box and for completely charming the judge, the jury and the audience, and for baffling the opposing counsel and making a fool of him till he scarcely knew whether his head was on his shoulders or off them. Of course she won her case, and we were all very triumphant, except Dada to whom it must have been torture, but I didn't realize that at the time, which just shows how young I was for twenty-one in the ways of the world. He had by then got rid of his stringy, wispy Lady Constance, and from now dates his friendship with another woman, Rebecca [Olive Rubens], who with her husband spent a lot of time at Knole.

Harold came back before the case was finished, and came down to the court with me during the last days. It was funny going there and seeing all Seery's family, whom I had known so well, especially his sisters, one of whom had broken to me the news of Grandpapa's death. I used to long for Seery to appear miraculously in court and tell them all what he thought of them, especially when they said that Mother and I had destroyed an unfavourable will of Seery's. I was frantic over that, and tried my best to show it when my turn came to go into the witness-box.

I ought to say that Violet was now back in England since a year, and I had seen her sometimes, but not very often, because Rosamund was even more jealous of her than of Harold and prevented me from going near her. So I really only saw her when she came to Knole for parties, but then I was always conscious of the same old undercurrent, and for that reason I never mentioned Harold to her; he was something separate. Once she came to my room in the middle of the night and asked me if I were in love; but that was sometime before, and I could say No quite truthfully. She always came like that when she had the chance, and she usually kissed me then – on my mouth, I mean – but we never did, even ordinarily, at other times. Violet was very amusing then and a terrible flirt, throwing over first one man and then another; she used to do all kinds of parlour-tricks, which I never saw, as she stopped immediately I came into the room, and if ever we met anywhere accidentally she would turn white to the lips. I used to amuse myself by taking her unaware in this way, and Dada in the innocence of his heart used to say, 'Did she turn pale?', as a joke.

Well, after the case was over Mother said we could be engaged and married in the autumn, so it was announced. Rosamund was miserable. She used to cry all night and every night, as I very well knew, because her bedroom was next door to mine at Knole, but as I had ceased to care for her and thought only of Harold, I was only exasperated by her tears and tried to stop them by getting angry, not by being sympathetic. I was cold as ice to her, and I see now what a beast I was, and how pathetic she was, because she really did adore me, and added to the misery of knowing that

I cared for someone else, she must have felt that she had no one who cared two straws for her — except an obscure sailor whom she didn't like. It was rather a relief to get away from Knole to Switzerland [Interlaken] with Mother and Harold and an elderly millionaire [W. W. Astor] whom Mother had in tow. She was feeling the strain of her two days in the witness-box, when everything that she said, although truthful in the letter, was certainly misleading in the spirit, and when one had to remember very carefully what one had said the day before, or even the hour before. She was, however, serenely happy in Switzerland, and as for Harold and me, we simply lived in heaven.

When we came back to Knole life became a jumble of letters, wedding-presents, and clothes, the whole being plentifully watered by Rosamund's tears. I have seldom seen anyone in such despair, but it didn't touch me. Mother lavished jewels on me. Harold and I grudged an hour spent away from one another. I hurry over this part, because it is the same for everybody. On the 1st of October [1913] we were married in the chapel at Knole, decked out like a theatre by me. Mother, who doesn't like being *émotionée*, stayed in bed. I had cried bitterly the evening before at the prospect of leaving Knole and giving up my liberty, but I had cried away all my regrets and had none left when the day came. Rosamund survived my wedding-day somehow, and rather splendidly rose to the occasion of hiding away her own sorrow; she is really rather splendid in some ways. Violet didn't come. I never told her anything about my engagement, and she learnt it through the papers and wrote me sarcastic letters through which I could read her anger.

That was my wedding.

We went away for three days to the country, and then came back to London for one night, which I spent with Mother and Dada while Harold went to his parents. I saw Rosamund, and said goodbye to her, which bored me very much, as I couldn't live up to the level of her emotion. Next morning early Harold came to fetch me in a motor and we left for Florence, where we lived in the little cottage I had shared with Rosamund eighteen months before. That is one of the things I am most ashamed of in my life. It was horrible of me. Besides being disloyal to Rosamund, it was a dreadful *manque de délicatesse*.

For sheer joy of companionship I should think the years that followed were unparalleled or at least unsurpassed. One side of my nature was so dormant that I believed it would never revive. I was really gentle, self-sacrificing, chaste; I was *too* good, if anything, because it made me intolerant of the frailties of other people. (Now, I feel I could forgive anyone anything.) We were a sort of by-word for happiness and union. We never tired of one another! How rescued I felt from everything that was vicious and violent! Harold was like a sunny harbour to me. It was all open, frank, certain; and although I never knew the physical passion I had felt for Rosamund, I didn't really miss it. This lasted intact for about four and a half years.

After a month spent in Italy and Egypt, we lived in Constantinople, and I found out there that I was going to have a child. I was pleased, but Harold was most pleased. His slightly medical attitude was the only thing that annoyed me, and I tried to counteract it by forbidding him to tell anyone except his own parents and mine. He wrote a letter to my mother about it which I tore up in a fury, which he couldn't understand at all. But on the whole I was very *bien-pensant* about it, as indeed about everything else – stagnantly *bien-pensant*! I don't think I regret myself as I was in those days; at least, I regret that the person Harold married wasn't entirely and wholly what he thought of her, and that the person who loves and owns Violet isn't a second person, because each suits each.

The correct and adoring young wife of the brilliant young diplomat came back to England in June. I remember a divine voyage by sea from Constantinople to Marseilles, through the Aegean, a second honeymoon. We met Mother in Paris, and both thought that she was going off her head, as she was obviously in an extraordinarily unbalanced state of mind. Then we went to Knole. War was declared on the 4th of August, and Ben was born on the 6th. Scenes immediately began with Mother over his name, and they culminated in our taking a house in London as it was impossible for us to remain with Mother. We spent the winter in

London, and I became quite sociable. I was, in fact, thoroughly tamed. I hardly ever saw Violet (who, at her own sarcastic request, was Ben's godmother), partly because she was jealous and partly because I was altogether too well tamed for her. That was the only period of my life when I achieved anything like popularity. I was no longer plain, I took adequate trouble to make myself agreeable, Harold was loved by everyone who met him — we were, in fact, a nice young couple to ask out to dinner. Oh God, the horror of it! I was so happy that I forgot even to suffer from *Wanderlust*.

And then, and then, those years: let me think. All that winter Mother was dreadfully and impossibly quarrelsome and queer, and no one could do anything with her. We thought she was going to Rome, but the day before she was due to start she said she wouldn't go. We were all frankly dismayed, having looked on Rome as a heaven-sent solution. Mercifully Dada was with his regiment, so he didn't suffer much from it all. She went at last to a nerve doctor who did her worlds of good. What else? We bought a country cottage [Long Barn] where we spent the summer and Harold went up to London every day. If he had to spend the night in London we thought it a tragedy. We had once been parted for three days while he went yachting — never more. Domesticity could go no further. Ben grew apace, and we were to have a second child at the end of September.

The nightmare of that September and October remains with me. Dada left for Gallipoli in September, and I waited and waited for the baby. I waited all October, and the days grew shorter and wetter; Harold had a fortnight's leave, which was the only bright spot. The baby was not born until the first week in November, and then it was born dead, and I was very ill myself, after two nights and days in which I seemed always to be watching the candles in the room grow paler in the light of the dawn.

As soon as I could be moved, we went away to London. I minded horribly about the baby, and it got worse instead of better. I never knew why it all happened like that, but I think it was owing to a shock I had had months before: there was a terrible gale raging, and we were all at dinner [at Knole], with screens round us to keep off the draughts, and the carpet rising gustily on the floor, and I for one was convinced that something would happen. (I was always, and still am, nervous about Harold.) Sure enough, the butler came in suddenly and said there had been an accident to the car. The car was bringing Rosamund from the hospital where she worked, and Harold from the station. I grabbed a coat and rushed out, but it was impossible to walk against the wind, and the night was black as pitch. I waited at the door, nearly dead with fright. Presently two men came, supporting Rosamund between them; she was covered in blood, her nose was pushed broken half across her face, and she was talking nonsense. There was no sign of Harold. For an hour I didn't know whether he had been in the motor or not; the chauffeur was carried in badly injured and Rosamund was completely out of her senses. However, after an hour he appeared, having walked from the station through that hideous night. It made a great impression on me, both my anguish about Harold and the really dreadful apparition of Rosamund, and I am sure that was responsible for the baby.

I want to get on, I want to finish those years that might have been the life of another person. I want to get to the present.

There are so few events in those years, except war events. In our personal life there was nothing except moving to London for the winter, to the cottage for the summer, watching Ben grow and learn to speak, and for me, writing. I should think it was hardly possible for two people to be more completely and unquestioningly happy. There was never a cloud, never a squabble. I knew that if Harold died, I should die too; it all made life very simple. I saw Violet from time to time, but she was more alien from me than she had ever been, and yet in a way our friendship was on easier terms; that strange undercurrent had never made itself so little felt.

She is very proud, and a first-class dissimulator.

In the winter [1917] Nigel was born, and shortly after that Rosamund's mother died of cancer. I was with Rosamund during the operation (which was only for appendicitis), and with her too when the surgeons told her with revolting details that they had discovered cancer. She left a letter for me, bequeathing to me the care of Rosamund. I have not fulfilled this trust.

We spent that summer in the country again, with Ben and Nigel. That was the last of our untroubled summers, but I didn't know it; there was nothing to foreshadow events. The war went on, and weighed on everyone; but no one could have been less affected than we were, except for Dada who had been out ever since 1915.

Chronology

PART ONE AND PART TWO

1827 'Old' Lionel Sackville-West born

1830 Pepita born in Malaga

1852 Lionel meets Pepita in Paris

1862 SEPTEMBER: Their illegitimate daughter, Victoria born in Paris

1871 Pepita dies at Arcachon

1873–80 Victoria in Paris convent

1881–8 Victoria in British Legation, Washington

1886 21 NOVEMBER: Harold Nicolson born in British Legation, Teheran

1888 SEPTEMBER: The Murchison letter ends 'old' Lionel's career

OCTOBER: Mortimer dies, and 'old' Lionel becomes Lord Sackville

1890 JUNE: Victoria and 'young' Lionel marry at Knole

1892 9 MARCH: Vita born at Knole

1894 JUNE: Violet Keppel born

1897 Victoria meets 'Seery', Sir John Murray Scott

1904 Vita meets Violet Keppel

1905–8 Vita at Miss Wolff's school, London

1906–10 Her early novels and plays

1908 MAY: Vita's first visit to Florence, with Rosamund and Violet

3 SEPTEMBER: 'Old' Lionel Sackville dies

1909 APRIL: Vita meets Pucci in Florence

AUTUMN: Vita goes with her mother and Seery to Russia

1910 FEBRUARY: Legitimacy case decided in Sackvilles' favour
APRIL–MAY: Vita in Italy with Pucci again
JUNE: Vita 'comes out'; she meets Harold
NOVEMBER: Vita in Monte Carlo with Lady Sackville and
Rosamund until April 1911

1911 JANUARY: Harold and Pucci visit her in Monte Carlo;
Harold goes to Madrid Embassy
CHRISTMAS: Harold at Knole

1912 17 JANUARY: Seery dies
18 JANUARY: Harold proposes to Vita at Hatfield ball
24 JANUARY: Harold leaves for Constantinople
APRIL–MAY: Vita in Florence with Rosamund
AUGUST: Harold home on leave
OCTOBER–NOVEMBER: Vita returns with Rosamund to
Italy

1913 APRIL-MAY: Vita goes to Spain and Italy
18 MAY: 'Crisis' telegrams between Vita and Harold
24 JUNE: Scott case begins
3 JULY: Harold returns to England
7 JULY: Scott case decided in Sackvilles' favour
5 AUGUST: Vita's engagement to Harold announced
MID-AUGUST: Interlaken
1 OCTOBER: Vita and Harold married at Knole; honeymoon
in Italy and Egypt
AUTUMN: Vita and Harold in Constantinople until spring
1914

1914 21 JUNE: Vita and Harold arrive back in England from
Constantinople
4 AUGUST: Outbreak of war
6 AUGUST: Benedict (Ben) born at Knole
28 DECEMBER: Accident to Rosamund at Knole

1915 MARCH: Vita and Harold buy Long Barn
3 NOVEMBER: Vita's second son born dead

1916 JANUARY: Vita and Harold buy 182 Ebury Street in London

1917 19 JANUARY: Nigel born at Ebury Street

1919 19 MAY: Lady Sackville leaves her husband and Knole for
ever

PART TWO
BY NIGEL NICOLSON

MY mother (whom I shall now call Vita, except occasionally) was understandably hazy about her own mother's origins, and it was only in 1936, when she read the contemporary documents for her book *Pepita*, that the facts replaced in her mind the legend on which she had been brought up. Pepita was not the illegitimate daughter of a gipsy and a Spanish duke. Both Vita and her mother would certainly have preferred it that way, and in a further dramatization of the legend, the duke was named as the Duke of Osuna. Nor was Catalina Ortega, Pepita's mother, an ex-acrobat. There was certainly gipsy blood in her, but she was happily married to a barber of Malaga, Pedro Duran, and after her husband's early death supported her family by patching and selling old clothes. Pepita was born in Malaga in 1830, and there was a younger brother, Diego. Her early career was not a great success. Her first contract, in Madrid, was cancelled, the ballet master saying in later evidence: 'In my opinion she was no artist at all as regards dancing, but no doubt her personal charms might fascinate the public abroad. She might perhaps be good enough for Germany, but not for Spain.'

One must take Pepita's beauty on trust. There is no photograph of her in her prime, and the oleographs which advertised her performances throughout Europe do scant justice to the 'Star of Andalusia', whose face and figure remained stamped on the memories of all who saw her. At the age of twenty, she married another Spanish dancer, Juan de la Oliva, but the marriage broke up in quarrels a few months later, and she was free to take as her lovers whomsoever she chose, and she chose many. Lady Sackville sometimes gave the story an extra twist by claiming Prince Yousoupoff as her natural father, and it could have been so, if the date of her birth, 1862, had corresponded with the dates of that brief affair, for her birth-certificate recorded that she was '*fille de père inconnu*', leaving her parental options enticingly open. However Lionel Sackville-West, who much against his will was obliged by the lawyers to leave the full facts on record, acknowledged his paternity of Pepita's three daughters and two sons, and of two other children who died in infancy.

Lionel and Pepita had first met in Paris when he was on leave from his diplomatic post at Stuttgart, and from that moment onwards, with some intermissions, they remained lovers until Pepita's death. They never lived in England, though Pepita once danced at Her Majesty's Theatre in London, but took a series of villas at places on the Continent which lay conveniently equidistant between Lionel's various legations and the cities which Pepita's charms were subduing one by one. She retired to Arcachon in southern France, and died there in 1871, giving birth to her seventh child, who lived only six days.

Vita's mother was christened Victoria Josefa Dolores Catalina, and she bore her father's surname, Sackville-West. Soon after Pepita's death he was appointed British Minister in Buenos Aires, and Victoria was sent with her sisters, Flora and Amalia, to the Convent of St Joseph in Paris, where she remained seven years, friendless, retarded and miserable. Her brothers, Maximilien and Henry, were sent first to Stoneyhurst and then to learn farming in South Africa. Victoria was not told of her illegitimacy until she was moved from the Paris convent to another in London in 1880, and it was then that she also heard for the first time that she had an uncle called Mortimer, Lord Sackville, who lived in a huge house called Knole, another uncle, Lord De La Warr, and two aunts, the Duchess of Bedford and the Countess of Derby. It was quite a shock. She knew nothing of the world. She could hardly speak English. She regarded herself as a waif, fit only to be a governess like Jane Eyre, and it was this waif whom her father suddenly proposed to translate to Washington as his hostess at the British Legation, where she would occupy the leading position in diplomatic society.

During his infrequent visits to Paris, Lionel must have seen in his eldest daughter latent qualities which convinced him that she would succeed in this alarming task, for the risks to his career were immense. He was obliged to admit officially what had long been common gossip, that although a bachelor he had five children; that his intended hostess was one of them, and she a totally inexperienced girl of nineteen. Queen Victoria gave her amused consent to this odd arrangement on condition that no objection was raised in Washington itself, and a Ladies' Committee was formed there to discuss it, headed by the President's wife, Mrs Garfield. 'A letter had come from Lady Derby, stating the situation', said one member of this tribunal subsequently, 'and that Mr Sackville-West was fond of his daughter and requested that she be received. The decision was that she should be received cordially as her father's daughter.' Victoria arrived in December 1881, alone, for Vita's autobiography is at fault in saying that her sisters went with her. Flora and Amalia did not join her until several years later, and their addition to the Sackville-West *ménage* America thought 'a bit too much', according to the same witness, but by then Victoria had won for her family a position immune to censure. They loved her.

My grandmother often spoke to me about her seven years in Washington as the first and greatest triumph of her life, and her boast was fully justified. I thought that she must be exaggerating when she told me that the second proposal of marriage which she received was from the President of the United States himself, President Arthur, a widower (Garfield having been assassinated before her arrival), but I have since discovered that it was true enough for an official denial to be issued by the President's brother: 'The story that the President is engaged to Miss West is absurd and without foundation, and the President has no idea of marrying now.' My grandmother said that she refused him late in the evening after her first banquet at the White House. 'I burst out laughing', she wrote in her Book of Reminiscences when she was aged sixty, 'and said, "Mr President, you have a son older than me, and you are as old as my father."'

What is beyond dispute is that she captivated Washington from the start. Contemporary Press comments could be merciless about other people – even about her father, who was described retrospectively as 'reserved and taciturn, and people who did not like him called him dull. He had at any rate an unusual power of silence.' But about Victoria they were unanimous. 'She has become the reigning belle. Her beauty and intelligence are alike remarkable. About both those rare qualities there is something exotic, which give both an added charm.' 'She is most pleasing in manner and appearance. She has the graceful figure of a very young girl and a most piquant face with large appealing dark-blue eyes.' 'She made an enormous impression by her beauty, charm, modesty, grace, clothes and taste.' 'The dignity of a woman with the unconscious sprightliness of a child.' On her unusual origin the Press remained gallantly dumb. Lionel was described as a widower, and the only reference to Pepita was that 'Miss West's harsh English angles are rounded off by the graces of her Spanish mother.'

Another quality soon developed – her efficiency. She took in hand the large staff of the Legation, diplomatic and domestic, and knowing exactly what she wanted, would tolerate no argument or disobedience. She was a natural organizer and hostess, gracious to the distinguished and, lacking all shyness herself, thoughtful for the shy. In the convent, dancing and deportment had not been taught, but she seemed to know it all, instinctively. In her first season she presided at five balls, with five hundred guests at each, and began to change the conventions and even the protocol of such occasions, to the delight of the young ensigns and attachés who flocked around her, first as a novelty, and soon as the leader of their improvisations. Finding that the Highland reel was unknown in Washington (she herself having first heard of it only six months before), she held classes in the Legation to which an invitation was an honour and a command. As the most popular of all the girls she found no difficulty in putting an end to the custom of 'bunching', by which young men were obliged to send to their partners bouquets which they could ill afford. She played tennis; rode horseback; shot rapids in a canoe; went fishing; discussed his campaigns with General Sherman; hunted with Red Indians; visited many parts of the United States; and spent two months every winter in Canada, where she broke another dozen hearts. For all that, she was a girl whom it was difficult to know well. When she drove out each evening in a stylish two-horsed carriage, attended by her coachman and footman, she was sometimes accompanied by her father or a girl-friend, never by young men. Any who attempted the mildest flirtation were brought up short: 'Please go away. I do not like this kind of conversation.' She was totally innocent until she married, and she remained all her life fastidious and proud.

The indiscretion which ended Lionel's career in 1888 is known in diplomatic history as the affair of 'the Murchison letter'. A man calling himself Charles F. Murchison, a former British citizen living in California, wrote to the Minister asking his advice on the forthcoming presidential election. Lionel was foolish enough to reply that he favoured the return of President Cleveland for a second term. His letter was published under such headlines as 'The British Lion's Paw Thrust into American Politics', and his recall was demanded by the State Department. Fortunately his brother Mortimer died a month later, and he was able to return to England with the excuse that his new responsibilites as Lord Sackville obliged him to retire. Victoria now exchanged the management of the Legation for that of Knole, the largest house in England still in private hands.

She chose from among her many suitors her first cousin Lionel, and married him in June 1890. Their only child, my mother, was born at Knole on 9 March 1892. She was christened Victoria Mary, but was known even before her birth as Vita, to distinguish her from her mother who shared the same name, Victoria Sackville-West, as did her father and grandfather, both Lionel Sackville-West and later Lord Sackville. To make clear the relationship between the two Victorias and the two Lionels, and as a key to the famous legitimacy case which followed, a simplified family-tree will be found useful:

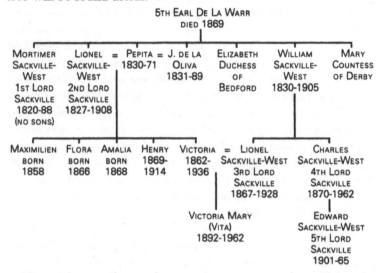

Victoria's marriage to her cousin was not welcomed by the family, except by her father, who saw in it an unexpected opportunity to keep his favourite daughter beside him at Knole and in a sense 'legitimize' at least one of his children, and by Lady Derby, who adored her niece. The others shook their heads at the extension of the family scandal into a new generation, deploring the perpetuation of the 'bad Spanish blood', and dreading the terrible progeny which this marriage might beget. They did not dare say these things to the two Lionels, but pointed out the unsuitability of cousin marrying cousin, their difference in age (she was twenty-seven, he twenty-three), and the disadvantage of a Protestant's union with a Roman Catholic. The latter difficulty Victoria boldly overcame by defying an edict from the Pope himself that any children of the marriage must be brought up in the Catholic faith. For this disobedience, she later claimed with pride, for it added another facet to her story ('*Quel roman est ma vie!*'), she was excommunicated by Cardinal Manning, with whom she had a stormy interview.

Vita, both in her autobiography and in *Pepita*, drew portraits of her parents which do too much honour to her father and too little to her mother. She emphasized her mother's eccentricity to the detriment of her truly remarkable personality and gifts. When she wrote the autobiography, she was still frightened of her; when she wrote *Pepita*, she was anxious to link the two halves of her story by arguing that the gipsy strain in her grandmother persisted in her mother, leading to wild fluctuations of generosity and parsimony, affection and selfishness, determination and incompetence. In fact Victoria Sackville was a woman of strong will softened by charm and oversweetened by sentimentality. She was master as well as mistress of Knole, both in her father's day and in her husband's. 'Old' Lionel was uninterested in the house and carelessly indifferent to his financial affairs, while young Lionel lacked bite and grasp. Victoria began her long régime at Knole by a programme of modernization – introducing electricity, central-heating and bathrooms, rearranging the furniture, and substituting cars for carriages; and when she found that her decisions on these matters went unchallenged, she began slowly to take over the management of the estate and its finances. She had her feet firmly on the ground. She was the family's strategist. When money was short it was she who speculated successfully on the Stock Exchange, she who opened in London a shop called Spealls for the sale of lamp-shades and stationery which became highly lucrative, she who was in constant consultation with the lawyers on the intricacies of the two great lawsuits, she who won both, she who saved Knole.

At first she was very much in love with her husband. He was the only man whom she ever loved absolutely. 'Lionel was perfect to me in those days', she wrote in her Book of Reminiscences. 'He gave me ten years of the most complete happiness and passionate love which I reciprocated heartily. I adored him, and he adored me.' Not until 1905 is there a word of criticism in her diaries of his growing neglect of her. Vita worshipped her father, seeing in him all the attributes of a country gentleman, of whom little was required but good manners and an interest in country pursuits. But she would have admired him less if he had not been her father and the current bearer of the Sackville title. For her that was enough: he *must* be good. For us grandsons he seemed invested with every *droit de seigneur*. Subsequently I have come to see him differently. He was certainly gentle and unostentatious, but he was a man who lived for pleasure, a snob (the prisoner as well as the beneficiary of his rank and times) who cast an indifferent eye at the labouring Midlands as he hurried northwards in his first-class carriage to shoot and fish. His duties on the Kent County Council he carried out without enthusiasm. It was only in his two wars that he discovered the dignity of achievement. For the rest of his life he amused himself. Vita writes that for years he was 'inexplicably' in love with Lady Constance Hatch. To me it is not inexplicable at all. He became increasingly off-hand with Victoria to whom he owed so much, uninterested in her pursuits, bored by her clever friends. He preferred an uncritical, undemanding society woman to the wife who was always asking necessary but uncomfortable questions about the estate, and who was growing stout with middle age. The eventual collapse of their marriage was as much his fault as hers. Of Vita he was fond, but he never began to understand her complicated personality, and discouraged all her wide-eyed enthusiasms as a girl. 'I wish', he was always complaining to Victoria, 'I wish that Vita was more *normal*.'

For years Victoria tolerated her husband's gallivanting and sullenness as she tolerated her father's taciturnity and rudeness. Gradually she began to form her own circle of more stimulating and attractive companions. There were no women among her intimates, and no younger men. She made a corner in millionaires and lonely elderly artists. The list of her conquests dispels the impression left by *Pepita* that she was nothing but a scatter-brained charmer, for men like Sir John Murray Scott, Pierpont Morgan, Kipling, Lord Kitchener, W. W. Astor, J. L. Garvin, Auguste Rodin, Sir Edwin Lutyens, Lord Leverhulme, Henry Ford and Gordon Selfridge would not have sought her company again and again after a first meeting unless she had as much to offer them as they to her. Even in her fifties she still had a great physical appeal. One of her old admirers, Cecil Spring-Rice, wrote to her: 'I tell you, you are charming, fascinating, heaven knows what. There is no end to your perfections ... You are an accomplished mistress in love. You play with it and use it and manage it, like a seagull the wind, on which he floats but is never carried away.' She throve on the unpleasant Edwardian convention of the touch of a finger from an old flame, and a bunch of orchids next day. She enjoyed adulation, but in her middle age was repelled by physical lust. She craved luxury, and was not too proud actually to beg. She loved power, but it must be given to her; she would not impose it. She could be cruel. She was both tender and fierce, quick to tears and quicker to sharp repartee.

Several of her new friends fell deeply in love with her, among them Pierpont Morgan, Astor and Rodin, but her diary, which is frank enough about their advances, is reticent about her response. She kept all her letters from William Waldorf Astor in an envelope marked, significantly (for, yes, she was vain), 'For Vita to read after my death', and in them he left little to the imagination: 'A woman in the flower of her prime needs a romantic attachment. It is the knowledge that someone is thinking of you, desires you, longs for the touch of your beautiful body, that keeps the heart young. Sweetheart, goodbye.' Of one meeting with Pierpont Morgan in 1912 she wrote in her diary: 'He holds my hand with much affection and says he will never care for me in any way I would not approve of, that he was sorry to be so old, but I was the one woman he loved and he would never change.' Undeterred by this, she invited him to Knole the following week: 'He has a wonderful personality. I have never met anyone so attractive. One forgets his nose entirely after a few minutes. He said he would be seventy-five next April.' She herself was then fifty, and weighed twelve stone. As for Rodin, it is quite clear from his letters, the extravagant compliments which he paid her in his studio (every one recorded at length in her diary) and his marble bust of her which illustrates this book, that he was for several years infatuated with her. She permitted him liberties but not licence. There is something distasteful about this side of her character. Lionel's flirtations with pretty young women were to be preferred.

Of all her admirers the most permanent was Seery, Sir John Murray Scott. Vita has described him so fully - in her auto-

biography and in *Pepita*, that there is no need to labour the point
that he was Lady Sackville's devoted companion from 1897 until
his death in 1912. Constantly quarrelling, they could not bear to
be apart, and when they were, wrote to each other twice a day.
They both had something of the Latin in them, she by birth, he
by long residence in France. It was fun to duel, and even more
fun to make up. They were a couple of aristocratic curators,
she of Knole, he of half the Wallace collection, buying, selling,
speculating, arranging, valuing – and knowing that there was
money enough, his money, to purchase anything which either of
them really wanted. They shared his purse: to buy for her was
like buying for himself. Of course she liked Seery for his money:
if he had been penniless half the fun would have been missing.
His wealth gave him grandeur – and what a *pied-à-terre* was the
rue Lafitte, what a country cottage Bagatelle, what a playground
Sluie! In London they were always in and out of each other's
houses, and he a constant visitor to Knole. At Sluie she had long
hours alone with him, while old Lionel slept, young Lionel shot
and fished, and Vita wrestled with the hall-boy on the moors.

That was the open side of their relationship. The hidden side
was not physical love, for I accept my mother's verdict that it
never existed apart from a little hand-patting, but his steady
financial subsidy to Knole. All the facts came out after Seery's
death. The Knole estate had an income of £13,000 a year, and
this was enough to maintain the fabric of the house, and pay the
staff of sixty indoor and outdoor servants and the household bills.
But it did not pay for Victoria's improvements, her large house in
Hill Street, Lionel's sporting expeditions, their constant weekend
parties, her extravagance in clothes and bibelots, and the enormous
expenses of the legitimacy case (£40,000 in lawyers' fees alone).
The estate was heavily in debt. When Seery came to hear of
their difficulties, he volunteered help, first by loans and then by
converting loans into gifts, and promised Victoria that by his Will
he intended to set her free from all financial worry. In his lifetime
he gave her and young Lionel £84,000. She never directly asked
for it, but never refused it, and was careful to let Seery know of
her embarrassments. Lionel encouraged her. 'I have had many

unpleasantnesses with my dear old Seery', she wrote in her diary for 1904, 'but Lionel advises me to be very diplomatic and put up with his humour. He says I must think of the future.' She knew that Seery could afford to help her and that it gave him pleasure, and she persuaded herself that it was not to her that he was being so generous, but to Knole, which he loved. Seery's family, watching his fortune melt away to a woman whom they regarded as an interloper and an adventuress, were not so charitable. They called the Sackvilles 'The Locusts', even before they knew about the will.

It was against a background of impending crisis that Vita grew up. There were three threats to her future: Grandpapa might have secretly married Pepita, as Vita's uncle Henry claimed, and if he could prove it, he would inherit Knole, not her father; secondly, her mother might one day quarrel so irrevocably with Seery that he would cancel his Will; thirdly, even if he did not, the Scott family might successfully dispute it. Vita gradually became aware of these family secrets, for they were endlessly discussed over the dinner-table, but her childhood, though lonely, was otherwise unruffled.

The surviving evidence supports in general her sketchy account of her earliest self. She was fractious with other children, though not so brutal as she suggests. When she was five, Lady Winchilsea wrote to her mother complaining that 'Vita was rough with little Mountjoy'; and six years later Victoria reproves her: 'Dada was telling me lately that he was afraid you had become a little abrupt and rough, so you must try, my very dear child, to copy Mama and remember that it gives people pain if they are not treated very kindly and thoughtfully.' But Victoria's attitude to Vita could be indulgent: 'She is extremely intelligent, and such a sweet child'; 'She is a very good child'; 'She speaks French so well, and is making good progress with her German.' Vita preferred the blacker picture of her childhood. Describing for Harold in 1912 what she was like ten years earlier, she wrote: 'I was an unsociable and unnatural girl with long black hair and long black legs, and very short frocks and very dirty nails and torn clothes. I used to disappear for hours up high trees, and they couldn't find me until I threw eggs out of the birds-nests onto their heads.' Violet Trefusis, then Keppel, recollected in her autobiography, *Don't Look Round*, her first impression of Vita:

> She was tall for her age, gawky, most unsuitably dressed in what appeared to be her mother's old clothes. We were both consummate snobs, and talked chiefly about our ancestors. I essayed a few superior allusions to Paris. She was not impressed. She digressed on her magnificent house in the country, her dogs, her rabbits. I thought her nice but rather childish. Vita at that age was stolidly, uncompromisingly, British. In her deep stagnant gaze there was no dawning Wanderlust.

Among the earliest documents in Vita's handwriting is a Will which she drew up in 1901, aged nine, and it confirms the impression of her exceptional tomboyishness:

> To Mama: A quarter of my bank money and my diamond V [a brooch in that shape].
> To Dada: A quarter of my bank money. My pony and cart. My cricket set. My football.
> To Seery: My khaki. My miniature. My claret jug. My whip.
> To Bentie [her governess]: My pearl V. Half my bank money. My ships.
> To Ralph [Battiscombe, a Sevenoaks boy]: My armour. My swords and guns. My fort. My soldiers. My tools. My bow-and-arrow. My pocket money. My target.

Ralph Battiscombe, apparently her residuary legatee, since the last three items were added in pencil as she acquired them, disappears from this story, but his existence shows that Vita was not entirely without favourites of her own age. '*Hier les Battiscombe sont venu prendre le thé*', she wrote to her mother in 1903. '*Nous avons joué au cricket, et après le thé, Ralph et moi, nous avons pris le fusil-à-air et pendant que Sylvia et Queenie se promenaient avec Fie* [Vita's new governess, after Bentie was sacked], *nous* stalked them.' One reads in her mother's diaries of nursery parties at Knole of up to twenty other children, and Vita was made presentable enough to be allowed downstairs each evening, and to attend, aged twelve, a banquet in the Great Hall at Knole for the West Kent Yeomanry, in which her father was an officer. She was twice a bridesmaid, at the weddings of her Uncle Charles and the Duke of Westminster.

Other sides of her nature soon began to appear. *'Je suis très contente de ne pas être à Londres'*, she wrote to her mother, a sentiment which she was to echo throughout her life. 'Vita', wrote Victoria, 'is busy gardening, and cultivates mostly salads and vegetables for her Grandpapa', and her first garden was a large V in cress. In 1904, at Sluie, 'I had to scold Vita severely for being so thoughtless when I give her any little commission to do. She forgets and dawdles terribly. She sobbed last night, a thing she rarely does. She minds me very much [Victoria never learnt to speak English faultlessly], is very obedient, but so absent-minded and careless and untidy.' A picture begins to form: Vita was tamed by her mother when with her, untamed when not, loving the country and its sports, pampered by nannies, very much the daughter of the house, with a streak of stubbornness and a yearning for solitary adventure. There is no mention in her mother's diaries of the 'two or three times I tried to run away', so the attempts cannot have been too serious. She was happy at Knole, which was certainly no prison. On the night before her wedding she looked back on her childhood:

> Pictures and galleries and empty rooms,
> Small wonder that my games were played alone;
> Half of the rambling house to call my own,
> And wooded gardens with mysterious glooms....
> This I remember, and the carven oak,
> The long and polished floors, the many stairs,
> Th'heraldic windows, and the velvet chairs,
> And portraits that I knew so well, they almost spoke.

Through Knole and her preferred solitude she discovered the joy of writing. The diary which she started in 1907 begins disconcertingly: 'R zn gl ivhgliv gsv uligfmvh lu gsv uznrob'. It is a code touchingly simple to crack, for it consisted in nothing more than substituting z for a, y for b, and so on, throughout the alphabet. When decoded it reads, 'I am to restore the fortunes of the family', having received that morning £1 for a poem published in the *Onlooker*, the first money she ever earned. The diary continues (transliterated): 'Mother scolded me this morning because she said I wrote too much, and Dada told her he did not approve of my writing. I am afraid my book will not be published. Mother does not know how much I love writing.' The book was *The King's Secret*, a novel of seventy-five thousand words about Knole in the time of Charles II. It contains a description, unmistakably autobiographical, of her boy-hero at the same occupation as herself:

> In a little arbour situated in the garden at Knole, a boy muffled up in a blue scarf was busy scribbling something in a ponderous book. The arbour was furnished only with a wooden seat and a table, and its sole occupants were the boy and a big hound who lay at his feet. His pen flowed rapidly over the paper. Outside the snow lay thick on the ground. The floor of the arbour was of stone, and the boy's foot tapped impatiently on it when he was in difficulties ... Never having been much with older children, in whose company he did not find himself at home, he had made his own thoughts his companions. He feared the shots of ridicule which might be fired at him did he air any of his opinions, so he held his tongue and committed his thoughts to paper only. He wrote from morning till evening.

In little over four years, between 1906 and 1910, Vita wrote eight full-length novels (one in French) and five plays, and nearly all the manuscripts survive at Sissinghurst. Her plots lay ready to hand, in the story of Knole and the Sackvilles. *The King's Secret* was not the first. She began her literary career at eleven years old with ballads in the *Horatius* manner,

> The good Queen Bess was wond'ring
> What noble she could send
> To take to Mary Queen of Scots
> The tidings of her end.
> When up rose Thomas Sackville,
> A doughty man and true...

continued with a bloodthirsty dramatization of the story of Ali Baba (the scene transferred, of course, to Knole), and then wrote *Edward Sackville: The Tale of a Cavalier*, a novel of sixty-five thousand words penned in a clear childish hand as easy to read as print, with scarcely a correction. Her fluency was remarkable. She taught herself the techniques of narrative and dialogue by careful observation of what she read, since she had no literary mentor and was yet to go to school. One can spot the strong influence of *Cyrano*. The Sackvilles, who were on the whole a modest family given to lengthy bouts of melancholia, were transformed by Vita into troubadours who played the most romantic roles at the most dramatic moments of English history, and behaved in every situation with the utmost gallantry. Here is Lord Dorset talking to his son:

'Never did I think', said the proud old Earl sadly, 'that I should have a son who would bring disgrace on our house. Tell me your name.'
'What mean you, my Lord?'
'What is your name?'
'Buckhurst', his son answered with surprise.
'I mean your full name. How are your letters superscribed?'
'To Richard Sackville, Lord Buckhurst.'
'And you can bear that name, the name of Sackville, and yet commit a disgraceful action? Out on you, my son, do you not blush to own it? Nay, but I blush myself for shame of you! Seek your own chamber. I will have no more of you.'
Buckhurst went without a word and threw himself on his bed, but sleep would not come to him. His father's words rang in his head. He had committed a disgraceful action; he who was a Sackville.

The disgraceful action was that he had been caught flirting with his cousin.

When Vita went to France and Italy, the novels and plays were about Richelieu and Robespierre and the Medici, but in every country and at every epoch her characters spoke the same nineteenth-century version of seventeenth-century English dialogue. The only novel left unfinished was *The Life of Alcibiades*, which she abandoned when even she realized that Periclean Athens must have been a rather different place from Cromwellian Knole. The novel bears no signs that she had yet read the *Symposium*. Alcibiades in his youthful manhood was firmly saddled with a wife.

At seventeen, having had her gloomy *Chatterton* privately printed at Sevenoaks, she attempted something more ambitious. It was a novel of 120,000 words called *Behind the Mask*, set in modern times. Her style had not yet matured. The book begins: 'The Baroness d'Arquailles owned a magnificent castle in the heart of the mountains of Auvergne. Far from any other house, far distant even from a large town, she might pace her ramparts like the fair lady of some brave knight of old'; but as she made progress with her story, her wings grew stronger. It is a love-story of unbelievable austerity, in which the key sentence reflects her contemporary attitude to men: 'She liked him for his respectful attitude of deference towards her, mingled with the cool authority of future possession.' Then this: 'It is better for us to live apart and love each other all our lives, than to marry and quarrel after a few months. Love is too tolerant. Love admits of no imperfections.' The moral is clear: you must never marry the person you love, for fear of spoiling it; you must marry someone you don't love, for then there is nothing to spoil. Again, 'There was no vulgar passion. Their love was too pure for that.' She says to him: 'I love you absolutely, completely and entirely, so much that I can renounce you without a pang.' He says to her: 'And I love you so much that I obey, and go.' It is a wildly romantic and foolish book.

At Knole in 1907 four people closely related to each other and linked by common forbodings, but totally different in character, were slowly moving apart. Victoria's diary gives this glimpse of their outwardly placid, inwardly uneasy, existence:

> I should like Vita to be more open. She seems indifferent: it is her life as an only child which is the cause of it. She is so wrapped up in her writings that it is apt to make her forget things. She is a very good child on the whole, but with a tendency to be too sure of herself, and a little bit hard. She has changed enormously since her 'things' have come on. If only she would become warmer-hearted. It has been rather hard to live all my life with Papa and Lionel who

are both so cold on the surface, and now I find the same disposition in my child. I like my old Seery because he is so *sympathique* and I want that so much, with my Spanish nature. I hate flirting and trifling with men, and Lionel knows it well enough. I have given up the hope of making him more outspoken; he is a dear, gentle, quiet nature, but he never takes the initiative or the lead, and is frightfully reserved. Papa is also hopeless in that way.

Next year, in September 1908, Lord Sackville died, and the abscess which had been gathering for years burst suddenly. Henry produced his carefully accumulated evidence that he was his father's legitimate son, the rightful heir to Knole. The case was heard in the High Court in February 1910. The story, for newspaper readers, had everything. A family which belonged to the highest Edwardian society were quarrelling publicly about inheritance – the inheritance of one of the most historic houses and titles in England, and a large sum of money – all because a young diplomatist had fallen in love with a Spanish ballerina sixty years before, and made her his mistress. Best of all, the new Lady Sackville was obliged to dispute her brother's evidence, and avow, openly and emphatically, that she and all her father's other children were bastards. If Henry could prove his legitimacy, she and her husband would be dispossessed of Knole and left destitute.

The weakness of Henry's case was that he could not show conclusively that Lionel and Pepita were ever married, and even if they had been, the marriage would have been invalid, because Pepita was already married to Oliva. There had been a separation but no divorce (and could not have been, in nineteenth-century Spain), and Oliva had outlived Pepita by eighteen years. Its strength was that Lionel had on several occasions legally claimed Pepita as his wife and five of her seven children as legitimate, including Henry himself. About Victoria no such claim was ever made ('*fille de père inconnu*'), nor about the eldest son, Maximilien, who had entered the world as 'son of Oliva and Pepita', a statement which was admitted by both sides to be untrue. All the others were described on their birth and baptismal certificates as children of 'Lionel Sackville-West and his wife Josefa (*Pepita*) Duran'. In 1869 old Lionel had signed a declaration before the Mayor of

Arcachon to the same effect, and on Pepita's death-certificate she was again named as his wife. When the girls were married, they were all described as the daughters of Lionel, without qualification. Fortunately all this evidence was known before old Lionel's death, and in 1897 he had put his name to a long *démenti*, beginning, 'I am a bachelor', and affirming that he had made these false declarations 'simply and solely to save the reputation of Pepita, and at her earnest request'. After her death he saw no reason to perpetuate the lie, for it now involved a considerable fortune, a peerage, and the laws of his own country – and he held a very senior position in the British Foreign Service. He wrote to Henry before leaving for Washington, telling him unequivocally: 'I never married your mother, and consequently you, as well as your brothers and sisters, are my illegitimate children.'

In face of this repudiation of the evidence by the man who should know best, and who could have had no other motive for depriving his son of the inheritance in favour of a nephew, Henry turned to fraud. He produced in court an alleged copy of Amalia's birth certificate, to which the words 'Parents married in Frankfurt-am-Main' had been added in a later hand, but the words did not appear on the original, and no record of such a marriage could be traced at Frankfurt. Secondly, he or his agents (but the handwriting experts said it was Henry) tampered with the register of the church in Madrid in such a way as to suggest that no marriage between Pepita and Oliva had ever taken place. Unluckily for Henry, many witnesses to the wedding were still alive, and it had been separately recorded in four other official registers which he had overlooked. His case collapsed. On the third day of the hearing he dismissed his Counsel, Sir Edward Clarke, for 'mishandling his testimony', and appeared, lamentably, in person, beginning his address to the Judge: 'If your Lordship will give me time, I will go on with this case myself. I know I shall lose it, but I will have a good try.' By the fifth day Henry had had enough: 'I can do nothing more, my Lord. I am done. I cannot defend myself any further. I retire my petition.' Judgement was given against him, with costs. To this day it is not known how Henry, an unsuccessful farmer, raised the money to fight his case, but it was probably

66

financed by speculators who hoped to profit from his victory. The Sackvilles' costs were never paid.

The now undoubted Lady Sackville and her husband and daughter were greeted on their return to Knole by a welcome more suited to someone who had just established her legitimacy instead of its opposite. The day was declared a public holiday in Sevenoaks. The horses were taken from their traces at the approaches to the town, and the local fire-brigade pulled the carriage through the streets and park to the very doors of Knole, under triumphal arches and between cheering crowds. Bands preceded the embarrassed cortège, and at intervals the carriage was halted for the presentation of illuminated addresses and bouquets of flowers. Vita says that she rather enjoyed it, but the photographs of the occasion are better evidence: she looked despondent and ashamed.

That was 'The Case'. It was followed three years later by 'The Other Case', which was even more dramatic, and the two in combination made the Sackvilles temporarily the most notorious family in the country, and Vita, to her dismay, the darling of the crowds. The nickname 'Kidlet', by which Seery had called her, was for several years enough to identify her in a headline, and the publicity and gossip which subsequently attended her activities and the publication of her early books went far beyond her wishes or youthful deserts. I shall describe the Scott case ahead of its proper chronological place in order to clear away from the narrative of Vita's personal life a massive landslide which could have wrecked it.

Seery died on 17 January 1912, collapsed in a chair at Hertford House. In his Will he left to Lady Sackville £150,000 in cash 'in gratitude for all your affection and kindness to me', and the contents of the house in the rue Lafitte, of which the value was estimated to be £350,000. To Vita he left a diamond necklace, and the 'expectation' that her mother would wish to pass on to her the bulk of his fortune when she died. These bequests were to be duty-free, the duty to be paid out of the residue of his estate, which he divided among his brothers and sisters, for he was a bachelor, together with his London house and its contents. Seery's family disputed the Will on the grounds that Lady Sackville had used undue influence to alienate their brother's affection from them, and to secure for herself a wholly disproportionate part of his property. The defence was that Sir John had every right to leave it to whomsoever he wished, and that being of sound, indeed agile, mind until the day of his death, he was quite capable of resisting any influence of that kind and could have changed his Will at any moment. His affection for Lady Sackville was simply that of a connoisseur for a charming companion who shared his tastes, and he wished to relieve her and Knole of financial anxiety after his death.

The case went on for nine days, starting on 24 June 1913. It attracted even larger and more glittering crowds than the Pepita case, for the two stars of the contemporary Bar, Sir Edward Carson and F. E. Smith, were appearing respectively for the Sackvilles and the Scotts, and the material was even juicier, being more recent and involving even larger sums of money and even greater scandal. The ladies in the public gallery dressed as if for Ascot, and brought with them cushions to ease the unaccustomed hardness of the benches and picnic-hampers to avoid vacating during the luncheon interval seats which might be filled by disappointed late-comers.

F. E. Smith's opening address lasted nine hours. He drew a picture of a grasping woman who would stoop to any device to lay her hands on Sir John's money. He recounted incident after incident during the fourteen years of their friendship to demonstrate how she had gradually edged the Scotts out of her way. She began by humiliating them in the guise of helpfulness. She rearranged the furniture in their houses; she asked her own friends to Seery's dinner-parties 'to make them more lively'; she then suggested to Seery that only one sister at a time, and later none, need attend these parties, 'for people don't come to meet your sisters'; she introduced their guests to each other 'because the sisters don't know who anyone is'; she acted as hostess at rue Lafitte when King Edward came to lunch, and the sisters were told to eat in a hotel; she chose the music for their soirées; she borrowed the Scotts' carriages without asking, and Seery's chef for Knole;

she kept the brothers away from Sluie. But it went much further than that. She flattered Seery, 'mesmerized' him, wheedled money out of him during his lifetime and more or less dictated his Will, working with her feminine strength upon his masculine weakness, not because she liked him (oh no, she found him rather boring), but because she was mercenary and he 'was a very innocent man, easily influenced'.

When the Scotts entered the witness-box one by one to corroborate these charges, the contrast between them and the lovely woman sitting in the body of the court was so apparent that Lady Sackville's case was won almost before she or her Counsel had uttered a word. She was like a yacht among a crowd of fishing-smacks. It was quite evident that the only reason why Seery had preferred her company to theirs was that they were dull and she delightful. It was quite true that she had thrown them into the shade, but they were shadowy people already, and their jealousy rendered them even more unattractive to him. She had remodelled his social life in the way that he most desired, and in doing so she could not help but expose his sisters' deficiencies. She let a ray of originality into his humdrum life, and he showed his gratitude to her in the best way he knew. Besides, it was not Scott money, nor family heirlooms, which he was leaving to an outsider: it was Wallace money and the Wallace collection (or the half of it which was not already in Hertford House). Had Seery gained that inheritance by 'undue influence' over Sir Richard and Lady Wallace? The sisters had certainly never said so during the many years when they had benefited from it. Yet it had come to him for exactly the same reasons as those which led him to leave part of it to Lady Sackville – because they had been fond of him, and he was fond of her. He was not cutting his brothers and sisters out of his Will; he was providing for them generously, as he had during his lifetime, allowing them to share his house and its superb contents, which were now bequeathed to them. If he had married and had children, they would have been fortunate to inherit anything from him at all.

These were the arguments which Carson put foward day after day, and his star witnesses were Lady Sackville and Vita. Lady

Sackville's cross-examination by F. E. Smith is one of the classics of English legal history. It lasted two whole days. It was not so much her tart repartees ('How dare you say that to me?' 'You don't seem to realize, Mr Smith, that Knole is bigger than Hampton Court') which impressed the jury, as her reasonable answers to brutal questioning about her private life, her most intimate letters, even her husband's friendship with Lady Constance. It was a performance equal to her triumph during her first few months in Washington, and it was based on inner calm, strong nerves and an acute memory for dates and figures, and (as Vita remarks) for 'what she had said the day before, or even the hour before'. Not once did she falter.

Vita considered that her mother's evidence 'although truthful in the letter, was certainly misleading in the spirit'. I believe that this is putting it too strongly. In her constant quarrels with Seery, Lady Sackville had never been the first to make peace, threatening time after time to leave him, and never more so than during the last years of his life, when her interest in preserving friendly relations was greatest. He held the Will over her like a threat, but she never capitulated. A few months before Seery died, she wrote to him: 'It would be much better if you refrained from reprimanding me and asking me constantly to make amends. I cannot and will not submit to it.' Six weeks later, when he renewed his threat to leave all his possessions to the Wallace Collection, she retorted: 'Well, make up your mind, and then we won't have any more talk about it. I will fill the gap by Spealls [her shop].' This was not the language of a sycophant or schemer. She certainly wanted his money, but on her own terms. 'You old silly', she would call him. 'You little rascal', he would reply. But neither meant it. The most that could be said against her was neatly put by the *Pall Mall Gazette* at the time: 'Sir John was ready to give, and Lady Sackville scrupled not to receive.'

Vita's part in the case was mainly concerned with the evidence of the most bizarre witness on the Scotts' side, a Major Arbuthnot, who testified that on a particular evening he had called on Seery at his London house, and opened by mistake the door into the library:

There were two ladies in the room, and they were going through the drawers of Sir John's desk, evidently searching for papers. I stepped back, and one of the ladies said 'Now!', and Lady Sackville came out followed by Miss Sackville-West, and they went down the passage on tiptoe hanging their heads down as if not to be seen. Miss Sackville-West put her hand up like that [*indicating*] as she went out. After dinner I told Sir John what I had seen. He looked dazed and wrung his hands. He said, '*Ah mon Dieu, c'est incroyable.*'

The clear inference was that they were searching for a Codicil which radically altered the Will. When Vita was asked about this incident, she was able to show by the evidence of her own diary and her mother's that she had been ill all that day, and Lady Sackville had stayed with her. Nor was there any mention of it in Seery's meticulous journal, and no servants came forward to support the Major's statement. It was as much Vita's appearance and manner in the witness-box — 'a tall dark girl, very young and very nervous, in a demure grey hat trimmed with cherries, and a deep white *fichu*' — as what she said, which convinced the jury that she could have had no part in such a ridiculous stratagem, and her mother, even if she were guilty of it herself, would have had more sense than to take with her so innocent a child. At the end of Vita's evidence, the Judge (Sir Samuel Evans) asked her kindly: 'Who gave you the name Kidlet?' 'I do not remember. I think it was Sir John.'

Sir Samuel's summing-up was strongly in the Sackvilles' favour. 'If it was the influence of friendship', he told the jury, 'the influence arising out of a community of tastes, out of the affinity of natures ... it was perfectly legitimate, and you ought to say so in your verdict.' They did. They conferred for only twelve minutes, and decided for the Sackvilles.

Lady Sackville was now a rich woman. She sold the contents of the rue Lafitte for £270,000, and this was perhaps the only shameful part of the affair, for Seery (as well she knew) had hoped that she would use his 'fine things' to enrich the Knole collection, not sell them to provide her with pocket-money.

Among those who gave evidence for the Sackvilles in the Scott case was Rosamund Grosvenor; and among those who heard Vita give hers were Violet Keppel and Harold Nicolson.

Rosamund was the daughter of Algernon Grosvenor, a relative of the Duke of Westminster, and until 1908 they lived at Sevenoaks. Daily she came to Knole to share Vita's lessons, though she was four years older, and old Lionel composed a little saying about her, 'Rosamund Grosvenor got nearly run ovner', which bothered Vita because she could not see how he got it to rhyme properly. Rosamund stayed frequently at Knole for weekends, and went twice to Sluie, and once to the rue Lafitte. Vita's early references to her in her diary are very tepid: 'She is likeable enough, but very ordinary.' 'She has no personality – that's all.' Rosamund's letters could not have been less suited to Vita's mood in what she calls in her autobiography 'my most savage years'. They began 'My sweet darling' and ended 'Your little Rose'. Even during their brief but intense love-affair, her letters never failed to strike the wrong note of deference, cloying sentimentality, possessiveness and mock anger. 'I do miss you, darling, and I want to feel your soft cool face coming out of that mass of pussy hair.' 'My poor little head begins to ache. I was miz, but I *do* forgive you.' 'How unspeakably lucky I am to possess you. I shall think of *you, you, you* and nothing else, tomorrow, next day, and Sunday and Monday, and every day and hour and moment!'

Violet was two years younger than Vita, but to pick up one of her childhood letters after Rosamund's is like handling rockets after sparklers. Take this, written when she was fifteen, in English for once, perhaps because it suited the Gothic theme, describing Vita's visit to Scotland after her grandfather's death the year before:

> I arrived here yesterday [Duntreath Castle]. I have also arrived at the conclusion that I love this place almost better than anywhere else. Do you remember it at all well? Do you remember the peacocks stalking round the house in the small hours of the morning uttering penetrating but unmusical cries, the gorgeous flaming sunsets that set the hills a-kindling for all the world like *cabochon* rubies? Do you remember the staid and stolid girl – a remote connection of mine –

whose birthday we celebrated at a place called Lennox Castle? Do
you remember the enforced exercise *à travers pluie et tempête* which
I considered it my duty to inflict on you? And the secret staircase
and Sonia's threats to accompany us although she had no clothes
on to speak of? And Willie's violent infatuation which he really
considered incurable at the time? And the haunted room and the
dumb Laird behind the dining-room screen? And the 'Viper of
Milan', and the deluge of Deucalion which inundated us all whenever we set foot out of doors? Don't you remember the purposeless
incessant tick-tock of pigeon feet upon the roof, and the jackdaws
flying from turret to window, and the desultory cries of the night-
owls?

This next letter, translated from her exquisite French, was
written in October 1910, when Violet was sixteen:

I love you, Vita, because I have had to fight for you so hard. I love
you because you never gave me back the ring I lent you. I love you
because you will never capitulate. I love you for your fine intelligence, for your literary ambition, for your innocent flirtatious-
ness. And I love you because you never seem to doubt my love. I
love in you what I know is also in me, that is, imagination, a gift
for languages, taste, intuition, and a mass of other things. I love you,
Vita, because I have seen your soul.

Here is Violet at seventeen:

*Ah Vita, je suis toute triste quand je songe combien nous ressemblons à
deux joueurs, avides de gain, dont l'un ne voudrait hasarder une carte qu'à
condition que l'autre avançât le sienne au même moment! Tu ne veux pas
me dire 'Je t'aime parce que tu crains à tort, la plupart du temps, que, d'un
élan simultané, je ne te le dise aussi!*
[Oh Vita, it makes me so sad when I think how like to two gamblers
we are, both greedy to win, one of whom will not risk throwing a
card unless the other simultaneously throws his! You will not tell
me that you love me, since you fear (wrongly, for most of the time)
that I will not make the same declaration to you at the same
moment!]

Finally this, in translation, a month later, anticipating so much
of what was to follow:

I would like to tear you away from your Italy, slap you on both cheeks and take you on a pleasure-trip with me far away, far from everything which could act like a narcotic on a nature which appears from your last two letters to be half-asleep. My God, my God, how can I shatter this Olympian calm which obliterates my purple and scarlet memories of you! First we must go to Spain, you as my pupil, I as your Cicerone. I will show you Manzanarès with its winding lanes; Irun, overshadowed by the Pyrenees, with its lovely cruel girls; Pamplona, flanked by eroded mountains; Burgos, sad and archaic. Follow me everywhere! I will show you eyes of dark velvet, the fandango, undulating bodies, the throbbing castanets, the magpies strutting between the olives, the sad plains, a fluttering mantilla. Follow me, follow me! I will force you to see a hand poised to strike, blood shed in secret, the calculated vendetta which is pitiless and has never been heard to speak of pardon. I will show you treason, infamy, women without scruple, without shame. I will show you madness, Vita (madness, do you hear?), which cracks from the fingers of a woman who saw her husband disembowelled last Sunday in the bull-ring!

Vita first met Violet Keppel in 1904 when she was twelve and Violet ten. She was the elder daughter of George and Alice Keppel and had one sister, Sonia, who was six years younger. Like Vita she had no friends until they met each other at a tea-party in London. They went to the same school in South Audley Street, Miss Helen Wolff's, where Vita carried off all the prizes, and met again in Paris, where they performed together Vita's interminable play La Masque de Fer before an audience of sleepy servants at the rue Lafitte. In 1908 Violet and Rosamund were Vita's companions on her first visit to Florence. 'It became quite clear', wrote Violet in Don't Look Round, 'that Vita's reaction to Italy was exactly what mine had been to France. She was bowled over, subjugated, inarticulate with love. She would wander from church to church, picture to picture.' They stayed at the Villa Pestellini, an ochre-coloured house with loggias and terraces and a cottage in the garden, and descended each day to the city, sightseeing with a rapture that few tourists have experienced. On her return, Vita poured her love of Italy helterskelter into her current novel.

It is a sense almost physical, so strong is it, a feeling of desire, saved from vulgarity by its very mysticism, the intoxicating repletion of beauty, in the mode of calm and sumptuous repose; it is the brilliant, mysterious, resplendent soul of the Renaissance, hovering still, infinitely sad beneath its peacock colours, in its unprobed depths.

She had suddenly grown up.

On her second visit to Italy, next year, she met Marchese Orazio Pucci, son of one of the oldest Florentine families, and he fell immediately and inconsolably in love with her. Vita, aged seventeen, was a little taken aback, but delighted to find that the Pucci name opened every door which had previously been closed to her, starting with the Palazzo Pucci itself. When she left Florence for Rome, Pucci followed next day, uninvited; on the Channel steamer when Vita and her mother were returning home, there was Pucci again. Lady Sackville liked him ('He is such a self-possessed and real gentleman', she noted in her diary. 'I feel so sorry for him, as I am sure he loves Vita and knows it is hopeless') and invited him to Knole. There he becomes 'Poor little Pucci ... He took heaps of photographs of Vita in her summer-house and at her writing-table. I let him see in a lot of little ways that he could never marry her. She does not in the least want to marry him; she knows that he would be too masterful for her, and the life too quiet.' At dinner that night he put on his uniform, 'to please Vita ... I don't think she was touched at all, poor little chap.' Next year, Pucci tried again, when Vita went to Florence for the third year in succession. She was still disconcerted by such homage, but now accepted it more easily, and they spent every day together, motoring through Tuscany and Umbria, with her old governess Fie as a chaperone. Vita's diary reveals her slightly warmer response:

There is difficulty with *il devotissimo O.*, who wants madly to come to Venice with us and is not allowed to. However, he and Fie make it up, and he can come as far as Bologna tomorrow. I suppose I ought not to have come here [Florence], because of him: he has got it really badly! This year he has made no secrets, but plunged into declarations the very first evening. I like him well enough, *en ami*. So I told him, which does not suit him at all.

He followed them to Venice nevertheless, but was ordered by Fie to stay at a separate hotel and made no further progress with his suit. He wrote to Vita constantly; she seldom replied. At Monte Carlo, in 1911, he finally gave up. He proposed again; she refused ('My God, how unhappy I would be with him!'), and on the following day, 'He says he will go to Africa. He is quite changed. He spoke coldly and seemed ill, lowering his eyes.' She next heard from him that he was in Tripolitania sublimating his love in desperate combat with the Senussi. I do not believe that they ever met again. He married happily and devoted the rest of his life to caring for the buildings of Florence. When I saw him there in 1944, he asked kindly after my mother, without mentioning his early adoration for her, but I felt his eyes upon my back as I left the room.

At eighteen Vita was more than just 'less plain'. She was lovely. The Laszlo portrait of her, painted in January 1910, confirms exactly the impression which she made upon Violet on her return from a long absence in Ceylon and Germany:

> I expected a representative Englishwoman, perpendicular, gauche, all knobs and knuckles. No one had told me that Vita had turned into a beauty. The knobs and knuckles had disappeared. She was tall and graceful. The profound hereditary Sackville eyes were as pools from which the morning mist had lifted. A peach might have envied her complexion. [*Don't Look Round*]

She was still secretive, and her friends remarked that she could hate as passionately as she could love. She was unpredictable, giving with both hands and then shutting her fingers tight into her palms. She was easily hurt by an unkindness, and nervous that she would be laughed at for failure, being desperately eager to excel. Although she tried to hide her feelings as much as possible, she had a craving for sympathy. With her parents she became increasingly reserved, and like them sought companionship elsewhere. She feared most her father's ridicule, because she loved him most, and would never allow him to read her books or accompany her to Italy, while he regretted (as he wrote to Lady Sackville) that 'Vita doesn't like more normal or ordinary things, but I see that it is no good trying to force her, and I am very much afraid that she will end by marrying a soul', by which he meant anyone with the slightest interest in the arts or general ideas.

Vita did her duty as the daughter of Knole and went to parties, sometimes to four balls a week and luncheons every day, and she enjoyed them if they were the sort of parties at which powdered footmen announced duchesses. Like both her parents she was a snob, in the sense that she attached exaggerated importance to birth and wealth, and believed that while the aristocracy had much in common with working people, particularly those who worked on the land, the middle class (or 'bedints' in Sackville language) were to be pitied and shunned, unless, like Seery or Lord Lever-hulme, they had acquired dignity by riches. When she was twelve years old, she could write to her mother, 'The little Gerard Leghs are not bedint, are they?', and, 'Yesterday we had a Sevenoaks girl to tea: she was rather nice, but a little bedint of course', and she never quite rid herself of this complex; her most famous novel, *The Edwardians*, written in 1930, was strongly influenced by it. She was a conforming rebel, a romantic aristocrat. The two sides of her character, the gipsy and the grandee, are well illustrated by the account she gives in her autobiography of her visit to Russia in 1909, and by a letter which she wrote to Harold during their engagement, describing a party at the American Embassy in London:

> Cambon and Imperiali [the French and Italian Ambassadors] sat on either side of me and made elaborate foreign compliments and said I ought to be an ambassadress. I said, No, I ought to live in a garret and be poor, and they threw up their hands and said, '*Ah mon Dieu quelle horreur!*' Then we went down the white marble staircase, and I felt a magnificent house wasn't to be despised. I liked it because it was so rich and unbedint and ambassadorial; and because I am a snob enough to love long dinner-tables covered with splendid fruit and orchids and gold plate, and people whose names I can find in the *Daily Mail* sitting all around. I get on with them so much better than with little dancing things in ballrooms. Except souls. I do like souls. They are amusing and easy and not heavy to talk to.

The little dancing things were the young men of noble birth whom her mother and father dangled before her. At least two of them were worth more than that description, Lord Lascelles and Lord Granby, each heir to one of the most magnificent houses in Britain, Harewood and Belvoir. Lascelles was much in love with her, but gossip had it that she would marry Granby. I do not believe that she was ever tempted. Her real friends were souls, but souls who had some breeding and a gun, who could make a fourth at bridge and knew the difference between claret and burgundy, young men like Robert Vansittart, Patrick Shaw-Stewart, Alec Cadogan, Duff Cooper, Archie Clark-Kerr, Philip Sassoon, the Grenfell brothers, Gerald Wellesley. It was the world in which Harold Nicolson had already found a natural place – with a significant difference: he had no gun; he could not play cards; he could not even dance.

Vita and Harold first met in the summer of 1910, at a dinner-party given by Anne Stanley before a Sherlock Holmes thriller, *The Speckled Band*. He was invited to Knole in June, as Lady Sackville's guest more than Vita's, and sat in the pouring rain to watch Vita's performance as Portia in the open-air Shakespearian masque. They met once or twice more in London during the season, but it was not until the autumn that she showed him any special favour:

Knole, 5 November 1910
My dear Mr Harold,
    I have been asked to 'ask a man' to dine on Thursday and go to a dance, so would you like to come? I promise you shan't be made to dance! Do come.
                            Yours very sincerely,
                                Vita Sackville-West
P.S. Mr Vansittart is here.

Harold was nearly twenty-four, Vita eighteen. His father was Sir Arthur Nicolson, recently British Ambassador in St Peters-burg, and now Permanent Under-Secretary of State at the Foreign Office; his mother was a sister of the former Vicereine, Lady Dufferin. After an unhappy boyhood at Wellington College,

Harold had suddenly blossomed at Balliol, and, to his father's astonishment, had succeeded in winning one of the coveted vacancies in the Foreign Office only the year before. Vita's first impressions of my father are given in her autobiography, and at this stage little need be added. His remarkable nature will gradually appear as this narrative progresses. He was immensely companionable, active, intelligent, very well-read, an undoubted soul, and had charming looks and excellent manners. Lady Sackville immediately took to him, but this was no recommendation to her daughter, for she had taken with equal warmth to Pucci and Lord Lascelles.

As Vita admits, her friendship with Harold developed slowly. In her diary (which for the next five years she kept in Italian, because her mother could not understand it) she recorded in January 1911 his departure after a brief visit to Monte Carlo as *cosa tristissima*, for she had found his company more than pleasing, and once, when they were playing draughts and she beat him, he said '*As-tu un franc?*', which thrilled her because he had *tutoyé*-d her. There is no further reference to him in her diary and no letters were exchanged between them, until September, when he came home from the Madrid Embassy and spent a weekend at Knole. He returned there for Christmas and the New Year, and it was then that he fell in love with her. Lady Sackville, who had a sharp eye for such things and their likely consequences, noted in her diary: 'I suspect the dear boy is very much in love with Vita; they have the same tastes and ideas – but where is the money to come from?' In his letter of thanks to Lady Sackville, Harold hinted at what she had already guessed, and in the manner which would most please her: 'No, I shan't find anyone in Constantinople [he had just been posted to the Embassy there]. I fear that I have an unfortunate faculty for admiring people who are far above me, and whom I can't marry. Perhaps it is lucky that I am going abroad.' He was to leave England on 24 January 1912. He had three weeks in which to prove to himself that his pessimism was unjustified.

Vita was whirled away from him by another round of parties to which he was not invited. *9 January*: Queen Anne's Mead,

Windsor, Lady Arran's house. Other guests: Diana Manners [Cooper], Patrick Shaw-Stewart, Lord Lascelles, Lord Nugent. *10 January*: Ball at Taplow – Lady Desborough. *12 January*: Eridge Castle. *14 January*: Ball at Tonbridge. Vita wrote to her mother:

> I enjoyed Taplow much more than any of the others. There were masses of people I knew, so many that I couldn't dance with half of them, though we stayed till 4! It was a shock to realize afterwards that I had danced almost the whole time with souls. What would Dada say? Lady Desborough was very amiable to me, and I like her son, Mr [Julian] Grenfell, who is enormously tall and danced with me and took me into supper.

On 16 January she went to stay with the Exeters at Burghley for the Stamford ball, and next morning Seery died. Vita heard the news from Lady Sackville on the eighteenth, and has described her quick dash to London and her relief that her own plans for that night were not cancelled, 'because by then I was sure that Harold meant to propose to me and I knew I should say yes'. Together they travelled down to The Grove, Watford, and changed there for the Salisburys' ball at Hatfield. Her diary gives a version of what happened different to that in the autobiography. Translated from the Italian, it reads:

> Until midnight I scarcely saw Harold, who then asked me to dance, and then we went up to the second floor where there was almost nobody. He asked me to marry him. I asked him to wait at least a year, because I am not yet sure. I seem to have dreamt it. For in the bottom of my heart I know that I *shall* marry him, and that we are virtually engaged. After having so much hoped that he would speak out before he went abroad, my only idea was to prevent him from speaking.

Lady Sackville's diary leaves little doubt that Vita did not 'say she would'. 'V. did not refuse him: but said that she would not give him any answer now ... Kidlet sat on my bed and talked by the hour about it all. She asked Lionel to let Harold come down to Knole for a last interview, as he is leaving for Constantinople at once.'

Harold came to Knole on 20 January. It was the day of Seery's funeral. Vita wrote that night: 'We said goodbye as ordinary friends, in front of Dada and Lady Connie [Lady Constance Hatch]. I don't understand it. I am quite dazed. Words are empty and faces expressionless.' Lady Sackville, as usual, took command:

> I told H. there can be no possible engagement for $1\frac{1}{2}$ years. Vita must be left absolutely free. He can come back and see her in July, and they can write to each other, not more than one letter a week each, but they must not correspond as engaged people, and no words like Dearest or Darling must be used. I discussed ways and means if the marriage comes off. He would like V. poor and to love him for himself, but I shall see to all that if I get poor Seery's money.

On 24 January Harold left for Constantinople. On the same day the Scotts began disputing the Will.

Well, were they engaged or weren't they? Harold thought they were, more or less. Vita couldn't remember exactly what she had said. Her mother was quite firm that they were not. Her father tried to pretend that nothing unusual had happened.

At the root of her parents' lukewarm response was disappointment that this was not a match good enough for their Vita, the only child of a famous family, despite herself the débutante of her year, a beauty, a scholar, and now (unless the Scotts upset the Will) an heiress. Even the Sackvilles could not pretend that the Nicolsons were bedint, for although they were descended from a long line of Edinburgh solicitors and an occasional rear-admiral, in their remoter ancestry were some robber-barons of Skye, which was a little better, and Sir Arthur was the holder of a baronetcy dating back to Charles I. He had reached the very peak of his exclusive profession, and was soon to be created Lord Carnock. But the Nicolsons did not move in society. Lady Sackville had never met Lady Nicolson in any of the drawing-rooms and country houses which she frequented, and Sir Arthur was too busy, and too crippled by arthritis, to fish or shoot. And they had no money beyond Sir Arthur's salary. Phrases like 'a penniless Third Secretary' began to circulate when the gossip spread.

Lady Sackville, however, was not entirely selfish about it, even in the privacy of her diary:

Vita telephoned Harold before he left London to say that I am not angry with him. Of course I am not, as I know she cares for him and he for her. She is such a difficult girl to please where men are concerned. It is not at present a good marriage, although he has a brilliant future before him as a diplomatist, and he is very attractive, and so intelligent and such a gentleman. But there is no money, and above all it is terrible for me, as she must live abroad if she takes him. My life will be very lonely, now that Seery has gone, if she goes too. I dread my talk with Lionel on the subject.

Lionel was less generous. He said that she saw only the sentimental side. 'Naturally he is very disappointed that she is not making a great match with a great title', when Lascelles and possibly Granby were offering her the historic names of Harewood and Rutland. But to Vita 'Dada was very sweet, though it is clear he had other dreams. He said that if in a year's time I still thought of nobody else but Harold, he would not make difficulties.'

Thus it was left. There could be no announcement of any engagement, for there was no engagement. Harold, exiled to Asia for at least six months, must attempt by infrequent and impersonal letters to maintain his tenuous hold on Vita, while she was courted by every little dancing thing in London, the two noblemen, the souls, and (did he but know it!) a girl, Rosamund Grosvenor, with whom she was passionately in love. All depended upon Vita, and Vita was now panic-stricken. On the very day when Harold left England, she wrote in her diary: 'I don't remember ever having been so unhappy. Only today have I begun to understand that I do not love him. He went to Constantinople this morning. I was in bed all day and have had time to think.' What he never understood was that his chief rival, even more possessive than Rosamund, even grander than Harewood, was Knole: 'I am all alone here, and all this big house is mine to shut up if I choose, and shut out all the rest of the world by swinging the iron bars across the gates ... It is so peaceful, and my little court so lovely in the moonlight. With its gabled windows it looks like a court on a stage, till I half expect to see a light spring up in one window and the play begin, with me for sole audience.'

Lady Sackville, knowing nothing of Vita's reservations, and of course nothing of the true situation concerning Rosamund ('She is such a nice companion for Vita'), began to enjoy herself, censoring 'their cold and reserved little letters', and flirting with Harold in the very way she denied her daughter. Harold was astute enough to spot the loophole. He could write to Lady Sackville from Constantinople all the things he was forbidden to write to Vita:

> Of course I am terribly jealous of Granby and all of them, but I hardly own this even to myself, and I ride alone over these beautiful hills and feel I could sing with happiness over what has happened and may happen. But then, in the evening, there are bad times when I go to parties here, and think she is at parties elsewhere, with eligibles all around her. And here I am, supremely ineligible, buried away in the Orient. But then my wiser self says it is better thus in the end, if I *do* win her, as then I shall feel that she does it with her eyes open.

To Vita he sent boxes of Turkish delight, and letters beginning Dear Vita and ending Yours Harold. For three months, until it became unendurable, he kept the rules.

In April 1912 Vita went with Rosamund to Florence, and they stayed in the cottage at the Villa Pestellini. From there she wrote to Harold: 'We went to pay a call on some people I used to know called Pucci [Orazio was still fighting in Tripoli] ... I've been so happy here, it is hot and the *grilli* [crickets] sing, and I love Rosamund, and somewhere in the world is you, and that is an undercurrent through everything else. I ought not to tell you so.' He did not read into the reference to Rosamund anything that he was not supposed to read. Nor in this: 'Rosamund knows about you and me. She is a very dear and sympathetic person, though she may not be particularly clever, and I am very fond of her. And she is a perfect tomb of discretion.'

Vita was suffering from the acute strain of what she euphemistically calls her dual personality. In love with Rosamund, she was teaching herself, willing herself, to love Harold too. She was playing for time, half-hoping that his ardour would cool, half-hoping that it would not. 'This is the first time I have lived at all and begun to make friends', she wrote to him, 'and if I let you take me away this year, it will all end. After all, I am only twenty. Let me be selfish for myself until next June [1913], and I'll spend the rest of my life being unselfish for you.' And then, a little more definitely, and breaking the rules: 'Do you want quite dreadfully to see me again? I don't know why I ask. It is a wild person you are going to marry.'

When Harold returned home on leave in August, the situation had scarcely changed since he had left in January. There was still great uncertainty. They met at Knole almost as strangers, partly because Lady Sackville ordained complete discretion, and partly because Vita was still in two minds (oh how literally!). When both Harold and Rosamund went away for a few days, he to visit his parents, her diary recorded '*Sono triste senza R.*', with no mention of him. But on 29 September: 'H. and I went through the show-rooms. In the Venetian Ambassadors' Bedroom he kissed me! He kissed me! I love him. *Io l'amo tanto, tanto* ... But I so much want to see R. again.' At the same time Lady Sackville's enthusiasm for Harold was beginning to wane:

V. is not suited to diplomacy and taking trouble about a lot of bedints. She ought to be a *grande dame*, very rich, where she could do what she likes and not have to do anything against the grain. She told me yesterday she would like to live alone in a tower with her books, and then she threw up her arms and said, 'Oh Mama, I really don't know what I want.' Poor child, of course she does not, and it is my duty to keep off the evil day of her marriage as long as I can, as she is not ready yet.

At the end of his leave, Vita and Rosamund went with Harold as far as Bologna, where he left them and continued to Constantinople. Although this was the moment when she was 'never so much in love with Rosamund', Vita could write to her mother, 'Oh Mama, I am so unhappy. I want Harold back so much. I can't believe I shan't see him come in at any moment', and at twenty such emotion cannot be feigned. But when she returned alone to Knole, only her diary received her secret: 'How I long to be back in Florence. This sporting life here bores me to tears. And I miss R, every moment, unbelievably.' When Rosamund did return: 'I talked to her very frankly about H. I do not think I love him enough to marry him [*non credo che l'amo abbastanza per sposarlo*]. Before talking to her like that, I had not really understood my own mind. But for a short time, I'll let things slide. Perhaps something will happen.' On 18 December 1912, she wrote: 'I ask myself if it would not have been better if Harold had married someone else. I can see nothing in the future but boredom and pain. I cannot, I cannot, leave everything for him – at least, I don't think I can. He will come back in April, and it makes me shiver. Oh why did he come to the Hatfield ball, and why didn't I refuse him at once? But he is so nice, so young, and he loves me, and we should be happy together.' 26 December: 'I spoke to Rosamund about H. She is the only person who knows the truth. Tonight I think I can never do it.'

It was almost a relief to her when the Balkan War temporarily stopped postal communication between Turkey and England, and when it was resumed, she wrote to Harold letters which gave no hint of her dilemma. She skirted the central problem by teasing him about diplomacy: 'Of course I shall hate the diplomatic life. After a few years when we get tired of solitude *à deux*, as we must, there will remain – what? Rio de Janeiro, boring old diplomats, no English friends.' But on occasions she could write to him as if she had reached an unalterable decision to marry him:

> If I don't seem to care much about all the others, you know why. If I leave my beautiful Knole which I adore, and my Ghirlandaio room which I adore, and my books and my garden and my freedom which I adore – it is all for you, whom I don't care two straws about. Now you deny a word of all that! But I want to sit on the arm of your chair and read your despatches over your shoulder, and rumple your curls which will make you cross. And I want to give dinner-parties in *our* house, when we will be so bored with the people because we would rather be alone.

To her diary she still spoke with her other voice:

> Harold has written that his father is probably going to be made Ambassador in Vienna, and that we shall go there too. The very idea of Vienna has appalled me. Am I to pass all my life abroad? I

can't do it. I let Mama see how I felt, and this was the first indication she has had of my change of mind. I could see that she was delighted. I simply can't leave Knole for Vienna!

In March 1913 Harold began to sense that something was wrong when her letters became shorter, less affectionate and very intermittent, but he failed to diagnose the seriousness of his situation because he had no inkling of its cause ('I walked three times round the park with Violet. She was crazy. She embraced me as she never has before, talking to me like a lover. Rosamund doesn't know that I was with Violet tonight'.) He wrote:

> No letter from you for ten days. This is dreadful for me. You can't be too lazy to write to me, and if you are, it means that you don't care one fig ... Is this a foolish letter to write? But it is only because my eyes are stinging with disappointment, and my heart is sore, sore, and you are so far away and I don't know what is happening. I can't bear it. You out there laughing with strange people – people I don't know, people who may have a power over your mind – and sometimes, before dinner, you write me a letter while Rosamund is having her bath, and it is written so lightly, and it goes so far. Oh Vita, *il pleure dans mon coeur comme il pleut sur la ville*.

She wrote to console him, 'Sometimes I think you are quite happy there with your friends and your wars, and that I am not all-important to you, and then I don't write ... Of course I love you', and much else, which produced a telegram in which one can sense his schoolboy relief, 'A ripping letter from you'. But worse was to come.

Vita went to Spain, and from Spain to Italy (*O Italia mia adorata!*), and returned to England in May 1913 drunk with the freedom she had tasted. The shallowness of her social life, the insipidity of Rosamund, had been exposed by contrast with the gipsies and bull-fighters with whom she had consorted in Seville, with the fishermen at Sorrento. How could she now tie herself to a husband, and tamely wait for him at a chancery door? 'I am happy to be in my old Knole', she wrote in her diary, 'but I am in a bad humour. I have a half-wish [*quasi-voglia*] to marry Harold this summer and finish with it ... Oh God, how will it end? And he returns at the beginning of July. I have no idea what to do. Today I wrote him a letter which will make him jump.'

This was the crisis. Her letter to Harold has not survived: he may have destroyed it. But he quoted its final sentence in his reply: 'Sometimes I feel it would be simpler to give it all up.' He immediately telegraphed: '*Dernière lettre incompréhensible et inquiétante. Dois-je la prendre au sérieux? Réponds télégraphiquement oui ou non. Très anxieux.*' She replied the same day: '*Non. T'en demande pardon. N'en crois pas un mot.*' From that moment until her death fifty years later her love for him never wavered.*

It may seem strange that a single telegram could have made so much difference. She partly explained it in the letter which she wrote next day:

> *Mea culpa! Mea maxima culpa!* My letter was just an ill-tempered storm from a wanderer who felt caged again after weeks of liberty, and was cross in consequence and rebellious of iron bars – and that is the person (you poor, rash, ill-advised Harold), that is the person you so lightly contemplate undertaking for life, someone you know nothing about. How much happier you would be with someone in the nature of Rosamund, not Rosamund herself, *mais dans ce genre là*, very gentle and dependent and clinging. Oh Harold darling, I am sorry. I didn't mean to upset you. I want you back frightfully. It was too awful you always being away, and eight months is a lifetime, and I don't know what I shall do if it has to happen again. I did write to you the very next day [after her 'simpler to give it up' letter], but I didn't dare send it, so I tore it up and waited to see what would happen. Now your telegram has happened, and I answered it. Harold darling, I do want you to forgive me.

But it was more than that. Her love for Rosamund was cooling, and Rosamund was half-engaged to a sailor named Raikes, whom she had met at Dartmouth while Vita was in Spain. Violet had not taken Rosamund's place. Vita was alone. She was genuinely anxious not to hurt Harold, for whom her feelings veered from

---

*His telegram: 'Your last letter incomprehensible and disturbing. Am I to take it seriously? Telegraph yes or no. Very anxious.' Her reply: 'No. Forgive me. Don't believe a word of it.' They telegraphed in French in order to conceal the sense of the messages from the post office in Sevenoaks.

tenderness to sudden spurts of genuine love. His letters affected her profoundly, his presence even more. Besides, she *must* make up her mind. Almost daily she heard from Lord Lascelles, who knew only of Granby as his rival, and there were others too who imagined that she could still be won. Her mother's anxious looks and none-too-discreet enquiries were becoming intolerable. She wanted a refuge, and Harold offered one. By her letter she had tested him. Had he faltered at that moment he would have lost her irretrievably, and this book would never have been written. His telegram was a cry of despair, but to her it was a lifebelt. The letter which he wrote before he received her answer confirmed everything: 'If you let me down, I feel I could kill you. I love you so much more than ever before, and the longing after you is like a stretched cord within me.' Here, at last, was the language that she could understand.

The effect of it is seen in her diary of 11 June: 'These days I think so much of Harold that I can't sleep. I so much want him to come home. I have an insane wish to see him again; and I cannot let him out of my life. I shall marry him.' She wrote to him frequently in the same strain, and when he returned from Constantinople on 3 July 1913, all that remained was to announce their engagement and fix the date of the wedding.

He travelled home through the Mediterranean, and the first European newspapers which he saw, at Marseilles, were full of the Scott case, which had just begun. In Paris, at Dover, he followed its progress, agonizingly, and at Victoria station the posters blazed with the latest news. He rushed to Hill Street, found Lady Sackville in tears, gathered Vita into his arms, and next morning went with Rosamund to the court to hear Vita give her evidence. When the Sackvilles won the case, they held a jubilant party in London, and then came an absurd anti-climax. The *Daily Sketch* identified Harold as 'Kidlet's constant companion at the court' and forecast that 'their engagement will be announced soon'. Lady Sackville, furious, issued a statement under her own name: 'The announcement of the forthcoming engagement of the Hon. Victoria Mary Sackville-West to Mr Harold Nicolson is entirely unauthorised', but not, it was noted, denied. Their tattered little secret was fluttering in the winds of publicity. Letters of congratulation began to arrive, and those from the three people who had most disturbed Vita's recent life were self-portraits of the writers. First, Lord Lascelles, gallantly lowering his flag:

> Dear Vita [until then she had been *Carissima mia*], It is not easy for me to sit down and congratulate you, although I hope you know that I do most really wish for your happiness. Nobody can say but yourself whether you have chosen right. I only know that H.N. seems very nice indeed, and I wish I knew him better. This is a sort of goodbye, but I hope that we may be good friends again after you are married.
>
> Yours ever,
> Harry

In 1922 he married Princess Mary, only daughter of King George V.

Secondly, Rosamund in despair:

> Don't ask me to visit you. I can't. I am so utterly miserable. I feel that you are going. I simply cannot begin to face it. I am ill with misery.

Thirdly, Violet, contemptuous:

> *Accepte mes félicitations les plus sincères à la nouvelle de tes fiançailles.* I never could write letters on this subject in any language, but somehow it seems less absurd in French. I wish you every possible happiness (et cetera) from the bottom of my heart (et cetera). Will you and Mr Nicholson [sic] come and have tea with me? ... I see in the evening papers that the rumour is contradicted, in which case this effusion would be (officially, at least) in vain. *Ma non importa.* You can keep it till the day when it ought publicly to be forthcoming. It will suit the same purpose at any age, with no matter whom.

Their engagement was officially announced on 5 August. Lady Sackville was generous to them. She gave Vita an allowance of £2,500 a year, of which the capital was to become hers on her mother's death.

The visit to Interlaken, between the announcement and the wedding, was farcical. The reason for it was not to give the couple a holiday together, but to provide Lady Sackville and William Waldorf Astor with chaperones. Astor suggested that they might meet 'by accident' in Switzerland, having failed to entice her to come 'veiled and unnoticed' to his office suite in London. Lady Sackville was prepared to come, provided that she might bring her daughter and her daughter's fiancé with her, and she enjoyed the escapade as much as Vita and Harold. The two pairs of chaperones left each other discreetly alone all day and reunited for dinner before withdrawing to their four strictly separated bedrooms.

As the wedding-day drew near, Vita felt no qualms, except about leaving Knole. She cried for a whole hour on her wedding-eve, comforted by Rosamund, who was struggling to suppress her own sobs:

To Knole. 1 October 1913

I left thee in the crowds and in the light,
And if I laughed or sorrowed none could tell.
They could not know our true and deep farewell
Was spoken in the long preceding night ...

So in the night we parted, friend of years,
I rose a stranger to thee on the morrow;
Thy stateliness knows neither joy nor sorrow,
I will not wound such dignity by tears.

(From *Poems of West and East*, 1917)

The wedding was not like other weddings. Rosamund was a bridesmaid. It was very grand and hugely publicized, for Kidlet was news, but the chapel at Knole was so small that only twenty-six people could fit in. It was a lovely day, the sun streaming through the chapel windows. While they waited, the other guests, who included by Lady Sackville's special invitation all the jurymen from the Scott case, milled around the Great Hall examining an array of six hundred wedding-presents. The only absentee was Lady Sackville herself, who remained in bed all day. She was genuinely ill, but could have roused herself if she had felt able to bear the strain of parting, or, as people unkindly said, if she had been the centre of attention. Vita was quite calm, dressed in a cloth of gold and veiled in Irish lace which her mother had worn at the Coronation of the Czar. That night she wrote in her diary, but not resignedly, '*Dunque si è culminato così!*' – 'So it has reached this conclusion!' Years later she told me that Harold had talked for so long about his uncle (Lord Dufferin), that she had to remind him that he also had a wife.

They spent a few days at Coker, a lovely Elizabethan house in Somerset, and then went to the cottage of the Villa Pestellini. To Vita's annoyance her mother had arranged that on their way to Constantinople they should spend a week with her friend Kitchener at Cairo. In *Passenger to Teheran* Vita recalled that visit, disguising that it was also her honeymoon:

> I had not wanted to stay with him; I had protested loudly ... The recollection survives with horror, a sort of scar on the mind. I had arrived at the Residency suffering from sunstroke and a complete loss of voice – not an ideal condition in which to confront that formidable soldier. Craving only for bed and a dark room, I had gone down to dinner. Six or eight speechless and intimidated officers sat around the table. Kitchener's bleary eye roamed over them; my own hoarse whisper alone penetrated the silence. Egyptian art came up as a topic. 'I can't', growled Kitchener, 'think much of a people who drew cats the same way for four thousand years.'

In Constantinople she was supremely happy and became reconciled even to diplomatic parties. She and Harold leased a Turkish house in Cospoli, overlooking the Golden Horn, and there she made her first garden:

> The gardens of her terraced hills
> Rose up above the port,
> And little houses half-concealed
> The presence of a light revealed,
> And here my journey's end was sealed.
> And I reached the home I sought.
> [*Poems of West and East*]

'Harold appears to me perfect', she wrote in her diary. 'So gay, so amusing, so intelligent, so *young*. I feel that until now I never really knew him.' Her father came to visit them; so did Rosamund (now bored with Raikes, but Vita was bored with Rosamund).* They went sailing on the Bosphorus and bought Persian pottery in the bazaars. Loaded with oriental treasures, they returned to England in June 1914, and Ben was born at Knole two days after the outbreak of war. Believing that she might not survive his birth, she wrote a letter to Harold to be opened if she died:

> If you marry again, which I expect you will, don't be just the same with her as you were with me; give her a place of her own, but don't let her take mine exactly. Don't teach her our family expressions. Darling, I hope I shan't die. I want years and years more with you as my playfellow. I love you so, my own darling husband. We are so young, and we have such fun together always that I refuse to believe that it can be cut off. If you ever get this, we shall have had nearly a year of absolutely unmarred happiness together, and you will know that I have loved you as completely as one person has ever loved another.

She left him everything – except a diamond watch to Rosamund, and a sapphire and diamond ring to Violet.

I do not intend to describe the war years in any detail, for they add nothing to the theme of this narrative. Harold was exempt from military service (what would she have felt if he had been sent to the trenches, and how did she feel about his not going?), and gained in the Foreign Office a reputation which made him the pet of successive foreign secretaries. They bought a house in London, 182 Ebury Street, where I was born in January 1917, and a tumbledown cottage, Long Barn, two miles from Knole, which they restored and extended with the advice of Sir Edwin Lutyens, who had now replaced Seery as Lady Sackville's constant companion.

At Long Barn Vita became seriously interested in gardening, and Harold in garden design; and she was busy writing, poetry mostly, but also a vast history of the Italian Renaissance which she rightly decided not to publish. The event which brought them

---

*Rosamund married Jack Lynch, a soldier, in 1924, and was killed by a German bomb in London, in 1940.

closest together (but then they were scarcely ever apart) was the death at birth of their second son on 3 November 1915, to which Vita refers in her autobiography, but attributes it to an unlikely cause, the accident to Rosamund which had taken place more than ten months earlier. In her diary it is simply recorded thus: '*La mattina alle dieci nacque il bambino, ma morto*'. She wrote to Harold a few days later a letter which illustrates what tenderness underlay her rebellious nature. She would, I suppose, have called it another example of her dual personality:

> Harold, I am sad. I have been thinking of that white velvet coffin with that little still thing inside. He was going to be a birthday-present to you next Sunday. Oh darling, I feel it is too cruel. I can't help minding, and I always shall. I mind more when I see Ben, how sweet and sturdy he is, and the other would have been just the same. I mind his being dead because he is a person. It is silly to mind so much. I can't bear to hear of people with two children. Oh Harold darling, why did he die? Why, why, why did he? Oh I wish you were here. I am in bed, and haven't got any more paper. [But she tears out of her Bible a map of St Paul's journeys, and continues on the back]: I try and stave it off, not to think about it, but when I am alone, it rushes at me. I am so frightened of being alone now. Harold, I want you so badly.

There was another event which must be mentioned at this point, for although it did not culminate until 1919, it had long been foreshadowed, and to give it its proper chronological place would only interrupt irrelevantly Vita's extraordinary story which follows. This was Lady Sackville's decision to leave her husband and Knole. In *Pepita* Vita gave a very guarded account of it, placing most of the blame on her mother for failing to understand that a man who had commanded troops at Gallipoli should wish, on coming home, to assert his authority in his own house. Lady Sackville, she says, 'suddenly lost her temper . . . and left the room never to return'.

Of course there was something in Vita's version of the story. Lady Sackville was a maddening person to live with, and she aggravated an already difficult situation by her tactlessness. Harold, who spent Christmas 1918 at Knole, gave Vita this example of it:

There was a terribly acrid row last night. It began this way. Just as B.M. ['Bonne Mama', the family name for Lady Sackville] was going to bed, she said suddenly to Dada, 'Did you tell your French officers about my passion for sitting out-of-doors?'. To which Dada rather crossly replied: 'Of course not. Why should I? I don't suppose that they knew I was married.'

Of course it was an idiotic question for B.M. to ask. I suppose she has some sentimental idea of stern-faced soldiers – *vaillants et alliés* – grouped round a camp-fire, with the silent sentry against the stars, and discussing their children and their homes in dear old England, and her own stern-faced warrior dwelling with silent emotion upon his dear one in the great ancestral home, and speaking lovingly and with gentle fancy of her qualities, the inflexions of her voice, and her dear personal idiosyncrasies.

And Dada, who is always irritated (like most men, mark you, Vita) by the *eau sucrée* of schoolgirl romance, and who, after all, would be most unlikely, in the intervals of telephoning, to pour out his heart to a French colonel however *vaillant* and however *allié*, felt a fool at the mere suggestion and answered her roughly and in a greater hurry than he intended.

Any how, B.M. threw up her head with a hard little laugh and went out of the room humming a hard little tune. We were left behind with the odd sense of something rather silly and rather cruel having happened. I slipped away, and with commendable courage crept into her room where she was sobbing away: '*Enfin, mon petit Harold, je m'en vais demain – c'est décidé* – and after all that I've done for Knole, and of course I shall not make a scandal – *tu sais que je suis trop grande dame pour ça* – *je dirai que je veux voir l'entrée du Président Wilson.*'

I soothed her down as best I could. I really don't know whether she is more hurt than angry. Anyhow, she decided not to go after all. But isn't it hopeless? B.M. keeps on saying, '*Je compte pour rien maintenant. Je ne suis que son* unpaid housekeeper.' Poor B.M.! Poor Dada! How happy each could be without the other! I don't know what will happen. But I have the impression that Dada wants to make Knole more or less impossible for B.M. Perhaps I am wrong, but I feel that he has come to the conclusion that it is only by being rather cruel that he can beat her. I think he is right, of course, because if he is nice to her, she will take advantage of it.

But there was something else. Since about 1905, Lionel had found his wife useful but no longer desirable. There had been Lady Connie, and now there was Mrs Walter Rubens, whom, with Mr Rubens, he intended to install in an apartment at Knole itself. The final scene came in May 1919, and the immediate cause of the breach seemed trivial. Lionel said that the Rubens were coming over to stay 'for a day or two'. Lady Sackville retorted that if they came, she would leave. They parted in anger. Vita, who was in the house at the time, went to her mother's room to make peace, but found that she had finally made up her mind. She packed up and left next day, with Lutyens, and went to Brighton, where she lived for the remainder of her life. Feminine jealousy was the reason for her leaving, dignified and complicated by her intense pride.

PART THREE
BY V. SACKVILLE-WEST

27 SEPTEMBER [1920]

IN APRIL [1918], when we were back in the country, Violet wrote to me to ask whether she could come and stay with me for a fortnight. I was bored by the idea, as I wanted to work, and I did not know how to entertain her; but I could scarcely refuse. So she came. We were both bored. My serenity got on her nerves, and her restlessness got on mine. She went up to London for the day as often as she could, but she came back in the evenings because the air-raids frightened her. She had been here [Long Barn] I think about a week when everything changed suddenly – changed far more than I foresaw at the time; changed my life. It was the 18th of April. An absurd circumstance gave rise to the whole thing; I had just got clothes like the women-on-the-land were wearing, and in the unaccustomed freedom of breeches and gaiters I went into wild spirits; I ran, I shouted, I jumped, I climbed, I vaulted over gates, I felt like a schoolboy let out on a holiday; and Violet followed me across fields and woods with a new meekness, saying very little, but never taking her eyes off me, and in the midst of my exuberance I knew that all the old under-current had come back stronger than ever, and that my old domination over her had never been diminished. I remember that wild irresponsible day. It was one of the most vibrant days of my life. As it happened, Harold was not coming down that night. Violet and I dined alone together, and then after dinner, we went into my sitting-room, and for some time made conversation, but that broke down, and from ten o'clock until two in the morning – for four hours, or perhaps more – we talked.

Violet had struck the secret of my duality; she attacked me about it, and I made no attempt to conceal it from her or from myself. I talked myself out, until I could hear my own voice getting hoarse, and the fire went out, and all the servants had long since gone to bed, and there was not a soul in the house except Violet and me, and I talked out the whole of myself with absolute sincerity and pain, and Violet only listened – which was skilful of her. She made no comments and no suggestions until I had finished – until, that is, I had dug into every corner and brought its contents out to the light. I had been vouchsafed insight, as one sometimes is. Then, when I had finished, when I had told her how all the gentleness and all the femininity of me was called out by Harold alone, but how towards everyone else my attitude was completely otherwise – then, still with her infinite skill, she brought me round to my attitude towards herself, as it had always been ever since we were children, and then she told me how she had loved me always, and reminded me of incidents running through years, which I couldn't pretend to have forgotten. She was far more skilful than I. I might have been a boy of eighteen, and she a woman of thirty-five. She was infinitely clever – she didn't scare me, she didn't rush me, she didn't allow me to see where I was going; it was all conscious on her part, but on mine it was simply the drunkenness of liberation – the liberation of half my personality. She opened up to me a new sphere. And for her, of course, it meant the supreme effort to conquer the love of the person she had always wanted, who had always repulsed her (when things seemed to be going too far), out of a sort of fear, and of whom she was madly jealous – a fact I had not realized, so adept was she at concealment, and so obtuse was I at her psychology.

She lay on the sofa, I sat plunged in the armchair; she took my hands, and parted my fingers to count the points as she told me why she loved me. I hadn't dreamt of such an art of love. Such things had been *direct* for me always; I had known no love possessed of that Latin artistry (whether instinctive or acquired). I was infinitely troubled by the softness of her touch and the murmur of her lovely voice. She appealed to my unawakened senses; she wore, I remember, a dress of red velvet, that was exactly the colour of a red rose, and that made of her, with her white skin and the tawny hair, the most seductive being. She pulled me down until I kissed her — I had not done so for many years. Then she was wise enough to get up and go to bed; but I kissed her again in the dark after I had blown out our solitary lamp. She let herself go entirely limp and passive in my arms. (I shudder to think of the experience that lay behind her abandonment). I can't think I slept all that night — not that much of the night was left.

I don't know how to go on; I keep thinking that Harold, if he ever reads this, will suffer so, but I ask him to remember that he is reading about a *different person* from the one he knew. Also I am not writing this for fun, but for several reasons which I will explain. (1) As I started by saying, because I want to tell the *entire* truth. (2) Because I know of no truthful record of such a connection — one that is written, I mean, with no desire to appeal to a vicious taste in any possible readers; and (3) because I hold the conviction that as centuries go on, and the sexes become more nearly merged on account of their increasing resemblances, I hold the conviction that such connections will to a very large extent cease to be regarded as merely unnatural, and will be understood far better, at least in their *intellectual* if not in their physical aspect. (Such is already the case in Russia.) I believe that then the psychology of people like myself will be a matter of interest, and I believe it will be recognized that many more people of my type do exist than under the present-day system of hypocrisy is commonly admitted. I am not saying that such personalities, and the connections which result from them, will not be deplored as they are now; but I do believe that their greater prevalence, and the spirit of candour which one hopes will spread with the progress of the world, will lead to their recognition, if only as an inevitable evil. The first step in the direction of such candour must be taken by the general admission of normal but illicit relations, and the facilitation of divorce, or possibly even the reconstruction of the system of marriage. Such advance must necessarily come from the more educated and liberal classes. Since 'unnatural' means 'removed from nature', only the most civilized, because the least natural, class of society can be expected to tolerate such a product of civilization.

I advance, therefore, the perfectly accepted theory that cases of dual personality do exist, in which the feminine and the masculine elements alternately preponderate. I advance this in an impersonal and scientific spirit, and claim that I am qualified to speak with the intimacy a professional scientist could acquire only after years of study and indirect information, because I have the object of study always to hand, in my own heart, and can gauge the exact truthfulness of what my own experience tells me. However frank, people would always keep back something. I can't keep back anything from myself.

29 SEPTEMBER [1920]

I think Violet stayed on for about five days after that. All the time I was in fantastic spirits; and, not realizing how different she was from me in many ways, I made her follow me on wild courses all over the country, and, because she knew she had me only lightly hooked, she obeyed without remonstrance. There was very little between us during those days, only an immense excitement and a growing wish to go away somewhere alone together. This wish was carried out, by arranging to go down to Cornwall for the inside of a week; it was the first time I had ever been away from Harold, and he obviously minded my going.

We went. We met again in London, lunched at a restaurant, and filled with a spirit of adventure took the train for Exeter. On the way there we decided to go on to Plymouth. We arrived at Plymouth to find our luggage had of course been put out at Exeter. We had only an assortment of French poetry with us. We didn't care. We went to the nearest hotel, exultant to feel that nobody in the world knew where we were; at the booking office we were told there was only one room. It seemed like fate. We engaged it. We went and had supper – cider and ham – over which we talked fast and tremulously; she was frightened of me by then.

The next day we went on to Cornwall, where we spent five blissful days; I felt like a person translated, or re-born; it was like beginning one's life again in a different capacity. We were very miserable to come away, but we were constantly together during the whole of the summer months following. Once we went down to Cornwall again for a fortnight. It was a lovely summer. She was radiant. But I never thought it would last; I thought of it as an adventure, an escapade. I kept telling myself she was fickle, that I was the latest toy; she used to assure me of the contrary. She did this with such gravity that sometimes I was almost convinced; but now the years have convinced me thoroughly.

She no longer flirted, and got rid of the last person she had been engaged to, when we went to Cornwall. But there was a man out in France, who used to write to her; she hardly knew him, and I wasn't jealous. He was called Denzil [Denys Trefusis]. She described him to me as fiery – hair like gold wire, blue eyes starting out of his head, and winged nostrils. I listened, not very much interested. I now hate him more than I have ever hated anyone in this life, or am likely to; and there is no injury I would not do him with the utmost pleasure.

Well, the whole of that summer she was mine – a mad and irresponsible summer of moonlight nights, and infinite escapades, and passionate letters, and music, and poetry. Things were not tragic for us then, because although we cared passionately we didn't care deeply – not like now, though it was deepening all the time; no, things weren't tragic, they were rapturous and new, and one side of my life was opened to me, and, to hide nothing, I found things out about my own temperament that I had never been sure of before. Of course I wish now that I had never made those discoveries. One doesn't miss what one doesn't know, and now life is made wretched for me by privations. I often long for ignorance and innocence. I think that if anything happened to bring my friendship with Violet to an end, I might have the strength of mind to blot all that entirely out of my life.

At the end of that summer Denys came home on leave, and I met him. He was very tall and slender, and had the winged look that she had described – I could compare him to many things, to a race-horse, to a Crusader, to a greyhound, to an ascetic in search of the Holy Grail. I liked him then (oh irony!), and he liked me. I could afford to like him, because I was accustomed to Violet's amusements. Even now I see his good points, and they are many; but I see them only by translating myself into an impersonal spectator, and I see them, above all, when Violet makes him suffer. I see that he is a rare, sensitive, proud idealist, and I recognize that through me he has undergone months of suffering, and that his profound love for Violet has been thwarted of its fulfilment. And I am sorry enough for him, at moments, just sorry enough to wish vaguely that he could have cared for someone other than Violet. I see his tragedy – for he is a tragic person. But none of this softens my hatred of him, which is certainly the most violent feeling I have ever experienced. I only hope he returns it in full measure; he has a hundred times more cause to hate me than I to hate him.

He was in London for about ten days. It was already arranged that Violet and I were to go abroad together that winter for a month. There were scenes connected with our going. Violet and I had a row over something; I refused to go abroad; she came round to my house and we made friends again; then I had a dreadful scene with Mother, who was furious at my going; however to make a long story short, we left for Paris at the end of November [1918]. I was to be away until Christmas!

5 OCTOBER [1920]

Paris ... We were there for about a week, living in a flat that was lent us in the Palais Royal. Even now the intoxication of some of those hours in Paris makes me see confusedly; other hours were, I admit, wretched, because Denys came (the war being just over), and I wanted Violet to myself. But the evenings were ours. I have never told a soul of what I did. I hesitate to write it here, but I must; shirking the truth here would be like cheating oneself

*Pepita at the height of her dancing
career in about 1852, when she
first met Vita's grandfather, Lionel
Sackville-West*

*Knole, near Sevenoaks, Kent,
which the Sackvilles had owned
since the mid-sixteenth century,
and where Vita spent her
childhood. Her room was the
middle window of the bay on the
right, next to the chapel*

Above (left), Vita's mother, aged thirty-five

Above, Sir John Murray Scott ('Seery')

Left, Vita and her mother in 1900, in the first car to be added to the Knole stables

Right, Lady Sackville in 1914. A bust (in the Musée Rodin, Paris) by Auguste Rodin, who for two years was much in love with her

Below, Vita aged nearly eighteen, painted by Laszlo in January 1910. This was the year when she 'came out' and first met Harold. The picture is now at Sissinghurst

*Above, (left to right)
Harold, Vita, Rosamund
Grosvenor and Lord
Sackville, on their way to
the courts on 4 July 1913
to hear Vita give her
evidence in the Scott case*

*Right, their wedding in the
chapel at Knole on 1
October 1913. Rosamund
is the bridesmaid on the left:
Harold's sister Gwen, on
the right*

Above, Violet Trefusis in the early 1920s

Left, Violet Trefusis, a portrait by Jacques-Emile Blanche, 1926 which she gave to Philippe Julian and is now in the National Portrait Gallery

Harold and Vita in 1919

Harold dictates to a secretary at the Paris Peace Conference in 1919

Long Barn, two miles from Knole, where the Nicolsons lived from 1915 till 1930, and made t' first garden

Geoffrey Scott at the Villa Medici, Florence, in 1923

Virginia Woolf at Knole in 1928 when she was writing Orlando

Above, Harold and Vita with Ben, left, and Nigel, at Long Barn in the summer of 1929, just before Harold's resignation from the Foreign Office

Right, Harold and Vita at Sissinghurst in 1932

Opposite, Vita in her sitting-room at Sissinghurst. The portraits on her writing table are of the Bronte sisters and Virginia Woolf

Sissinghurst from the air.
The Priest's House, left,
contained the kitchen and
dining-room, and the first
floor of the tower was
Vita's sitting room

Vita at the foot of the to⦙
in about 1950

playing patience. I dressed as a boy. It was easy, because I could put a khaki bandage round my head, which in those days was so common that it attracted no attention at all. I browned my face and hands. It must have been successful, because no one looked at me at all curiously or suspiciously — never once, out of the many times I did it. My height of course was my great advantage. I looked like a rather untidy young man, a sort of undergraduate, of about nineteen. It was marvellous fun, all the more so because there was always the risk of being found out. Of course it was easy in the Palais Royal because I could let myself in and out by a latchkey; in hotels it was more difficult. I had done it once already in England; that was one of the boldest things I ever did. I will tell about it: I changed in my own house in London late one evening (the darkened streets made me bold), and drove with Violet in a taxi as far as Hyde Park Corner. There I got out. I never felt so free as when I stepped off the kerb, down Piccadilly, alone, and knowing that if I met my own mother face to face she would take no notice of me. I walked along, smoking a cigarette, buying a newspaper off a little boy who called me 'sir', and being accosted now and then by women. In this way I strolled from Hyde Park Corner to Bond Street, where I met Violet and took her in a taxi to Charing Cross. (The extraordinary thing was, how natural it all was for me). Nobody, even in the glare of the station, glanced at me twice. I had wondered about my voice, but found I could sink it sufficiently. Well, I took Violet as far as Orpington by train, and there we found a lodging house where we could get a room. The landlady was very benevolent and I said Violet was my wife. Next day of course I had to put on the same clothes, although I was a little anxious about the daylight, but again nobody took the slightest notice. We went to Knole!, which was, I think, brave. Here I slipped into the stables, and emerged as myself.

Well, this discovery was too good to be wasted, and in Paris I practically lived in that role. Violet used to call me Julian. We dined together every evening in cafés and restaurants, and went to all the theatres. I shall never forget the evenings when we walked back slowly to our flat through the streets of Paris. I, personally, had never felt so free in my life. Perhaps we have never been so happy since. When we got back to the flat, the windows all used to be open onto the courtyard of the Palais Royal, and the fountains splashed below. It was all incredible – like a fairy-tale.

It couldn't go on for ever, and at the end of the week we left for Monte Carlo, stopping on the way at St Raphael. The weather was perfect, Monte Carlo was perfect, Violet was perfect. Again as Julian, I took her to a dance there, and had a success with a French family, who asked me to come and play bridge with them, and, I think, had an eye on me for their daughter, a plain girl whose head I tried to turn with compliments. They said '*On voit que monsieur est valseur*', and their son, a French officer, asked me about my '*blessure*', and we exchanged war reminiscences.

I didn't go back at Christmas. I didn't go back till nearly the end of March, and everybody was very angry with me, and I felt like suicide after those four wild and radiant months. The whole of that time is dreadful, a nightmare. Harold was in Paris, and I was alone with Mother and Dada, who were both very angry, and wanted me to give Violet up. (There had been a lot of scandal, by then.) On the other hand, Denys had been in England a month, and was agitating to announce his engagement to Violet. Violet was like a hunted creature. I could have prevented the engagement by very few words, but I thought that would be too outrageously selfish; there was Violet's mother, a demon of a woman, longing to get her safely married, and having told all London that she was going to marry Denys. She had already so bad a reputation for breaking engagements that this would have been the last straw. Besides, we both thought she would gain more liberty by marrying, and Denys was prepared to marry her on her own terms – that is, of merely brotherly relations.

I was absolutely miserable. I went to Brighton, alone, in a great empty dust-sheeted house, and all night I used to lie awake, and all day I used to wonder whether I wouldn't throw myself over the cliffs. Everyone questioned me as to why I looked so ill. On the fifth day Violet's engagement was announced in the papers; I bought the paper at Brighton station and nearly fainted as I read it, although I had expected to find it there. Not very long after that I went to Paris, to join Harold, who by that time knew the whole truth of the affair. I was terribly unhappy in Paris. When I came back to London, Violet began to declare that nothing would induce her to go through with the thing, and that I must save her from it by taking her away; in fact I believe she used Denys very largely as a lever to get me to do so. Living permanently with me had become an obsession in her mind. I don't absolutely remember the process in detail, but I know that I ended by consenting. After that we were both less unhappy; I could afford to see her ostensibly engaged to Denys when I knew that instead of marrying him she was coming away with me. I really intended to take her; we had every plan made. We were to go the day before her wedding – not sooner, because we thought we should be overtaken and brought back. It was of course only this looking-forward which enabled me to endure the period of her engagement.

Then about five days before her wedding I suddenly got by the same post three miserable letters from Harold, who had scented danger, because, in order to break it to him more or less gently (and also because I was in a dreadful state of mind myself during all that time), I had been writing him letters full of hints. When I read those letters something snapped in my mind. I saw Harold, all sweet and gentle and dependent upon me. Violet was there. She was terrified. I remember saying, 'It's no good, I can't take you away.' She implored me by everything she could think of, but I was obdurate. We went up to London together, Violet nearly off her head, and me repeating to myself phrases out of Harold's letters to give me strength. I telegraphed to him to say I was coming to Paris; I had only one idea, to fly as quickly as I could and to put distance between me and temptation. I saw Violet twice more; once in my own house in London; she looked ill and changed; and once in the early morning at her mother's house, where I went to say goodbye to her on my way to the station. There was a dreary slut scrubbing the doorstep, for it was very early, and I stepped in over the soapy pail, and saw Violet in the morning-room. Then I went to Paris, alone. That is one of the worst days I remember. While I was in the train going to Folkestone I still felt I could change my mind and go back if I wanted to, for she had told me she would wait for me up to the very last minute, and would come straight away if I appeared, or telephoned for her. At Folkestone I felt it becoming more irrevocable, and tried to get off the boat again, but they were moving the gangway and pushed me back. I had Harold's letters with me, and kept reading them until they almost lost all sense. The journey had never seemed so slow; it remains with me simply as a nightmare. I couldn't eat, and tears kept running down my face. Harold met me at the Gare du Nord. I said I wanted to go straight back, but he said, 'No, no', and took me out to Versailles in a motor. The next day was Sunday, and he stayed with me all day. By then I had got such a reaction that I was feverishly cheerful, and he might have thought nothing was the matter. I gave him the book I was writing [*Challenge*], because I knew Violet would hate me to do that, as it was all about her. I was awake nearly all that night. Next day was Monday, 16 June [1919]; Harold had to go into Paris, and I sat quite dazed in my room holding my watch in my hand and watching the hands tick past the hour of Violet's wedding. All that time, I knew, she was expecting a pre-arranged message from me, which I never sent.

I was so stunned by all this at the time that I could not even think; it is only since then that I have realized how every minute has burnt itself into me.

On Tuesday night Violet and Denys came to Paris. On Wednesday I went to see her, at the Ritz. She was wearing clothes I had never seen before, but no wedding ring. I can't describe how terrible it all was – that meeting, and everything. It makes me physically ill to write about it and think about it, and my cheeks are burning. It was dreadful, dreadful. By then I had left Versailles, and was living alone in a small hotel. I took her there, I treated her savagely, I made love to her, I had her, I didn't care, I only wanted to hurt Denys, even though he didn't know of it. I make no excuse, except that I had suffered too much during the past week and was really scarcely responsible. The next day I saw Denys at an awful interview. Violet told him she had meant to run away with me instead of marrying him; she told him she didn't care for him. He got very white, and I thought he was going to faint. I restrained myself from saying much more. I wanted to say, 'Don't you know, you stupid fool, that she is mine in every sense of the word?', but I was afraid that he would kill her if I did that. That night I dined at the Ritz, and from the open window of her room Violet watched me, and Denys sobbed in the room behind her. That day seems to have made a great impression upon him, as he constantly referred to it in his letters to her afterwards.

After that they went away to St Jean de Luz, and I went to Switzerland with Harold, and then back to England alone. After three weeks Violet came back. Things were not quite so bad then. She had a house in Sussex, and Denys only came there for the weekends, and I spent all the rest of the week there. He and I never met, because in Paris he had said to me it must be war or peace. We met once, when he arrived earlier than was expected; I was just leaving, and Violet threw some things into a bag and came with me. I never saw anyone look so angry as he did. He was dead white and his lips were shaking. I tried to make Violet go back, because I thought it was really humiliating the man too much, but she wouldn't. On the whole, however, she was on friendly terms with him, and I am bound to say that he was friendly as an angel to her, and above all he kept the promises he had made, which I think few men would have done. I think on the whole that that was the period when Violet liked him best.

21 OCTOBER [1920]

But she was incessantly trying to get me to come away with her. For a very long time I wouldn't, because I thought she had played me a mean trick over her marriage, and I wouldn't sacrifice Harold to someone whom I thought unworthy. I thought she had played Denys a worse than mean trick too, marrying him like that and accepting his devotion, and deceiving him all the time, and I held myself in almost equal contempt for being a party to the deception, and altogether I was pretty miserable and sickened of the whole thing. My only consolation was that Harold knew all about it; and so did Mother, for I had told her the whole truth about myself the evening I came back from Paris; and if Violet didn't choose to be as frank as I had been, it wasn't really my business. It wasn't my business to look after Denys and see that he wasn't deceived. So I tried to argue, but without bringing myself much satisfaction.

It was not till the end of August that I agreed to go away with Violet. Harold was still in Paris, and I could leave Ben and Nigel at Knole, so it was comparatively easy. We were to go to Greece, because my book was about Greece, and that provided a reason; and there wasn't much opposition except from Mother at the last minute, but I went in spite of that. We started in October – not a very propitious departure, because Violet was so ill that we had to spend the night at Folkestone. Once we got to Paris it was different, and we led the same life as the year before, of cafés, theatres, and 'Julian'. There was no abatement, rather the reverse, in our caring for one another; there was no abatement either in my passion for the freedom of that life. I used to stroll about the boulevards as I had strolled down Piccadilly, I used to sit in cafés drinking coffee, and watching people go by; sometimes I saw people I knew, and wondered what they would think if they knew the truth about the slouching boy with the bandaged head and the rather *voyou* appearance, and if they would recognize the silent and rather scornful woman they had perhaps met at a dinner-party or a dance?

I never appreciated anything so much as living like that with my tongue perpetually in my cheek, and in defiance of every policeman I passed.

We didn't stay very long in Paris, but went on to Monte Carlo en route for Greece. It was divine, returning to Monte Carlo where we had been so happy, and we stood at the open window of our old rooms looking out over the lights and the night and the sea, and really it was one of those moments when one can hardly believe one is alive for sheer happiness. For complicated and merely practical reasons we never went to Greece after all, and although I was disappointed I wasn't heartbroken, because it was delicious at Monte Carlo and Violet so loved being there. A complication arose over Denys announcing his arrival at Cannes. Violet didn't want to go; she wanted to make off, but I thought that if he arrived at Cannes confidently expecting her and then found she had bolted, he might do anything in a fit of despair. So I took her to Cannes, and went on myself to Paris; she was to tell Denys and I Harold, we hated leaving one another, even for (as we thought) a few days. We had then been together two months. But when I got to Paris I found Harold with an abscess in the knee, and he had to be operated, and had a great deal of pain, so of course I dismissed every idea of letting him know anything was amiss. I stayed with him a fortnight (Mother was there too), and then went to England to see after Ben and Nigel. Violet came back to England a day or two later, and Harold was to follow. In the meantime Violet, Denys and I met at a grotesque interview in London, when he asked me how much money I should have to keep Violet and myself on if we went away, so that I felt like a young man wanting to marry Violet and being interviewed by her father. Denys, who had come to see me by his own request, was very quiet and business-like, and looked like death. We did not shake hands. He turned to Violet and asked her if she wished to renounce everything and live with me. She was frightened, and asked for a week. We both agreed to that, and to abide by her decision, and he went away.

On the day that Harold came home Violet tried to rush things. She telephoned to me and told me Denys had said we must be gone by the following evening or not at all. Like a fool I believed her. This entailed telling Harold the moment he arrived. I met him at Victoria; he was very lame and on two sticks; the recollection of him goes through me like a stab even now. We dined at his parents' house, and after dinner I went upstairs to his room and told him I was leaving England with Violet next day. He broke down and cried. Then his mother came in, and I told her what I was going to do, and why; and of course she implored me not to; she had taken off her false hair, and although she didn't realize it a bit, was one of the most pathetic and sincere figures at that moment I have ever beheld. I felt so alien from the whole kindly, law-abiding house; I felt like a pariah, and his mother's tolerance

ly increased my shame; she didn't push me away, but put both
arms round me and said that nothing I could do was wrong
only mistaken. I felt blackened, and I was so unhappy, and
felt my alienation from them and my affinity with Violet so
keenly that I only wanted to fly where I would not pollute their
purity any longer. I went away to a little hotel, where I had got
a bedroom already, and sat up half the night writing letters. The
room was full of white lilac that Violet had sent me. Next day I
went round to see Harold. He pleaded his illness, and asked me
at least to spend the fortnight of his sick leave with him. In order
to arrange that, I went to find Violet. I was harsh to her as I never
have been to Harold; I absolutely refused to go with her that day.
After luncheon I took Harold to see her. He told her that at the
end of the fortnight he would let me go with her if I still wanted
to. Then he and I went to Knole, and the subject was not renewed
between us. I don't know what he thought about during all that
fortnight – I don't even know whether he took the danger of my
leaving him at all seriously. There were he and I, Ben, Nigel, and
Dada; because I was so preoccupied with my own affairs that I
forgot to say that in the May of the previous year Mother had
left Dada and Knole, and had never returned. So there were only
us five, and to me at least it was pretty fantastic, and not the least
fantastic part was the fact that Harold never made any allusion to
my going.

On the very last day (it was January), I went up to London
with him and still he wouldn't talk about it except when I forced
him to. He went back to Paris, and I to Knole, wondering
when, if ever, I should see him again. At Knole I made every
arrangement, and next day went up to London with my luggage.
Violet behaved in an extraordinary fashion, which I have never
been able to explain. She said she must have that evening in which
to talk business with Denys, but I then discovered that she had
arranged to go to a play with him. However we agreed to go the
next day. I would go back to Knole for the night. Violet came to
the station with me, with her luggage, wanting to come away
then and there; but she had given her word of honour to Denys
that she would be at home that evening, and I said she must wait

until next day. She implored me not to make her go back, and I almost had to push her out of my train, where she had forced her way into my carriage. As soon as I got to Knole she rang me up from a hotel in Trafalgar Square, saying that nothing would induce her to return to Denys, but as I couldn't bear to think of her alone in goodness knows what *bouge* of an hotel I persuaded her to go back. She wanted to come to the inn at Sevenoaks. I understood nothing then, and understand no more of it now; but I ought in justice to her always to remember that she tried desperately to get to me that night, and that she had told me for days that she was terrified of Denys breaking his promise.

Next day I called for her in a taxi in London, and we left for Lincoln.

It was bitterly cold, but we were happy in Lincoln. I took her with me to the fen country, which I was writing a book about; that was the object of going to Lincoln. Then we came back to London to the Liverpool Street hotel, and she telephoned for Denys, who came, and she told him she was leaving England next day. I was not present, but I saw him. As we were waiting for a taxi with our luggage in the hall of the hotel next morning, he came in again. He asked her to go and speak to him, but I don't know what he said. He gave her a long letter he had written her, and she gave it to me to read in the taxi on the way to Victoria, and having read it did the only thing I am in the very least proud of: I said I would give her up if she would go back to him. She refused vehemently and said nothing would induce her to, not even my leaving her. I urged her — I really did urge her; he had written her a letter that really touched me. I travelled down to Dover with her, and all the way I tried to persuade her. But she was adamant. The only concession she would make was to start for France by herself, because she seemed to think he would mind that less. So I saw her off, absolutely firm in her resolution, but childishly terrified of the journey on the boat, and I was to join her at Amiens the next day.

I remained alone at Dover, watching her boat out of sight, and then I went to a lodging house and got myself a room for the night. I lunched, and feeling very disconsolate I walked down to the station and stood staring out over the sea, when turning round I saw Denys coming towards me. He looked very anxious, and wore big motor gloves. He said, 'Where's Violet?', and I answered that she had gone. He wanted to follow her. I took him back to my lodging house, and he paced up and down my bedroom there for the rest of the afternoon. At first I would not tell him where she had gone, but as he threatened to stay with me until I left Dover, saying that he knew I was going to join her, I told him I was leaving next day. He promised not to steal a march on me, and we said we would go together and give her the choice between us. I did not hate him in the least then; I was only very sorry. We stalked out together to the post office, and sent telegrams to Violet's family and to mine, and then parted with extreme grimness. During the evening I got a panic-stricken telegram from Violet, which I telephoned through to Denys.

During the night a gale got up, and as I lay in bed I could feel the whole house – which was old and probably frail – shaking under me. I couldn't sleep. I lay in a sort of waking nightmare; at one moment I was convinced that the house would catch fire, that the wind would blow it instantly into a roar of flame, and that as my bedroom was at the top of the house I would stand no chance of escape. I got up, and went to peer over the well of the staircase; gas-jets burnt on every landing, flickering in the draught, and I thought nothing more likely than that the fire should be started by one of them. I took some aspirin, went back to bed, and presently slept; I dreamt horribly, and woke once with the tears running down my face. I woke constantly, until the dawn began to show behind the blinds, and I got up and dressed.

It poured with rain, and the wind seemed stronger than ever; I went out, and was blown clean across the road. The sea was mud-coloured, and very rough; even the ships in the harbour rocked violently, and outside the harbour the waves flung showers of spray over the piers. I never remember such a gale. I went to the boat to get a cabin, and there encountered Denys on the same errand. The sight of us both bribing for cabins in the purser's office was so comic that it made us less grim to one another. I don't know what Denys thought, but personally I was rather exhilarated at the prospect of steaming out into that storm and insecurity after the nervous and inactive hours I had lived through. Once out there, there could be no weakness or turning back; one might pray for a respite but one would pray in vain; one wouldn't be let off or eased for a minute; one would have to fight one's way to the other side before one could find peace. Very salutary to one who, like me, had been fighting with human affairs that could be shelved or postponed when one felt one's strength failing one! Out there one was given no time to breathe or recover; the ship ran again right down under the grey valleys of waves; water broke all over her, running blackly off her decks; everything was wet, uncomfortable, and quite remorseless; the wind buffeted one, shook and raged at one, noise and tumult bewildered one; one had to think primarily of keeping one's feet and fighting for one's balance; all the hair-splitting niceties that assailed one on dry land, were, thank heaven, in this good rough world of elements entirely out of the question.

Anyhow, that symbolic crossing beat cordiality into Denys and into me, and we joked about sea-sick remedies, and he dared me to smoke, and by the time we drew alongside at Calais he was asking me to lunch with him in the buffet. He then said he would look after my luggage if I would go on and get a table. I went into the buffet, and there Violet rushed up to me, white and shaking and nearly hysterical. I said, 'Good God, why aren't you at Amiens? Denys is with me', and she said she must get away at once, but at that moment he came in. We realized at once that she was ill and starving (she had had nothing to eat since twenty-four hours or more), so we made her sit down and eat chicken and drink champagne. She said she had left all her possessions at Amiens, but there was no question of taking her there that day, or of anything except putting her to bed and getting a doctor. We all three trundled across Calais in a shut cab, found a hotel, and started putting her to bed; but it was so dirty that we took her to another one. She was completely docile in our hands, and we were too busy getting her hot-water bottles, sponges, soup, and a doctor, to realize the absurdity of the whole thing. What made it more ridiculous, was that Denys and I were given communicating rooms, while she was a little way off. When we had got her safely to bed, we both sat in her room and beamed at her with relief. She had recovered then, and amused us by telling us stories of her adventures on the way to Amiens. We had both been anxious about her, and were conscious of nothing but delight in merely having her safe; at least I know that was what I felt, and I am sure from Denys's manner that he felt the same. The immense problem that the three of us had got to solve, and all the agony and heartburning its solution must entail for one of us – all that was set aside by triple consent. We were all gay, we were even light-hearted, not negatively, but positively; it was as though time were suspended, and all human relations suspended too, except Denys's and my common love for Violet. We had no hostility, I think, towards one another. We were foes who, while our enmity was in abeyance, were prepared to love one another. Our enmity was an extrinsic, not an intrinsic thing. We argued and discussed upon all the detached topics that were as dear to Denys as they were to me; we discussed music, poetry and immortality, and all the while Violet lay like a princess propped up by a pillow in an enormous bed and listened to us with a *narquois* expression of amazed amusement, and frank relish at the farcical turn affairs had taken. This was after dinner. We had all three dined in her bedroom, and Denys and I had, in turn, waited upon her. She was altogether charming and amusing that evening. At the beginning of dinner our lips were twitching with the tempation to *fou rire*, and Violet alone saved the situation. After dinner, as I have said, it was Denys and I who talked. I saw that evening how intelligent he was, how absorbed in un-sordid things; I even saw with regret what good friends we might have been under other circumstances; and above all I was touched by his very naive joy at having Violet safe, and present; I was touched by this, because I shared and could understand it.

Next morning Violet was better, and we three breakfasted together, and afterwards got a motor to go across to Boulogne. Still the essential subject had not been raised, except as a joke on the previous evening by Denys, who suggested that we should go to Jamaica and grow sugar. We were both grimmer again now, realizing that the discussion could not much longer be put off. The motor drive was a dreary business. It was a black day, and the road lay across bleak country, hedgeless, monotonous country, and once we nearly got smashed up, and Denys said to me, 'Perhaps that would be the best solution after all.' We lunched at Boulogne, then took the train to Amiens. We had agreed to discuss it at Amiens, but in the train in the midst of writing limericks and jokes, Denys wrote on a piece of paper that he knew Violet's mind was made up, and that he would leave us at Amiens and go on himself to Paris, never to see Violet again. Everything was tragic again in an instant. I was tongue-tied, and could say nothing. We were then about two hours distant from Amiens, and feeling that the journey would really be too painful, I went away and sat in the compartment next door. Denys cried the whole way to Amiens, and at Amiens Violet and I got out, and so did he, as he had to get into another train; he looked awful as he went away, and Violet and I were alone.

That was a bad two hours.

We went to the Hôtel du Rhin, where Violet's things already were. I think I was more sorry for Denys than she was. If he had not made up his mind like that in the train I had meant to urge her again to go with him, although I knew it would be quite useless. I could not understand her indifference towards him, for even I was oppressed by the thought of what he must be suffering, and of what he would suffer next day on his way through from Paris to London, when he passed through Amiens knowing that Violet was still there with me. I was so much disturbed by all this, that I telephoned myself to Paris to find out if he was all right, and was told that he had already left for London.

We spent that day looking at the devastations of Amiens and at the very lovely cathedral. I telegraphed to Harold where I was in case he should be anxious. (I did not know that he had had no letters or telegrams from me at all, as he was by then looking for me in England, having crossed in the same gale, only in the opposite direction.) Violet and I meant to motor past Paris (I couldn't bear to go actually into Paris where I thought Harold was), and then to get a train and go to Sicily. If she had been well we should probably have done this the same day, but she was still ill from the effects of her fright and starvation, so we stayed in Amiens. After dinner that night her father [Colonel George Keppel] arrived at our hotel. He was pompous, theatrical, and unimpressive. He stormed at us, and it was all we could do to keep from laughing. The tiresome part was, that he had wired for Denys, and refused to leave us lest we should slip away.

Now comes the worst part. Denys and Harold arrived together by aeroplane early in the morning [14 February 1920]. I was very much astonished, because of course I had thought Harold was in Paris all this time, getting letters more or less all the time from me. He came up to my room, hard on Violet's heels, and told me to pack. Then there was an unpleasant scene. I sat on the window-sill, and Violet stood near me, and we defied first Harold and then Denys, and then both together. This sounds absurd and childish, and so I dare say it was. Denys was the most silent of all; he just looked at Violet while she abused him. The upshot of it was that we refused to leave each other, and Harold said we should be starved out by having someone always with us till we gave way – it was all undignified and noisy to a degree, and I hated it, and was rude to Harold, and he said a lot of silly things that showed him in a wrong light to Violet, and I was sorry about that too. Then Violet and I went together and met Denys in a passage, and he leaned against the wall looking like a stained-glass window saint, very pale and frail, and quite golden-haired, while she said she loathed him, and never to my dying day shall I forget the look on his face. He said nothing at all, but again only stared at her, and if he had slipped down and died at our feet I should scarcely have been surprised.

Then I went upstairs again, to where Harold was sitting in my room, and he tried to talk to me sensibly, and I was less rude, but firm. Then he said a thing which made all the room spin round my head. He said, 'Are you sure Violet is as faithful to you as she makes you believe? Because Denys has told your mother quite a different story.' I thought I should go mad when he said that. I rushed downstairs, and at the foot of the stairs I met Denys. I stopped him and said, 'I am very sorry, but I must ask you the most terribly indiscreet question: have you ever been really married to Violet?' He answered, 'I refuse to tell you; that is a matter which lies entirely between Violet and myself.' (I can remember every single one of the words we all spoke at that time.) I caught his sleeve; I kept him; I insisted. I said, 'If you tell me you have, I swear to you I will never set eyes on Violet again.' He hesitated a little at that, and then said again, 'I can't answer'.

I let him go; I went into the restaurant where Violet was sitting at a little table waiting for her breakfast. I went straight up to her and said (as though the words were being put into my lips), 'Why have you not told me you have deceived me with Denys?' I never saw such absolute terror leap into anyone's face. She stammered something, I don't know what. I said, 'You have belonged to him.' She said 'Yes.' I said 'When?', and she said, 'The night before we went to Lincoln.' Yet I knew she was a virgin.

I don't know what I said then; I only know that I broke away from her as she tried to hold me, and said quite wildly that I was going away from her. She followed me, and we got into the sitting-room; somehow the doors and woodwork of the sitting-room were pocked with bullet marks. Denys was there too, and she kept saying all kinds of wild things, like, 'Let me explain', or, 'Tell her it isn't true', and I kept saying only that I wanted to go. I was half mad with pain and not understanding. She was crying, and held me so strongly that I couldn't get away till Denys helped me. Then I rushed upstairs while he held her in the sitting-room, and I packed my things, blind with passion and pain, not able to think or speak, but only thinking that I must get away at all costs. I went downstairs, and found that Harold was with her. Denys was guarding the door. I had just enough sense left to beg him not to leave her for a moment. When Harold came out I went in, although they tried to prevent me. I kissed Violet. Then I went away as quickly as I could, in a motor, with Harold. We had to get his bag out of the aeroplane, and we waited a long time on the aerodrome. That was awful, as Amiens was so near, and we had to drive through Amiens again to get to the station, but I heard Harold tell the chauffeur to avoid the street where the hotel was, and we went by slums. There was no train for Paris for about an hour.

22 OCTOBER [1920]

Harold had lunch in the buffet, but I couldn't eat anything. I saw Violet's father also going to Paris by the same train, so I knew she was alone with Denys, and I hated him then as I never had before. But I couldn't think of anything clearly at all. Harold took me to his hotel in Paris; I didn't care where I went or what became of me. I couldn't cry. I don't remember when we got to Paris, or what I did until it was time for dinner. I had not swallowed a mouthful of food all day, and I was beginning to feel slightly light-headed, so I went down to the restaurant and had some soup. I began to get the usual reaction after one has gone through too much strain, and in consequence I started talking to Harold and making jokes, and all the time a hammer in my head went 'Violet! Violet!', and it was rather like the day before her wedding, when I was at Versailles with Harold.

We hadn't been in the restaurant long when I saw Violet come in. I dropped my knife and fork, and went to her; it was like warmth rushing back when one has been deadly cold, because for the first second I forgot that something much worse than mere distance had parted us. Harold told me take her upstairs, and I was shut into the sitting-room alone with her. I got behind a chair so that she shouldn't come near me; I was shivering all over. I don't remember our conversation very distinctly; I remember saying over and over again, 'You mustn't ask me to think; I've been stunned and I haven't recovered.' She was very urgent and desperate, and said that if I cast her off altogether she would throw herself into the river, and I am sure this was true. She also said that things had not been quite as I had first believed. She had never belonged to Denys, although matters had gone halfway in that direction. I still kept shivering and saying that I couldn't think. At that moment Harold and Denys came in. She asked Harold to go out, and asked Denys to corroborate what she had just told me. He walked up and down the room and seemed to be struggling with himself. Then he said, 'This must never go further than this room; I promise you that there has never been anything of that kind between Violet and me.' I could have cried with relief, but still it was bad enough that she should have deceived me even to a certain extent – especially on the very night when I was innocently making every disposition to give up everything in the world for her next day. That was what hurt me most bitterly. When I was again alone with her I said I could not bear to see her for at least two months.

Next day she left Paris for the south of France, and every day she used to telephone to me from the various provincial towns where they stopped for the night; and every day her voice was fainter as the distances increased. It must have been a nightmare journey – Denys collapsed and fell ill, but she urged on the motor as though she had been driven by a demon, and it was on that journey, I think, that Denys finally lost what slight hope he still had that she might come to care for him.

I won't say what I went through during the six weeks that passed before I saw her again. I seemed to know every variety of torment – that of longing and aching miserably for someone in whom I had lost faith, that of loving to desperation someone in whose worth I no longer believed. Before I had always buoyed myself with the thought that although she might hold no other moral precept, at least she was whole-hearted and true where she did love. To this day I don't understand what prompted her to give in, even so little. I think it was a mixture of pity and remorse because she knew she was intending to leave him for good the next day and she had certainly told me for weeks that he was increasingly importunate. Anyhow I don't want to speculate, it's too painful.

I stayed in Paris for some time, then came back to England. Violet was at Bordighera, living in a villa, while he lived in an hotel. In March I went out to join her at Avignon. I hadn't seen her for six weeks, and I travelled straight through. It ought to have been a good meeting, but it wasn't. Three hours after my arrival we were already quarrelling because she had apparently thought she could persuade me to stay with her for good, and was angry when she found she couldn't. We motored from Avignon to Bordighera, and quarrelled the whole time, and I was acutely wretched. Then at San Remo I lost my head and said I would stay, and for a few days we were happy. We went on to Venice, but I don't really look back on that journey with much pleasure. She was ill, with a touch of jaundice, a most unromantic complaint, and I could do nothing with her, especially after I had gone back on what I had said at San Remo. I admit that I behaved badly over that. One ought not to allow oneself the luxury of losing one's head.

26 OCTOBER [1920]

She wanted to remain abroad by herself, but I couldn't allow that – she is as helpless as a child, and would happily have entrusted her passport, her ticket, her jewels, and her money to the first person who offered to relieve her of the responsibility of looking after them, and anyway I saw the sort of life she would lead, ranging from hotel to hotel, quite irresponsible, and horribly lonely, so I dragged her reluctant person back to England with me.

Then began a very unsatisfactory summer; we each bitterly resented the other living officially with someone else, and our brief and comparatively infrequent meetings were stormy with quarrels, and the additional worry of having no place where we could spend a little time peacefully together got upon our nerves, and that added to the ever-renewed wound of parting, made us the more irritable to one another. I have a confused recollection of hours spent in the writing-rooms of various London hotels, where we would order coffee to enable us to remain there for a little; lingering over lunches in restaurants, because a restaurant too, was a place where one could sit and talk; going to plays, for that, also, provided chairs and a roof over our heads. All this contributed to our discomfort and dissatisfaction. Sometimes we met in the National Gallery, sometimes in the flat of a friend; but wherever it was, we felt the sordidness and the humiliation of the whole thing, for we cared far too deeply to derive the slightest amusement out of any excitement of danger or difficulty. We wanted far too thirstily to be uninterruptedly together. She very rarely came to stay with me. Whenever she did come, the antagonism between her and the house was ludicrous and painful. The country would seem deliberately to drape itself in tenderness and content, and she, feeling the place to be an enemy, would turn yet more fierce, yet more restless, while I stood bewildered and uncertain between the personification of my two lives. When I passed from one to the other, keeping them separate and apart, I could just keep the thing within my control; but when they met, coincided, and were simultaneous, I found them impossible to reconcile. My house, my garden, my fields, and Harold, those were the silent ones, that pleaded only by their merits of purity, simplicity, and faith; and on the other hand stood Violet, fighting wildly for me, seeming sometimes harsh and scornful, and riding roughshod over those gentle defenceless things, but sometimes piteous and tragic, reduced to utter dependence upon me, and instantly defeated by any rough word of mine, until I really knew not where the truth lay. No sooner did I hit her where alone she was vulnerable — in her caring for me — than her harshness and pitilessness vanished, leaving her at my mercy. No plea, no exhortation could touch her; I had only one weapon that she understood.

Those were very cruel weeks, when our only preoccupation seemed to be the desire to score off one another, or to catch one another out. The Amiens incident had (not unnaturally) destroyed all trust on my part, and the temporary death of the possibility of our living together drove her into the usual embittering despair. She tried again to get me to go away, by making me believe that Denys threatened to break his promises to her; but I was more wary now, and before making any promise I made her write to Denys, a letter whose reply showed quite clearly that he had not attempted to break his promises nor had any intention of doing so.

There was a strange period when Denys went away by himself to Devonshire, and wrote her daily letters from there telling her that he no longer cared for her. In fact when he returned to London he refused for a long time to set eyes on her, and she spent that time with me, chiefly at Hindhead (Harold was in Paris), but of course when Denys saw her, everything began again.

He cared for her too fatally for it to die like that. There was one evening when she was staying with me, and he telephoned to her to come at once; it was after dinner; I got out my car and drove her to the station, but the last train had gone, so I drove her on to London, to the hotel where Denys was waiting for her, and went myself to lodgings I knew of, where I had to have the room of someone who was away; I had nothing whatever with me, and it took me ages to find anywhere to sleep. Of course I dared not go to Mother's house [Hill Street], as it was after midnight.

The whole summer was made up of episodes like that. We weren't happy – how could we be? We were happy once for five days when we went motoring; we went from Hindhead to Rye, and it was a great success, but it didn't make up for all the wretchedness and jealousy and turmoil we went through at other times. Other people were wretched too; I mean, Denys, who actually fell into consumption, and had to go and do a cure in Holland, where Violet's mother had a house, and Violet of course had to go too, for five weeks. During the whole of those five weeks we didn't quarrel by letter, and when she came back it was like two flames leaping together. She arrived from Holland at one station, and drove straight across London to another station where I was waiting for her, and we went down to her house in the country where we spent four absolutely unclouded days.

28 MARCH [1921]

I am writing now in the light of later events, and writing in the midst of great unhappiness which I try to conceal from poor Harold, who is an angel upon earth. It is possible that I may never see Violet again, or that I may see her once again before we are parted, or that we may meet in future years as strangers; it is also possible that she may not choose to live; in any case it has come about indirectly owing to me, while I remain safe, secure and undamaged save in my heart. The injustice and misfortune of the whole thing oppresses me hourly; it gives me an awful sense of doom – Violet's doom, which she herself has consistently predicted.

Chronology

PART THREE AND PART FOUR

1918 18 APRIL: Vita and Violet at Long Barn: beginning of their love affair

28 APRIL: Vita and Violet in Polperro, Cornwall, till 10 May

14 MAY: Vita begins writing *Challenge*

4–23 JULY: Second visit to Polperro

OCTOBER: 'Julian' in London

11 NOVEMBER: The Armistice

26 NOVEMBER: Vita and Violet go to Paris

6 DECEMBER: Vita and Violet go to Monte Carlo, and remain there till mid-March

CHRISTMAS: Harold at Knole, without Vita

1919 JANUARY: Harold on British staff, Paris Peace Conference, till June

15 MARCH: Vita leaves Monte Carlo, rejoins Harold in Paris

19 MARCH: Vita returns to England

26 MARCH: Violet's engagement to Denys Trefusis announced

19 MAY: Lady Sackville leaves her husband and Knole for ever

16 JUNE: Violet marries Denys; Vita with Harold at Versailles

19 OCTOBER: Vita and Violet return to Monte Carlo

18 DECEMBER: Vita joins Harold in Paris: operation on his knee

1920 2 JANUARY: Vita returns to Knole

     17 JANUARY: Harold returns on leave; Vita tells him she intends to elope with Violet

     18–31 JANUARY: Vita and Harold at Knole

     1 FEBRUARY: Harold returns to Paris, now on League of Nations staff

     3–8 FEBRUARY: Vita and Violet in Lincoln

     9 FEBRUARY: Violet crosses to France, leaving Vita at Dover

     10 FEBRUARY: Vita, with Denys, joins Violet at Calais

     11–13 FEBRUARY: Vita and Violet in Amiens

     14 FEBRUARY: Crisis day: Harold and Denys fly to Amiens, and take their wives separately to Paris

     16–20 FEBRUARY: Violet and Denys motor to Toulon

     28 FEBRUARY: Vita returns to London

     20 MARCH: Vita joins Violet in Avignon; they go to San Remo and Venice

     10 APRIL: Vita and Violet return to England

     23 JULY: Vita starts writing her autobiography

1921 JANUARY–MARCH: Vita and Violet at Hyères

     SUMMER: Gradual end of their love-affair

     AUTUMN: Violet returns to Denys

PART FOUR
BY NIGEL NICOLSON

THERE is one essential matter which must be explained, and I prefer to do it at the outset. Vita has described her nature quite frankly: she was physically attracted by women more than by men, and remained so all her life. She was by no means frigid, but she came to look upon the 'normal' act of love as bestial and repulsive. In one of her novels, *Grand Canyon* (1942), she gives expression to this feeling: 'One wonders how they ever brought themselves to commit the grotesque act necessary to beget children.' Once, when she was a child, a gamekeeper's son at Sluie had initiated her, by demonstration, into the physical differences between boys and girls, and she had run away, dreadfully shocked. Her mother's fastidiousness and her father's reluctance to discuss any intimate subject with her deepened her sexual isolation. With Rosamund she tumbled into love, and bed, with a sort of innocence. At first it meant little more to her than cuddling a favourite dog or rabbit, and later she regarded the affair as more naughty than perverted, and took great pains to conceal it from her parents and Harold, fearing that exposure would mean the banishment of Rosamund. It was little more than that. She had no concept of any moral distinction between homosexual and heterosexual love, thinking of them both as 'love' without qualification. When she married Harold, she assumed that marriage was love by other means, and for a time it worked.

The very existence of myself and my brother is proof of it, and there is ample evidence in the letters and diaries that for the first few years of their marriage they were sexually compatible. After 1917 it gradually became clear that their mutual enjoyment was on the wane. Lady Sackville refers in her diaries to frank conversations with Vita on the subject ('She remarks about H. being so physically cold'). When I myself married, my father solemnly cautioned me that the physical side of marriage could not be expected to last more than a year or two, and once, in a broadcast, he said, 'Being "in love" lasts but a short time – from three weeks to three years. It has little or nothing to do with the felicity of marriage.' Simultaneously, therefore, and without placing any great strain upon their love for each other, they began to seek pleasure with people of their own sex, and to Vita at least it seemed quite natural, for she was simply reverting to her other form of 'love'. Marriage and sex could be quite separate things. In a letter which she wrote to Harold in 1960, two years before she died, she said:

When we married, you were older than I was, and far better informed. I was very young, and very innocent, I knew nothing about homosexuality. I didn't even know that such a thing existed, either between men or between women. You should have told me. You should have warned me. You should have told me about yourself, and warned me that the same sort of thing was likely to happen to myself. It would have saved us a lot of trouble and misunderstanding. But I simply didn't know.

When she said 'I simply didn't know', she must have meant that she didn't know how strong and dangerous such passion could be, until Violet replaced Rosamund. Of course she knew that 'such a thing existed', but she did not give it a name, and felt no guilt about it. At the time of her marriage she may have been ignorant that men could feel for other men as she had felt for Rosamund, but when she had made this discovery in Harold himself, it did not come as a great shock to her, for she had the romantic notion that it was natural and salutary for 'people' to love each other, and the desire to kiss and touch was simply the physical expression of affection, and it made no difference wheth it was affection between people of the same sex or the oppos

It was fortunate that both were made that way. If only one of them had been, their marriage would probably have collapsed. Violet did not destroy their physical union; she simply provided the alternative for which Vita was unconsciously seeking at the moment when her physical passion for Harold, and his for her, had begun to cool. In Harold's life at that time there was no male Violet, luckily for him, since his love for Vita might not have survived two rivals simultaneously. Before he met Vita he had been half-engaged to another girl, Eileen Wellesley. He was not driven to homosexuality by Vita's temporary desertion of him, because it had always been latent, but his loneliness may have encouraged this tendency to develop, since with his strong sense of duty (much stronger than Vita's) he felt it to be less treacherous to sleep with men in her absence than with other women. When he was left stranded in Paris, he once confessed to Vita that he was 'spending his time with rather low people, the *demi-monde*', and this could have meant young men. When she returned to him, it certainly did. Lady Sackville noted in her diary, 'V. intends to be very platonic with H., who accepts it like a lamb.' They never shared a bedroom after that.

Harold had a series of relationships with men who were his intellectual equals, but the physical element in them was very secondary. He was never a passionate lover. To him sex was as incidental, and about as pleasurable, as a quick visit to a picture-gallery between trains. His a-sexual love for Vita in later life was balanced by affection for his men friends, by some of whom he was temporarily, but never helplessly, attracted. There was no moment in his life when love for a young man became such an obsession to him that it interfered with his work, and he had no affairs faintly comparable to Vita's. Their behaviour in this respect was a reflection of their very different personalities. His life was too well regulated to be affected by affairs of the heart, while she always allowed herself to be swept away.

He saw Vita as the companion of a lifetime. Each brought as a dowry to the other new interests (he French literature, she English domestic architecture), and others, like gardening, they discovered

d output of novels and poetry encouraged him
never in rivalry, for the style and subjects of
quite different, and jealousy was a handicap he
en her first novel *Heritage* was published in 1919
usual acclaim, he wrote to her:

done it. The Secretary of the Marlborough Club,
otherwise an intelligent and quite polite man, has just said to me:
'By the way, are you any relation to the Nicolson whose wife wrote
Heritage?' Now look here: I don't mind being Hadji [her use of that
name dates from about this time]; or you being Vita; or my being
your husband. I might even put up, from foolish people, with being
called 'Vita's husband' or 'V. Sackville-West's husband'. I might
(though I'm not sure) put up with being 'that fellow Nicolson
whose wife wrote *Heritage*'. But I *will not be asked* if I am 'by any
chance' (by *any* chance mark you) 'a *relation* of *the*' (just think, *the*)
'Nicolson whose wife etc . . .'

That's as far as it went. His pleasure at her literary success was
unforced. So was his sympathy with the romantic side of her
nature. He loved the countryside of England as much as she did,
and shared her yearning for places abroad where they might live
in solitude and discomfort, on holiday, or even permanently.
They discussed seriously buying a ruined castle in the Abruzzi,
another on a tiny island called Giglio in the Tyrrhenian Sea, or
the island of Herm in the Channel Islands, and at one moment
during the height of Vita's affair with Violet all was temporarily
forgotten in their excitement at discovering that Bodiam Castle,
the shell of which rises so unexpectedly from the hop gardens of
the Sussex Weald, was for sale. But for the moment they remained
content with Long Barn, the calm centre of their harassed lives,
the symbol of their marriage.

Harold soon abandoned any expectation that Vita would take
any interest in his career. She was pleased, vaguely, that he was
doing well in it, and would pass on to him any compliments
which she heard, but scarcely noticed the award to him of the
CMG at the early age of thirty-four. Her ignorance of foreign
policy was profound, and she made no effort to acquire even a
headline-reader's familiarity with the crises that absorbed Harold'

every working day, and they would never discuss such things on his return home. To her a new crisis meant simply that he would be kept late at the Foreign Office, or be sent to Lausanne or Prague. The middle stages of the Violet affair coincided with the Paris Peace Conference, when Harold was in almost daily consultation with world-leaders like Lloyd George, Clemenceau, President Wilson and A.J. Balfour, and his narrative of those days in *Peacemaking* makes poignant reading when one knows the concurrent drama of his private life. In his letters to Vita he rarely referred to political events, knowing that they would bore her, but one obtains an occasional glimpse:

> There is such a thunderstorm brewing here against the P.M. [Lloyd George]. It is all about this Asia Minor business, and it is difficult for me to guide my row-boat safely in and out of these fierce Dreadnoughts. Even A.J.B. is angry: 'Those three all-powerful, all-ignorant, men sitting there and partitioning continents with only a child to take notes for them.' I have an uneasy suspicion that by the 'child' he means me. [*17 May 1919*]

> I really feel that this bloody bullying peace is the last flicker of the old tradition, and that we young people will build again. I hope so. [*1 June 1919*]

To these remarks she never responded. When, after the signing of the Treaty of Versailles, Harold was appointed to Sir Eric Drummond's staff on the nascent League of Nations, Vita did not even know what the League of Nations was.

My father's was a gentle nature. If he had fought in the First World War, he might have returned a slightly different man, like Lord Sackville, but his character remained as rounded and supple as a rubber ball. He was in no sense indecisive or frivolous. He took his professions, diplomatic and literary, very seriously, and throughout his life worked extremely hard, but his resilience had a puppyish quality, an innocence and playfulness, and he tended to avoid direct confrontation with unpleasant truths. Just as in his two earliest biographies he toned down the homosexuality of Verlaine and the masochism of Swinburne, so in the crisis of his own life, he hoped that by joking about it he could make it go way. His sense of fun, his literary arabesques, his capacity always to see the other person's point of view, softened his indignation, weakened its impact. A letter of mild reproach to Vita would immediately be followed by another, or by a telegram, telling her to ignore it. He suggested that she might buy Violet as a Christmas present 'a copy of Sappho's poems – I believe you can get one quite cheaply in Tauchnitz'. He invited Violet to stay at his flat when she came to Paris. His distress at Vita's behaviour alternated with disconcerting tolerance; 'come back at once' with 'enjoy yourselves'; hatred of Violet with sympathy for her predicament. He could write to Vita, 'I really don't feel that anything so deep or so compelling as her love for you can be called unnatural or debasing.' So Vita never knew how much he minded, and guessed, correctly, that no matter what she did, she would always be forgiven. She thought his melancholy partly unreal, or at least fitful, knowing that he knew that she would always come back to him in the end. Here is one of his crosser letters:

I have never loved you so much as during the last few months, when you have been slipping away from me. Violet in her clever way has made you think I'm unromantic. Oh dear, how can a middle-aged civil servant [he was only thirty-one!] deal with so subtle an accusation? You see, if I were rich, I could have a valet and an aeroplane and a gardenia tree, and it would all be very Byronic; but not being rich or successful, it is just Poor little Hadji. I wish Violet was dead. She has poisoned one of the most sunny things that ever happened. She is like some fierce orchid – glimmering and stinking in the recesses of life, and throwing cadaverous sweetness on the morning's breeze. Darling, she is evil, and I am not evil.

Oh my darling, what is it that makes you put her above me? We seemed, you and I, to be running hand-in-hand on the Downs, and now I am wandering about alone and rather frightened in the fog. What is it? It may be your bloody Sackville looniness, or it may be a sort of George Sand stunt, or it may be that I am just a bad, futile, unconvincing, unromantic husband. Is it that I am not amorous enough? How can I even think such things! And against me I have that little tortuous, erotic, irresponsible, irremediable and unlimited person. I don't hate her. No more than I should hate opium if you took it. [10 September 1918]

He followed this letter by two others written on the same day, telling her to pay no attention to the first, 'as I was writing in a depressed mood. I get cold panics in the rain. I am not in the least depressed really.'

He was nervous lest she should think that he was too safe for her, too domesticated; that she should feel 'your glowing youth is being wasted on a curate'. He realized that she needed a 'safety-valve for your gipsy instincts', the chance to escape occasionally from the 'yoke' of marriage. This was true. Vita had Wanderlust. The desire to be free from interruption, free from being available, was as real and painful to her as love or jealousy. She longed to be in new places where nobody would ask her to order luncheon or pay house-bills or come to her with a grievance against someone else. In a sense she had at Long Barn everything which her romantic heart desired:

> My Saxon Weald! My cool and candid Weald!
> Dear God! the heart, the very heart, of me
> That plays and strays a truant in strange lands,
> Always returns and finds its inward peace,
> Its swing of truth, its measure of restraint,
> Here among meadows, orchards, lanes and shaws.
> [*Orchard and Vineyard* 1921]

But she could rebel against the tameness of the English landscape, where the hills are small hills, the lakes small lakes, and at night the stars are small stars. At these moments the whole countryside appeared to her a horrible compromise, like its smug society, and she longed for a crueller climate, a more tempestuous people, and to shake the mud of 'this beastly grey place' off her shoes.

In *Heritage* she wrote: 'Serenity of spirit and turbulence of action should make up the sum of man's life'; and in the character of the Romany-Kentish Ruth, the heroine of her novel, she drew her self-portrait. Ruth's lover says: 'What am I to believe — that she is cursed with a dual nature, the one coarse and unbridled, the other delicate, conventional, practical, motherly, refined? Can it be the result of the separate, antagonistic strains in her blood, the southern and northern legacy?' Vita believed that the Spanish blood ran even more strongly in herself than in her mother. She felt it to be the more vehement strain, the source of her creative talent; but she also acknowledged that it was wild and irresponsible, and conflicted with the stability which she also coveted. Violet was the Mediterranean in her; Harold was Kent. She felt for his patience a mixture of admiration and pity. She would have liked him to pull her back by the hair, as a Spaniard would have done, but loved him because he would not do so. She found in Violet a fascinating and passionate girl who awoke all the adventurousness of her spirit, her hatred of the *Gemütlichkeit* of domestic life, her fear that her youth would pass before she had lived it, and lived it recklessly. 'Women', she wrote to Harold,

> ... ought to have freedom the same as men when they are young. It is a rotten and ridiculous system at present; it's simply cheating one of one's youth. It was alright for Victorians. But this generation is discarding, and the next will have discarded, the chrysalis. Women, like men, ought to have their youth so glutted with freedom that they hate the very idea of freedom. [*1 June 1919*]

Periodically she felt ashamed of these ideas. When Harold asked her, 'What has happened to you?', she couldn't honestly answer, or couldn't answer honestly.

Towards us, her children, she felt distant affection. Babies were an interruption, a reminder of duty, of her place in the home, a reminder of their innocence compared to her guilt, a reminder, even, of maternity, which by then, under Violet's influence, she found distasteful. But Violet never shook her love for Harold:

> Oh Hadji, I couldn't ever hurt someone so tender and sensitive and angelic and loving as you are – at least, I know that I have hurt you, but I couldn't do anything to hurt you dreadfully and irrevocably. What a hold you have on my heart; nobody else would ever have such a hold. I love you more than myself, more than life, more than the things I love. I give you everything – like a sacrifice. I love you so much that I don't even resent it. [*8 June 1919*]

> You have met and understood me on every point. It is this which binds me to you through every storm, and makes you so unalterably the one person whom I trust and love. Oh Hadji, what more can I

say? Appearance and facts are so hopelessly at variance, I know. But when I say I love you, it is true, true, true. You are the best and most sacred and the most tender thing in my life. [*1 November 1919*]

I hear her unmistakable voice across more than fifty years. Before she steeled herself to tell him the whole truth about Violet, the deceit was agony to her. She wrote this scrap of a poem on her return from their first visit to Cornwall:

I wish you thought me faithless, whilst within
My heart I knew my innocence from sin.
This I could bear; I cannot bear that you
Should think me faithful, when I am untrue.

When she did tell him, she looked to him for strength. The victim of her love-affair must rescue her from it:

Hadji, my darling, there is only one thing left in which I unshakeably believe, and that is your essential goodness. I don't know what is going to happen or become of me, and I simply cling and cling to the thought of you. You are my only anchor. I hate myself. Oh, I do crave to be with you. I feel like a person drowning who knows there is an absolutely safe boat somewhere on the sea, and if they can only keep up their strength long enough, they will reach it. Hadji, I am so frightened sometimes. [*25 May 1919*]

At first she thought the division within herself 'so neat'. She could love Harold, she thought, and be 'in love' with Violet. Then she realized that it was not neat at all, for she was swept away by the current while he remained lonely and miserable on the shore. Such was her shame that she gave up writing to him, telling him in response to his heartbroken reproaches that she felt it 'indecent' to write to him while she was with Violet: a sort of *pudeur* prevented her from mingling her two lives. Harold saved her from isolation by writing every day even when he received no answer, keeping himself and his love for her constantly in her mind, cherishing her when he thought her brutal, trusting her when he knew that she was not to be trusted. It was not 'his' struggle, but 'their' struggle. He never thought of leaving her, only of showing her the way back. Slowly she responded, but the ordeal lasted three whole years.

Violet Keppel suffered from no such conflicts of loyalty. Vita and Harold had five years of married happiness behind them when the affair began. Violet had no equivalent, and when she married it was on the impossible condition that the affair must be allowed to continue. Her marriage was a spur to infidelity; to Vita marriage was its only rein. Acknowledging no responsibilities, Violet was the more reckless of the two, the leader of their truancy, the more insistent that they break all their ties. Hers was the stronger character, and she used her strength not to dominate, but to seduce. She converted Vita's surrender to her into her surrender to Vita. She was attractive in its most literal sense: she drew people after her, men and women. Brilliantly gifted, richly subtle, loving everything that was beautiful, she had all the qualities which Vita most admired, and many of which she shared. Violet taunted her, dared her to practise the excesses of their joint imaginations, while remaining submissive to her in love. She was a true rebel, conscious from an early age of the hypocrisy of the society in which she had been brought up, and wished to shock it by openly violating the code which society violated in secret. She would show the world what love really meant, what sacrifice meant, what moral courage meant, and how shallow were the conventions that ruled the boring lives of the great majority. She would break open the cast of respectability which imprisoned her lover. Vita called her Lushka; she called Vita Mitya; their very names must be changed to something more suited to their rebellion:

The fact remains, my beautiful romantic Mitya, our scruples are not worthy of our temperaments. Think of the life we could have together, exclusively devoted to the pursuit of beauty. What have we to do with the vulgar, prattling, sordid life of today? What care we for the practical little *soignées* occupations of our contemporaries? You know we're different – gipsies in a world of landed gentry. They've taken and burnt your caravan, they've thrown away your pots and pans and your half-mended wicker chairs. They've pulled down your sleeves and buttoned up your collar. They've forced you to sleep beneath a self-respecting roof with no chinks to let the stars through. But they haven't caught me yet! Come! Come away! I'll await you at the crossroads. [*15 September 1918*]

Once again you have gone and left me — left me for Brighton, hard, mechanical, vulgar Brighton, and the joys of domesticity, *la rentrée au bercail*, correct comfortable *Familienleben*. My wildlife, devil-may-care Mitya is no longer, Mitya is ousted by Vita, someone gentle, affectionate, considerate, nice, someone inordinately fond of her husband, her mother and her children ... It is the incongruity of the whole thing that I mind so much. It's like playing the *Walkürenritt* on a piccolo and a penny trumpet; it's like hanging the *Nachtwacht* in a housekeeper's room; it's like a panorama of the Dolomites painted on the back of a menu. And then there's my jealousy. All the time I see how different it might be — the wild hawk and the windswept sky. I can see you splendid and dauntless, a wanderer in strange lands, in the inviolable chastity of inspiration. [*22 October 1918*]

For sixteen nights I have listened expectantly for the opening of my door, for the whispered 'Lushka!' as you entered my room, and tonight I am alone. How can I sleep? This can't go on. We must once and for all take our courage in both hands and go away together. What sort of life *can* we lead now? Yours an infamous and degrading lie to the world, officially bound to someone you don't care for [Harold!], perpetually with that someone. And I, who don't care a damn for anyone but you, am condemned to lead a futile existence. [*22 July 1918*]

Mitya, do you think I am going to waste any more of my precious youth waiting for you to screw up sufficient courage to make a bolt? Not I. Damn the world, and damn the consequences. [*24 August 1918*]

Heaven preserve me from littleness and pleasantness and smoothness. Give me great glaring vices, and great glaring virtues, but preserve me from the neat little neutral ambiguities. Be wicked, be brave, be drunk, be reckless, be dissolute, be despotic, be an anarchist, be a suffragette, be anything you like, but for pity's sake be it to the top of your bent. Live fully, live passionately, live disastrously. Let's live, you and I, as none have ever lived before. [*25 October 1918*]

Her daily letters, unpremeditated, uncorrected, scrawled in pencil with no address and no date (but Vita fortunately kept them in their postmarked envelopes), no beginning (like two intimates telephoning) and no ending except occasionally a huge

L splashed across half a page, intoxicated both the writer and the troubled woman to whom they were written. Vita's replies do not survive: they were destroyed by Denys. But one can imagine her response to this insistent drum-beat, for her actions prove it.

The best evidence of Vita's feelings for Violet is contained in her novel *Challenge*, which is dedicated to Violet and is about her. She began it in May 1918 within a few days of their return from Cornwall, and finished it in Monte Carlo in November 1919. It was never published in England. Both Vita's and Violet's parents insisted that it be suppressed (much to Violet's fury), since the portrait of her was too easily recognizable and they feared a scandal. But it was published in the United States in 1924, and I have the manuscript at Sissinghurst. While Vita was writing it, she was living her life on two levels, the actual and the fictional, and as her love for Violet intensified, so did that between Julian and Eve in the novel, with incidents, conversations and letters lifted into the book from reality. Every evening Vita would read to Eve's model the pages which she had written during the day, and Violet loved the game, glorying in the splendidly romantic situations in which she found her fictional self, suggesting extra touches to the drama and her own portrait, and adding from time to time huge chunks of her own invention.

It is the story of Julian, a rich young Englishman living in a small republic on the Greek coast, who incites the offshore islanders of Aphros to revolt, and becomes their illegal president. Eve, his cousin, lovely, wayward, contemptuous of all other suitors, joins him there, and they become happy lovers, until jealousy of Julian's commitment to Aphros leads Eve to betray him. Eve wants Julian absolutely, and to hell with convention and his political beliefs:

> I understand love in no other way. I am single-hearted. Is is a selfish love. I would die for you gladly, without a thought, but I would sacrifice my claim on you to no one and to nothing. It is all-exorbitant. I make enormous demands ... Freedom, Julian, romance! The world before us to roam at will! ... Tweak the nose of propriety, snatch away the chair on which she would sit down!

Julian is Vita; Aphros stands for Harold, the rival for Eve's love; Eve is Violet to the very inflexions of her voice, the tossing of her dark hair, 'turbulent, defiant, courting danger, and then childishly frightened when danger overtook her, deliciously forthcoming, inventive, enthusiastic, but always at heart withdrawn ... She lives constantly, from choice, in a storm of trouble and excitement.' 'She was spoilt, exquisite, witty, mettlesome, elusive, tantalizing, a creature that from the age of three has exacted homage and protection.' 'Was Eve to blame for her cruelty, her selfishness, her disregard for truth? Was she, not evil, but only alien, to be forgiven all for the sake of the rarer, more distant, flame? Was the standard of cardinal virtues set by the world the true, the ultimate, standard?'

> Julian sprang up. He caught Eve by the wrist.
> 'Gipsy!'
> 'Come with me gipsy', she whispered.
> Her scented hair blew near him, and her face was up-
> turned, with its soft sweet mouth.
> 'Away from Aphros?', he said, losing his head.
> 'All over the world!'
> He was suddenly swept away by the full force of her wild
> irresponsible seduction.
> 'Anywhere you choose, Eve.'
> She triumphed, close to him and wanton.
> 'You'd sacrifice Aphros to me?'
> 'Anything you asked for', he said desperately.
> She laughed and danced away, stretching out her hands
> towards him.
> 'Join in the saraband, Julian?'

'Vagabond', says Julian in another passage: 'Is life to be one long carnival?' 'And one long honesty', Eve replies. 'I'll own you before the world and court its disapproval.'

Challenge is Vita's defence of Violet, and of herself. Vita was twenty-six in 1918, Violet twenty-four. When together their feet barely touched the earth. They were carried on the breezes towards the sun, exalted and ecstatic, breathing the thin air of the apyrean. Violet seemed to her a creature lifted from legend, deriving from no parentage, unprecedented, unmatched, pagan. Their bond of flesh was so compelling that it became almost a spiritual, not a bodily, necessity, exacting so close and tremulous an intimacy that nothing existed for them outside. It swept away their careful training, individual and hereditary, replacing pride by another pride. They loved intensively, with a flame that purged all from their love but the essential, the ideal, passion. Marriage was nothing to this: marriage was only for husbands and wives. When Eve betrays Julian, his final insult is to offer her marriage. And she, proud to the end, drowns herself. It is very reminiscent of *Behind the Mask*, which Vita had written as a child.

Let me retrace the story of the second part of Vita's autobiography, and add some of the detail which she omits.

Her rediscovery of Violet at Long Barn on 18 April 1918 is simply recorded in her diary as 'How eventful a day!', and her account of their subsequent holidays together at Polperro in Cornwall is equally reticent. They went there twice, and the cottage where they stayed belonged to Hugh Walpole, the novelist. One can recover the picture from one of Violet's later letters, when she remembered with anguish how happy they had been:

> That little room of Hugh Walpole, with the sea almost dashing against its walls, the tireless cry of the seagulls, the friendly books, the friendlier atmosphere, the complete liberty of it all. And I was yours, yours to bend over and kiss as the fancy seized you. And sometimes we loved each other so much that we became inarticulate, content only to probe each other's eyes for the secret that was a secret no longer. [*10 July 1919*]

Lady Sackville was quite without suspicion ('they have gone to see the spring flowers'), and Harold wrote Vita six letters on the day of her departure, the very number suggesting his light-heartedness (at his office, before dinner in his club, during dinner, after dinner and so on), and in one of them he drew caricatures of Violet enjoying the simple life, paddling, shrimping, cooking, hiking, her Mayfair dresses tucked up to her knees. But that both Vita and Harold acknowledged that there was something a litt' more serious behind it is shown by the letter which she wrote him just before she left:

> Yes, I have got Wanderlust, and got it badly. I want to go away with you, where no one knows where we are, where no letters can follow. It's absurd. I have everything I want — you, two little boys, a cottage, money, flowers, a farm. Of course I know you will trace it to Violet, but you're wrong. I want to be free with you, a thing I can't have until the war is over. In the meantime I feel that people like Violet can save me from a sort of intellectual stagnation, a bovine complacency. So don't be jealous of Violet, darling silly.
> [27 April 1918]

It was on her return from Polperro that Vita had her portrait painted by the Scottish artist, William Strang. Violet was in his studio throughout the sitting, her eyes fixed upon Vita. How different it is from the Laszlo! Here no longer is Vita the dusky beauty, but Vita an Elizabethan youth, straight and arrogant, hand on hip, resting a moment, one could imagine, before leaping onto horse or pinnace. 'Julian' began that autumn, in London, Julian the bandaged subaltern, escorting his girl from Ebury Street to Piccadilly and down to Knole, Julian who was living another life of parallel adventure in Challenge. 'Julian!' Vita wrote in her diary. 'Oh the wet dark evening at Hyde Park Corner! This is the best adventure!' But the risk they took! For though Vita thought her disguise impenetrable, Violet was herself, a fashionable society girl, a little scatter-brained, it was generally considered, but not vicious, and here she was in company with this disreputable boy in public places where at any moment she, or both, might be recognized. On the day when her acknowledged suitor, Denys Trefusis, went back to the front, Violet wrote to Vita:

> You could do anything with me — or rather Julian could. I love Julian overwhelmingly, possessively, exorbitantly. For me he stands for all emancipation, for all liberty, for youth, for ambition, for attainment. He is my ideal. There is nothing he can't do. I am his slave, body and soul. Horrible thought what friends Denys and Julian would be! They would be in open competition for Lushka.
> [14 October 1918]

In fact, they already were. Both were desperately in love with Violet. In character Denys and Vita were not unalike. 'It was impossible to look better bred, more audacious', wrote Violet in *Don't Look Round*. 'Slim and elegant, he could not help dramatizing his appearance. Intrepid, rebellious, he had led an adventurous exciting life, having run away to Russia when he was little more than a schoolboy.' Thence he had returned on the outbreak of war, and was now commanding a company on the western front. Almost contemptuously he won the Military Cross, and when on leave in London disdained the amusements of other men. When Sonia, Violet's sister, first met him, 'He had a Crusader's flare to his nostrils and a cold bright eye which I felt would unhurriedly size up an enemy.' (*Edwardian Daughter*, 1958). Vita, on the other hand, took to him immediately. 'I can't tell you how much I like him,' she wrote to Harold. 'I really, really do. He is very intelligent.' Violet set her cap at him, as she confesses in her book: 'Never did I work so hard. At long last he began to respond, taking care to explain that, like Julian [but this was Julian Grenfell, killed in the war, who had also been in love with her] he was anti-matrimony.' This was the wayward side of Violet's nature: some would call it by a harsher name. She could set out to capture the devotion of a proud man, while her own was utterly committed elsewhere. Denys for her was chiefly important as a baited hook, a rival with whom to tease Vita.

In the autumn of 1918, two weeks after the Armistice, Vita and Violet carried their love to Monte Carlo. It was not easy to obtain permits, and incongruously it was Harold who did so, with his special influence in the Foreign Office. He thought that Vita needed a holiday, and 'it would be nice for you to have Violet as a companion'. He cannot have been ignorant of what was going on, for by this time Lady Sackville was feeding him with her fears, but he thought that their holiday was intended to last no more than a fortnight. It lasted four months. As soon as they reached Paris, Violet began to extract promises from Vita that she would stay with her indefinitely, threatening to kill herself if she did not agree, and these scenes were repeated whenever Vita tried to escape. But Vita did not try very hard. She experienced i

Monte Carlo during 'those wild and radiant months' a repetition of the delirious happiness she had enjoyed with Rosamund in Florence, with the added pleasure that their absence was now illicit, and they must fight for their freedom. Very quickly they ran out of money. They moved from the Hôtel Bristol to the less expensive Hôtel Windsor, but found themselves by mid-December quite penniless ('We have fifty centimes between us', says Vita's diary), and they were obliged to pawn their jewels to pay the hotel bill and raise enough money to gamble, successfully, at the Casino. Harold then cabled them £130. They spent their days reading, writing *Challenge*, playing tennis, walking in the hills and the garden of Château Malet, and their evenings at the tables.

Christmas came, which Harold spent miserably at Knole attempting to reconcile the quarrelling Sackvilles. It was in the New Year that he began to grow really anxious and, for the first time, angry, particularly when Vita's letters almost ceased,

> ... but I know how extremely busy you are and how much of your time is taken up by playing tennis and talking to your dirty little friend. At times I get racked with longing for you, and the slightest thing gives me a *crise de jalousie*, not jealous of you loving other people (you know I am calm about that), but jealous simply of your *being* with other people *dont je ne connais pas la puissance sur ton coeur*. [*8 January 1919*]

Vita replied with her 'indecent' argument, which was quite hollow, for if it was indecent to write to Harold when she was with Violet, was it not even more indecent to write to Violet when she was with Harold?

> It is dreadful of me not to write to you. I know. Don't think it is indifference or forgetfulness – it is not. But as I have so often said to you in talking, it's so difficult for me to write to you when I'm staying with Violet. It seems so *indecent*. Oh do, do, do, try to see it. [*11 January 1919*]

Still she would not come home. It was the moment of her greatest cruelty: it was worse than Amiens, for at Amiens at least she made no attempt to conceal the truth. Harold rented a flat in Paris to entice her back, brought over their silver and a few of her very personal possessions from Long Barn, hired two servants, and told her that all was ready. He expected her on 1 February, for she had given him a promise to come. At the last moment she chucked, pleading that Violet was too ill and miserable to be left alone. He wrote to her what seems to me the most heartrending letter in their entire correspondence – heartrending because it was so generous:

> I woke up so happy this morning, thinking you were perhaps at that very moment getting into the train to come to me. And I got out my box and began packing to go round to *our* flat, where we should be together again and sit over the fire. Oh God, how it hurts me to think of it! And then they brought me your two letters – with Violet's. Poor Vita. Poor Hadji. Poor *poor* Violet. After all, what does our pain mean in comparison with hers? It isn't fair that people should be made to suffer so. My disappointment is terrible. I feel quite ill with it. But our love is an eternal thing, like the sea and the wind, and what is time, a few days, a few weeks, to that? And what does all the gossip matter compared to Violet's suffering? I have destroyed her letter. How sad it was. I shall write to her. How I like her to love you like that, darling – it is the best thing she has ever done.

He added a postscript:

> Being a woman, you will say when you put this letter down, 'Well, he can't love me very much, as he would have made more fuss'. Good God! More fuss! When my heart feels like a *pêche Melba*. [*1 February 1919*]

Two days later he wrote:

> Don't think I shall be permanently miserable. I am only feeling crushed and sore and sad today. But it is childish of course; disappointment is after all a very transitory thing, and nothing compared to poor Violet's tragic and hopeless position. But all the sun has gone out of Paris, which has become a cold grey meaningless city, where there is a Conference going on somewhere. I feel you are slipping away, you who are my anchor, my hope and all my peace. Dearest, you don't know my devotion to you. What you do,

can never be wrong. I love you, in a mad way, *because* of it all.
[*3 February 1919*]

He should, of course, have taken the night-train to Monte Carlo, if only to quell the mounting gossip. All London, all Paris, hummed with it. Nothing appeared in the newspapers, but both Vita and Violet were well known, and this was something entirely new: the unmentionable had become mentionable. Lady Sackville took perverse pleasure in defending her daughter against 'that viper', 'that sexual pervert', writing to all her friends that Vita was bewitched, thus spreading still more widely the news which she was anxious to suppress.

To her the most distressing aspect of the affair was Vita's unnatural neglect of her children. Ben was four and I was two, far too young to know what was happening, and already accustomed to spending most of our time in nurseries. We did not feel neglected. I should like to be able to inject a note of pathos at this point, telling how childish letters brought our mother home, but no such letters were written, because neither of us could write. We stayed at Knole; and when Lady Sackville dismissed our nanny and simultaneously the pipes froze, we were sent to a hotel in Eastbourne, which we enjoyed enormously (so her diary says), then to the Carnocks, Harold's parents, in Cadogan Gardens, and finally to her own house in Brighton, which Lutyens was converting in his lavish style. She now began sending angry telegrams to Monte Carlo: 'Come back immediately; Katie Carnock and I cannot accept any more responsibility for the boys' [26 February 1919]. Vita replied that it was quite impossible for her to return before 15 March, as she couldn't get seats on the train. This did not ring true. But on 15 March she did return, and described to Harold our touching reunion at Brighton:

Ben plays in the bathroom, and every now and then I hear him say, 'Tell Mummy to come'; and then there is a scuffle and a shuffle, and I hear something come trotting along very busily, like the White Rabbit in *Alice*, muttering to itself, 'Tell Mummy . . . Tell Mummy . . .', and sticky fingers tug at me to come and see the miraculous Ben. I can't see in Nigel the faintest resemblance to anyone. He calls me 'darling' in an absent-minded way when I ask him if he loves me. He is extremely polite, even to Ben and inanimate objects like wooden ducks and cows, to whom he says 'Please'. Ben is not the criminal we were led to expect; he is just as sweet as ever. They are both absolute darlings. [*22 March 1919*]

The purpose of this quotation is to show, not what darlings we were, because we were almost certainly not, but how fond, basically, she was of us.

Vita was forgiven by Harold, scolded by her mother, incessantly pursued by Violet. A new twist to their story was now given by Violet's engagement to Denys Trefusis. It was announced on 26 March 1919, and the Keppels and the Sackvilles sighed with relief, brightly telling everyone that there had never been anything to worry about, for Violet was as deeply in love with Denys as Vita was with Harold. If only they could have read Violet's panic-stricken letters:

It is so awful, Mitya, being constantly with someone whom one doesn't care two rows of pins about, a someone incredibly grim and silent, and who I obscurely feel only wants to marry me out of revenge. We are not even on friendly terms. I feel there is something implacable about him. We don't talk to each other, and all the time I think tortured thoughts of you. I ache for you, Mitya. What is going to happen? Are you going to stand by and watch me marry this man? It's unheard of, inconceivable. You are my whole existence. How am I to get out of it? What is this hideous farce I am playing? If we could go away, even for a few months, I could get out of it. It would be so infinitely cleaner if we were to run away openly together. [*21 March 1919*]

I don't care if you were married six times over, or if you had fourteen children. In my desperate plight I have more right to you than anyone on this earth. Last night on the telephone you murmured something about a month. What are you made of, that for a whole month you want me to undergo this hell – this hell of having to endure the caresses of someone I don't love? He is adamant; nothing in this world will move him. He has got the will of a thousand fiends. [*24 March 1919*]

How could Violet, how could Denys, have involved themselves open-eyed in this grotesque engagement? It became all the stranger when Denys agreed that their marriage would be one in name only: they were to have no sexual relations whatever. Here were an intelligent proud man, an intelligent proud woman, binding themselves to a marriage which was nonsensical and humiliating from the start. One must allow for Violet's exaggeration in her letters to Vita: she was, as usual, dramatizing her dilemma. People who saw Violet and Denys together were unanimous in saying that they behaved towards each other with an affection that could not have been simulated. There was also family pressure. Alice Keppel insisted on the marriage taking place, and Violet adored her mother. Denys was genuinely in love with his fiancée: she was the only woman whom he ever loved deeply, and he was prepared to let her have her way. He knew all about Vita, of course, but thought that such an affair could be no more than transient, and that his pledge of continence would sooner or later be broken by Violet herself. There was another possible reason, of which a hint is contained in a letter from Violet to Vita written in 1920. Denys may have been at least partially impotent. Violet had been to see his doctor, and the doctor told her certain things about him, which, when she repeated them to Denys, drove him to an outburst of anger and despair. It is therefore conceivable, though by no means proved, that at the time of their marriage Denys was not too anxious to have his virility put to the test. But when all these reasons have been given, it remains the most inexplicable part of the whole story:

Denys said that he would marry me on any terms I chose to make, that he would consent to anything rather than that I should leave him. He said that if I left him he would kill himself. He gave me his word of honour as a gentleman that he would never do anything that would displease me – you know in what sense I mean. What am I to do? What can I say? There is only one thing to be done – that is to run away, without saying anything to anyone. Wretched man. He cares for me drivellingly. His one *chic* was that I thought he didn't. [*30 March 1919*]

By running away she meant elopement with Vita:

> I want you more than ever for my very, very own, for always. It
> is quite beyond my control. Mitya, fly, fly, fly – fly with me now,
> before it is too late. Why don't you assert your claim on me before
> all the world? You know that you have only to say the word. Away
> we'd go, away from the pretty countryside with its neat hedges and
> decent revelry. Away! Away! [14 April 1919]

'We were to go the day before her wedding', Vita says in her
autobiography. Harold was now too experienced to overlook the
danger-signals, but he did not know the worst. Vita had told him
jocularly that she would go to the wedding, and when the vicar
put the question, 'If any man can show just cause or impediment
why these two may not be joined together, let him now speak',
she would rise to her feet and say, 'Yes I can.' But it was not quite
a joke, as he well knew. He told her that he did not expect her to
break entirely with Violet, but he would not allow them to go
away together for a long period. She must cease sacrificing her
reputation and happiness to a hopeless passion, this 'scarlet adventure'. He understood what a terrible thing it was for Violet to
marry a man she didn't love, but Denys might in the end be her
salvation, and Vita's, if Violet could grow fond of him. Of the
intended elopement Harold had no idea. He was far away, in
Vienna, Budapest, and Prague, attempting with Smuts to sort out
the political confusion of Central Europe, while Violet spent much
of her time alone with Vita at Long Barn.

In May *Heritage* was published; and Lady Sackville left Knole.
Harold returned to England for a week's leave, and Violet was
enraged by his very presence, 'with its Hadji this, and Hadji that,
and you and he strolling about arm in arm (God I shall go mad!).
And I, who love you fifty times more than life, am temporarily
forgotten, set aside.' She began to load on Denys new conditions,
hoping that they would break him, but he agreed to everything,
even to Vita sharing their honeymoon, even to the two women
remaining abroad together when he returned. Violet felt trapped
and desperate. Reproached by Vita for telling people that she and
Denys were in love, she replied: 'Of course I told them that. Bu

why? To camouflage our going away ... I hate men. They fill me with revulsion, even quite small boys. Marriage is an institution that ought to be confined to temperamental old maids, weary prostitutes, and royalty.' When she thought Vita was weakening in her resolution to elope, she wrote: 'They have taken you from me, Mitya. They have taken you back to your old life; you are so prone to take fakes for the genuine article. Julian is dead.'

It was a measure of Vita's fidelity to Harold that Violet became so hysterical with jealousy. But Vita knew that she could only save herself from total surrender by escaping to Paris before the wedding, which was now fixed for 16 June. Her decision to 'betray' Violet was reached quite suddenly. She says that it was due to three letters which she received from Harold at that time. She had written to him:

> I can't believe that the wedding will come to pass. A great solemn social set-out wedding – it seems too grotesque. And I know that I could prevent it even now. I can't be in England, *or it will never take place*. I AM ABSOLUTELY TERRIFIED. I tell you about it in order to protect myself from myself. I shall do something quite irretrievable and mad if I stay in England. You are my only anchor, as I told you. If it wasn't for you, I'd give London something to talk about [*1 June 1919*]

Here is one of his replies:

> I know that we will win through this terrible struggle one day – both of us – but I don't want you to come out of it changed and broken, like France out of the war. Darling, when you are in London, you write so cynically, but the babies and the cottage seem to touch the ice to tears, and you write in a way that wrings my heart but doesn't break it. You say it is only for my sake that you are making this sacrifice, and it frightens me that you should say that. Why do you imagine that there is nothing between eloping with Violet and cooking my dinner? Oh what am I to do to win you back to calm and sanity? My love for you is certain; but yours for me sometimes seems so frail that it could snap. [*9 June 1919*]

Vita, rushing to Paris as if to an asylum, sent this reassurance
head:

Oh my Hadji, of course I love you. I love you unalterably. You don't know how I respond to any letter of yours. *Je m'humilie devant toi.* I have no words for my contempt for myself. Oh Hadji, you will never know. No one on this earth has the power to touch me as you have. One word from you moves me instantly, more than the tears or lamentations of anyone else. You don't know your power over me; you don't know it. [*13 June 1919*]

Violet Keppel and Denys Trefusis were married in London on 16 June 1919, while Vita was at Versailles. Violet wrote her a single line before she left her mother's house for the church: 'You have broken my heart. Goodbye.'

Never can such letters have been written during a honeymoon as those which Violet wrote to Vita:

Oh give me back my freedom! I was so happy once, so irresponsible and free. What am I now? A heartbroken nonentity, a lark with clipped wings. I feel desperate. The rows have begun worse than ever; we have been odious to each other. I can't help it. I don't care. [*23 June 1919*]

And constant telegrams from Saint Jean de Luz: 'Tell Julian Lushka loves him as much as ever.' This was dated 28 June 1919, the day when the Germans signed the Peace Treaty at Versailles.

When they returned to England, Violet and Denys lived at Possingworth Manor, near Uckfield in Sussex, and Violet renewed her efforts to persuade Vita to go away with her. She drew heartbreaking comparisons between Vita's marriage and her own, the one affectionate, intimate, secure, the other stony and sterile. Already she was talking of a legal separation from Denys, who had told her that he no longer cared for her. She gave him all Vita's letters to read so that he should have no illusions left, and then he burnt them. Vita eventually agreed to go abroad with her, and Harold, astonishingly, consented. The excuse was that *Challenge* was about Greece as well as about Violet, and Vita had never seen Greece except from the rail of the steamer when she returned from Constantinople in 1914:

I suppose that you will want to take Violet with you, so as to get both your copies at the same time? Anyhow, you can't go alone, and Violet is the obvious person, and I trust you, dearest, not to let her make you hate me. You said in the car, 'I shall be beastly to Violet after seeing you', and I feel you are cold to me after seeing Violet. You know that you can rely on my love for you, on my understanding everything. I get an odd vicarious pleasure from feeling that you will be in lovely places. Think of me as someone who enjoys you enjoying yourself. [*9 August 1919*]

They did not leave till 19 October, and travelled slowly, by Paris, Carcassonne and Saint-Raphaël, to Monte Carlo. Harold immediately began to regret his tolerance. All his anguish of ten months before revived, particularly when he heard that they were not going to Greece after all, because there was rioting there, and Vita explained that since the Mediterranean was much the same everywhere, she could draw her local colour as easily from one part of it as from another. Fireworks at Monaco one day became fireworks on Aphros the next. They resumed their old life: the Casino, tennis, and (once in Vita's diary) *Thé dansant: Julian*. The same reproaches began to flow to the Hôtel Windsor from Knole and Paris — scandal, neglect of children, cruelty to husbands (now two of them), refusal to answer letters. Vita was at last driven to jolt Harold into accepting the fact that her conduct was more fundamental than mere naughtiness:

I don't think you realize, except in a very tiny degree, what's going on. I don't think you have taken the thing seriously. You have looked on it as more or less transitory and 'wild oats' — your own expression. But surely, darling, you can't think that I've gone away from you and risked all that I have risked — your love, Mama's love, Dada's love and my own reputation — for a whim? (I really don't care a damn about the reputation, but I do care about the rest.) Don't you realize that only a very great force could have brought me to risk these things? Many little things have shown me that you don't realize it: 'wild oats'; you talk about my being away as 'a holiday'; you write of V. as 'Mrs Denys Trefusis' — don't you realize that that name is a stab to me every time I hear it, every time I see it on an envelope? Please never refer to it again.

Then, oh Hadji, my darling, darling, Hadji (you *are* my darling

153

Hadji, because if it wasn't for you, I would go off with Violet), there is another thing. You say you want to make love to me again. But that is impossible, darling; there can't be anything of that now – just now, I mean. Oh Hadji, can't you realize a little? I can't put it into words. Is isn't that I don't love you. I do. I do.

The whole thing is the most awful tragedy, and I see only too clearly that I was never fit to marry someone so sane, so good, so sweet, so limpid as yourself. It wasn't fair on you. But at least I love you with a love so profound that it can't be uprooted by another love, more tempestuous and altogether on a different plane.

[*5 December 1919*]

She rejoined Harold in Paris, alone, on 18 December, to find him laid up with an abscess on his knee, and Lady Sackville spoiled their reunion by her tactless solicitude towards both.

Things then built up quickly towards the climax. Vita was infatuated by Violet. Her audacity gave an impression of strength which she did not really possess. As Harold wrote to her, 'When you fall into Violet's hands, you become like a jellyfish addicted to cocaine.' She succumbed to an overwhelming temptation. She was angelic to Harold during his pain and sickness, but as soon as she and Violet were reunited in London in early January 1920, they began to plot their elopement, this time for good. She told Harold of their intention as soon as he arrived. Her diary adds a few details to her autobiographical account:

17 Jan. 1920. A perfectly awful day. Go round early to Cadogan Gardens and stay until midday talking to H., who refuses to agree to my going off today. Go round to see L. [Lushka]. Lunch with Harold and take him to Grosvenor Street [the Keppels' house] afterwards. L. agrees to wait a fortnight, and then, when H. has gone, she says she won't. Come back to Knole in a state of collapse.

The next fortnight was spent at Knole, and Harold avoided any reference to the crisis, returning to Paris on the first day of February without any idea whether he would ever see his wife again, consoling himself with the thought (as he wrote to her in the London–Dover train), 'I do feel that we are really closer than any two people have ever been, and that whatever happens w

shall come together in the end.' At the same moment Vita was
writing to him from Knole:

> Hadji, Hadji, I feel lonely and frightened. There is so much in my
> heart, but I don't want to write it, for *à quoi bon?* Only if I were
> you, and you were me, I would battle so hard to keep you – partly,
> I dare say, because I would not have the courage and the reserve to
> do like you and say nothing. Oh Hadji, the reason why I sometimes
> get you to say things, to say that you would miss me, is that I long
> for weapons with which to fortify myself; and when you do say
> things, I treasure them up, and in moments of temptation I say them
> over to myself, and I think 'Then he *does* mind, he *would* mind, you
> *are* essential to him. It *is* worth while making yourself unhappy to
> keep him happy', and so on. But when you say things like you don't
> miss me in Paris, and that scandal matters, I think, 'Well, if it is only
> on account of scandal and convenience and above all *because I am
> his wife* and permanent and legitimate – if it isn't more personal than
> that, is it worth while my breaking my heart to give him, not
> positive happiness, but mere negative contentment?'
>
> So I fish and fish, and sometimes I catch a lovely little silver trout,
> but never the great salmon that lashes and fights and *convinces* me
> that it is fighting for its life. You just say, 'Darling Vita', and leave
> me to invent my own conviction out of your silence.
>
> But I *have* struggled. I tore myself away and came to Paris in June
> last year. And it was only, only, out of love for you; nothing else
> would have weighed for me the weight of a hair, so you can see
> how strong a temptation it must have been to sweep everything
> aside, and you must see also how strongly my love for you must
> be. My darling, I shall love you till I die; you know I shall.
> [*1 February 1920*]

It is important to give Harold's reply, lest it be thought that he
had grown indifferent:

> When did I say that I didn't miss you in Paris? Darling, I miss you
> all the time. I suppose I said I didn't miss you in Paris as much as in
> England. If I said that, I meant that it was rather as if I was a soldier
> and said I didn't miss you in the trenches. It would be quite true –
> but it wouldn't mean that I didn't *want* you. I want you all the time,
> wherever I may be – and if I were not to see you again, I cannot
> contemplate what my attitude would be. It would be despair like

one can't imagine – a sort of winter night (Sunday) at Aberdeen, and me in the streets alone with only a temperance hotel to sleep in.

Then about my general attitude. You see, what appeal can I make except that of love? I can't appeal to your pity and it would be doing that if I let you see what I feared and suffered. It would be ridiculous to appeal to your sense of duty – that's all rubbish. So what is there left except to appeal to love – my love for you, and yours for me? How can that appeal be anything but inarticulate? If you left me, I should never love anyone else. I see that quite clearly. I should be so lonely, so terribly lonely; it would be worse than that, for even my memories would be painful.

And you are all wrong to think that I look on you as my *légitime*. You are not a person with whom one can associate law, order, duty – or any of the conventional ties of life. I never think of you that way – not even from the babies' point of view. I just look on you as the person whom I love best in the world, and without whom life would lose all its light and meaning. [*4 February 1920*]

Then came Lincoln: and after Lincoln, Amiens.

The excuse for Lincoln was Vita's new novel, *The Dragon in Shallow Waters*, which was set in the Fen district, but she also told her mother that she was taking Violet to the country to escape Denys, who was threatening to shoot her. People were now telling each other so many lies to protect themselves that it is difficult to know where the truth lay. Lady Sackville recorded in her diary this account of a conversation with Denys:

5 Feb. 1920. I had an extraordinary interview with Denys Trefusis. He hates Vita – that's obvious. He said that he wished he could confront people who gossiped about his marital relations with Violet. He was her husband absolutely. It was a pity she didn't want a child – she hated children – but she was very fond of him physically, and they were very happy together. It was Vita who had taken Violet away from him. He said they were very bad for one another, and that this friendship and their 'jaunts' together ought to be stopped; and that if Violet went away with Vita, she would get bored in three days and would return to him. Violet had been telephoning to him to say how bored she was in Lincoln. What *am* I to believe!

The truth was that Vita and Violet were very happy in Lincoln, staying at the Saracen's Head Hotel. There they made their plan to fly the country together. It was a hot-blooded plot, and Vita was a willing partner to it. Harold was in Paris, busy with the Adriatic question and the fate of war-criminals, quite unconscious, in spite of all Vita's warnings, that the climacteric moment had arrived. He knew that she was in Lincoln, but he did not know that Violet was with her. He thought that Vita was collecting local colour for *Dragon*.

Vita and Violet returned to London, saw Denys, spurned his pitiful entreaties, and travelled together to Dover. Violet crossed that night to France, leaving Vita in Dover to follow next day (an odd concession to respectability), when they were to meet at Amiens, never to return.

Vita has described what happened next. Denys confronted her on the Dover quayside, and she told him what was afoot. She spent that night in the King's Head Hotel, most of it writing letters. First to her mother:

> I daren't think what you must imagine now after my telegram. Briefly, I got back from Lincoln late last night, and Violet saw Denys and told him that she wanted to leave him. I travelled with her as far as Dover and honestly did my utmost to persuade her to go back to him, but she wouldn't listen to a word of it. I honestly, honestly tried, though it was torture for me to do so, as you will appreciate better than anybody, knowing as you do all the true facts. Anyway, she left Dover by the afternoon's boat and promised to wire to me. This afternoon, Denys arrived, and he and I are going out to France tomorrow (what a ridiculous journey! I can't help seeing that, even at this moment), and he will ask her to return to him, and I alas! shall again do all I can to make her, but whether I shall succeed, I very much doubt. If she does go with him, I think I shall go to Paris for a few days with Harold. But if she refuses, God alone knows what is going to happen. I have never been in such an extraordinary situation in my life, and the *décor* is all so much in keeping – a howling gale, and my awful little lodging-house room with a single gas-jet – it seems very unreal, and the only real thing is the anguish which he [Denys] and I both endure.
>
> Oh Mama, don't think I am not taking it seriously. I know only

too well that somebody's heart will be broken tomorrow night, probably mine – I *hope* mine – and I think of you. [*9 February 1920*]

To Harold she wrote:

Perhaps I shall try to find V. Nothing will induce her to remain with Denys, even if I never saw her again. In the most absolute and sacred confidence I will tell you why: he is no longer willing to keep his original promises to her. If she goes back to him, I will come to you. I am trying to be good, Hadji, but I want so dreadfully to be with her. Oh darling, it's awfully lonely here. [*9 February 1920*]

She never said what she would do if Violet refused to go back to Denys. But she hinted at it in another letter to Harold written from Dover early next morning. It was a sort of Will, and she sent it to Paris registered:

I am leaving in an hour's time. It is terribly rough, but the ships are going, so I must go, and if it were not for the ignominy of being seasick, I would not be sorry to have the battle with the sea and wind; it would be rather a relief. Look here, darling, I am sending you a few facts, in case I get drowned or anything.

(1) I send you a blank cheque by which you will be able to get all the money at present in my Sevenoaks bank.

(2) The rates and taxes on Ebury Street are paid up to date.

(3) Then the gardeners' wages at Long Barn are paid, and

(4) The interest on the money which Dada lent us to buy Long Barn has been paid.

I leave you everything: and will you be my literary executor?
I suppose this is sufficiently legal. Perhaps I'd better sign it.

She signed it 'Victoria Nicolson' over a 1½d stamp.

'In case I get drowned or anything.' In case I never come back.

Vita has described in her autobiography what happened on the Channel crossing, and when she and Denys reached Calais. Nothing is suppressed. No doubt is left that at this moment she and Violet had decided to live together for the rest of their lives. They took money with them to buy a house, perhaps in Paris, as she says in her diary, perhaps in Sicily, as she says in her autobiography. Her promise to persuade Violet to return to Denys was qualified by her hope, the virtual certainty, that Violet would refuse. What sort of life did they imagine lay ahead of them? Was everything to be abandoned — children, homes, husbands? Apparently, yes. They were utterly defiant. By chance the poem which Vita scribbled on the train between Boulogne and Amiens has survived:

> We have cleared the Northern seas
> While you thought we took our ease,
> But you won't be mistaken very long.
> And you think that you will win,
> But that's just where you are wrong, wrong, wrong.
> Here we come swinging along;
> We will lead you such a dance
> If in Belgium or in France,
> But we aren't going to trifle very long.

On arrival at Amiens Denys left them, giving up hope, and the sentry-duty was taken over by George Keppel, Violet's father, with whom the two runaways had a ridiculous and abusive scene. As soon as he had heard of their elopement, he had gone to Scotland Yard and 'had the ports watched to prevent them leaving the country' (Lady Sackville's diary), but his precautions had been singularly ineffective. Now he was in Amiens, totally unable to cope with a situation beyond his comprehension, and he hung around the Hôtel du Rhin for the next two days, while Vita and Violet went sightseeing.

Vita's mother now took the leading role in organizing the salvage operation from Brighton and Hill Street. In a perverse way she was enjoying herself: her daughter was proving herself worthy of Pepita.

13 Feb. 1920. Harold has just arrived from Paris. He told me that he had no idea where Vita was. I persuaded him to see Denys, which he agreed willingly to do. He is in a most pitiful state. After he had left me to go to his conference [League of Nations], I went straight to Grosvenor Street and interviewed Denys ... He is going to fly to Amiens tomorrow morning at 7, and I asked him to take Harold, as he had a two-seater aeroplane, and he most readily said he would. I took him to Cadogan Gardens where he saw Harold and arranged everything with him. Denys was very cool and collected, and fully determined either to bring Violet back or have done with her.

I wish I knew more about that flight. How did Denys happen to have a two-seater aeroplane? From which airfield did they take off? When had he learnt to fly? What plan did they concoct? Lady Sackville's diary, the only source, is silent on these matters:

> *14 Feb. 1920.* No news from Vita. I have been thinking all day of those two husbands flying to Amiens to try and each get his wife back; quite like a sensational novel.

About the events in Amiens itself I should know little but for Vita's full autobiographical record. In her diary for that culminating day, she wrote simply this, enigmatically:

> *14 Feb. 1920.* Denys and Harold arrive together by aeroplane from London, landing at Amiens. Return to Paris with H. In the middle of dinner L. [Lushka] comes in, and I feel restored to life to a certain extent. My God, what a day! I am broken with misery, and if things were as bad as I had at first thought, I should have put an end to myself. I *had* to go. I should have killed her if I had stayed an instant longer. I have told her I cannot even see her for two months. She calls it banishment – it is *not*. It is simply the impossibility of bringing myself to see her for the moment.

Let it not be supposed that Violet's infidelity (the infidelity of sleeping with her husband) had destroyed Vita's love for her. They felt themselves defeated, not by each other, but by convention, by 'them', by what today would be called the Establishment, the Establishment of two such totally un-Establishment figures as Harold and Denys. In 1921 Vita published in *Orchard and Vineyard* this remarkable poem, which must have been written in Paris at that time, for her fury could not have lasted much longer at that pitch. The simple change of pronoun does nothing to disguise her anguish. The poem's very title is *Bitterness*:

> Yes, they were kind exceedingly: most mild
> Even in indignation, taking by the hand
> One that obeyed them mutely, as a child
> Submissive to a law he does not understand.
> They would not blame the sins his passion wrought.

No, they were tolerant and Christian, saying, 'We
Only deplore ...', saying they only sought
To help him, strengthen him, to show him love; but he
Following them with unrecalcitrant tread,
Quiet, towards their town of kind captivities,
Having slain rebellion, ever turned his head
Over his shoulder, seeking still with his poor eyes
Her motionless figure on the road. The song
Rang still between them, vibrant bell to answering bell,
Full of young glory as a bugle; strong;
Still brave; now breaking like a seabird's cry 'Farewell!'
And they, they whispered kindly to him, 'Come,
Now we have rescued you. Let your heart heal. Forget!
She was your danger and your evil spirit.' Dumb
He listened, and they thought him acquiescent. Yet
(Knowing the while that they were very kind)
Remembrance clamoured in him: 'She was wild and free,
Magnificent in giving; she was blind
To gain or loss, and loving, loved but me – but me!'

I did not know Violet. I met her only twice, and by then she
had become a galleon, no longer the pinnace of her youth, and I
did not recognize in her sails the high wind which had swept my
my mother away, because I did not know that she had been swept
away. I did not know that Vita could love like this, had loved
like this, because she would not speak of it to her son. Now that
I know everything, I love her more, as my father did, *because* she
was tempted, *because* she was weak. She was a rebel, she was Julian,
and though she did not know it, she fought for more than Violet.
She fought for the right to love, men and women, rejecting
the conventions that marriage demands exclusive love, and that
women should love only men, and men only women. For this
she was prepared to give up everything. Yes, she may have been
mad, as she later said, but it was a magnificent folly. She may
have been cruel, but it was cruelty on a heroic scale. How can I
despise the violence of such passion? How could she regret that
the knowledge of it should now reach the ears of a new generation,
one so infinitely more compassionate than her own?

So they came from Amiens to Paris – Vita and Harold to the Alexandre III, Violet and Denys to the Ritz. By letter and telephone between the two hotels, Violet tried desperately to correct the misunderstanding which had lost her Vita, to retrieve her fatal admission, to persuade her that nothing conclusive had happened the night before Lincoln:

> I am absolutely dazed and sodden with pain. How can I bear it? My God, and happiness was so near, Mitya. We'd gone, we'd gone, we'd got away! What is so perfectly awful to me is the feeling that our separation is due to a misunderstanding. There has never, never, never in my life been any attempt at what you thought from that person – *never*. Oh Mitya, why didn't you give me time to explain? [*14 February 1920*, Paris]

Next day Denys supported Violet's version of what had occurred. But later he told Harold that he had 'perjured himself' (Lady Sackville's diary), 'which Harold thought meant that he had told some big lie to Vita, such as he was not really married to Violet', to save Violet from suicide. We shall never know the truth – and what does it matter now?

Violet and Denys began their nightmare journey by road from Paris to Toulon, scarcely speaking to each other except to sob out some extra insult, some additional reproach, and at every town Violet stopped the car to telephone or wire to Vita. A shabby packet of French telegram-forms preserves her anguish: '*Viens! Viens!*' 'Oh Julian! Julian!' And each night she wrote agonizing appeals:

> I am going mad with longing for you. Half my day has been spent in a dead stupor, the rest in tears. I have hardly eaten and hardly slept since I left Amiens ... I have still got the money, *our* money, that was to have been for our house. [*17 February 1920*]

> He is abhorrent to me with his tears and his servility, I told him that I looked upon him merely as my jailor, and that my one ambition was to get away from him. I hate him. I *hate* him. I have never belonged to him in any sort of way. I look on men as animals. [*18 February 1920*]

At Toulon they met Mrs Keppel, who treated her daughter with great consideration. She did not insist that Violet should remain with Denys, nor that she should break completely with Vita, who could, if she wished, stay with them in England from time to time; and she offered her an allowance of £600 a year. But Violet was untouched by her generosity and soft persuasion. She wrote to Vita, 'I shall bolt from Bordighera at the first opportunity. You must meet me in a town in the south of France.' Vita calmly returned to England, even agreeing, as an act of renunciation more than of contrition, to abandon the publication of *Challenge*, now in proof. She appeared with Harold at the theatre, at lunch parties, without betraying by word or look what they had both been through, and they were almost the only people not to speak about it.

In March she joined Violet at Avignon. Harold encouraged her to do so, sensing that the crisis was past. But it was not, as her diary shows:

San Remo. 23 March 1920. L. horrible to me all day, and makes me very miserable and exasperated. After dinner I lose my head and say I will stay with her. Paradise restored.

Venice. 28 March 1920. Everything is black again. I have had to tell L. that I should only be followed and brought back. It is horrible. She is in the depths. So am I. I feel the Grand Canal, in spite of slime and floating onions, would be preferable.

On Vita's return in April, the spring held no pleasure for her. 'Beastly grey country', she wrote again. When she tried to pick up the threads of *Dragon*:

Oh my good Lord, I can't write nowadays. It drives me mad to remember my fluency once upon a time – ten or twelve sheets a day! And as for poetry, it's gone, gone, gone from me. How I envy Harold his clear-cut intellect. I must shake myself out of this inertia. I wish I was poor, dirt-poor, miserably poor, and obliged to work for my daily bread or go without. I need a spur. I am a rotten creature.

She sought distraction and a temporary escape from Violet's incessant letters ('We shall have to fight tooth and nail for each other') by sailing in the Channel on her father's yacht *Sumerun*. The day after her return to Long Barn, she sat down in the corner of a field, opened a notebook, and began writing: '*23 July 1920*. Of course I have no right whatsoever to write down the truth about my life . . .'

The end of the story can be told quite quickly. As Vita was writing her autobiography, the last scenes were being enacted, so that it became in its final stages a running commentary. At the end of 1920 Violet's passionate love for Vita was unabated; Vita's was cooling off, as the opening paragraph of her autobiography shows. Apart from flares and flickers, it never survived the shock of Amiens.

> Oh Mitya [wrote Violet reproachfully], you don't know how unhappy I am. It seems to me that we are completely severed from one another. You do not know what the human heart can suffer. You were so stiff on the telephone: it was the last straw. I mind so much. Think how much happier your life is than mine. If you let me down, what will there be left for me? Do try to love me. This time last year it wasn't necessary for me to say this. It breaks my heart to have to say it now. [*31 December 1920*]

'Think how much happier your life is than mine.' That was the rub. They had been accomplices, yet one returned to warmth and love and freedom, while the other was imprisoned and despised. There was nothing in Violet's life comparable to Harold's love, to Lady Sackville's love. She had no children. She had no other close friends. Denys would have nothing more to do with her; nor, temporarily, would her mother. Every post brought Vita new evidence of her isolation. Let us compare two letters written within less than a week of each other. The first, from Denys to Violet, was forwarded by Violet to Vita, in order, one can only suppose, to arouse her pity:

> It is nothing short of monstrous to start reproaching me with coldness after the absolutely inhuman and abominal way in which you have treated me. You think the hardness and coldness of a few

days comparable with the absolute cruelty of a year! I will endure it no longer. *Voici la vraie vérité – je ne t'aime plus.* [*21 July 1920*]

The second was from Vita to Harold:

I have been gardening and writing a lot. I've been alone on purpose. I do love you so – it's like a well, so deep that if you went to the very bottom, you would see stars. [*26 July 1920*]

Harold had won, though he never thought of it as winning. He had been winning not only during the past few months, but during the last ten years.

Of course so great a furnace could not die down at once. In January 1921 Vita yielded to Violet's entreaties sufficiently to go with her to Hyères for six weeks, and on her return she wrote the last paragraph of her autobiography, dated 28 March 1921. She was trying desperately to make the final break.

I am dead with grief [wrote Violet]. I am utterly alone. You cannot want me to suffer so. You had to choose between me and your family, and you have chosen them. I do not blame you. But you must not blame me if one day soon I seek for what escape I can find. [*26 March 1921*]

By that she meant suicide. Vita was seriously worried. She felt her responsibility dreadfully, and this was the hold that Violet had on her during the whole of that year. I don't quite know how it ended. Violet's letters tail off in misery and sad recollection. By the end of the following year, 1922, Vita was sure enough of Violet's resilience to be cruel. She wrote to Harold:

Not for a million pounds would I have anything to do with Violet again, even if you didn't exist, you whom I love fundamentally, deeply and incurably. Oh yes, I know you will say, 'But you loved me then, and yet you went off with her'. It's quite true. I did love you, and I always loved you, all through those wretched years, but you know what infatuation is, and I was mad. [*8 December 1922*]

Four years later, she wondered, not for the first time, whether Harold had been too gentle with her.

You have never understood about Violet: a) that it was a madness of which I should never again be capable: a thing like that happens only once, and burns out the capacity for such a feeling: b) that you could at any moment have reclaimed me, but for some extraordinary reason you wouldn't. I used to beg you to: I *wanted* to be rescued, and you wouldn't hold out a hand. I think it was a mixture of pride and mistaken wisdom on your part. I know you thought that if you tried to hold me, I should go altogether. But in this you were wrong, because I never lost sight of how you were the person I loved in the sense of loving for life. Only I suppose you either didn't believe this, or else you wouldn't take the risk. [*17 August 1926*]

'You wouldn't hold out a hand.' Oh, but he did, over and over again. It should be rephrased: 'You wouldn't *seize* my hand'. There she was right. It was pride and mistaken wisdom; and one should add his respect for her, his courtesy towards her. He had given her all his love, and if that was not enough, it would be selfish to hold her back by force.

It may be wondered what Violet had to say about the affair, for several times I have quoted from her autobiography *Don't Look Round*. Simply this:

Marriage can be divided into two categories: those that begin well and end badly, those that begin badly and end well. Mine came (roughly) under the latter heading. It was not until a full year had elapsed that we were able to establish a *modus vivendi*. I hasten to add that the fault was entirely mine. I was spoilt, egocentric, insensitive, odious.

Denys and she came back to each other. 'We both loved poetry, France, travel. We were both Europeans in the fullest sense of the term. The same things made us laugh. We quarrelled a lot, loved not a little. We were more to be envied than pitied.' They had no children, but they lived together in Paris until Denys's early death, from consumption, in 1929. Violet's life was a full one. She became a distinguished novelist, a focus of Parisian intellectual society. She was well known for her wit and verve, retaining until the end of her life something of the grand manner of the Edwardian age. She was always a bird-of-paradise, different, electric, a brilliant, exciting woman, whose character is summed up by her two houses, St Loup near Paris, strong and Gothic, and the Villa Ombrellino outside Florence, dreamy, sunlit, scented and seductive. I remember her springing gait when she visite

Sissinghurst, her elegant French clothes, her power. She looked at us with curiosity, which I did not then understand.

She and my mother did not meet or correspond for eighteen years. Then in 1940 another war brought them together again. Violet fled from France to England, and telephoned to Vita. Vita's terror is a measure of how much Violet still meant to her:

> Lushka, what a dangerous person you are. I think we had better not see too much of each other. We loved each other too deeply for too many years, and we must not play with fire again. We both upset the other's life; we mustn't do it again. The very sound of your voice on the telephone upsets me. I loved you and I think you loved me. Quite apart from those three years of our passionate love-affair, we had years and years of childhood love and friendship behind us. This counts. It makes you dear to me. It makes me dear to you.
> [31 August 1940]

Violet came to Sissinghurst. Vita wrote afterwards:

> It is as though great wings are beating round me – the wings of the past. Am I at Carcassonne? At Avignon? In Venice? (How I wish we had been more enterprising, instead of always ending up at Monte Carlo!) Yes, it was good to see you ... The past does not worry me ... I told you I was frightened of you. That's true. I don't want to fall in love with you all over again ... My quiet life is dear to me ... But if you really want me, I will come to you always, anywhere.

Ten years later, in 1950:

> The time when we were in love has gone by, leaving us with this queer deep love, that seems to have lasted from the time we were at Duntreath. There is a very odd thing between you and me, Lushka. There always was.

How ignorant we were in our childhood of these events, seeing in our parents' marriage unruffled conjugal bliss. Surely, we thought (if we thought of it at all), it must always have been so. Then one day Lady Sackville told my brother, inexcusably, all about it. I have asked him, as his contribution to this book, to describe what happened. Let Ben take over, and end, the story:

'On leaving Eton and before going up to Oxford, I started a diary. I was eighteen. Out of a back shelf I have pulled my first dusty volume bound in *carta Varese*. I can hardly bear to repeat the flat, childish words I found. We were still children at eighteen in those days, not really interested in the ways of the adult world:

> *Tuesday, 9 May 1933.* Went alone to see G. [Lady Sackville] at White Lodge [Roedean, Brighton]. She was not in a bad temper but merely tired. She spent the whole time saying things about M. and D. [Vita and Harold] to put me against them – stories about M. getting hold of women and D. of men – about Violet Keppel, Virginia Woolf etc. All quite without foundation. I should have prevented her, but meekly listened. When she had finished, she made me promise not to tell M. and D. Stopped at Hawkhurst golf-club on my way back and saw the pro. Of course told M. and D. all about it. D. said she was like Iago, and that nobody would ever believe that such a person could exist. M. said she was a genius gone wrong. I don't think I understand.

> *Wednesday, 10 May.* After I wrote yesterday's account, M. came to my room at midnight and said that what G. had said was true. My bookshelves have come ...

and so it continues about my golf-lesson that afternoon, quite unconcerned.

'That was all I felt fit to record. And yet that day forty years ago, at Brighton, and its aftermath over the dinner-table at Sissinghurst, are engraved more sharply on my mind than the events of last week. Nigel had gone back to Eton, and that is why I motored to Brighton alone. I was proud of my first two-seater. My grandmother was then living in a windswept house on the cliffs near Roedean School. She was bedridden and going blind. Every two months or so Nigel (when he was at home) and I would spend the day with her, never knowing what to expect when we drove up: abuse, wild generosity, lunch cooked by the gardener at her bedside or on an icy terrace at half-past three, a cheque for £10, or dismissal after a five minutes' stormy interview. This day her exhaustion provoked the wicked revelations. Either my mother had "stolen all her jewels" or had not written for six months (she wrote every day): I seek some explanation for her outburst. There might easily not have been a cause, real or imaginary, of any kind; she may just have wished to give vent to her misery and loneliness – this blind old woman with a gardener on a cliff, with nothing to keep her alive but dreams of Washington, Knole and her lost beauty – by poisoning an innocent grandson's mind: so she hoped.

' "How ignorant we were in our childhood of these events", my brother has written above. I never thought much about my parents because they were grown-up, but if I thought at all, I had no reason to suspect that their conjugal bliss had ever been interrupted. Then for hours on end my grandmother disillusioned me, by unfolding the whole Violet story; explaining how my mother had been determined to desert her husband and two little boys for a "Circe", how she would have succeeded, had she (my grandmother) not taken resolute steps at the last moment to prevent it; how a few years later a second woman entered my mother's life and again almost wrecked the marriage. ("That Mrs Woolf, who described in that book [*Orlando*] how your mother *changed her sex!*"). Then she turned on her angelic son-in-law, describing the boys he had had in Persia and in all the capitals of Europe. And – shame upon me – I was too indifferent to protest or to leave the house in a huff. After tea she must have thought she had gone too far, because she made me promise not to repeat it. I left unruffled, partly because I did not believe a word of it, partly because I was more worried about next day's mashie shots than about my parents' peccadilloes. I would have made a puzzling patient on the psychiatrist's couch.

'Anyhow, the impulse to repeat it was stronger than my pledge of secrecy. There were only the three of us at dinner at Sissinghurst that night, my parents and myself. They listened in silence to my adventure, and occasionally cast enquiring glances at each other as the cruel words poured out. It was they who were deeply embarrassed, not I. I took their embarrassment to mean that they were shocked that Lady Sackville should do anything so monstrous. It never occurred to me that they were also distressed that the central drama of their lives was being played back to them by their own adolescent son.

'I can imagine the conversation that took place as they left the dining-room. The truth was out, but which of them was to confirm it? The argument cannot have gone on very long: for my father with his fastidiousness could never have brought himself to enlighten me; by letter, perhaps, but not face to face. It was my mother who sat on my bed at midnight and into the small hours, and I suppose it was the first intimate talk we had ever had. She told me that everything was true except the part about Virginia endangering their marriage, but none of it mattered a hoot because the love they bore each other was so powerful that it could withstand anything.

'My diary entry for Sunday, 28 May, three weeks later, reads:

Virginia and Leonard came to lunch. Virginia looking well and happy after her Italian trip. She listened to the whole story of my visit to Brighton with her head bowed. Then she said: "The old woman ought to be shot".'

PART FIVE
BY NIGEL NICOLSON

VITA's elopement with Violet Trefusis was the only crisis of her marriage. Having survived it, she and Harold were able to confront with equanimity many later incidents so menacing that each separately would have broken up most homes. After Amiens there was six foot of water under their keel, and their rowboat, which had nearly foundered on the rocks, slid easily away from the shoals which it touched offshore. Violet had shown them that nothing could destroy their love, which was actually enhanced by the complete freedom they allowed each other. Both were completely frank about it, in speech and letters. It no longer required argument: simply a statement of fact and current emotion. Harold would refer to Vita's affairs as 'your muddles'; she to his as 'your fun'. No jealousy ever arose because of them. On his side there was only a concern that she might break the heart of someone else, a rival or the woman's husband, while she was more amused than worried by what was happening to him, knowing that he had these things under greater control. To scandal, or, in his case, to the law, they seem never to have given a thought, for their intellectual friends were infinitely tolerant, and they did not mind what was said by outsiders.

I suppose [wrote Vita], that ninety-nine people out of a hundred, if they knew all about us, would call us wicked and degenerate. And yet I know with absolute certainty that there are not ninety-nine people out of a hundred less wicked and degenerate than we are. I don't want to boast, but we *are* alive, aren't we? And our two lives, outside and inside, are rich lives – not little meagre repetitions of meagre cerebral habits.

So carefree were they that quite often at Long Barn Harold's friend and Vita's would join the same weekend party, and the four of them would refer to the situation quite openly. Lady Sackville gives in her diary this instance of their attitude, her embarrassment leading her to an unfortunate choice of phrase:

23 Sept. 1923. Vita is absolutely devoted to Harold, but there is nothing whatever sexual between them, which is strange in such a young and good-looking couple. She is not in the least jealous of him, and willingly allows him to relieve himself with anyone. They both openly said so when I was staying at Long Barn, and Reggie Cooper [who had been at Wellington and in Constantinople with Harold] was there too. It shocked me extremely . . .

To this easy relationship they gave a moral base, both having analytical minds, and they evolved a 'formula' for their marriage, 'a firm, elastic formula', said Harold, 'which makes it so easy for us both to duplicate the joys of love and life, and to halve their miseries'; or, as she put it to him, 'We are sure of each other, in this odd, strange, detached, intimate, mystical relationship which we could never explain to any outside person.' The formula ran something like this: what mattered most was that each should trust the other absolutely. 'Trust', in most marriages, means fidelity. In theirs it meant that they would always tell each other of their infidelities, give warning of approaching emotional crises and, whatever happened, return to their common centre in the end. Vita once put her 'little creed' for Harold in these words: 'To love me whatever I do. To believe my motives are not mean. Not to credit tales without hearing my own version. To give up everything and everybody for me in the last resort.'

The basis of their marriage was mutual respect, enduring love and 'a common sense of values'. There were certain things which were wrong absolutely, and so long as they agreed on what those things were, it did not matter much if in other ways they behave differently or even (in the eyes of the world) outrageously. When we were children, they divided misdemeanours into 'crimes' and 'sins', and applied the same rule to themselves. Crimes were naughtinesses, for which we were punished. (My mother was not very good at that. When I broke the greenhouse windows, she decided to spank me on the bottom with her hairbrush, but never having done such a thing before, she used the brush bristle side downwards, and the bristles were very soft.) Sins were so dreadful that for them we were never punished at all: their very exposure was enough. There were only three sins: cruelty, dishonesty and indolence. Vita herself had been guilty of the first in 1919–20; never again. Harold was innocent of them all. Their morality can be summed up as consideration for other people, particularly for each other, and the development of their natural talents to the full. It was an amalgam of the Christian virtues and the eighteenth-century concept of the civilized life.

In 1929 they debated on BBC radio their ideas about marriage, and this was their conclusion:

Harold: You agree that a successful marriage is the greatest of human benefits?

Vita: Yes.

Harold: And that it must be based on love guided by intelligence?

Vita: Yes.

Harold: That an essential condition is a common sense of values?

Vita: Yes.

Harold: That the only things that will stave off marital nerves are modesty, good humour and, above all, occupation?

Vita: Yes.

Harold: And give and take?

Vita: And give and take.

Harold: And mutual esteem. I do not believe in the permanence of any love which is based on pity, or the protective or maternal instincts. It must be based on respect.

Vita: Yes, I agree. The caveman plus sweet-little-thing theory is long past. It was a theory insulting to the best qualities of both.

Marriage, they thought (but not for a BBC audience in 1929), was 'unnatural'. Marriage was only tolerable for people of strong character and independent minds if it were regarded as a lifetime association between intimate friends. It was a bond which should last only as long as both wanted it to. (Both, for this reason, were strongly in favour of easier divorce.) But as a happy marriage is 'the greatest of human benefits', husband and wife must strive hard for its success. Each must be subtle enough to mould their characters and behaviour to fit the other's, facet to facet, convex to concave. The husband must develop the feminine side of his nature, the wife her masculine side. He must cultivate the qualities of sympathy and intuition; she those of detachment, reason and decision. He must respond to tears; she must not miss trains.

As it happened, mutual adjustment was particularly easy for them, because they already possessed these qualities. Vita since her childhood had never ceased to regret that she was not born a boy. Once she quoted to Violet Queen Elizabeth's magnificent phrase: 'Had I been crested not cloven, my Lords, you had not treated me thus.' She had inherited from her mother the aristocratic gift of command, and in most things was very competent. Harold had certain feminine attributes, his emotionalism and his clemency. Vita could be intimidating. Harold rarely was, though in social and diplomatic London he was a young lion. If they witnessed together an act of cruelty, such as a Greek peasant beating his donkey, he would express his horror; she would furiously intervene. He obeyed regulations with the instinct of a trained civil servant; she would protest, sometimes refuse. Harold had a sentimental side to his nature which she did not. He could be moved to tears by a film or play in which virtue was triumphant or innocence abused; she took both in her stride. She was the calculated-risk-taker in their marriage, sometimes to the peril of them both. The risks which he took were more spontaneous, motivated by a sudden surge of emotion, personal or political. But because they knew each other so intimately, and loved each other so deeply, neither was in the least irritated by these opposites. Vita would sometimes reproach him for being too mild, 'put upon' she said (for instance by the low fees he accepted from

editors), and he would tease her about the odd gaps in her knowledge of the world, like her total inability to understand an Income
Tax form or add up a simple column of figures, or her ineradicable
belief that rivers like the Nile which flow northwards must run
uphill. Never, never did I see them lose their tempers with each
other, and my mother told me that it happened only once. The
incident was typical.. She came into his room one evening and he
shouted, 'Go away!' Hurt and angry, she flung at him the lilies
which she was carrying, and slammed the door. He rushed after
her to explain that his birthday-present — a bust of Hermes —
which he was to give her as a surprise the next morning was
sitting unwrapped on his table.

No reader could fail to be convinced of their love for each
other if I were to give constant quotations from their letters spread
over fifty year, but such an anthology would become tedious and
cloying in the mass. In most marriages love after a time becomes
inarticulate, or is expressed in bed. In their marriage there was no
bed, but both, being writers, found infinite pleasure in analyzing
their emotions. As they were so often apart, they wrote to each
other thousands of letters, and these formed the warp and woof
of their marriage, which was thus continuously enriched and
rewoven. She spoke of 'the great triumph of being loved by you',
and both were perpetually amazed at their good fortune. Each
loved most in the other the qualities which she or he did not
possess, Vita his leniency, Harold her wildfire romanticism, and
it amused them to identify the differences between them in order
to highlight the qualities they shared. They had many common
interests: literature and travel and gardening; their children; their
cottages; their possessions; their tastes; their plans, past and present;
memories of joy and near-disaster. All these things formed a
rich *pot-pourri* which never staled. Separation sharpened its tang.
Painful as it was, absence often seemed to them like an illusion:
the other might be in the next room. 'Your letter', he once wrote
to her from Persia, 'makes me feel that distance does not matter,
and that loneliness is only a physical, not a spiritual, displacement.'
They could reach out over continents to feel the other's pulse and
measure it exactly. They could be together at Long Barn for

hours, reading in silence, and then both speak suddenly at the same moment. This communion of feeling was as expressive as a touch or glance. If one were ill or in imagined danger (and to Vita every taxi seemed like a threat to him, every aeroplane certain murder), they would undergo tortures of anxiety. Harold would cable across half the world for the latest news of her mild attack of sciatica. A hostile paragraph about him in a newspaper would drive her to despair, while he would worry agonizingly about one of her lectures or broadcasts which alarmed her. It was their constant involvement in each other's lives and feelings, caring without interfering, which was both the expression of their love and its strength. In the middle of the Second War, Vita wrote for Harold a poem which was read by the Poet Laureate, Cecil Day-Lewis, at their joint memorial service in 1968:

I must not tell how dear you are to me.
It is unknown, a secret from myself
Who should know best. I would not if I could
Expose the meaning of such mystery.

I loved you then, when love was Spring, and May.
Eternity is here and now, I thought;
The pure and perfect moment briefly caught
As in your arms, but still a child, I lay.

Loved you when summer deepened into June
And those fair, wild, ideal dreams of youth
Were true yet dangerous and half unreal
As when Endymion kissed the mateless moon.

But now when autumn yellows all the leaves
And thirty seasons mellow our long love,
How rooted, how secure, how strong, how rich,
How full the barn that holds our garnered sheaves!

That poem was written at Sissinghurst; but for fifteen years, until 1930, their home was Long Barn, which lies at the edge of a village known after its district as Sevenoaks Weald, halfway down a slope which overlooks a quilted pattern of fields and small woods. When they first found it in 1915, it was a battered cottage in which Caxton, it was said, had been born, and a coin of 1360 found behind the plaster was evidence of its antiquity. So was its condition. The floors sloped crazily, so that every piece of furniture appeared crippled, and the roof was held together less by construction than by natural angles of repose. In place of a garden there was a chute of rubble and a tangle of briars and nettles. They restored the cottage, transformed it into a house by adding a new wing at a right angle (the timbers coming from an old barn which lay askew at the foot of the hill), and made a garden in a series of lawns and walled terraces, leading by gradual descent from formality to the artlessness of the surrounding copses. Long Barn was not simple. There were seven main bedrooms, four bathrooms and a sitting-room fifty feet long. There were always at least three domestic servants, and two gardeners. It could put up three or four guests at a time, and was sunny, pretty, romantic and comfortable. But it retained an atmosphere of fourteenth-century rusticated innocence. Vita's writing-room was low, timbered and nooked, and her bedroom above it seemed always on the point of collapse, though it still stands. Harold built his own study at the far end of the new wing; and we, the children, were set firmly apart in a cottage higher up the hill. This physical separation of the family was symptomatic of our relationship. Each person must have a room of his own, but there must be, and was, a common room where we could periodically unite.

Ours was a strange childhood, though we did not think it strange. Our parents were remote, and therefore admirable. Every day until we went to school was spent under a nanny's eye. Meals, lessons, walks, the nursery routines of bedding and awakening shaped our lives. The highpoint of each day was our descent to the house at 6 pm, when we would find our mother bent over her current book, patient of our interruption, uncertain how to amuse us. Only now, when I read the manuscript of *The Land*, can I understand what these daily incursions must have cost her in concentration. But she was pleased to see us; we to see her. My father was different. He showed more demonstratively his affection for us, took us for walks, drew funny pictures, read us Conan Doyle, studied us (though we did not notice it), wondering how he could help. Vaguely we realized that we could claim but a small share of their attention; dimly we acknowledged that the part of their lives that we saw was not the whole. What was the whole?

Vita was always in love. I do not know of any moment in her life when she was not longing to see or hear from the only person who could satisfy that longing. One of the first, after Violet, was a man, Geoffrey Scott. He had known Vita since her childhood, and was linked in her mind with its happiest period, for they had first met in Italy in 1911. He had a part-time job at the British Embassy in Rome, but was primarily a writer. His first book, *The Architecture of Humanism* (1914), was perhaps the most important contribution to the history of aesthetics since Ruskin. His second, *Portrait of Zélide* (1924), is still regarded as one of the most charming biographies in the language. He was a tall, black-haired, short-sighted, sallow man, rather saturnine in expression and with a strong streak of melancholy, but he was humorous and witty, polished and profound, learned and inspired, critical and affectionate – the finished product of a high civilization. In 1923 he was forty. He was married to Lady Sybil Scott, and they lived in the Villa Medici, at Fiesole, overlooking Florence.

It was there that Vita went to stay in October 1923. Harold, who had been in Greece writing his book on Byron, joined them for a few days, but neither his presence nor Lady Sybil's did anything to deflect Vita's passionate response to Geoffrey's sudden declaration of love. On a hillside, one lovely evening, when the moon rose above a sea of olives, he took her into his arms. I cannot begin to explain (unless it was Florence and the moon) what reawoke her acceptance of a man's physical love which had lain dormant in her for five years, but there is no doubt that for a few weeks at least it was absolute. She returned to England dazed, telling Geoffrey, 'My love and tenderness is a bank on which you can draw unlimited cheques', and her mother that

... she missed Geoffrey atrociously ... She says he is very passionate. She is sure Harold does not mind, and Sybil says that if it had to be anyone, she's glad it's Vita. Geoffrey has had many affairs, but naturally she and he think that this is *the* one. He knows all about

Violet, and says his love will redeem Vita's reputation. [Lady Sack-ville's diary, *3 November 1923*]

It was true about Sybil. Her marriage had not been going well. She wrote to Vita pathetically, 'You are in love with each other, and he is not in love with me. He must feel free, and I don't ever want to come between you.' She gave Geoffrey an 'unwedding' ring to symbolize her renunciation. Lady Sackville was also right about Harold. He knew about the affair from the start, and in a curious way was rather pleased. He had an inner conviction that this was not a serious threat. He admired Geoffrey, liked him, and found him refreshingly different from Violet. If Violet was clever, Geoffrey was intelligent; in place of Violet's hypnotic influence, here was Geoffrey's candid adoration. He enriched Vita's mind instead of confusing it. His letters were like an invigorating shower after a torrid breeze. He discovered quickly the importance to her of Harold and Long Barn, and never challenged it. He touched her most sensitive chords, echoing her love of Italy, honouring her writing by his gentle criticism:

> You are a poet, not a poetess. An unforgivable word always, but applied to you, odious. My dear, keep your *apartness*. There is real aloofness in your best work, the inward and solitary-minded quality which at all costs you mustn't smear. I'm terribly ambitious for you. Oh the joy of talking the same language as you, of being made the same way! [*23 November 1923*]

Vita was beginning to write *The Land*; Geoffrey was writing *Zélide*. Each was writing for the other, and as they completed key passages, they paid each other the supreme compliment of sending their manuscripts for the other's comment. He nursed her poem with vicarious pride as carefully as he cherished her:

> I feel the Georgics is our poem [the title *The Land* was chosen only at the last moment], just as *Zélide* is our book. 'The little sullen moons of mistletoe' and 'Clean as a cat in pattens, smelling good' – oh Vita I could hug you! Bless you for having it in you to write like that, for being so stored with memories, older than any personal memories ... Be very shy of moralizing your subject. Agriculture and husbandry ought to be sparingly moralized; it tends to weaken

the impression. What you must never do is to pat your peasantry approvingly on the back. The bumpkin gesture – each muddy foot – must be placed inevitably and precisely right. No matter how heavy, how slow, how 'dull', one must never feel that you have relaxed one inch of your severity ... I worry about your work as if I had your gifts and the problem was my own. [*10 November 1924*]

What excellent advice, how tenderly conveyed! But behind it was a love which was strengthening in Geoffrey, as it weakened in Vita. Some months after her return to England she appeared aghast at the salmon she had hooked. In absence she could not match his mood, needing always (except with Harold and Virginia) the presence of the beloved to evoke her response. While Geoffrey wrote to her that their love was eternal, she in her replies became disconcertingly restrained. He could not fail to notice it. It was only when he returned to England early in 1924 that he was able to reassure himself temporarily that nothing had changed. They met constantly, stayed some weekends at Knole, others, with Harold, at Long Barn, and they shared a room at Hill Street. Lady Sackville watched them with protective eyes: '*22 Jan. 1924.* V. went again to Knole with G.S. I am so afraid of gossip.' '*24 Jan.* Went to Hill Street, and found V. and G.S. together. She looked very shy. I am shocked that he shows so much proprietorship over her.' '*4 Feb.* Went to Long Barn. I fear it is much more than a flirtation. People are talking unkindly.' '*16 Feb.* Everybody calls him a bounder.' Nobody was less of a bounder than Geoffrey Scott. He felt for Vita something greater than infatuation but never nurtured the hope that he might wrest her from Harold. His love was doomed, because of Harold, because of her restraint, because of his own chivalry. It was a proposition more than a proposal. When he returned to Florence in mid-February, he found a loving letter from her, written while he was still at her side. Then again her letters began to cool, and one can sense his anxiety in his attempts to fan her love into a fiercer flame:

Now that we have found each other, for God's sake let us keep it and make it a kind of dazzling light ahead. Our love has to be 'domesticated' and made reasonable and commonsensical – against its very nature – and yet I don't have the reward of a shared life, as the dear reasonable Harold gets. You will help, won't you? It is going to be difficult to keep the edge of it firm, with blunting time and absence rusting it. Keep the feeling, the knowledge, that I would at any moment chuck everything else in my life for you, if that would help. [*11 March 1924*]

You won't let difficulties come between us, will you? They do so easily, and love gets cold-shouldered by degrees by the presence of other people who are *always* against it. You see, you are very conciliatory by nature. I think of you always as you were the first time you said ... [the rest of the sentence is heavily scored out by Vita]. So long as you really, unalterably, unhesitatingly feel that, I'm ready to be as good as a lamb. But remember the pressure to divide will be steady and persistent. However 'good' I am, I shall never be allowed to share your life in any real sense, like Harold ... You and I mean the same thing by love, something absolute and final, and if needs be, merciless. You know you want it that way; you want me to love you like that. [*16 March 1924*]

The trouble was that she didn't. Her affair with Geoffrey Scott lasted for a few days, followed by another period of a few weeks. It spurted, but never flowed. Her moderate love was killed by his greater love. It became for her something too demanding, too disruptive, and once she had begun to feel like that, her distaste gathered into disgust. If only he would stick to literature!

They met several times again, in England and in Italy, and she tried to calm his ardour by degrees, using Harold (who was half-amused) as her lightning-conductor. Long Barn was the scene of Geoffrey's final despair. He would look across the angle formed by the two wings and see the neighbouring lights of her bedroom and Harold's, symbols of their intimacy and his exclusion. I just remember him. I was seven. I thought him rather fierce, but this must be because I once burst into his bedroom by mistake when he was changing for dinner, and he was naked. He was very angry. How little did I realize that my trivial existence was a reminder of his hopelessness. He slowly gave up. In 1927 he and Sybil were divorced and he spent the last years of his life in New York, where he edited Boswell's papers. There he died in 1929, aged forty-six.

Vita had not been kind to Geoffrey – she had smashed his life and finally wrecked his marriage – but what part does kindness play in love? For him their pledge had been cut in granite; for her it had been written in chalk on slate. Her love for Geoffrey had been an experiment in love, an experiment which failed. It failed because he was a man, because he was an impossible rival to Harold, and because he was replaced by someone to whom he could not hold a candle, a woman, a genius, Virginia Woolf.

Virginia was the most remarkable human being I have ever known. She could attract, yet she could also remove to a distance. She did neither deliberately, for she was without conceit, being on the contrary anxious to please, anxious to discover (she was very inquisitive) and touchingly sensitive to praise or reproach, but one was aware of her occasional withdrawal, and never quite knew how deep to penetrate, how shallow should be one's own response. We were children then, and the uncomprehending casualness of childhood soon mellowed our relationship with her. To us she was not Virginia who had been mad and could go mad again, nor Virginia Woolf who had uncovered a whole new seam of literary perception. She was Virginia. Virginia who was fun, Virginia who was easy, who asked us questions about school and holidays (gathering copy, though we did not know it), and who floated in and out of our lives like a godmother. 'Virginia's coming to stay.' 'Oh good!' We knew that she would notice us, that there would come a moment when she would pay no attention to my mother ('Vita, go away! Can't you see I'm talking to Ben and Nigel'), and then she spoke to us about our simple lives, handing back to us as diamonds what we had given her as lumps of coal. I think of her as delicate, but in the cobweb sense, not the medical. I think of her as an autumn, indoor, person, though she loved the summer and the Downs, stretching tapered fingers towards the fire, elaborating her fantasies, provocative, delicious, matching gestures to her words, drawing back her long hair from her forehead as a new fantasy occurred to her, smiling often, laughing seldom, and with never a giggle in her laugh. I think of her at Knole, leaning S-curved against a doorway, finger to her chin.

contemplative, amused. She instinctively assumed attitudes expressive of her moods.

Vita first met Virginia on 14 December 1922, with Clive Bell; and four days later she invited her to dine at Ebury Street, with Clive and Desmond MacCarthy. She wrote to Harold (who was with Curzon at Lausanne):

I simply adore Virginia Woolf, and so would you. You would fall quite flat before her charm and personality. It was a good party. They asked a lot about your *Tennyson*. Mrs Woolf is so simple: she does give the impression of something big. She is utterly unaffected: there are no outward adornments – she dresses quite atrociously. At first you think she is plain; then a sort of spiritual beauty imposes itself on you, and you find a fascination in watching her. She was smarter last night; that is to say, the woollen orange stockings were replaced by yellow silk ones, but she still wore the pumps. She is both detached and human, silent till she wants to say something, and then says it supremely well. She is quite old [forty]. I've rarely taken such a fancy to anyone, and I think she likes me. At least, she's asked me to Richmond where she lives. Darling, I have quite lost my heart. [*19 December 1922*]

The growth of their intimacy is recorded in Vita's diary:

22 Feb. 1923. Dined with Virginia at Richmond. She is as delicious as ever. How right she is when she says that love makes everyone a bore, but the excitement of life lies in 'the little moves' nearer to people. But perhaps she feels this because she is an experimentalist in humanity, and has had no *grande passion* in her life.

19 March 1924. Lunched with Virginia in Tavistock Square, where she has just arrived. The first time that I have been alone with her for long. Went on to see Mama, my head swimming with Virginia.

Then there was a pause. They wrote to each other a lot, saw each other quite often, but Virginia grew alarmed to think where all this was leading. As Quentin Bell puts it from Virginia's corner: 'She probably became aware of Vita's feelings and perhaps acquired an inkling of her own at that first encounter; she felt shy, almost virginal, in Vita's company, and she was, I suspect, roused to a sense of danger.' There was also Harold, and Leonard, and from October 1923, Geoffrey Scott. Vita was too well aware of the delicacy of Virginia's mind and body to press her strongly, and their friendship developed affectionately, starting with small tendernesses by the fireside. (Vita liked to sit on the floor by Virginia's chair) which gradually, so gradually, led to something a little more.

Virginia's influence on her is shown best, I think, in Vita's short novel *Seducers in Ecuador*, which she wrote for the Hogarth Press in 1924, for it is the most imaginative of all her fiction, as if she had wanted to write something 'worthy' of Virginia, in Virginia's alusive style, tuned to a new vibrancy by the thought of so critical an editor whom she was meeting almost every day. The effect of Vita on Virginia is all contained in *Orlando*, the longest and most charming love-letter in literature, in which she explores Vita, weaves her in and out of the centuries, tosses her from one sex to the other, plays with her, dresses her in furs, lace and emeralds, teases her, flirts with her, drops a veil of mist around her, and ends by photographing her in the mud at Long Barn, with dogs, awaiting Virginia's arrival next day.

Her friendship was the most important fact in Vita's life, except Harold, just as Vita's was the most important in Virginia's, except Leonard, and perhaps her sister Vanessa. If one seeks a parallel to Vita–Harold one can find it only in Virginia–Leonard, although one must admit differences, for Virginia was sexually frigid and Leonard was not homosexual. Their marriages were alike in the freedom they allowed each other, in the invincibility of their love, in its intellectual, spiritual and non-physical base, in the eagerness of all four of them to savour life, challenge convention, work hard, play dangerously with the emotions – and in their solicitude for each other. How well do I recall Leonard's look as he watched Virginia across a sitting-room to see that she did not grow tired or over-excited, caring for her much as Joseph must have cared for Mary, for their relationship was biblical. There was no jealousy between the Woolfs and the Nicolsons, because they had arrived independently at the same definition of 'trust'. Leonard, perhaps, was a little less tolerant than Harold, fearing not that Virginia might cease to love him, but that the strain on her emotions might again unsettle her mind. Harold feared this too.

But let them speak for themselves. First, Virginia in her diary, still slightly defensive:

> Vita for three days at Long Barn . . . I like her and being with her and the splendour — she shines in the grocer's shop at Sevenoaks with a candle-lit radiance, stalking on legs like beech-trees, pink glowing, grape clustered, pearl hung . . . What is the effect of all this on me? Very mixed. There is her maturity and full-breastedness; her being so much in full sail on the high tides, where I am coasting down backwards; her capacity I mean to take the floor in any company, to represent her country, to visit Chatsworth, to control silver, servants, chow dogs; her motherhood (but she is a little cold and off-hand with her boys), her being in short (what I have never been) a real woman. Then there is some voluptuousness about her; the grapes are ripe; and not reflective. No. In brain and insight she is not as highly organised as I am. But then she is aware of this and so lavishes on me the maternal protection which, for some reason, is what I have always most wished from everyone . . . [Quentin Bell. *Virginia Woolf*. Vol. II. pp. 117–18]

Professor Bell speculates on how things may have developed from there: 'There may have been — on balance I think there probably was — some caressing, some bedding together.' I can add a little to that from Harold's and Vita's letters. Harold was then in Teheran. 'V.' had become another V.

> *Vita to Harold:* I fetched V. and brought her down here [Long Barn]. She is an exquisite companion, and I love her dearly. Leonard is coming on Saturday. Please don't think
> a) I shall fall in love with Virginia
> b) Virginia will ,, ,, me
> c) Leonard ,, ,, ,, ,,
> d) I shall ,, ,, ,, Leonard
> because it is not so. Only I know my silly Hadji will say to himself *Ça y est*, and so on. I am missing you dreadfully. I am missing you specially because V. was so very sweet about you, and so understanding. [*17 December 1925*]

> *Vita to Harold:* Virginia read the Georgics [*The Land*]. I won't tell you what she said. She insisted on reading them. She read them

straight through. She likes you. She likes me. She says she depends on me. She is so vulnerable under all her brilliance. I do love her, but not b.s.ly.* [*18 December 1925*]

Vita to Harold: I think she is one of the most mentally exciting people I know. She hates the wishy-washiness of Bloomsbury young men. We have made friends by leaps and bounds in these two days. I love her, but couldn't fall 'in love' with her, so don't be nervous! [*19 December 1925*]

Harold to Vita: I am not really bothered about Virginia, and I think you are probably very good for each other. I only feel that you have not got *la main heureuse* in dealing with married couples. [*8 January 1926*]

Harold to Vita: Oh my dear, I do hope that Virginia is not going to be a muddle! It is like smoking over a petrol tank. [*7 July 1926*]

Vita to Harold: Darling, there is no muddle anywhere. I keep on telling you so. You mention Virginia: it is simply laughable. I love Virginia – as who wouldn't? But really, my sweet, one's love for Virginia is a very different thing: a mental thing; a spiritual thing, if you like, an intellectual thing, and she inspires a feeling of tenderness, which is, I suppose, owing to her funny mixture of hardness and softness – the hardness of her mind, and her terror of going mad again. She makes me feel protective. Also she loves me, which flatters and pleases me. Also – since I have embarked on telling you about Virginia – I am scared to death of arousing physical feelings in her, because of the madness. I don't know what effect it would have, you see: it is a fire with which I have no wish to play. I have too much real affection and respect for her. Also she has never lived with anyone except Leonard, which was a terrible failure, and was abandoned quite soon. So all that remains an unknown quantity; and I have got too many dogs not to let them lie when they *are* asleep. Besides *ça ne me dit rien*; and *ça lui dit trop*, where I am concerned. I don't want to get landed in an affair which might get beyond my control before I knew where I was.

Besides, Virginia is not the sort of person one thinks of in that

---

*The initials 'b.s.' stood for 'back-stairs'. But the expression changed its original meaning of 'gossipy', 'giggly' in Sackville shorthand to mean 'homosexual attitudes or behaviour'.

way. There is something incongruous and almost indecent in the idea. I *have* gone to bed with her (twice), but that's all. Now you know all about it, and I hope I haven't shocked you. My darling, you are the one and only person for me in the world; do take that in once and for all, you little dunderhead. [*17 August 1926*]

Harold to Vita: Thank you for telling me so frankly about Virginia. It's a relief to feel that you realize the danger and will be wise. You see, it's not merely playing with fire; it's playing with gelignite. Don't let's worry about these things. I know that your love for me is central, as is my love for you, and it's quite unaffected by what happens at the outer edge. [*2 September 1926*]

Vita to Harold: I know that Virginia will die, and it will be too awful. I went to Tavistock Square yesterday, and she sat in the dusk in the light of the fire, and I sat on the floor as I always do, and she rumpled my hair as she always does, and she talked about literature and Mrs Dalloway and Sir Henry Taylor, and she said that you would resent her next summer. But I said, No you wouldn't. Oh Hadji, she *is* such an angel. I really adore her. Not 'in love' — just love — devotion. Her friendship has enriched me so. I don't think I have ever loved anybody so much, in the way of friendship; in fact, of course, I know I haven't. She knows that you and I adore each other. I have told her so. [*30 November 1926*]

Harold to Vita: I am far more worried for Virginia's and Leonard's sake than for ours. I know that for each of us the other is the magnetic north, and that though the needle may flicker and even get stuck at the other points, it will come back to the pole sooner or later. But what dangers for them! You see, I have every confidence in your wisdom except where this sort of thing is concerned, when you wrap your wisdom in a hood of optimism and only take it off when things have gone too far for mending. [*3 December 1926*]

He need not have worried. These letters tell all there is to tell. Vita and Virginia did no damage to each other, and Harold was grateful to her for opening up in Vita 'a rich new vein of ore'. The physical element in their friendship was tentative and not very successful, lasting only a few months, a year perhaps. It is a travesty of their relationship to call it an affair. When they went Burgundy together two years later:

Virginia is very sweet, and I feel extraordinarily protective towards her. The combination of that brilliant brain and fragile body is very lovable. She has a sweet and childlike nature, from which her intellect is completely separate. I have never known anyone who was so profoundly sensitive, and who makes less of a business of that sensitiveness. [*27 September 1928*]

Virginia did not admire Vita as a writer, and said so in a way which Vita would not mind. By *The Land*,

... she was disappointed, but very sweet about it. She says it is a contribution to English literature, and is a solid fact against which one can lean up without fear of its giving way. She also says it is one of the few *interesting* poems – I mean the information part. [*26 January 1926*]

But *Orlando!* Imagine those two, seeing each other at least once a week, one writing a book about the other, swooping on Knole to squeeze from it another paragraph, on Long Barn to trap Vita into a new admission about her past (Violet, whom Virginia met once, comes into the book as Sasha, a Russian princess, 'like a fox, or an olive tree'), dragging Vita to a London studio to have her photographed as a Lely, tantalizing her, hinting at the fantasy but never lifting more than a corner of it – until on the day before publication, *Orlando* arrived in a brown-paper parcel from the Hogarth Press, followed a few days later by the author with the manuscript as a present. Vita wrote to Harold: 'I am in the middle of reading *Orlando*, in such a turmoil of excitement and confusion that I scarcely know where (or who) I am!' She loved it. Naturally she was flattered, but more than that, the novel identified her with Knole for ever. Virginia by her genius had provided Vita with a unique consolation for having been born a girl, for her exclusion from her inheritance, for her father's death earlier that year. The book, for her, was not simply a brilliant masque or pageant. It was a memorial mass.

By scattered references I have already landed Harold in Persia. He was sent to Teheran in October 1925 as Counsellor at the British Legation, and remained there for the next one and a half years. At first he seems to have hoped that Vita would go with him.

Persia was one of the few places in the world where she would find the diplomatic life tolerable, for it was 'unsmart' (Lady Sackville's phrase) and there were the compensations of a beautiful country and a proud romantic people. But she preferred not to. She would visit him there, but she would not be lodged in a Legation compound as his *légitime*, and be made to sit at dinner-parties in her correct order of precedence with a white card beside her plate proclaiming her 'The Hon. Mrs Harold Nicolson', when she could be V. Sackville-West at Long Barn, with her writing, her garden and Virginia. This sounds selfish, but neither of them thought it so. She cared so deeply for her independence that for both of them it outweighed everything else, even their agony at being parted for months on end. There is no suggestion in their hundreds of letters that their misery could be ended at any moment by her joining him permanently in Teheran. Instead they exchanged commiserations about his 'bloody profession' which forced them apart, and he began to consider seriously throwing it up for something less divisive. He went as far as to apply for a job in the Anglo-Persian Oil Company – the London end – but it came to nothing.

Lest it be thought that I exaggerate their unhappiness when separated, I will cite one incident – their parting at Rasht – which they saw afterwards as a watershed in their marriage, because it convinced them that never again must they expose each other to such pain. Vita went to Persia (the journey which she described in *Passenger to Teheran*) in March 1926, driving across the desert from Baghdad to meet Harold in a snowbound village on the Persian frontier late one night, the headlights of the car lighting up his figure on the road, suddenly. She much enjoyed her visit, and attended the coronation of the Shah ('a Cossack trooper' she described him in the book, which appalled Harold, for this was the sovereign to whom he was accredited), but in May came the dreadful moment when they must part. They had arranged that she would return home via Russia, crossing the Caspian from a northern Persian port near Rasht to Baku. Harold drove with her from Teheran to Rasht, and Raymond Mortimer went with them. They spent the night there, and early next morning Harold and Raymond left her to return to Teheran. Here is Harold's account in his letter written next day:

> When I closed your bedroom door at Rasht, I stood for a moment on the landing with a giddy agony, which made the whole house swing and wobble. With a great effort I stopped myself bursting into your room again – where I should have found your dear head bowed in tears, and your green pyjamas still wet from them. I went down the stairs into the garden and looked back at your window. I longed to call, 'Vita, Vita, I can't bear it!'. I got into the motor with Raymond, and gradually I found my voice again. We talked of indifferent things ... We stopped for lunch by the roadside, and put the water-bottle to cool under a spring. I went to wash a fork. Raymond said, 'Here's a tin of Ovaltine'. I said 'Yes, there are some little cakes in it.' I had put those cakes in before leaving, and you had had one of them. I crouched there, holding the fork in the stream – tears pouring down my face. I went up behind the rock and leant against it and shook and shook with sobs. Raymond was infinitely tactful ...

Late that night they arrived back in Teheran:

> I found your fur cap in my cupboard. I flung myself on the bed in an agony of suffering such as I have never known. I walked up and down in the dark saying, 'Vita, Vita, Vita, Vita, Vita!', with the tears splashing on the dark floor. I felt that this is not to be borne. One can't be as unhappy as this. This morning I broke down completely. I leant against the window with my back to Raymond. He said, 'I would give my head to have in my life a love such as you and Vita have.' That comforted me. Oh my dear, we can't go through this again. It is mad to inflict such suffering on each other.
> [7 May 1926]

From Rasht Vita wrote to him before the boat sailed:

> I heard the motor start after what seemed an endless interval, and then I heard it hooting a long time through the streets. Oh my dear, God keep you safe. Life is empty and silent. I feel lightheaded with pain. Never, never, never again. I cannot bear it, and if Providence forgives me for having tempted it and allows me to be with you again, we will not leave each other any more. There is no one in

the world who counts for me but you, and never will be. I simply can't live without you. [*6 May 1926*]

The strange fact is that there was nothing imperative to take her home. We, her children, were well cared for; Lady Sackville's selfish insistence that Vita must remain near her could have been ignored; Vita had enjoyed the easy intelligent company of Raymond and Gladwyn Jebb, who was Third Secretary at the Legation; she had even been able to write in Persia the concluding lines of *The Land*, invoking her Kentish Weald and the ghost of Virgil. I find it difficult to explain. Virginia was not the draw: Virginia could come alive in letters. But absence is something more endurable than separation. When Vita arrived back in England, she took up her old occupations, and the wound healed. The sense of unbroken communion with Harold was renewed by correspondence. Her letters to Persia were the best she ever wrote to him, perhaps because the long time-lag between posting and delivery (two weeks, at least, sometimes four) gave them a perspective and a rhythm, like a slow procession of waves advancing to a distant shore. She was able to be franker — a blush cannot last three weeks — and she became more contemplative:

I got a letter from Virginia, which contains one of her devilish, shrewd psychological pounces. She asks if there is something in me which does not vibrate, a 'something reserved, muted ... The thing I call "central transparency" sometimes fails you in your writing'. Damn the woman, she has put her finger on it. There *is* something muted. What is it, Hadji? Something that doesn't come alive. I brood and brood, feel I am groping in a dark tunnel. It makes everything I write a little unreal; gives the effect of having been done from outside.

There is no doubt about it, as one grows older, one thinks more. Virginia worries, you worry, I worry. Yet I would rather do this and become introspective than rattle about London, where people's voices become more and more devoid of meaning. [*20 November 1926*]

Harold gained much from Persia. He loved the country, learnt the language, and professionally his grasp became more incisive — so much so for the taste of some of his superiors in the Foreign

Office, for he could never bring himself to write his dispatches in the approved guarded manner. He also wrote *Some People*, his most original book, in the same months as Vita was putting the finishing touches to *The Land*, her most distinguished. *Some People* was autobiographical to the extent that he traced his intellectual development by placing himself in a series of confrontations, some real, some imaginary, with his nanny, a schoolboy hero, a French intellectual, a diplomatic pundit, Lord Curzon and so on – from all of which encounters he emerged slightly on top. In style the book owed something to Lytton Strachey, something to Max Beerbohm, but its amused detached analysis of the nudging and jostling of people in their relations with each other was wholly his own. He always regarded *Some People* as a lightweight book, and groaned inwardly whenever some acquaintance began, 'Now let me see, I read something of yours the other day – something about Lord Curzon's valet and a pair of trousers, was it?', but on the day when he finished writing it in Teheran, he obviously thought it contained a little more than mere entertainment:

> This evening I wrote the last words of *Some People*. I then walked across to see Gladwyn, wishing to clear my mind. He was tired by his day's shooting and had a cold, and didn't in the least want to talk about the soul. But I made him. I said that the intellect was the only thing which made man a higher animal, and therefore virtue should simply mean the development of the intellect. He said I was leaving out the emotions. 'You know, Harold, you'd be an awful cad if it weren't for your emotions.' I said, 'No, you're completely wrong.' So then I came back and sat in my bath and realized that he was completely right. I mean, I *like* Gladwyn because he is intelligent; but I am *fond* of Gladwyn because he is sensitive and shy and reserved and distinguished. So my theory has broken down. [*20 December 1926*]

In February 1927 Vita returned to Persia by the Russian route, and their reunion at Rasht almost (but never quite) effaced in family legend their parting at the same place nine months before. This time they arranged things better. After a month in Teheran they went south to Isfahan, and thence, on foot, with Gladwyn, they crossed the Bakhtiari Mountains to the oil-fields, in hail an rain, pushing against sheep and tribesmen, for they had chosen the season of the annual migration. When they reached the plains of Abadan, the bungalows, Fords and telephones of the Oil Company were to Harold 'the joy of civilization', to Vita 'the horrible resources of modern ingenuity'. She wrote in her second book of Persian travels, *Twelve Days*: 'A wave of regret swept over me. I forgot the exhaustion of our toiling days. I would have turned back then and there into the mountains and be lost for ever.' Instead, Harold took her home to Long Barn. In his diary on the day of their arrival he wrote:

> *4 May 1927.* It is a different place: wide lawns and tidy edges; tulips and aubretia, phlox, lilac, irises – a sea of colour. It is so exciting that I am violently sick and have to be given brandy. I have never felt so happy in my life. All the weary months of exile are wiped away as if by a sponge.

Odd things coincided during that summer and autumn. Maurice Couve de Murville, the future Prime Minister of France, came to Long Barn for six weeks, a shy youth brittle as a biscuit, dressed in midsummer tweeds, to teach us French. Vita was awarded the Hawthornden Prize for *The Land*. Virginia started to write *Orlando*. Roy Campbell, the poet, and his wife Mary, were lent the gardener's cottage, and Vita fell in love with Mary, to the fury of Roy, who wrote *The Georgiad*, a highly uncomplimentary portrait of Long Barn and the Nicolsons, in revenge. And Harold advanced another step towards his decision to leave the diplomatic service:

> *24 Aug. 1927.* I can now envisage the prospect of resignation without a pang. I have Vita and the boys. I have my home and my love of nature. I have my friends. I have my energy and my talent for writing. I shall be free. I can tell the truth. There is no truth now which I cannot tell.

Instead, when he was asked in October to go as First Secretary to Berlin, 'I accept, gloomily.'

The importance of Berlin in their personal lives was to confirm Harold's growing conviction that for Vita's sake he must abandon his diplomatic career at mid-point for another which would allow him to live in England. Berlin was nearer home than Teheran, near enough to send tulips from Long Barn with a chance that they would revive in water, but it was uglier and smarter. Vita went there several times and loathed it. Harold did not loathe it quite so much, because he found the work interesting (he was soon promoted Counsellor), and he made many new friends among the Germans and visiting English, but 'I am far more homesick than I was in Persia, for Persia did appeal to my nature-love, but here there are no works of God at all'. Once again it was taken for granted between them that while he was in Berlin she would stay most of the time at Long Barn, writing him letters of mounting indignation against those who kept him there:

> Oh God, how I hate the Foreign Office! How I hate it, with a personal hatred for all that it makes me suffer! Damn it, damn it, damn it – that vile impersonal juggernaut that sweeps you away from me. [15 November 1928]

More profoundly:

> I am not a good person for you to be married to. Men and women who marry ought to be positive and negative respectively – complementary elements. But when two positive people like us marry, it resolves itself into a compromise which is truly satisfactory to neither. You love foreign politics; and I love literature and peace and a secluded life. Oh my dear, my infinitely dear Hadji, you ought never to have married me. I feel my inadequacy most bitterly. What good am I to you? [13 December 1928]

And he replied, What good was he to her? She should have married Lord Lascelles.

He heard that it was likely that after two years in Berlin he would be sent as Minister to Washington. The prospect made less appeal to Vita than it had to her mother fifty years before. She could not, she *would* not, do it. While Harold had been able to explain her long absences when he held more junior posts ('It rather amuses me that people think we don't get on'), as he rose to be in charge of Legations and then Embassies, her refusal to join him as his hostess (the word made her shiver) might be awkward for him. It would be an overstatement to say that

Vita wrecked Harold's career, because he himself, on additional grounds, had for some years been thinking of chucking it. *Some People* had sown distrust in his 'soundness', and his 'too clever' dispatches from Teheran had ruffled feelings in Downing Street. He felt himself to be under a slight cloud. He disliked exile as much as she did, and was not at ease on formal diplomatic occasions, which would grow more formal as he became more important. He loved his work, and in a non-pushing way was ambitious. This was one of Vita's grievances: 'How I wish you weren't ambitious; how I wish you preferred books to politics, me to Hindenburg!' Literature was his second string (while he was in Berlin he wrote the life of his father, Lord Carnock, who died in 1928), but there was something feeble, he thought, in the idea of 'lotus-eating at Long Barn, writing books, at the age of forty-three', and even Vita might come to despise him for it. Not at all, replied Vita: 'I am all for some people doing public duty, but I think it ought to be reserved for those who can't do anything else, and people like you who can write marvellously should not waste themselves in a lot of humbug and fubsiness', by which she meant the preliminaries to the Second World War. The importance of his work made no great impression on her when he was appointed to take charge of the Berlin Embassy between two Ambassadors.

Again and again they returned to the central problem of their separation, although they met far more frequently than during the Persian years. Harold often came home on leave, and we spent several of our school holidays in Germany, skating in the Tiergarten, sailing on the Heiligesee and playing badminton in the Embassy ballroom, while Vita managed to avoid most diplomatic parties and was able to work on her books: she began the first chapter of *The Edwardians* in the restaurant of Cologne railway-station. But more meetings meant more separations:

> I spent most of the evening in tears. It is sheer misery for me, these perpetual departures ... I simply feel that you are me and I am you – exactly what you meant by saying that you became 'the lonely me' whenever we parted.

This could have been written by either of them. In fact, it was written by Vita, in the spring of 1929.

When in June of that year Bruce Lockhart asked Harold out of the blue whether he would care to join the staff of the *Evening Standard*, he accepted, not impetuously, not very happily (for he thought journalism sordid), but gratefully. The salary which Lord Beaverbrook offered him, £3,000 a year, would make them independent of Lady Sackville, who was turning nasty about the allowance which she owed them as a legal right. He could come home, for good. He could write books as well as paragraphs for the Londoner's Diary. He asked Leonard Woolf's advice, and Leonard agreed. Vita, who was walking in the Val d'Isère with Hilda Matheson (Talks Director at the BBC) when she heard the news, was delighted, feeling in an obscure way that his resignation was a snub to the Foreign Office. As the time drew near for his departure, he felt no regrets. He referred to it as 'the great liberation'; and the last words of his last letter to Vita from Berlin were: 'How glad I shall be when the train moves out of the Friedrichstrasse!' In his diary, when that day came (20 December 1929), he wrote: 'I am presented with a cactus. It symbolizes the end of my diplomatic career.'

Their marriage had now lasted sixteen years. Vita was to live another thirty-two, Harold another thirty-eight. It may be wondered why I should devote only a thirtieth part of a book entitled *Portrait of a Marriage* to an account of two-thirds of it. There are two reasons: first, because the remainder of the story has already been told in the three published volumes of Harold's diary, which he began to keep regularly in 1930; second, because there was no change in their relationship from that time forward, no threat to their married happiness. It simply deepened. I can summarize the events of those years quite shortly.

For eighteen months Harold compiled the Londoner's Diary for the *Evening Standard*, hating it. After the Foreign Office, with its pride in itself, its lofty intellectual aspirations and its discretion, daily journalism appeared to him trivial and squalid. He became closely involved with Sir Oswald Mosley's New Party in 19~

editing its newspaper *Action*, and stood unsuccessfully for Parliament in its name. It was the most depressing period of his life. On 'descending to the market place', as he put it, he had made two false starts. He found himself obliged to part in quick succession first with Beaverbrook, then with Mosley, and was left without a job, without money, and his reputation (so he believed) shattered. It wás no consolation to him that during those same years he achieved sudden notoriety by his weekly talks on BBC radio under the title *People and Things*; nor that Vita was able to keep their home together and us at Eton by writing three best-selling novels, *The Edwardians, All Passion Spent* and *Family History*. Harold made his contribution with *Public Faces*, a brilliantly amusing novel about the Foreign Office, and together in 1933 they went on a joint lecture tour of the United States. On their return, Harold settled down to more serious books, *Peacemaking*, and *Curzon, the Last Phase*, and a biography of the American financier and statesman, Dwight Morrow, but he still believed himself to be a failure. Privately, without telling Vita, he bitterly regretted his resignation from the Foreign Office. His worst fears had been justified: he was 'lotus-eating'. Then in 1935, everything changed. He was elected to Parliament as National Labour member for West Leicester, and remained there for the next ten years.

Too little has been made of Harold's years in the House of Commons by potted accounts of his career. It has been tempting to write him off as a political lightweight because he gained no Government office higher than Parliamentary Secretary to the Ministry of Information in 1940-1, and could never bring himself to engage in party in-fighting. He should have been a Liberal, it was said, or sat for one of the University seats. But he had two great advantages in the House. He was almost the only back-bench Member to have had direct experience of the higher conduct of foreign policy; and he was exceptionally astute and personally very popular. His diffidence, his apparent lack of ambition, his geniality, his wit made his cleverness acceptable in a place where dexterity is usually more honoured than intelligence. He never advertised himself at Question-time, never snubbed the less well educated Members, and spoke rarely and shortly on the subjects he knew best. He had the courage to stand up to the Conservatives with whom his tiny splinter-party was nominally allied, protesting eloquently against their refusal to recognize the Nazi danger. He found himself in the pre-war years aligned with Churchill and Eden against Chamberlain, and reached the peak of his Parliamentary career in his speech against the Munich settlement of 1938. When war came, and his friends were in power, he should have been rewarded for the stubborn rightness of his judgement, but his year of junior office was abruptly ended by Churchill, not because Harold had been found wanting, but because the Parliamentary Secretaryship was needed for someone else in the Party share-out of offices, and Harold was considered dispensable because he was not formidable. For the remainder of the war he was a Governor of the BBC, and devoted his Parliamentary gifts mainly to reconciling the British Government to the Free French. What an Ambassador to Paris he would have made when the war ended! But he did not have that sort of push. In the General Election of 1945 he lost his seat, and never returned to public life.

Vita all this time was gardening and writing books. If in the early years of their marriage things happened to Vita more than they happened to Harold, in the later years it was the other way round. She became solitary – a recluse would be too strong a description – finding happiness in country things and the periodic company of her family and a few close friends. She played no part whatever in Harold's political life, visiting Leicester on only one occasion during his ten years as its Member, and as far as I know never set foot in the House of Commons. She went to London as seldom as possible, but often abroad on holiday, to Italy and in later years to the Dordogne district of France. After the American tour of 1933 she appeared rarely in public, for she was a nervous lecturer though she enjoyed broadcasting, and social functions became increasingly abhorrent to her. She accepted one or two semi-public positions such as membership of the National Trust's Gardens Committee, and she became a Justice of the Peace, more because she liked the medieval sound of the title than the twentieth-century actuality of the work involved. During the war years she lived at Sissinghurst under the umbrella of the RAF, and helped to organize the Women's Land Army, whose history she wrote.

After the war Harold divided his time between weekends writing at Sissinghurst and week-days in London, where he served on many committees and enjoyed a dazzling social life as an eligible single man, his hostesses having long given up hope that Vita could be induced to come too. Once he tried to re-enter politics by joining the Labour Party and standing as its candidate at the Croydon by-election in 1948, but he was not elected, and the mortification of the experience ('I was certainly not intended by nature or by training for one of the central figures in a harlequinade') decided him to abandon politics for literature. Soon after Croydon he was invited to write the official biography of King George V, and this was the most massive literary undertaking of his career, earning him a knighthood which he felt it ungracious to decline. Vita hated being Lady Nicolson even more than she hated being Mrs Nicolson, and anyone who addressed her as such would be startled by a freezing look.

To end the factual part of this narrative, a word should be added about my brother and myself. Both of us went to Balliol College, Oxford, after Eton, and both served in the army in North Africa and Italy during the war, from which we emerged unscratched by the enemy. Ben thereafter dedicated his gifts to the history of art, becoming in 1947 Editor of the *Burlington Magazine*, the leading journal of the history of the fine arts, a position which he still (1973) retains, and wrote major books on the painters Terbrugghen, Wright of Derby and Georges de La Tour. I entered publishing as George Weidenfeld's partner in 1947, and politics as MP for Bournemouth East in 1952, losing my seat seven years later mainly because I differed from most of my constitutents about the Suez crisis. Ben and I both married and had children, but our marriages (in spite of the example which this book records) did not succeed, nature having endowed us with a greater talent for friendship than for cohabitation, for fatherhood than for wedlock.

The centre of our lives during later boyhood and adolescence was Sissinghurst Castle, near Cranbrook in Kent, where both our parents lived for more than thirty years and where both died. I remember well (but my memory is perhaps gilded by too frequent recital of the event) my first visit there in April 1930. I went with my mother and Dorothy Wellesley, the poet, to view 'an estate' recommended by a local agent. Vita and Harold had been disturbed by the rumour that the meadows around Long Barn were about to be sold to a chicken-farmer who intended to raise a cantonment of huts within view of the terrace, and were looking for another place where they could live in peace and make a new garden. Sissinghurst appeared to my eyes (aged thirteen) quite impossible. It was the battered relic of an Elizabethan house in which not a single room was habitable. The future garden was a rubbish-dump. The day was a wet one, and I trailed my mother between mountains of old tins and other unexplained humps from one brick fragment to another, each more derelict than the last. She suddenly turned to me, her mind made up: 'I think we shall be very happy here.' 'But we haven't got to live *here*?' I said, appalled. 'Yes, I think we can make something rather lovely out of it.'

My father came down with Ben the next day, and recorded in his diary, 'I am cold and calm, but I like it.' But it was Vita who pressed the audacious plan, she who had the money to buy Sissinghurst, she who organized the rehabilitation of what had once been the finest architectural ornament of the central Weald. They repaired the surviving buildings, making two bedrooms for themselves in one of the cottages, one for Ben and me in another (which we shared until we were both at Oxford), and most important of all, separate sitting-rooms for each of us. There were no guest-rooms, deliberately, and only one common sitting-room, a room like Long Barn's fifty feet long, which we used only occasionally. They had achieved by the accident of the physical separation of the buildings the perfect solution to our communal lives. Each of us could be alone for most of the day, and we could unite for meals.

Vita's own sitting-room was on the first floor of the Elizabethan

tower which rose slim and solemn from the centre of this dis-
jointed compound. It had been the room in which we all four
slept at weekends on camp-beds until the cottages were ready,
breakfasting off sardines and honey on a packing-case. One
morning my father took the butter-knife and prised loose a brick
in the wall which sealed off the neighbouring turret-room, and
Vita, peering through the hole, at once exclaimed, 'That will be
my library; and this', waving a teaspoon around the wall, 'will
be my sitting-room.' Within a month or two it was, and it
remained hers for the next thirty-two years. Few were ever
admitted to it. We would go to the foot of the staircase in the
opposite turret and shout that lunch was ready or that she was
wanted on the telephone, but by an unspoken rule we never
mounted it. She filled the room with her books and personal
mementoes – a stone from Persepolis, a photograph of Virginia,
one of Pepita's dancing slippers – and as the wallpaper peeled and
faded, and the velvet tassels slowly frayed, she would never allow
them to be renewed. Her possessions must grow old with her.
She must be surrounded by evidence of time. When after a short
absence I returned with her to inspect the repairs to her bedroom
in the South Cottage, we found the workmen applying a skin
of white plaster to the Elizabethan bricks. She stopped them
immediately (she could be imperious, like Bess of Hardwick), and
ordered them to undo all that they had done so far. 'But surely,
madam, you don't want to have bare bricks in the mistress's
bedroom?' 'That's exactly what I do want.' To this day the room
remains as she rightly ordered it, the red and purple bricks forming
a tapestry against which hang the mirrors of a later age. Her
sitting-room too is quite unchanged. For a week or two after her
death, I tried to use it as my own. I could not endure it. I ceased
to be myself: I became a ghost of her.

One day, perhaps, a book may be written about the making of
the garden at Sissinghurst, and it could well bear the same title as
this book, for the garden is a portrait of their marriage. Harold
made the design, Vita did the planting. In the firm perspectives
of the vistas, the careful siting of an urn or statue, the division of
the garden by hedges and walls and buildings into a series of

separate gardens, the calculated alternation between straight lines and curved, one can trace his classical hand. In the overflowing clematis, figs, vines and wisteria, in the rejection of violent colour or anything too tame or orderly, one discovers her romanticism. Wild flowers must be allowed to invade the garden; if plants stray over a path, they must not be cut back, the visitor must duck; rhododendrons must be banished in favour of their tenderer cousin, the azalea; roses must not electrify, but seduce; and when a season has produced its best, that part of the garden must be allowed to lie fallow for another year, since there is a cycle in nature which must not be disguised. It is eternally renewable, like a play with acts and scenes: there can be a change of cast, but the script remains the same. Permanence and mutation are the secrets of this garden.

Let the author of the future book understand well that it emerged from their leisure hours. They created it in the intervals of earning enough money to create it. The garden was an extravagance. For both of them it was an accompaniment to their books, like the left hand on a piano to the right. When Harold returned to Sissinghurst each Friday evening, he would look round the garden in London suit and with swinging briefcase, the first of all his concerns, a sump to drain off the week's despair, a wineglass to hold the weekend's delights. She, alone all week, would plan and toil, committing to a vast notebook (for ink and paper were her adjutants) her plans, her self-interrogation, and when he came back, she put to him her ideas, her worries, her triumphs and disappointments. 'Come: come and look. What shall we do?'

Vita, I have said, withdrew into preferred solitude. Before the war, because of it, and after it, she retreated to Sissinghurst. In her young womanhood she had been vigorous, alert for new excitement. She had constantly made fresh friends, and was anxious to make more. She searched for experience, gambled with life. Now she was content with what was familiar, people and places, and her new adventures were tuned to a gentler key, measured by a slower tempo. Her loves lasted five, seven, years, not one or three; they were no longer rockets, but slow-burning fuses with no explosive at the end. She loved more deeply, less passionately, as she became more contemplative. Religion, which hitherto meant little to her, began to puzzle and worry her. Why had she not reflected more? In *Saint Joan of Arc* and *The Eagle and the Dove* she explored the mysteries in which she could not believe, finding at the end of her long enquiries only a greater question mark. To her, nature was the dumb expression of what she could never satisfactorily explain – flowers and cattle, crops and birds – and her poem *The Garden*, a profounder commentary than *The Land*, was her attempt to reconcile the known with the unknowable, probing ever deeper and never reaching the bottom of the well.

This was her secret life, the life of the tower, into which we never attempted to penetrate. Often we would not know the title or subject of her latest book until we saw it advertised, while Harold would discuss his work-in-progress over lunch. More superficially she was very companionable. Occasionally her two worlds overlapped, and we became aware how easily, how deeply, we could wound her by an unconsidered remark. It was Christmas Eve 1933. I was sixteen. I came early to the dining-room, switched on the radio, and listened to the bells of Bethlehem which were being broadcast live by the BBC for the first time. I leant casually against the mantelpiece, munching a banana. My mother came in. 'What's that?' she asked. 'Oh, it's only the bells of Bethlehem,' I replied. It was the word 'only', my stance, the banana, which cumulatively shocked her. How could her son be so indifferent? She rushed out of the room, in tears, and it took an hour for my father to persuade her to return.

Such was the gap between her and us. It had been there since we were babies. When we were at school she dutifully tore herself away from her work to visit us on half-terms at Summer Fields and Eton, and was always sweet to us, but she could not disguise the effort which it cost her to find new subjects to talk about when we had exhausted the garden and the dogs, and she was touchingly different from the other mothers, dressed (as my father once said) in the sort of clothes that Beatrice would have worn had she married Dante, and at a complete loss to keep her end up in their smart society gossip. Later she always took an interest in what was happening to us, and during the war wrote to us very regularly, but her letters were more constrained than those which she wrote to Harold. Her pen had needed pushing, we felt, instead of keeping pace with her thoughts. She was guiltily conscious that she never managed to establish an intimacy with her sons, and thought herself a failure as a mother, but it was as much our fault as hers. We never made the necessary effort to know her well.

With our father it was quite different. I can express our relationship in no better words than those I used in the Introduction to the first volume of his Diaries:

> His attitude ... was one of open enthusiasm for anything that we were doing. He read, for instance, the whole of Aeschylus' *Seven against Thebes* because it was my set-book at school. He hired a boat to visit the islands which I bought in the Outer Hebrides [the Shiant Islands]. He encouraged us to discuss with him anything that amused, interested or worried us. I once wrote to him from Eton about the problem of switching from surname to Christian-name terms with my close friends. He replied from the United States in a six-page letter of advice, the gist of which was to smother the explosive word: 'Don't begin by saying, "James, have you borrowed my Latin dictionary?" Say, "Oh by the way, James, have you borrowed my Latin dictionary?"' This was exactly the sort of problem that delighted him. He always claimed that it was impossible for a father to transmit experience, but in fact he did so, for his advice was always very practical, and by understanding the exact nuances of our dilemmas, he dissipated them.

I do not think that it will unbalance these concluding pages if I quote a complete letter which he wrote to Ben at Eton in 1931, when Ben was seventeen, for Harold has been overshadowed in this book by Vita, just as he overshadowed her in his Diaries, and his whole nature is contained in this letter:

My darling Benzie,

I thought your sonnet excellent – really good. And the absurd thing is that the 'swallow' passage, which you made up yourself, was far the best passage in the whole thing. The rest was a clever imitation and adaptation. But the swallows were observed.

I think that your weakness in writing is not technique but originality. You need not bother about writing well. That comes naturally to you. But you must bother about thinking well. That has not come to you yet. I sometimes wish that you did not agree with Mummy and me so much. Of course, *of course*, we are always right. But a boy of your age should sometimes think us wrong.

It is no use *trying* to be original. That ends by being merely contradictory — and people who are merely contradictory are the worst of all sorts of bore. But you should think things out for yourself. Do not start merely by disagreeing in principle with whatever other people think. They are probably right. But work out slowly, carefully, quietly, you own ideas about everything.

I think in some ways you have an original and courageous mind. You were very good indeed about confirmation and Holy Communion. That was the real Ben. It was not *just* trying to be original: it was a deliberate and perfectly sensible attitude or gesture of thought. Now that you are becoming less bothered about what Hanbury thinks, or Sevelode thinks, or Tiddliumpty thinks, you might begin to be bothered about what Ben thinks.

My darling, I am so glad that you are less bored at Eton and less unhappy. Seek out the things you enjoy and forget the things you hate. You are beginning to realize that your independence is not just because you are a freak, but because you are a person. The same idea is occurring to your contemporaries. Go on being the same, only with a smile on your lips. They may tease you about it, but at the bottom of their hearts they respect you. Being 'odd', being 'different', is a sign of individuality. It exposes you, when a young boy among other young boys, to the jeers of the herd. But the herd is growing older even as you are growing older. They will come to look on you with a 'vague surmise' (or is it 'a wild surmise'?). They will begin to wonder whether after all Nicolson *ma* is not Benedict Nicolson — a person, who in spite of much suffering, has emerged as himself from the crude machinery, the crushing uniformity, of the lower boy ideals. You may find that the stand you have taken, which seemed so odd to them at first, seems to them now a rather courageous thing — a thing far finer than their own subservience to the course of the stream.

I repeat, be nice to the lower boys. I know that this may expose you to misunderstanding, and I do not wish you to flaunt intimacy with the more handsome youths of fourteen. But I beg you, when you see a person as shy and as unhappy as you were yourself, to give him a kind word, a look of understanding. You will answer, 'Daddy doesn't know the conditions at Eton'. I reply, 'Yes, I do.'

They were just the same in my day at Wellington. Human nature doesn't change. And I know that in my case I found that when I got to your position in my house, the opportunity of being kind to little miseries, made up for all the unkindness and cruelty which I had received myself.

Boys are generally insensitive. You are far too sensitive. One act or word of kindness on your part will compensate for all the jeers of the worthless people who have laughed at you in the past. Try it and see. It will give you a warm feeling, in place of that cold sore feeling which you know.

Bless you, my own darling. Your very loving,

H.G.N.

This was the person Harold had become in his maturity. His virtues are self-evident from what has already been said and quoted. His faults were that he had a slight insensitiveness (in spite of what he wrote about lower boys) to people who were not born with his advantages. His dislike of Jews and coloured people, the persistent 'bedint' prejudice, were characteristics which he shared with Vita, and against which Ben and I later reacted. It could also be said that he lacked mettle, which Winston Churchill once defined as the most estimable quality in a man, and he would smooth his path by concessions to a stronger will unless his deepest beliefs or emotions had been aroused by a political event like Munich or Suez, or a personal one like an act of cruelty. I have already mentioned the streak of sentimentality in him, which occasionally distorted his view of people, and its opposite, an acidity which could creep into his judgements. It seems strange that someone of so loving a disposition could cause pain, but there are people who knew him slightly who still think of him as rather formidable, a verdict which would have astonished him. He wanted always to repay, like a debt, the pleasure which he had gained from work and friendship. When he reached the age of fifty, he wrote in his diary:

I have dispersed my energies in life, done too many different things, and have no sense of reaching any harbour. I am still very promising and shall continue to be so until the day of my death. But what enjoyment and what interest I have derived from my experience! I suppose that I am too volatile and fluid, but few people can have extracted such happiness from fluidity, and when I look back upon my life, it is as gay as an Alpine meadow patinated with the stars of varied flowers. Would I feel happier if I had stuck to a single crop of lucerne or clover? No!

He and Vita had long ago reconciled their different temperaments, and they created for themselves a life which suited both perfectly – separation during the week, reunion at weekends. She when alone would garden all day, and write half the night: he in London, first at King's Bench Walk in the Temple, and after the war at Albany, Piccadilly, was busy, social, industrious. He would carry up from Sissinghurst on Monday baskets of flowers, bring down on Friday the London news which still entertained her so long as she was not involved, and in between, every day, they wrote to each other, and each kept all the other's letters. Few marriages can be better documented. What cannot be preserved except in memory is the gentleness of their reunions. They did not 'leap together like two flames', as when Violet returned from Holland, but berthed like sisterships. There was always a certain bustle, the business of unpacking and tea, the tour of the garden and the changing of clothes, but soon they settled down to their easy companionship, allowing words to trickle into the crevices of the other's mind, feeding each other with impressions of what they had read or heard, stimulating, reassuring, teasing by turns – a process which was half solicitous, half provocative, always tender. It was the alternation of excitement and calm in their lives, the 'succession of privacies' as Harold described the charm of Sissinghurst itself, the sense that each was always available to the other though neither would intrude unasked, which made the later years of their marriage so consecrated and serene. When Virginia drowned herself in 1941, Harold came down to Sissinghurst at once to be with Vita, but during the whole of that long evening, Virginia's name was never once mentioned by either of them. In 1960 Vita wrote to him:

> I was always well trained not to manage you. I scarcely dare to arrange the collar of your greatcoat, unless you ask me to. I think

that is really the basis of our marriage, apart from our deep love for each other, for we have never interfered with each other, and strangely enough, never been jealous of each other. And now, in our advancing age, we love each other more deeply than ever, and also more agonizingly, since we see the inevitable end. It is not nice to know that one of us must die before the other.

It was she who died first. In January 1962, at the outset of the last of several winter cruises which they made together, she had an internal haemorrhage, but managed to conceal it from Harold throughout their voyage. On her return she could do so no longer, and underwent an operation which revealed advanced cancer. She barely survived the operation, but regained sufficient strength to return to Sissinghurst in late May. There she died on 2 June 1962.

I ended the last volume of my father's Diaries with Vita's funeral. During his lifetime I did not wish to dwell on his agony. 'Oh Vita, I have wept buckets for you', he wrote three weeks later. And he did, quietly at the dinner-table, clamourously when he thought himself out of earshot in the garden. I was awed by his desolation, giving him the comfort of my familiar presence, but fearing to increase his flow of tears by attempting to staunch them by words of consolation or remembrance. He never recovered from Vita's death. His gaiety gradually subsided into gentle good humour, his intellectual vitality to vague contemplation. He had two strokes in quick succession, which further dulled his mind. He gave up writing, then reading, and became very silent in his last two years. His decline was more painful to us than for him, for I do not think he was aware of it. When the earlier volumes of his Diary became unexpected best-sellers, he remarked to me with a flash of his old humour, 'It's sad to think that of all my forty books, the only ones that will be remembered are the three that I didn't realize I'd written.' But when I gave him the typescript of the third volume, he did not have the interest or energy to glance at more than half-a-dozen pages. Sometimes I would ask him about the past, but his responses became fewer. He told me that he had no wish to live longer, and I believed him.

The end was sudden and merciful. He died at Sissinghurst on 1 May 1968, of a heart attack, as he was undressing for bed.

Index

Ben Elton's television credits include *The Young Ones*, *Blackadder* and *The Thin Blue Line*. He has written three hit West End plays, a film and two musicals, *The Beautiful Game*, with Andrew Lloyd Webber and *We Will Rock You*, with Queen. He is also the author of a string of major bestselling novels, including *Popcorn*, which won the Crime Writers' Association's Golden Dagger Award, *Blast from the Past* and *Inconceivable*.

Ben Elton lives in London with his wife Sophie and their three children.

'Elton again underlines his mastery of plot, structure and dialogue. In stand-up comedy, his other forte, it's all about timing. In writing it's about moving the narrative forward with exciting leaps of imagination and, as before, he seems to have the explosive take-off formula just about right. This literary rocket burns bright'
Sunday Times (Perth)

'The dialogue is as sharp as a razor and the plot as slippery as an eel'
Yorkshire Post

'Ben Elton plucks at the foibles and preoccupations of the insecure '80s with sly humour – and creates a compelling thriller'
She magazine (Australia)

'Riddled with intrigue and steamy, sexual tension, this is a lively thriller of sexual politics and morality, questioning whether people's past relationships should affect their present. Elton's best book yet'
Elle

'This is not a book for squeamish readers; others will relish its pace, its satire, its comic verve. I did'
Canberra Sunday Times

'A witty, observant thriller with some great plot twists'
Sainsbury's magazine

'*Blast from the Past* is a wicked, rip-roaring ride which charts the fine lines separating hilarity from horror; the oily gut of fear from the delicious shiver of anticipation'
West Australian

'As always, Ben Elton is topical to the point of clairvoyancy... Fast, funny and thought-provoking'
The List

Also by Ben Elton

STARK
GRIDLOCK
THIS OTHER EDEN
POPCORN
INCONCEIVABLE
DEAD FAMOUS

Ben Elton

BLAST FROM THE PAST

BLACK SWAN

BLAST FROM THE PAST
A BLACK SWAN BOOK : 0 552 99833 8

Originally published in Great Britain by Bantam Press,
a division of Transworld Publishers

PRINTING HISTORY
Bantam Press edition published 1998
Black Swan edition published 1999

10

Set in 11/14 pt Sabon by
Falcon Oast Graphic Art.

Black Swan Books are published by Transworld Publishers,
61–63 Uxbridge Road, London W5 5SA,
a division of The Random House Group Ltd,
in Australia by Random House Australia (Pty) Ltd,
20 Alfred Street, Milsons Point, Sydney, NSW 2061, Australia,
in New Zealand by Random House New Zealand Ltd,
18 Poland Road, Glenfield, Auckland 10, New Zealand
and in South Africa by Random House (Pty) Ltd,
Endulini, 5a Jubilee Road, Parktown 2193, South Africa.

Printed and bound in Great Britain by
Clays Ltd, St Ives plc.

For Sophie

1 ★

It was 2.15 in the morning when the telephone rang. Polly woke instantly. Her eyes were wide and her body tense before the phone had completed so much as a single ring. And as she woke, in the tiny moment between sleep and consciousness, before she was even aware of the telephone's bell, she felt scared. It was not the phone that jolted Polly so completely from her dreams, but fear.

And who could argue with the reasoning powers of Polly's subconscious self? Of course she was scared. After all, when the phone rings at 2.15 in the morning it's unlikely to be heralding something pleasant. What chance is there of its being good news? None. Only someone bad would ring at such an hour. Or someone good with bad news.

That telephone was sounding a warning bell. Something, somewhere, was wrong. So much was obvious. Particularly to a woman who lived alone, and Polly lived alone.

Of course it might be no more wrong than a wrong number. Something bad, but bad for someone else, something that would touch Polly's life only for a moment, utterly infuriate her and then be gone.

'Got the Charlie?'

'There's no Charlie at this number.'

'Don't bullshit me, arsehole.'

'What number are you trying to call? This is three, four, zero, one . . .'

'Three, four, zero? I'm awfully sorry. I think I've dialled the wrong number.'

That would be a good result. A wrong number would be the best possible result. To find yourself returning to bed furiously muttering, 'Stupid bastard,' while trying to pretend to yourself that you haven't actually woken up; that would be a good result. Polly hoped the warning bell was meant for someone else.

If your phone rings at 2.15 a.m. you'd better hope that too. Because if someone actually wants you you're in trouble.

If it's your mother she's going to tell you your dad died.

If it's some much-missed ex-lover who you'd been hoping would get back in contact he'll be calling drunkenly to inform you that he's just been diagnosed positive and that perhaps you'd better have things checked out.

The only time that bell might ring for something good is if you were actually expecting some news, news so important it might come at any time. If you have a relative in the throes of a difficult pregnancy, for instance, or a friend who's on the verge of being released from a foreign hostage situation. Then a person might leap from bed thinking, 'At last! They've induced it!' or, 'God bless the Foreign Office. He's free!' On the other hand, maybe the mother and baby didn't make it. Maybe the hostage got shot.

There is no doubt about it that under almost all normal circumstances a call in the middle of the night had to be bad. If not bad, at least weird, and, in a way, weird is worse. This is the reason why, when the phone rang in Polly's little attic flat at 2.15 a.m. and wrenched her from the womb of sleep, she felt scared.

Strange to be scared of a phone. Even if it's ringing. What can a ringing phone do to you? Leap up and bash you with its receiver? Strangle you with its cord? Nothing. Just ring, that's all.

Until you answer it.

Then, of course, it might ask you in a low growl if you're wearing any knickers. If you like them big and hard. If you've been a very naughty girl. Or it might say . . .

'I know where you live.'

That was how it had all begun before.

'I'm watching you right now,' the phone had hissed. 'Standing there in only your nightdress. I'm going to tear it off you and make you pay for all the hurt you've done to me.'

At the time Polly's friends had assured her that the man was lying. He had not been watching her. Pervert callers phone at random. They don't know where their victims live.

'He knew I was wearing my nightie,' Polly had said.

11

BEN ELTON

'He got that right. How did he know that? How did he know I was wearing my nightie?'

'It was the middle of the night, for heaven's sake!' her friends replied. 'Got to be a pretty good chance you were wearing a nightie, hasn't there? Even a fool of a pervert could work that one out. He doesn't know where you live.'

But Polly's friends had been wrong. The caller did know where Polly lived. He knew a lot about her because he was not a random pervert at all, but a most specific pervert. A stalker. That first call had been the start of a campaign of intimidation that had transformed Polly's life into a living hell. A hell from which the law had been unable to offer any protection.

'Our hands are tied, Ms Slade. There's nothing actually illegal about making phonecalls, writing letters or ringing people's doorbells.'

'Terrific,' said Polly. 'So I'll get back to you when I've been raped and murdered, then, shall I?'

The police assured her that it hardly ever came to that.

2

He'd been a client of hers. At the council office where she worked, the office that dealt with equal opportunities and discrimination. His was one of those depressing modern cases where sad white men who have failed to be promoted claim reverse discrimination, saying that they have been passed over for advancement in favour of less well qualified black lesbians. The problem is, of course, that often they are right: they have been passed over in favour of less well qualified black lesbians, that being the whole point of the policy. To positively discriminate in favour of groups that have been negatively discriminated against in the past.

'But now I'm being negatively discriminated against,' the sad white men inevitably reply.

'Specifically, yes,' the officers of the Office of Equal Opportunity (of whom Polly was one) would attempt to explain. 'But not in general. Generally speaking, you are a member of a disproportionately successful group. There are any number of sad white men who achieve promotion. It's merely that you are not one of them. You're being negatively discriminated against positively, and you'll feel the benefits in a more socially cohesive society.'

Not surprisingly, this argument was never much of a comfort, but Polly's failure to help her client did not cause the man to do as so many disappointed clients had done before him and dump the entire weight of his confusion and impotent anger on top of Polly's innocent head. He had not called Polly a communist slut and stormed out of her office. He had not threatened to bring death and pestilence upon her. He had not promised to starve himself to death on the steps of the town hall until he got justice.

If only the man had behaved like that. How much better it would have been for Polly. Instead, he had become infatuated with her.

At first she had not been unduly alarmed. He sent one or two cards to her office and one day, on discovering that it was her birthday, he went out and returned with a single rose. On their final consultation he had given Polly a secondhand book, an anthology of post-war poetry, rather a tastefully chosen selection, Polly thought. He'd inscribed the book, 'To dearest Polly. Beautiful words for a beautiful person.' Polly had not much liked that, but since the gift could not have cost more than a pound or two she had felt it would be more trouble to refuse it than accept. Particularly considering that it was, she thought, to be the last time they would meet.

But the following evening the man knocked on the door of the house where she lived and greeted her as if he was a friend.

'Hi, Polly,' he said. 'Just thought I'd drop round and see what you thought of the book. Hope it's not inconvenient. I mean, if it is, just say.'

Of course, Polly knew then that she had a problem. She just did not know how big. 'Well, yes, it is inconvenient, actually, besides which . . .'

'Don't worry, don't worry at all. How about later? Maybe we could have a drink?'

'No, Peter,' she said. Peter was the man's name. 'That's not a good idea at all. Now I don't know how you got my home address, but you mustn't come here again. What you've got to understand is that we have a professional relationship. It's not at all acceptable for you to try to enter my private life.'

'Oh dear.' Peter looked surprised. 'Sorry.' And he turned and scurried off.

Five minutes later he was back.

The change in the man was shocking. His face seemed to have been physically transformed. The muscles and the contours appeared to do different things, point in different directions. He still looked pathetic but now he also looked demonic.

'And what you've got to understand, Polly, is that you can't just be fucking friends when *you* want to! All right? You can't just fucking use me – talk to me at the office and then refuse to speak when I call.'

Now Polly knew who had been phoning her. The tone, the voice, they were unmistakable. Polly wondered how she'd failed to notice it before, but then he'd always been so mild to her face.

He was mild to her face no longer.

'You can't just take my fucking presents and then think you can make all the rules! A relationship cuts two ways, you know!'

That was the thing. The terrible, terrible thing. Right from the very beginning Peter had thought he and Polly had a relationship. His anger at her rejection was the vicious, righteous anger of one who felt betrayed. Peter had invested so much in his fantasies of Polly that it was impossible for him to believe that his feelings were not in some way reciprocated. Everything Peter did he did with Polly in mind, and in his unbalanced state he had come to believe that despite her denials Polly was equally conscious of him.

'*Dear Polly*,' he would write, '*I watched you at the bus stop. Thank you for wearing that blue jumper. I was so thrilled to think that you had remembered I liked it.*'

And Polly would rack her brains and remember the time back in her old life, when Peter had been just another sad case, when he had remarked on how much he liked the top she had been wearing.

The appalling thing was that after only a short period of harassment Polly did of course have a kind of relationship with Peter. Everything *she* did she did with Peter in mind. Thus the stalker feeds his need, becoming central in the life of someone who should be a stranger to him. For the victim – Polly – it was like being in love, except the emotion she felt was hate. Like a besotted lover, she thought about her torment the whole time. Of course to Peter this was only right. For he was giving everything – his time, his passion, his every living breath – so why should not the person he loved give something back? Surely a true and deep love is worth that at least?

Eventually Peter got his wish. He and Polly were brought together, if only in court. Bringing matters to such a pass had not been an easy process for Polly. Naturally the law had been as concerned for Peter's rights as it had been for hers and, as the police had pointed out, you cannot prosecute people for being annoying and rude. The law at the time did not even recognize stalking as a crime.

Neither did it recognize the fact that Polly was being driven mad.

It was not, it seemed, illegal for Peter to repeatedly write to Polly expressing his wish that she would get AIDS (which was all a bitch like her deserved). It was not illegal for him to stand outside her house and stare up at her window until late into the night. It was not even illegal for him to ring her front doorbell in the small hours of the morning. Polly's distress was in fact almost irrelevant to the courts. What they wanted to know – what Polly was required to show – was that Peter's actions had dealt her *material harm*. Money, it seemed, was the bottom line. The law required Polly to establish that Peter's activities had left her out of pocket. Had the mental torment she was suffering rendered her unfit to work? Could she demonstrate that Peter was preventing her from making a living?

If she could, the law would be in a position to act; otherwise she would simply have to learn to live with her problem.

Polly produced her doctor's letter, her employer's testimonial, the diary of harassment the police had advised her to keep. She told of her sleepless nights, her clouded days, the tears and the anger that blighted her life.

Across the courtroom Peter luxuriated in every detail, thrilled, finally, to have proof that she was as obsessed with him as he was with her.

When it ended Polly had won a victory of sorts. The judge granted her an injunction. Peter was to neither approach nor contact Polly for an indefinite period, and should he try to do so he risked a custodial sentence. It did not stop him completely, but after further warnings from the police his hysterical intrusions on Polly's life slowly began to diminish and for Polly life started to resemble something like a nervous normality.

He was still with her, of course. She felt he always would be. She still glanced up and down the street when she left the house in the morning, still checked in the communal hallway when she got home at night. Still wondered as she had always wondered whether one day he would try to stick a knife into her for betraying his love.

'Actually, I don't think he would ever have turned violent,' Polly would say to her friends.

'No, definitely not,' they would reassure her.

'Actually I read that those type of people almost never do.'

But she always wondered.

And now, three months since he had last surfaced, it was 2.15 in the morning and Polly's phone was ringing.

3

On the previous evening, as the dark clouds had gathered over the grim hangars of RAF Brize Norton and an invisible sun had set behind them, a small party of military men (plus one or two civil servants) assembled in the grizzly, drizzly gloom. They were awaiting the arrival of an American plane.

Inside that plane, suspended high over England, sat a very senior American army officer, deep in thought. So preoccupied was the general that he had scarcely uttered a word in the five hours since his plane had left Washington. The general's staff imagined that he was considering the meeting that lay before him. They imagined that the general had been wrestling with the delicate problems of NATO, the ex-Soviet states and the New World Order. After all, it was to debate such weighty issues that they had crossed the Atlantic. In fact, had the general's staff been mindreaders, they would have been surprised to discover that their commander was thinking about nothing more momentously geopolitical than a young woman he had once known; scarcely a woman – almost a girl, in fact, a girl of seventeen.

Back on the ground the British coughed and stamped and longed for the bar. There were always mixed emotions involved for British officers when dealing with their American cousins. It was a thrill, of course. The undeniable thrill of being on nodding terms with such unimaginable power. Most of the officers standing waiting, shuffling their feet on the tarmac at Brize Norton, thought themselves lucky if they got the occasional use of a staff car. Their professional lives were couched in terms such as 'limited response', 'tactical objective' and 'rapid deployment'. When they described themselves and their martial capability they spoke of 'an élite force', a 'highly skilled, professional army'. Everybody knew, of course, that these phrases were euphemisms for 'not much money', 'not many soldiers'.

The Americans, on the other hand, measured their budgets in trillions.

'Can you believe that, old chap? *Trillions* of dollars. Makes you weep.'

Their ships were like cities, their aeroplanes not only invincible but also apparently invisible. They had bombs and missiles capable of destroying the planet not once but many times over. Traditionally within the scope of human imagination only gods had wielded such mighty influence on the affairs of men. Now men themselves had the capacity, or at least some men, men from the Pentagon.

There was no denying that to other soldiers, soldiers of lesser armies such as the British who stood waiting

21

on the cold, damp tarmac, such power was attractive. It was sexy and compelling. It was fun to be around. Fun to tell the fellows about.

'I read somewhere they were developing ray guns.'

'Bloody hell!'

But alongside the sheepish admiration there was also jealousy. A deep, gnawing, cancerous jealousy born of grotesque inequality. The difference in scale between the American armed forces and those of its principal and most historic ally are so great as to render Britain's military contribution to the alliance an irrelevance. In truth, Britain's role is nothing more than to add a spurious legitimacy of international consensus to US foreign policy. That is why Britain has a special relationship. That is why Britain is special and why the Americans let it remain special. They certainly can't trust the French.

The general's plane was beginning its descent. Looking out of the window, he could just make out the fields below. Grey now, nearly black. Not green and gold as he liked to remember them, as indeed they had been on that fabulous summer's day half an army life-time ago. Before he'd blown his chance of happiness for ever.

He took from his pocket a letter he had been writing to his brother Harry. He often wrote to Harry. The general was a lonely man in a lonely job and he had few people in whom he could confide. Over the years he had got into the habit of using his brother as a kind of confessional, the only person to whom he showed anything like the whole of his self. His brother sometimes wished that he would unload his woes onto someone else. He always knew when he saw an airmail letter in his mailbox that somewhere in the world his celebrated and important brother was tormented about something.

'The little shit never writes to say he's happy,' Harry would mutter as he slipped a knife into the envelope. 'Like I care about his problems.' Although of course Harry did care; that's what families are for.

As the plane began slowly to drop towards England and its undercarriage emerged, rumbling and shaking from its belly, noisily pushing its way into the gathering night, the general took up his pen. Contrary to all accepted safety practices, he also lowered the tray table in front of him and laid the unfinished letter out before him.

'*Olde England is outside of the window now, Harry,*' he wrote. '*Funny, me returning this way. Back in those sunny, glory days when I was last in this country, all I could think about was becoming a general. All I wanted was my own army. Now I'm a general, a great big general, the biggest fucking general in the European Theatre. Strange then that all I can think about is those sunny, glory days. And her. I'll bet you're laughing.*'

General Kent paused, then put down his pen and tore the letter into pieces. He had never lied to Harry and he did not wish to start now. Not that anything he had written was untrue. Quite the opposite. His thoughts were indeed filled with memories of halcyon days long gone and the girl with whom he had shared them, and he was certainly cursing the army that had torn them apart. But that was only half the story of what was on General Kent's mind, and Harry would see that immediately. With Harry, omission was tantamount to deceit. Harry would know that his brother was holding out on him, as he always did. Harry had known that Jack wanted to be a soldier even before Jack had known it himself. It had been Harry who had broken the news to their parents after Jack had chickened out and left home without a word. Christ, what a scene that must have been.

The general stuffed the torn pieces of his letter into the ashtray that was no longer allowed to be an ashtray and returned to staring out of the window.

Down below, the chilly Brits were assuring each other that, despite its undisputed position of global dominance, the American army was not what one would call a proper army.

'They're either screaming abuse at each other, singing silly spirituals or bonding in a big hug. I mean really, I ask you, what a way to run a show.'

The Brits all agreed that, despite having more fire power than Satan and more influence than the God in whom they trusted, the armed forces of the United States were not what one would call a formidable fighting machine. No, no, the damp, miserable, khaki-clad figures felt, much better to be lean. Lean and hungry, like the British forces. Much better to be under-funded, undermanned and undervalued, like they were.

That was character-building. That was what made a soldier a soldier.

'They can't even get the uniforms right,' the jealous Brits assured each other. 'They seem to be dressed either as hell's angels in leather jackets and sunglasses or as Italian lift attendants with more brass and braid than a colliery band.'

Everybody agreed that it was a shocking state of affairs, but in truth there was not a man amongst them, itching in his damp khaki blouse, who would not have dearly loved to swap places and be dressed half as stylishly as the Americans.

A far-off noise in the gloomy sky announced the imminent arrival of the loved and hated allies.

'On time, at least,' remarked the senior British officer in his best patronizing drawl. 'Thankful for small mercies, eh?'

It started to rain.

'Look at them,' said the general, staring out of the drizzle-dotted window as his plane taxied towards the little RAF terminal and the forlorn-looking British reception committee. 'Nothing ever changes in the British army, you know that? They're actually proud of it.'

One of the crew handed the general his coat.

'They always look the same. Down at heel but defiant. Like they just got off the boat from Dunkirk. The worst thing about being a great power is when you're not one any more. It takes centuries to get over it. Look at the Portuguese. They just gave up altogether.'

'Sir! Yes, sir!' said the young airman, not having the faintest idea what the general was talking about.

Jack turned to General Schultz, his chief of staff, who was sitting respectfully two seats behind, playing on a gameboy.

'Let's make this piece of bullshit as quick a piece of bullshit as any bull ever shitted. OK?'

4 ★

Polly turned on her bedside lamp and felt her irises scream in protest at the sudden light.

The phone was on her desk, on the other side of the room. Polly had put it there so that if ever she booked an alarm call she would have to get up in order to answer it. It was too easy to just reach out from under the duvet and clunk the receiver up and down in its cradle. Polly had missed trains that way. You didn't wake up, your dreams just changed gear.

The phone rang again. Somehow it seemed to be getting louder.

Through Polly's watery eyes the room looked strange. The phone, her desk, the crumpled shape on the floor that was her jeans, everything looked different. It wasn't, of course, just as the phone wasn't getting any louder. Everything was exactly the same as it had been when she'd gone to sleep the previous evening.

The phone kept ringing.

Polly got out of bed and padded across the room towards it. Across almost her entire home, in fact. Polly's landlord claimed that Polly lived in a studio-style maisonette and had set the rent accordingly. Polly thought she lived in a bedsit and that she was being ripped off.

The phone was set to ring six times before the answerphone kicked in. Polly watched the machine as it completed its cycle.

She was more angry than scared.

Very angry, terribly angry. Anger had seized hold of her whole body, which was the one thing she knew she must not let it do if she wished to get back to sleep before dawn. In vain she struggled to regain control of herself, but it was too late. The anger had released its chemicals and they were surging through her nervous system like a drug, making her muscles twitch, her stomach squirm and her heart expand like a balloon against her ribs. An anger so powerful because it was born of fear.

The Bug was back. Great holy shit, hadn't the bastard had enough?

'The Bug' was what Polly called Peter. She had given him that title in an effort to depersonalize him. To resist the relationship that was growing between them. Polly had realized from the beginning, as every victim of an obsessive does, that the more she knew about her tormentor the more difficult it became to remember that he had absolutely nothing to do with her. Every extra detail that she accumulated of the man's hated existence clouded the basic fact that he had absolutely no business in her life at all. He was a stranger, an aggressive stranger of course, but that did not mean she had to get to know him.

Even when the whole ghastly business became a matter for the police and solicitors, Polly had strenuously avoided sharing in the information that was unearthed about her foe. She did not want to know what he was like or where he came from. She did not want to know if he had a job or friends. She had learnt the bitter lesson that the more she knew about this man the more there was for her to think about, and the more she thought about him the greater was her sense of violation.

Which was why Peter had become the Bug. A bug is a thing that annoys you. It buzzes into your life and is difficult to get rid of, but it can't hurt you or kill you; all it can do is buzz. A bug is also a minor virus, a thing you accidentally pick up, like a cold or the flu. It could happen to anybody. If you catch one you're just unlucky, that's all. It has nothing to do with you.

Above all, it is not your fault.

A bug is something that you shake off. That you determine will not ruin your day and if you cannot shake it off you accept your misfortune philosophically and cope the best you can. You do not become obsessed with a bug. It does not cloud your thoughts and bleed an undercurrent of tension and unhappiness through your every waking moment.

A bug cannot own you.

The 'thing' that was Peter was not a friend or an enemy, or an acquaintance, or even a man. He was a bug and only a fool rails and rants and weeps over a bug; only a fool feeds its malignant symptoms with their anger and hurt.

Polly stood waiting for her answerphone message to start and struggled to control her fury.

She scarcely even noticed that she had begun to cry.

5

General Schultz, General Kent's chief of staff, was not a very good hustler and there followed what seemed to be an interminable period of introductions and hand-shaking as the British and American parties greeted each other on the tarmac. Eventually, just when Kent was beginning to suspect that he would be expected to bond even with the man who waved the ping-pong bats, he found himself sitting alongside the senior British officer in the first of a convoy of army staff cars heading for London.

Kent was silent, preoccupied, deep in thought. Despite this, however, his host felt obliged to make some effort at conversation.

'I had the privilege of serving under a colleague of yours,' the senior British officer said. 'During the Gulf War. I was seconded to the staff of General Schwarzkopf. Your famous Stormin' Norman.'

Kent did not reply.

'Splendid name, don't you think?' Actually the senior British officer thought it an absolutely pathetic name. He despised the way Americans felt the need to attach silly macho schoolboy nicknames to their leaders. 'Iron' this, 'Hell bugger' that; it was bloody childish.

General Kent knew exactly what his host was think-ing and in his turn thought it was pathetic the way the British compensated for their massive inferiority complex by forever sneering at the Yanks. There had once been a time when British soldiers were equally world famous and equally popularly revered, 'Fighting Bobs Roberts' of the Boer War, the 'Iron Duke' of Wellington himself, but that had been in another century, when . . . General Kent stopped his train of thought. He did not wish to be pondering the inanity of his companion's comments. He wished to be left alone to concentrate on his own deep and tormented feelings. To dwell once more upon the summer of his love.

What would she be like? Would she remember? Of course she would remember. She would have to be dead to have forgotten, and he knew she wasn't dead.

'Not your first trip to Britain, I imagine.' Once more the senior British officer's voice crashed into Kent's thoughts. The man was not giving up. He had been instructed to make the American feel welcome and by hell he was going to make him feel welcome even if that also meant annoying him utterly.

'I said, not your first trip to Britain, I imagine . . .' he repeated loudly. 'Been here before, I suppose.'

He had blundered into General Kent's very train of thought. General Kent had been in Britain before and it had changed his life for ever.

'Yeah,' Kent acknowledged at last. 'I was here

before.' But his tone suggested that he did not wish to elaborate.

'I see. I see. Here before, you say? Well, I never. Splendid. Splendid.'

Another few cold, dark miles slid by outside the windows of the car.

'Plenty of friends this side of the pond, then, I imagine. People to look up and all that. Old pals to visit?'

Again the Englishman had got it right. There certainly was an old pal to visit, but General Kent did not choose to discuss it. He had never once in over sixteen years discussed the one love of his life with anyone apart from his brother Harry, not a soul, not ever and he certainly did not intend to start now. After this the British officer gave up and the conversation, such as it was, lapsed completely until the Englishman delivered his American through the gates of Downing Street.

'Well, goodbye, General. It's been a privilege and a pleasure to meet you,' said the senior British officer.

'Yes, it's been very real,' replied General Kent. 'Thank you so much for the trouble you've taken.'

'Not at all. Goodbye, then.'

'Goodbye.'

The two soldiers shook hands and parted.

'Surly bastard,' thought the senior British officer.

'Pompous creep,' thought General Kent.

Kent stood outside the famous front door for as long as he dared, breathing in the cold night air, attempting to marshal his thoughts. He must pull himself together.

He had an important meeting ahead of him. It was his job to brief the British on White House plans for the eastward expansion of NATO. He needed to be thinking about Poland and the Czech Republic, not about making love in a sundrenched field to a seventeen-year-old girl. He stamped his feet; he must concentrate! It was time to put away the past and think about the present. The past could wait. After all, it had waited these many long years; it could stand another few hours.

'General?'

Kent's party had now all assembled on the pavement and were awaiting their commander's lead. A bobby was standing expectantly, ready to open the door.

'OK, let's do it,' Kent said and led his officers across the familiar threshold.

6

Polly was smiling.

Polly was frowning.

She was yawning. She was walking. She was standing.

She was walking to her bus stop. She was standing at her bus stop. She was walking away from her bus stop. She was standing at her front door searching for her key.

A hundred tiny, near-identical moments from Polly's life, frozen in time, developed, printed and stuck on Peter's wall.

'Well, I don't see as how it can do any great harm really,' Peter's mother would say, more for her own comfort than that of the next-door neighbour with whom she would share the occasional pot of tea. 'Lots of boys have pictures of their favourite women on their bedroom walls. Pamela Anderson or *Playboy* girls, stuff like that. In fact, I think Peter's more normal than those other boys because at least he's gone all funny over a real woman. Not just some fantasy figure.'

Peter had taken the pictures in defiance of the court injunction against him.

He had not begun to lose interest over the previous three months as Polly had been hoping. Quite the opposite. He had acquired a different car from the one known to the police and he would park it in Polly's street at about seven in the morning. There he would wait, hiding behind a copy of the *Daily Mirror* until he could watch and photograph Polly beginning her journey to work. Once she had boarded her bus he would start up his car and follow it until it got into the local high street, where Polly got off. Peter could not take any photographs at this end of her journey because there was too much traffic and too many people, and it was a red route, anyway, so he couldn't stop his car.

Once when Polly got off the bus Peter saw her throw a sucked-out Just Juice box into a dustbin.

Of course, he had to have that box, even if it meant getting a ticket. He put on his hazard lights, pulled over and pushed his way across the crowded pavement towards the rubbish basket. When he got there a homeless person was already inspecting the contents of the bin in the hope of finding something to eat or read. The homeless person was not interested in Peter's box. Fortunately for him.

Sometimes before he went to sleep Peter caressed the box, putting his fingers where hers had been in that moment when she had squeezed it and crushed it up. He imagined her delicate fingers squeezing and crushing at him in the same way.

Then he would put his lips to the little bent straw and gently suck at it.

'I think she's still on his mind a bit,' Peter's mother would tell her friend, 'but he's not made contact, not since, not since . . .' Peter's court appearance remained a painful memory for his mother. Whenever she thought of it she became angry. Angry with Polly.

'That bitch. She didn't need to tell the police, did she? She could have come to me, talked to me. I could have stopped him. And anyway, what harm was he doing? He loved her, didn't he? It's not as if she had anything to be afraid of.'

In fact, Peter's mother knew very well that from the tone of Peter's letters and messages Polly had had every reason to be afraid of him. He had never actually threatened her directly but the things he said about her and wished upon her would have scared anyone. Peter's mother had rationalized this. She reasoned that if the Bitch had only been pleasant – just said hello to her son and smiled occasionally, perhaps replied to one or two of his letters – then he would not have become upset. Peter's mother felt, as Peter did himself, that devotion such as Peter's deserved some sort of reward. After all, it isn't every girl who's worshipped the way Peter worshipped Polly.

'He brought her presents. Flowers and CDs. She never said thank you, not once. Not so much as an acknowledgement. Well, of course he was hurt. Of course he was upset. I don't blame him. I nearly wrote to the Bitch myself.'

As far as the Bug's mother was concerned, Polly wasn't Polly any more. She was 'that woman' or, when she felt particularly distressed, 'the Bitch'.

'Anyway. He's promised me he'll let it go now, stop approaching her and all that. Well, he has to. Otherwise it's prison, and what would I do then? It's her loss, anyway. She doesn't deserve a boy like my Peter.'

But Peter could not let it go. How could he? You can't just let love go. Love is something beyond a person's control. You don't ask it to come and and you can't make it leave. Only iron discipline can control an obsession, and Peter had none.

Even as his mother spoke Peter was at his computer. Inside his computer, like the bug he was. It was exciting to reach out to her through the silence of cyberspace. He was banned from e-mailing Polly, but that didn't stop him making a connection. A palpable physical connection. His fingers touched the keyboard, the keyboard touched the modem, the modem touched the Telecom network, the network touched Polly's phone, and so he touched her!

He could hack into her.

He had read her Sainsbury's loyalty card account. He knew that she had bought most of her furniture at IKEA; he even knew the styles and colours she'd chosen. Likewise he knew the brand of abdominizing exerciser that she'd ordered in an insane moment of optimistic piety from the back of a colour supplement. He imagined her rolling back and forth upon it in a leotard, though he'd got that wrong; she'd never even assembled it. He even knew her ex-directory telephone number. Sitting in his bedroom reading Polly's Telecom account on his computer screen had felt so good. It was a little invasion of her privacy, a violation of her secrets. Finding out the things she did not want him to know.

Peter's mother sometimes opined that Peter seemed to love that computer more than he loved the Bitch. She did not understand that to Peter his computer was an extension of Polly, a means of penetrating her.

7

General Kent's meeting had long since finished and he was alone, sitting at the wheel of a car parked in a small residential street in the Stoke Newington area of London. The car was unmarked, there were no military or diplomatic plates, no official driver, no bodyguard. Just Jack and the girl on his mind.

On Kent's lap was a file marked, 'General Kent: For sight of. Secure file. Absolute discretion required. No non-authorized viewing whatsoever'.

A few years before, it would have simply said, 'General Kent: Private'. Kent reflected that military industrial complex bullshit was now expanding at such a rate that soon there would be no room on a file for the description of what was in it and they would have to attach extensions to the cover.

The contents of the file were biographical. Details about the life and current circumstances of a thirty-four-year-old Englishwoman: Polly Slade. There were photographs too, old ones and new. The new ones were very similar to those that had been taken by the Bug. Polly walking, Polly standing, Polly at the bus stop, etc. The pictures in the file were rather better than the Bug's blurry efforts, having been taken by professionals, but they were no more revealing. Just a woman in a street. That was all. Of course the Bug did not know of the general's photographs and the general did not know of the Bug's. How astonished they would have been to find out the other's existence. After all, the chances of the same woman being covertly photographed at the same time and in the same place by two completely separate and unconnected people must be millions to one. But that is what had happened.

General Kent looked at the face in the pictures. Such a nice face. A little careworn, perhaps, but very pretty. Not everyone would have thought the woman beautiful, but General Kent did, ravishingly so.

The file also contained a telephone number.

Kent carried a mobile phone, but this he left in his pocket. Instead he took up the little stock of ten-pence coins that his security contact had furnished him with and got out of the car. Nearby was a public phonebox. Not one of the solid red ones that Jack remembered, but a phonebox none the less, not merely a phone in a hood on a pole.

It was very late and the street was quiet. Empty almost, save for one other man, a nervous-looking fellow loitering further up the street. The other man appeared to have been making for the phonebox himself, but when he saw Kent he stopped.

Kent wondered whether the man had been planning to call one of the extraordinary number of girls who advertised their sexual services on little cards inside the phonebox. Judging by the pictures on the cards, some of the most impossibly glamorous and attractive women in Britain were advertising cheap fucks in Stoke Newington. Kent suspected that if the fellow ever did pluck up courage to call he would be disappointed.

He pushed twenty pence into the machine and dialled. It was 2.15 a.m.

8

The phone was on its fifth ring. After the next one Polly's answerphone would start. She sat on the floor and assumed the lotus position. When the Bug spoke she wanted to be ready.

Polly's yoga teacher, a Yorkshireman called Stanley, had said that yoga was the process whereby the superior, conscious element in a person was freed from involvement with the inferior material world. A tough trick to pull when you're being stalked in the small hours of the morning, but Polly was determined to give it a go. And so she sat, as the answerphone began to clunk, her feet crossed, her knees spread like a wing nut, her elbows on her knees and her fingers and thumbs set in the required position.

She was calm, she was at ease, she was relaxed.

Her bottom was freezing.

The problem was her nightie. It was an old shirt of her father's, and was too short for the situation; it did not properly cover her backside from the cold floorboards on which she sat. She did not wish to break position at this crucial moment of calm; on the other hand the whole point was to be comfortable, and a cold bum was not comfortable. Besides which, some ancient memory was whispering to her that this was the best way of getting piles. It was no good, she would have to move onto the rug. While remaining absolutely calm, at one with herself and in the lotus position, Polly shuffled over to the rug using only her buttock muscles to motivate her.

'Hello,' said Polly's voice as Polly shuffled. 'Nobody's answering at the moment, but please leave a message after the tone. Thank you.'

A defiantly unfunny and matter-of-fact message. Polly's days of using music, cracking gags and pretending to be the Lithuanian Embassy had ended the day that the Bug had first discovered her phone number. During the worst period of harassment she had got a male friend to record her outgoing message, but this had just made genuine callers think they had the wrong number.

There was no incoming message.

The caller hung up and the answerphone clicked and clunked accordingly. Furious, Polly leapt up from her lotus position (an effort which nearly broke both her ankles), grabbed the phone off its cradle and shouted, 'Fuck off!' at the dialling tone. Stanley would not have been pleased.

'Now, d'you think 'indu philosophers'd go abaht 'ollering "Fook off!" into't pho-an?' he would have enquired. 'No fookin' way.'

Polly struggled to prevent her blood from boiling. Calm was required. Calm. She had work in the morning.

Perhaps it had been a wrong number after all.

Perhaps the drug baron on the other end of the line had heard Polly's voice on the machine, realized his mistake and had gone on to deliver his threats elsewhere.

Inside the phonebox Jack put down the phone. He had been expecting her to answer personally; he hadn't prepared himself for an answerphone. She couldn't be out. He'd specifically had that checked. She must be screening her calls. Or else she had become a heavy sleeper over the years.

A little further up the street Peter was watching Jack. For a moment he thought that the man must have finished his calls but then, to Peter's fury, the man picked up the phone a second time.

Polly was just about to return to bed when the phone rang again. This time she didn't bother with the lotus position; she just stood in the middle of her room, shaking with anger and fear, and waited.

'Hello,' said Polly's voice again. 'Nobody's answering at the moment, but please leave a message after the tone. Thank you.'

This time the machine did not clunk to a halt. Polly could hear the faint electric hiss of an open but silent line. He was there but he wasn't speaking. Standing there, alone in the night, Polly watched the phone like it was a hissing snake. Like it was going to pounce. She itched to grab up the receiver again and scream further

45

obscenities, but she knew that she mustn't. If there was one sure way to give the Bug satisfaction it was to share her emotions with him. Do that, shout at him, let him hear your fear and he would be nursing an erection for a week.

'Polly?'

It wasn't the Bug. She knew that within those first two syllables.

'Polly. Are you there?'

Within four words she knew who it was.

'Are you there, Polly?'

It was the last voice in the world that she had expected to hear.

'Listen, don't freak out,' said General Kent. 'It's Jack, Jack Kent.'

9

Jack and Polly had met many years before, in a roadside restaurant on the A34 near Newbury. Jack was a captain, serving with the American forces in Britain. Those were the days when the Cold War was still hot, which was more than could be said for most of the food in the restaurant. The moment he'd walked in, Jack had regretted his decision to stop off for a cup of coffee, and as he brushed the crumbs from the orange plastic seat he very nearly turned around and walked straight out again. His uniform had already attracted attention, however, and he did not wish to appear foolish. He was, after all, an ambassador for his country.

Jack cleared a space for his newspaper amongst the debris left by the previous occupants of his table. There was an election on, not that he cared much about British politics. Mrs Thatcher was in the process of pulverizing some whitehaired old boy in a donkey jacket. It didn't look like a very equal contest to Jack; he'd been under the impression that the Brits believed in fair fight.

A hormonally imbalanced teenaged lad approached Jack's table and offered him a menu.

'Just coffee, please,' Jack said.

'Coffee,' the lad repeated, and Jack knew immediately that he would not be brought coffee. He would be brought that beverage the British chose to call coffee but which the rest of the world recognized as the urine of the devil's dog. This dark and bitter brew would be accompanied by a small, sealed plastic pot of white liquid marked 'UHT Cream', which Jack knew to have been squeezed straight from the colon of a sick seagull.

Jack took in his surroundings. Great Christ, what hellish imagination had conceived of such places? These 'Little Shits' and 'Crappy Cooks' and 'Happy Pukers'? These pale imitations of another, more vibrant culture plucked from the highways and byways of America and dumped down, dowdy and deflated, upon the A roads of Britain? In the three years that Jack had been in the United Kingdom he had viewed the inexorable advance of these gastronomic ghettos with increasing alarm. They were everywhere. Every turn in the road seemed to reveal another ghastly vision of red, yellow and orange identikit architecture plus a huge plastic elephant for the kiddies. Any day now Jack expected to find one of these cheery hellholes installed at the gates of his base, possibly even outside his office door.

Jack's 'coffee' arrived, about half of it still in the cup, the rest in the saucer, lapping around the grimy thumb of Jack's server.

'One coffee,' the server said. 'Enjoy your meal.'

The fact that Jack was clearly not having a meal was

of no concern to this boy, whose instructions were to say 'Enjoy your meal' on delivery of every order, and that was what he did. Jack reflected on the problems of imposing a corporate culture. There was simply no point attempting to make English kids into Americans. You could put the silly hat on the British teenager, but you still had a British teenager under the silly hat. You could make them say, 'Enjoy your meal,' 'Have a nice day,' and 'Hi, my name is Cindy, how may I help you right now?' as much as you liked, but it still always came out sounding like 'Fuck off.'

Jack was restless. He could not be bothered with the newspaper. Mrs Thatcher would win the election and she would probably stay in power for ever. The Brits weren't stupid; they had a winner there. Hadn't she just won a war, after all? A war! Even a year after the event Jack could still scarcely believe the good fortune of his British colleagues. It was so unfair. America was the world's policeman; they had the best army, they should have got to fight the wars. And yet all of a sudden, just when everybody least expected it, those lucky bastard British had arranged themselves a real live, proper, non-nuclear, blood-and-guts, old-fashioned war. Jack and his comrades had suffered agonies of jealousy when it happened and, of course, being in Britain at the time had made it a hundred times worse. There they were, young eager members of the most powerful army on earth, and they had had to sit around in Britain, of all places, guarding cruise missiles while the dusty, down-at-heel old British sailed off halfway round the world to defend the Queen's territory in the South Atlantic.

Jack put the frustrations of the previous year from his mind and took a sheet of writing paper from his pocket. Perhaps he would pass the time by writing to his brother. Jack had been meaning to write for some time but had kept putting it off because it was too depressing. What had he to say for himself? Only that it was starting to look as if Harry had been right all along. Harry had always said that joining the army was throwing your life away.

'*OK, Harry, I admit it,*' Jack wrote in his small, precise hand. '*You were right all those years ago and you've been right ever since. The army is a pain in the ass. It's boring and there isn't any glory any more. Are you pleased, you son of a bitch? Maybe you should put it in one of your damn poems!*'

This was a cheap shot. Harry no longer wrote poems, although for a brief period as a teenager he had attempted to. Jack had never, ever let Harry forget this.

'*Yeah, I'll bet you're pleased,*' Jack continued. '*Tell Mom and Pa the black sheep is bored. Tell them they saw more action shouting slogans at LBJ and fighting cops in '68 than I've seen in the fifteen years since I joined the fucking army.*'

This was not true at all. In fact Jack had seen plenty of action, having served with distinction in Vietnam, but Jack was in a sour mood. Besides, Jack's South-East Asian service had been at the end of the war, beating the retreat, so to speak, a great power cutting its losses. The US disengagement from that bloody adventure had not felt very glorious at the time and it still rankled with Jack. It was one of the many things for which he some-how managed to blame his parents, an attitude his brother Harry found pathetic.

'*What?*' Harry would exclaim. 'It's Mom's fault you didn't get enough Vietcong to shoot at! Jesus, Jack, you are such an asshole.'

'Well, it was the enemy at home that stopped the war, wasn't it?' Jack would counter. 'Those students and hippies and campus fucking heroes! They had their Vietnam War, oh yeah! Outside the White House and on the steps of the Lincoln Memorial! And then they ruined it for me! I didn't get sixties Vietnam, no, not me. I got seventies Vietnam. I didn't get to play Beach Boys music and fight a jungle guerrilla war. No, I finally get out there in '73, just in time to help load a bunch of fat fucking failures onto helicopters in the compound of the Saigon Embassy. That was my introduction to the new global reality. Even the music was shit. You can't fight a war with Donny and Marie at number one.'

Jack and Harry had fought all the time as kids and they still did whenever they got the chance. Harry certainly had no sympathy for Jack's frustrations with army life. He had never made any secret of the fact that he thought Jack's life choices incomprehensible. As far as Harry was concerned, in the army there could only be two states – bored and terrified – and neither seemed very attractive to him. Harry's theory of why Jack had chosen the course in life that he had was the old favourite that he had done it to spite their parents. They had been teenagers during the sixties and while their mother and father had not embraced the counter-culture entirely, they had certainly inhaled. Being college teachers, it would have been almost impossible for them not to. The sixties had been a very difficult decade to opt out of. Even the Brady Bunch and the Partridge Family had hippy values. Almost overnight unorthodox behaviour had become the new orthodoxy, long-haired weirdos became the norm and patriotic boys with crew cuts started to look like freaks. Jack felt like a stranger in his own home. He had wanted proper parents at a time when the concept of formal generations was breaking down. Anybody could be hip; greyhaired old men were on the TV extolling the glories of drugs, and grizzled beat poets and blues men were becoming folk heroes. Whereas traditionally adults had encouraged young people to act like grown-ups, suddenly grown-ups were acting like kids. Jack was fifteen and he felt like the only adult in his house. He had cringed away his teens while his mother swapped dresses for caftans and his father's thick wavy hair got longer and longer and stupider.

Jack's mind had wandered. He returned to his letter and current dissatisfaction with army life.

'I bet you're laughing to read this,' he wrote. 'I know you think I'm in this situation because I wanted to embarrass Mom and Pa. I still can't believe that. You actually think I joined the army because Mom wore a see-through blouse to my high school graduation! You're such a jerk, Harry. You just can't bear the simple *fact that however bored I may feel right now I love the army. You hate the fact that somebody with virtually identical DNA to yours actually loves and respects the armed forces of his country. Just like you love your damn chairs or washstands or whatever it is you whittle out of trees in your stupid wood in Ohio. I didn't join the army because all the guys in my class got to see my mother's nipples. I joined because I want to kill people in the cause of peace and freedom, OK? Something I am unlikely to get the chance to do at RAF Greenham Common, the shithole of the planet. If England had haemorrhoids, believe me they'd be here.'*

Jack had hated the Greenham base the day he had arrived, and the three grim years he had spent there since had done nothing to change his mind. Three grinding years. Years that lived in Jack's memory as one, long, wet miserable winter's afternoon. He supposed that the sun must have shone at some point during the previous thirty-six months but if it had it had made no impression on him. Concrete and steel, steel and concrete, that was what the camp meant to Jack, and the very sky itself seemed to be constructed of the same joyless stuff. A Cold War sky, grey, flat and impenetrable, like the belly of a vast tank. Jack had spent a thousand ghastly hours of duty staring up at that gloomy canopy. He often thought that if ever the missiles for which he and his comrades were responsible were to be fired, they would just bounce off that sky and fall right back to earth, blowing them all to hell.

He took an absentminded sip at his coffee and immediately wished he hadn't. He continued with his letter.

'Then, of course, there's the singing. Harry, that awful, awful singing beggars belief. Worse than when you were trying to learn "The Times They Are a-Changin'" on the guitar. From dawn to dusk, and back again from dusk till dawn. Whenever a guy gets remotely near to the wire his ears are assaulted by those seemingly endless dirges. I cannot believe it, Harry. The one thing I thought was when I got in the army I would not have to listen to any more fucking hippies. Now I'm surrounded by them! They'll be singing now, those appalling women, if singing isn't too grand a word for it. Keening, I've heard them call it, which sounds to me like something cats do in alleys, which would be about right as far as I'm concerned. They stop around midnight, but some nights I still can't sleep for the din. Those damn dirges are still running around my brain, like a tone-deaf rat with a megaphone is trapped inside my head. I can hear them even now, Harry, even as I try to concentrate on writing this letter. Here's what they were singing yesterday. Show Mom. She'll probably think it's beautiful.

> You can't kill the spirit
> She is like a mountain.
> Old and strong.
> She goes on and on and on.
> You can't kill the spirit.
> She is like a mountain.

Old and strong.
She goes on and on and on.
You can't kill the spirit . . .

You get the idea, Harry. They repeat it ad nauseam,
and believe me, the emphasis is on nauseam . . .'
A woman struggled past carrying two children and
leading a third. One of them managed to spill orange
fizzy stuff onto Jack's letter. He sighed and called for the
check. He could sit in that restaurant no longer. The
noise and the smell were getting on his nerves. Old chip
fat and baby sick were competing for supremacy in his
nostrils, and BBC Radio One was clashing with the
dirges running round his head. The song playing was
called 'Karma Chameleon', sung by some kind of trans-
vestite called Boy George who seemed suddenly to have
become more famous than God. Jack had noticed that
when the British liked a song they liked to hear it a
lot and 'Karma Chameleon' had been number one for
ever. Jack had liked it at first, but in that depressing place
it seemed as tinny and irritating as the three girls who
were singing along to it while simultaneously drinking
milkshakes and smoking cigarettes. Jack liked to smoke
himself but he never ceased to be amazed at the smoking
capacity of the British teenage girl. He bet they could do
it underwater. Jack finally gave up on his grubby coffee
cup, scarcely having tasted its gloomy contents, and got
up to go. For all its soulless concrete and its dreadful
women, RAF Greenham Common was beginning to
look preferable to his current surroundings.

Then, rather abruptly, Jack sat down again.

An old couple looked up from their all-day breakfasts and stared. They were no doubt glad of a moment's diversion from eating their meal, from the unpleasant task of consuming the formless mess they had unwittingly ordered under the mistaken impression that they would be brought food. They were more than happy to take a break from fossicking about on their plates to find a bit of bacon that had actually been cooked. They were grateful for the chance to look, if only for a moment, at something other than the snot-like puddles of raw eggwhite that surrounded the chilly yokes of their partially fried eggs. What a disaster. Yet they would no more have dreamt of complaining than of robbing a bank.

They stared at Jack for a moment and turned wearily back to their disappointing meals. Jack had not noticed them anyway. His attention was absorbed elsewhere. The reason he had sat down again was because, just as he had risen, a young woman had entered the restaurant. She was accompanied by a middle-aged couple, probably her parents, but Jack scarcely glanced at them. He was only interested in the girl. He recognized her the moment he saw her.

She was the interesting one, the beautiful one.

The one with the pink streaks in her hair. The one he always looked out for when he drove into the base, slowing his jeep down in plenty of time to make sure he got a good look. Each time Jack surprised himself at just how attractive he found this girl. He had certainly never been taken by any of that monstrous muddy regiment before, and the young woman in question was scarcely what he might have thought was his type. Her eyes were often surrounded by great dark purple circles of eyeshadow, which made her look like a negative photograph of a Panda. On some occasions she had the female gender symbol painted on both cheeks. Jack feared that she might be colour blind because of the green lipstick she sometimes wore, although usually it was a garish, aggressive red. None the less, despite all of this, the girl's fresh, sparkling beauty never failed to shine through. She had the sweetest face that Jack had ever seen, and the neatest of bodies, like a dancer. Jack always tried to get a good long look at her as he drove past and now fate had afforded him the opportunity to absorb her properly. The more Jack looked, the more absorbed he became. In fact it would not be putting it too strongly to say that he was transfixed. His mouth watered and his eyes became lost in dreamy contemplation.

The women at the till wondered if perhaps the coffee was improving.

10

'Don't freak out,' his voice said. 'It's Jack. Jack Kent.'

Polly was freaking out. She stood shaking in her nightshirt, staring at the answerphone machine as it delivered a voice into her life that she had not heard for more than sixteen years.

She had met him in a roadside restaurant on the A34. She was seventeen and a committed political activist. What is more, she had been a committed political activist in a way that only a seventeen-year-old can be. More committed, more political and more active than any committed political activist had ever been before her, or so she thought. She would have made the secret love child of Leon Trotsky and Margaret Thatcher look like an uncommitted, apolitical layabout.

Polly described herself as a feminist, a socialist and an anarchist, which of course made her an extremely dull conversationalist. Smalltalk becomes wearisome when no two sentences can be negotiated without the words 'fascist', 'Thatcher' and 'capitalist conspiracy' being crowbarred into them. So when Polly had announced her intention of joining the women's peace camp at Greenham Common her parents had secretly been extremely pleased.

'It's only for the summer,' Polly assured them, under the impression that they would be devastated.

'Yes, dear, that's fine,' her parents said.

'It's just something I feel I have to do,' Polly continued. 'You see, white male eurocentric hegemony has developed a culture of violence, which . . .'

Polly's parents' eyes glazed over as she spoke at length about the socio-political development of her commitment to the anarcho-feminist peace movement. They had very much preferred it when she had been obsessed with Abba.

The problem with idealism in the young is that, like sex, they think that they are the first people to have thought of it. Polly's parents were lifelong liberals and would have assured anybody who cared to listen that they were very much against the world being destroyed by nuclear war. Yet their daughter bunched them in with Reagan and Ghengis Khan and seemed to feel that it was her duty to convert them from the warmongering ways of all previous generations.

'Did you know that the US defence budget for just one day would feed the whole Third World for a year?' Polly would tell them at breakfast over her fourth bowl of muesli, 'and what are we doing about it?'

By 'we' Polly's parents knew that really she meant them and the truth was that, apart from maintaining a standing order to Oxfam, they were not doing very much.

Therefore, although they were certainly going to miss

their beloved daughter, it was none the less going to be rather a relief to be able to enjoy breakfast again without feeling that by doing so they were shoring up the Pentagon and murdering African babies.

And of course Mr and Mrs Slade were very proud of their daughter. They admired her moral zeal. Other kids were going off grapepicking in France or working in supermarkets to pay off the hire purchase on their motorbikes, or having it off in Ibiza. Their daughter was saving the planet from complete annihilation. Mr and Mrs Slade felt that if she could do that and complete the prescribed reading for her A-level year then she would have spent a useful summer.

And, of course, one thing they did not have to worry about now was boys. Polly was a headstrong girl and between the ages of fourteen and sixteen had alarmed her parents by bringing any number of extremely off-putting young thugs home for tea. Scrumpy-swilling, long-haired bumpkins who kept falling off their mopeds; snarling rude boys in sixteen-hole Doc Martens; cocky New Romantics who wore far too much make-up – and, for a brief, distressing period, a green-haired lad who called himself Johnny Motherfucker and claimed to have eaten a live pigeon. Mercifully, since Polly had discovered politics there had been fewer of these horrible youths hanging about the place, although Mr and Mrs Slade lived in fear that on some rally or other their daughter would get involved with an anarcho-squatter peacenik punk with a tattooed penis and rings through his scrotum.

There would be no risk of such disasters at Greenham Common. The Greenham Peace Camp was separatist, women only. Men were not allowed to stay overnight. Mr and Mrs Slade thought it all sounded splendid. Summer camping, with plenty of time for reading, in the company of serious and idealistic women, struck them as a very good idea indeed. Of course the first mass evictions and the sight of their daughter on the news being carried away by policemen was rather a shock, but still, better a bobby man-handling her than some dreadful yob who rode a motorbike and washed his jeans in urine.

★ 11

Jack skulked behind his newspaper and watched the girl as her parents ordered tea and teacakes. He watched as they attempted vainly to spread the lump of icy butter that had been crushed into the centre of the bun by some joyless jobsworth in a stupid white hat, dry teacakes with a bit of butter in the middle being a speciality of the restaurant chain they were in.

When they'd finished the father figure asked for the bill. Jack sighed to himself, his pleasant diversion nearly over. The little ray of sunshine was about to be extinguished. He hoped the girl would be the last to leave so that he would be able to look at her legs as she walked out.

Then the two older people got up, kissed the girl and left without her.

This was a surprise. Until that point Jack's interest had been entirely passive. He was merely passing a few minutes of his dull day on his dull tour of duty, eyeing up a pretty girl. Now things were different. The girl was alone and devilish thoughts were playing on his mind Should he say hello? Of course it was madness. He wa a US army officer and she was a peace protes dedicated to the confusion of all that he held dear. What was more, she was at least ten years his junior.

On the other hand, she was gorgeous and it could do no harm to say hello. She would probably tell him to shove it anyway and there would be an end to the matter.

Polly did not notice Jack approach. She was lost in her own thoughts and was feeling rather sad. This had been her parents' first visit since she had joined the camp and now that they had gone she suddenly felt rather homesick. Strange, she thought, that having spent most of the last five years imagining that all she desired was to leave home she was now discovering that home had its advantages. The devoted love and affection of her parents and a regular supply of clean knickers were two that sprang immediately to mind.

'Can I buy you a cup of coffee, ma'am?' said Jack. 'If you can dignify the swill they serve in these places with such a name.'

Polly couldn't believe it. An American soldier! She had only ever seen them at a distance before, or whizzing by in their cars. The Americans were a different, more glamorous breed, officers and technicians and the like. It was poor little teenage British squaddies who actually guarded the fence and got sung at.

Having overcome her initial shock, Polly asked Jack to sit down. She was certainly not going to let an opportunity like this go by. Here was her chance to convert the enemy. Jack ordered the coffee and asked if 'd eaten. Polly said that although she had, she'd be happy to do so again. In fact she was starving, having only allowed her parents to order a snack lest they think she was not eating properly at the camp.

If Jack had been at all concerned that his impulsive gesture would result in an awkward silence he need not have worried. While ordering the food the girl managed to call him a fascist, a mass murderer and a zombie-brained automaton. She also asked him if he ever thought about what he did, appealed to him to desert the army and enquired whether he knew the temperature at which a human body combusted. From there it was, of course, a short step to a detailed description of the Hiroshima shadows.

'Those people were burned into the walls, you know. Babies' skin peeled away like parchment while their eyeballs literally melted.'

Vainly did Jack protest that he too wished only for a peaceful world and that it was his opinion that the vigilance and armoured might of NATO's forces had prevented such horrors occurring more often.

'Oh, sure,' Polly sneered. 'You want to stop nuclear war so you build more bombs. Brilliant. That's like fucking for virginity. You're just a bunch of sweet old peace-loving hippies, aren't you? Do you realize that one day's budget for the US military would feed the entire Third World for an entire year?'

Polly had ordered a three-course meal at Jack's invitation and at this point the tomato soup arrived. Jack was impressed to discover that this girl could even be furious about that. She had good cause to be. This w the time when microwave ovens were still a relatively recent invention, when the microwaves actually continued to be generated even when the door was open, thus making it possible for teenage wage slaves to contract bone cancer while at the same time failing to heat up the food.

'It's hot on the top and cold in the middle. With a skin on it! I mean, how do you do that? It's almost as if it was deliberate.'

Jack just nodded and stared. He simply could not get worked up about the soup. He was feeling too happy. She really was beautiful, this wild English rose, and so angry. He loved how angry she was, passionately angry, angry about everything. Angry about nuclear bombs, angry about soup. 'The system' certainly had a lot to answer for.

How astonished would Polly's parents have been had they returned at this point. Polly had found a boy, after all. Or, rather, a man, and no punk or hippy either but an American army captain. Their daughter would, of course, have explained that she had only just met the bloke. That he had nothing to do with her at all. But something in the eagerness of her manner, and the way she was blushing beneath the female gender symbols on her cheeks, would have warned them that this was to be no brief encounter.

And how astonished would Jack's parents have been to see their deeply conservative son hanging upon the ɔs of such a strange-looking girl. A radical girl, a py girl, a girl not so different from the students whom Jack Senior had taught in the sixties and whom Jack Junior had despised as traitorous apologists for Hanoi. How they would howl with laughter when, later, they heard from Harry the extraordinary news that their little soldier son had fallen for a subversive! A peacenik! Their Reagan-loving, Red-bashing, Liberal-hating offspring, for whom it was and always would be hip to be square, had come under the spell of the enemy.

Because that is certainly what happened. Jack fell for Polly like a man with no parachute. Even at that first meeting he was already half besotted. He wanted their lunch to go on for ever. He could not remember having ever been in the company of such an exuberantly free spirit. This girl was the opposite of everything he wanted in his life, and yet he loved it. She was rude, untidy, undisciplined, unfettered and anarchic, and he loved it. How happy Polly made him feel, how liberating it was just talking to her. Of course Jack knew that he was taking a considerable risk sitting openly in a restaurant with her. She was quite definitely not a suitable dining companion for an army officer, and were he to be spotted it would mean a severe reprimand. But on that special day Jack did not care. In fact, he gloried in the risk he was taking. Polly was making him feel as free-spirited as she was herself.

Polly's second course arrived: chips, baked beans, peas and carrots. She had asked if they had anything vegetarian but this being the days before that type of option was common in British catering the unpleasant youth the silly hat had said the best he could do was to take the meat out of a meat and potato pie for her.

Polly squirted red sauce out of a large plastic tomato all over her food and seethed at the fascistic, Thatcherite injustice of it all.

'They might at least offer something that isn't dripping with blood. I think we should protest.'

'I thought you just did,' Jack replied. After all, Polly had announced loudly that she resented being forced to eat in a fucking charnel house. This had sounded like protest to Jack. The manager (who had enough to worry about what with having arrived at puberty only that morning) scuttled over and told Polly that she was not being forced to eat anywhere and that she was welcome to leave at any time, the sooner the better, in fact.

Polly told the manager that in fact she was being forced to eat in his establishment because multinational capitalism had ensured that the only food available on the roads of Britain was supplied by the owners of the dump in which they sat.

'And when I say food,' Polly added, 'I mean of course shit.'

A pretty comprehensive protest, Jack thought. Certainly enough to be going on with. Polly, however, had other ideas and, taking out the superglue with which she was wont to block up police padlocks and car doors, she glued the sauce bottles to the table.

'Well, that'll certainly show them,' said Jack.

'Non-violent direct action. Anarchy, mate. You have to do it,' Polly assured him.

'Yeah. I'll bet they're really gonna rethink their policy on animal welfare once they find out you vandalized their ketchup.'

'Protest is accumulative,' Polly assured him.

'Protest is self-indulgent and pointless, pal,' said Jack. 'Believe me, I know. My parents tried it. They spent the sixties knocking their country over dinner and waving banners at a liberal president. What did they get for their trouble? Richard Nixon. Ha! That showed them. Now they've got Reagan! Jesus, are they pissed. I phone them every time he cuts welfare just to rub it in. They're a couple of sad, fucked-up anachronisms who don't have the sense to see that God is a Conservative and the Gospel is money. The only way you're ever going to change anybody or any institution is to hit 'em in the head or hit 'em in the pocketbook. If you want to hurt these people you take their money.'

'Well, ye-es,' said Polly, slightly confused.

Jack looked about him. 'So, let's go.'

'What?' Polly enquired, not yet catching on.

'When I say run,' said Jack, 'we run.'

'You don't mean . . .' Polly began.

'Run!' said Jack.

12

If Jack had been trying to find a way to impress Polly
he had hit the nail on the head. *This is the stuff!*
Polly thought as they charged out of the restaurant and
ran for Jack's car. She could scarcely believe that her
despised enemy, a member of the US military, could
ever do anything so cool as to run out of a restaurant
without paying. Never judge a book by its cover, she
might have reflected, had she not been so breathless
with excitement.

They tumbled into the car and as Jack hit the ignition
the sound system leapt into life along with the engine.
It was playing Bruce Springsteen, Jack's preferred
driving companion, and by a happy chance the tape
was cued up on 'Born To Run'. Suddenly Polly found
herself bang in the middle of the Boss's runaway
American dream and she shouted with delight as, with
tyres screeching and Bruce pumping, Jack pulled out of
the carpark and onto the road.

'This is brilliant!' Polly shouted as Jack kicked down
the accelerator, hammered through the gears, cranked
up the Boss and left any pursuers to eat his dust.

About a mile along the road, which they seemed to

cover in about fifteen seconds, Jack slammed on the brakes and executed a spectacular handbrake turn off the main road, which nearly threw Polly out of the car. Suddenly they found themselves bumping along what was little more than a dirt track.

'Think I'll give the main roads a miss for half an hour,' he remarked casually. 'That manager kid is bound to have called the cops by now. Wish I had my off-road jeep four by four. Then we could have some fun.'

'Four-wheel drive cars are destroying the country-side,' said Polly.

'Yeah. So?' Jack enquired.

They soon arrived at a gate that led into a field and Jack was forced to stop. After that it was all rather spontaneous. They scarcely spoke, just grabbing each other with passionate fury and feeding on each other's mouths and faces, tearing at each other's clothes. Later on, Jack would remember thinking that Polly even kissed angrily or at least with the same kind of serious commitment that she seemed to put into everything else she did. Polly was not thinking anything at all. Her mind had been emptied by this sudden and completely unfamiliar surging physical desire. Nothing like it had ever happened to her before. She had often wondered over the past three or four years what true passion felt like and whether she would ever experience it herself. She would wonder no more.

Then had come the inevitable environmental frustrations. It just isn't easy to make love in cars. In his efforts to get to Polly Jack very soon found himself with his knee in the glove compartment and his stomach impaled upon the gear stick. It was most frustrating. Jack had not experienced anything like it since high school and his body had been suppler then. He was halfway to being on top of Polly but he could get no further, not without major organ removal.

'Fucking gear stick,' Jack growled, speaking for the first time since they had fallen upon each other.

'It's your own fault for driving a TR7,' said Polly, feeling rather self-conscious because Jack had one of her breasts in his hand. 'Everyone knows a TR7 is a wanker's car.'

'Well, it would need to be,' Jack replied, extricating himself. 'You certainly can't fuck in one.'

It was no good. They would have to go elsewhere. Then, as if by magic, the sun burst through what had until then been a rather grey day. The field beyond the gate turned golden. A glorious meadow carpeted with long, swaying grass with butterflies hovering lazily above it. Had that field been candlelit, strewn with red velvet cushions and with Barry White's greatest hits wafting softly from speakers hidden in the hedges, it could not have seemed more like a good place for sex.

'Come on,' said Jack.

They climbed the gate and fell together into their five-acre bed.

Deflowered amongst the flowers, Polly thought to self, being not quite out of her teenage poetry stage. was a disaster. Making love in a field is almost as

difficult as doing it in a car, especially if it's been rain-
ing the night before and you have a problem with
pollen and what looked like soft grass turns out to be
some kind of organic barbed wire. It's probably just
about possible if you've brought a groundsheet, a
mattress, a blanket, some DDT and a scythe. Otherwise, forget it. Pretty soon Jack's elbows and knees
were in cowpats, Polly's knickers were in shreds and
something with two hundred legs and fifteen sets of
teeth had crawled up his backside.

For the second time since they had begun their
desperate groping Polly and Jack were forced to put
their passion on hold. With Polly's virginity still pretty
much intact, Jack suggested a hotel.

'OK,' said Polly, getting up and putting what was left
of her knickers back on. 'But I haven't got much money,
so I'll have to pay you back later for my half of the bill.'

Jack laughed, feeling a tremendous wave of affection
sweep over him for this strangely intense girl. At that
point the sun, which had disappeared into some clouds,
came out again behind Polly and all of a sudden she
was bathed and silhouetted with an almost luminous
golden glow. She looked like some kind of pure and
lovely teenangel and Jack's conscience began to trouble
him.

'Polly, how old are you?' he asked.

'Seventeen,' said Polly defensively.

'Oh, Christ,' said Jack.

'But I'm a lot more mature than you, mate,' Po'
added. 'I know that it's dangerous to play with gun

Seventeen. Jack had been hoping for at least nineteen, possibly twenty, although he knew that twenty would be the absolute limit.

'Polly. I'm thirty-two. I'm fifteen years older than you.'

Polly shrugged.

'Are you a virgin?' Jack asked.

'What if I am?'

It was worse than Jack had thought.

'I can't do this to you,' he said.

Suddenly it was not the sunlight that made Polly glow but righteous indignation. Her cheeks reddened and her eyes took on a fiery glint.

'Listen, you patronizing bastard,' she said. 'You aren't doing anything *to* me. I do things for myself, all right? If I choose to go to bed with you – or in this case to a field with you – if I choose to use your body for my pleasure, then that's my business. I am a woman and males do not have a say in my life. In fact, emotionally and politically I'm a lesbian. It just happens to be my misfortune that I fancy men, that's all.'

Jack had never been overly receptive to radical feminism in the past, but he was warming to it. 'OK,' he said.

They got back into the car and drove to a nearby hotel. It was a large, redbrick, eighties place, built on a roundabout in the middle of nowhere with toytown turrets and pastel-coloured Roman pillars in the foyer. Polly wanted to hate the place as a prime example of reckless urbanization of the countryside, but she could not because in fact she found it all desperately romantic. This, considering that the hotel was really just a large carpark with a leisure complex, conference centre and executive miniature golf course attached, Jack found very touching.

There was some trouble at the check-in desk, not because of Polly's age – she was, after all, perfectly legal and did not look particularly young. It was the T-shirt she was wearing that required careful negotiation, the objection being that it had a picture of a cruise missile on it that had been altered to make it resemble a penis. Polly explained that this was a comment on the masculine nature of war.

'I'm afraid that other guests might find it offensive,' the receptionist explained.

'Oh, and I suppose nuclear arsenals aren't offensive?' Polly enquired.

'Nobody is attempting to bring a nuclear arsenal into the hotel,' said the receptionist. 'Perhaps the gentleman could lend you his coat?'

Jack could not do this because he did not wish to advertise the uniform he was wearing underneath. Polly was clearly a loose cannon and a troublemaker and Jack did not want the manager phoning his colonel and complaining about the type of girl American officers brought to the hotel. In the end a compromise was reached. Polly reluctantly agreed to keep her arms folded across her chest while she remained in the public parts of the hotel, thus covering the offending political statement.

'I thought this country was supposed to have freedom of speech. I don't think!' Polly muttered as Jack led her away.

And so began a relationship which very soon was to become an intense and all-consuming love affair. A love affair which, although in some ways desperately brief, would last a lifetime. Two people of different ages, different backgrounds and, most importantly, utterly different principles and values, were to be bound together from that ecstatic moment on.

Newton said that for every action there is an equal and an opposite reaction. Jack and Polly certainly lent substance to that observation.

A few days after Jack's first encounter with Polly he wrote to Harry, angrily anticipating the sibling ridicule he knew he must endure.

'*Oh, yeah, ho, ho,*' he wrote. '*You think this somehow proves your piss-weak psychological theories, huh? You think that this girl is like Mom, am I right, Harry? Of course you do. You're so transparent. Well, forget it. In fact before you forget it, shove it up your ass, then forget it. This girl is not a bit like Mom, or Pa, or you. She's like me! Yeah, that's right, like me, because she's a fighter, the real thing, a two-fisted bruiser with poison for spit. OK, maybe what she fights for is a bunch of crap, in fact it is a bunch of crap. Quite frankly I hear less woolly thinking when sheep bleat. But so what? She's got guts and she fights. She doesn't sit on her ass smoking tealeaves like Mom. doesn't think that stuffing envelopes for the*

Democrats once every four years makes her an activist. What is more, Harry old pal, she hasn't hidden away from life making dumb furniture which a factory could make better and at a tenth of the cost, like you, asshole! Polly is a soldier, she's out there, punching hard and kicking ass for what she believes in. Besides which, she's the sexiest thing I ever saw in my whole life, so screw you.'

When Harry read the letter he was pleased. Despite its abrasive tone it was by far the most romantic letter Jack had ever written. In fact it was the only romantic letter he had ever written. The only time Harry could remember his brother being even half as excited was when he had been promoted to captain at a younger age than any of his West Point contemporaries. Jack had never been enthusiastic about anything except sport and the army. He had certainly never talked about being in love and yet now his entire soul seemed to be singing with it. Of course Harry was happy for Jack, but in the midst of that happiness he was also uneasy. It seemed to Harry that his brother now loved two things – soldiering and this English girl. It did not take all of Harry's intellectual powers to work out that these two things were not compatible. Harry could see that in a very short time the crunch would come and that Jack would have to decide where his loyalties lay.

It was Newtonian physics again; for every action there is an equal and opposite reaction. Jack's current happiness was surely storing up an equal quantity of unhappiness for someone.

13

'Polly? Polly! Are you there? Are you there, Polly?' The long-lost but still familiar voice breathed out of Polly's answerphone. It was rich and low and seductive as it had always been.

'Are you there?' Jack said again into the telephone.

A little way along the street Peter was getting frustrated. He'd been surprised to see the telephone box occupied. It never had been before at that time of night. He felt angry. It was 2.15 in the morning. People had no business using public telephones at 2.15 in the morning. Particularly his own private, public telephone, a telephone with which Peter felt a special bond. Many times on that very phone Peter had heard the voice of the woman he loved. The cold mechanics within its reciever's scratched and greasy plastic shell had vibrated with her adored tones. That phone, his phone, had been the medium through which Polly's precious lips had caressed his senses.

'It's you, isn't it?' she would hiss. Hiss directly into his ear, so that he could almost imagine he felt her breath. 'Fuck off! Fuck off! Just fuck off and leave me ⌐ne, you disgusting little prick!'

Peter didn't mind Polly's anger at all. Some relationships were like that, fiery and tempestuous. After all, he certainly gave as good as he got. Peter liked Polly's fury. It was passionate, exciting. So many nights he had stood listening to those blistering, heavenly tones. Looking at the photographs he'd laid out on top of the tattered telephone directories, sucking on his precious straw and masturbating into the lining of his overcoat.

That telephone box was where Peter had had sex with Polly. It was his telephone box and now some bastard was using it.

Peter felt the knife in his pocket.

A flick-knife he had bought in Amsterdam one night when he had not had the guts to go into one of the shops that had women in the windows. Peter liked to carry that knife about with him for his protection and also because he fantasized that one day he would find himself in a position to use it in defence of Polly. He imagined himself chancing upon her in the street; she would be surrounded by vicious thugs who would be taunting her, pulling at her clothes. She would be weeping with terror. He would kill them all before claiming his reward!

Peter fondled the flick-knife in his pocket.

Still Polly did not pick up the phone. In fact she did not move. She couldn't; she was too shocked. The only animation she could have managed at that point of supreme surprise would have been to fall over. She avoided this by gripping onto a chair back for support.

'It's Jack,' she heard him say again. 'Jack Kent.'

She knew it was Jack Kent, for heaven's sake! She would never forget that voice if she lived to be two hundred and fifty years old. No matter what was to happen to her, be it premature senility, severe blows to the head, a full frontal lobotomy, she would still be able to bring that voice instantly to mind. Its timbre was resonant in her bones. Jack's voice was a part of her. But what was it doing broadcasting out of her answerphone in Stoke Newington at 2.15 in the morning? His was quite simply the last voice in the world that Polly had expected to hear. If the Queen had woken her up to ask her round to Buck House for a curry and a few beers it would have seemed a more natural occurrence than this.

Still receiving no reply, Jack's voice continued. 'Weird, huh? Bet you're surprised . . . Me too. I'm surprised and I knew I was going to call! How surprising is that? I just got into town. It's only ten p.m. in New York, so it's not late at all. Don't be so parochial, we live in a global village now.'

It was the same old Jack, still cool, still cracking gags. Still vibrant with sensual promise.

'I can't believe I just heard your voice, even on a machine. It's just the same . . .' Jack's voice was even softer now. Even softer, even lower. 'Are you there, Polly? Look, I know it's late . . . real late . . . but maybe not too late, huh?'

Too late for what? Surely he didn't mean . . .? Polly ould not begin to think what he meant. She could rcely begin to think at all.

79

14

Jack kept talking. He knew she could hear him.

'I want to see you, Polly. Are you there, Polly? I think you're there. Pick up the phone, Polly. Please pick up the phone.'

Across the street Jack could see that the man he had noticed earlier was walking slowly towards the phonebox. In his hand was what looked like it might be the hilt of a knife, but there seemed to be no blade. The man walked right up to within a yard or so of the phonebox and then stood and stared. Perhaps he wanted to use the phone. Perhaps he wanted to use the phonebox as a lavatory. Perhaps he did not know what he wanted. Whatever was going on, it did not take the instincts of a soldier to work out that this man meant Jack no good.

Their eyes met through the cloudy plastic of the window. Peter and Jack, two men from opposite sides of the world, connected by a woman whom they had both wronged, with whom by rights neither should have been having anything to do at all.

Jack kept his eyes fixed on Peter's. Matching him stare for stare. Meanwhile, he spoke again into t phone. Delivering his voice back into Polly's life.

'I think you're there Polly. Are you there? Pick up the phone, Polly.'

He imagined her standing in her flat, staring at the machine. Its red light blinked back at her.

'Are you there? Pick up the phone, Polly.'

Suddenly Polly did as she was bid and snatched up the phone, fearful that in her hesitation the voice would disappear again, back into the locked vault of her memory, where it had resided for so many years. Clunk. Whirr. Clunk. The answerphone announced its disengagement.

'Jack? Is it really you, Jack?'

Down in the street, outside the phonebox, there was a glint, a flash of orange streetlamp light reflected on shining metal. Peter had pressed the button on his flickknife and its wicked blade had leapt out into the night, thrusting itself forward from within the hilt, from within Peter's clenched fist. It glowed orange in the night like a straight, frozen flame.

'Yes, Polly, it's me,' said Jack. 'Listen, can you hold the line for just one second?'

It was not what Polly had expected to hear, and it was not, of course, what Jack had expected to say. You do not, after all, return from the dead, wake someone up in the middle of the night, give them the shock of their life and then put them on hold. Circumstances, however, had forced Jack's hand. At this supreme moment in his plans, in his life, fate had suddenly dealt a wild card. A mugger had clearly blundered into his life and the situation would have to be dealt with.

Jack kicked open the door of the phonebox. It was a good kick, firm and accurate. A confident kick, which connected with the frame of the door rather than the windows and sent the whole thing swinging outwards at speed and into the man who stood outside. Peter had been in the process of reaching for the door at the time and the force hit him first in the hand and then in the face, surprising him considerably and making him drop his knife.

As Peter leant down to pick up the knife the door swung closed and Jack kicked it again. This time the door hit the top of Peter's head and he went over into the gutter. Jack left the phone hanging, stepped outside and with one final bit of confident footwork sent Peter's knife down a convenient drain.

'If you want to make a call you wait, OK?' said Jack to Peter. 'I thought the British were supposed to be good at standing in line. If you disturb my call again you'll regret it.'

With that, Jack returned to the box and picked up the phone.

'Sorry, Polly, some guy thought he owned the call-box.'

Peter decided not to wait. He got up and ran. He was unbalanced and inadequate in any number of ways but his instincts of self-preservation were entirely healthy. He hadn't wanted a fight anyway and he had not intended to use the knife, he had just wanted to scare the fellow off. Since that was now clearly out of question Peter decided to get himself away and consider his position.

Perhaps he would not telephone Polly tonight after all. His hand stung and his head hurt and he felt in no shape to begin the delicate task of restarting their relationship. What is more, he had promised his mother faithfully that he had no current plans to call her. She had made him promise again only that night. He had been trying to sneak out of the house quietly, but she had heard him and had come running from her room in her nightie. Peter hated seeing his mother in her nightie; she seemed so much older and more shapeless.

'It's gone midnight, Peter. Where are you going? You're not going to phone that bitch, are you?'

'I'm going for a walk, and don't call her a bitch. She's all right.'

'I'll call her what I like, lad, and as long as you live in my house you'll leave her alone.'

Peter had shrugged and headed for the door but she'd grabbed him by the ear.

One day she would do that one too many times.

'Do you promise?'

'Yes, Mum, I promise.'

In fact, Peter's promises to his mother were pretty worthless. He had also promised that he would not obtain Polly's new ex-directory telephone number. Computer hacking was something that the law took more seriously than swearing at people over their inter-ms. Peter's mother was worried that if Peter did it 'n he would be put away. He had done it again, though, and Polly's number had been burning holes in his thoughts for weeks now.

But he would not phone her tonight. The tough American in his phonebox had spoilt it. He would just walk up the street, round the corner and past the building in which Polly lived. Peter liked to stand there in the emptiness of the night and stare up at her window. Imagining her alone in her bed. Imagining himself beside her.

Polly was not in bed. She was standing, phone in hand, shaking with shock.

'It can't be you, Jack. That's insane,' said Polly. 'What, now? You want to visit now?'

'Yeah, I'm in town.'

'In town!'

He had said it like it explained everything.

'This is insane.'

'Don't keep saying it's insane, Polly. Why is it insane?'

There were so many reasons why it was insane that Polly couldn't begin to answer that question adequately. It would have taken her all night, all week, the rest of her life.

'I'm coming round,' said Jack.

'No! Where are you? How long will you be? How long is not long? Jack! Jack!'

But the line had gone dead.

Polly put down the receiver and slumped into h~~ office chair, which was actually one of her kit~

chairs. Polly only had four upright chairs, one of which was kept permanently by her desk, except on the rare occasions when it was required for a dinner party. If Polly ever entertained more than three people at the same time someone had to bring their own chair.

Polly's insides were doing somersaults. What could be going on? Why had Jack come back? Where had he come from? What could he possibly want with her now?

Such were the larger questions that tormented Polly as she sat there, shaking, in the shadowy half-light of her room, but they would have to wait. There were practical considerations to be dealt with and she must pull herself together. First and foremost she was in her night attire, if night attire was not too grand a term to describe the slightly ratty, threadbare old man's shirt she was wearing. She must get dressed and quickly. No matter how weird the situation, Polly had standards. She did not receive visitors dressed only in a shirt.

Rushing to her knickers drawer she grabbed a vaguely current-looking pair and put them on. The jeans she had worn on the previous day were still concertinaed on the floor where she had stepped out of them a few hours earlier. She stepped back into them and began hurriedly to pull them up. Then she had second thoughts. With her jeans already lodged halfway up her legs, she waddled across her flat and, flinging open a cupboard, began pulling out dresses. She held one up to herself in the mirror and, finding it unsatisfactory, tried another. Then a third and a fourth.

Finally she chose the shortest and most flattering of the selection. She told herself that it was simply the smartest and most practical choice, but actually it was the sexiest.

Polly was about to remove her nightshirt and put on the dress when the front door buzzer buzzed.

'Christ's buggery bollocks!'

Polly stepped back out of the jeans and rushed over to the front door of her little flat. She lived on the top floor of a large house, one of the thousands of houses that once were home to prosperous Mary Poppins families. Places built to house twelve people and which ended up providing for twelve households. 'There's room in this conversion for four decent-sized flats or six small ones,' the property developers of the early eighties would say. 'So what do you reckon? Fourteen? Or is that pushing it?'

That particular speculative bubble had, of course, long since burst, and there were now a mere six buttons on the front of Polly's building. One of which led right up to the attic of the house, which was Polly's home.

Polly gingerly took up the receiver of the entryphone intercom that hung on the wall beside her front door. Her hand was shaking. This was insane. Why had he come back? She was furious, of course, all the old emotions returning, the ancient wound exploding open, but she was thrilled as well. How could she not be? Never had she expected to hear his voice again, and yet here he was, only four floors below, standing at her own front door.

'Hello,' she said, attempting a noncommittal, matter-of-fact tone and failing entirely. 'Is that you?'

Suddenly she was half her age. A young girl again, young and nervous and excited.

'Is that really you?'

'Your light was on. It's never been on this late before.'

Polly stepped back as if she had received a blow. She nearly fell. The receiver dropped from her hand and bashed against the wall, swinging on its curly flex.

'Can't you sleep?'

The hated voice, the hated and shocking voice drifted up from the dangling receiver.

'I thought you might want company. If you tell the police I came round my mum will say I was at home with her. Are you wearing any clothes, Polly? Have you got a bra on? What colour are your knickers? I bet you aren't wearing any this late at night, are you?'

Polly's eyes were full of tears now. Through the watery mist she focused on the red panic button that stood out upon the wall behind the door. It was so located that should an intruder ever push open the door, forcing Polly backwards into her flat, the button would then be in immediate reach. There was another one on the wall by her bed. Polly wanted to push those buttons, she wanted to alert the whole house to her persecution, to set alarm bells ringing there and in the local police station, but she knew that she must not do it. Her enemy was not at the gate, he was in the street and would no doubt soon scurry off as he always did. He was no physical threat. There was no justification in summoning a screaming squad car, and the police did not take kindly to having their services abused. One does not cry wolf with panic buttons. When you push them you need to be believed.

Blinking back her tears, Polly grabbed up the receiver.

'I'm calling the police. I am calling the fucking police right now! Fuck off! Please fuck off!'

'You use that word a lot, don't you, Polly?' said Peter. 'Is that because you like it, Polly? Fucking? Is that what you like?'

15

Downstairs the Bug turned and scurried away. He had taken a big risk ringing her doorbell like that. He'd certainly not intended to do it. He knew it would probably mean a police visit, more social workers, his mum in tears. But seeing her light shining so late, knowing that she, like him, was still awake in the small hours of the night, perhaps even thinking about him, that had been too much for him to resist. Now, however, he must retreat. If Polly did call the police and he were found in her street no denial from him or testimony from his mother would prevent his arrest.

Leaning against the wall beside her door Polly struggled to control her pounding heart and the tears that she could feel beginning to prickle up into her eyes. Her legs felt weak. Slowly she slid down the wall, her back cold against the plaster until she sat upon her haunches. Jack and the Bug? Within minutes of each other? What could be going on? What was happening?

Perhaps half a minute went by before the front door buzzer sounded again. She was waiting for it but it still made her jump. Like the phone, the buzzer seemed much louder than it did in the day. Even in Polly's emotional state she found herself wondering if it could be heard in the flat below. She hoped not. She was currently in dispute with the man downstairs. He was a milkman who rose every morning at four and put on his radio, a habit which had caused Polly to voice numerous complaints. She did not want to arm the man with counter-accusations of late-night comings and goings.

The buzzer buzzed again.

She would not answer it. It would be the Bug again. Polly knew his pattern well enough. He tended to attack (which was how Polly privately described the Bug's intrusions into her life), then attack once or twice more before disappearing, long before any policeman might deign to turn up. On the other hand, supposing it wasn't the Bug? Supposing it was him, Jack? Unlikely, of course. After all, it was only a minute or two since Jack had telephoned, but he'd said he wouldn't be long . . . If indeed it had been Jack at all . . . In her distraught state Polly found herself prey to the most paranoid of musings. Had the Bug found out about Jack? Was he somehow playing a terribly cruel trick on her? Had she merely imagined that the voice had been that of her former lover?

Buzz.

She had to answer it. So what if it was the Bug? She would call him a sad no dick. What was more, if she did not feel justified in using her panic button she could certainly let off her rape alarm into the intercom. Sod the milkman, sod everyone else in the house if it woke them up. They weren't being stalked. She would shatter the Bug's eardrum. Polly went to her bedside table and took up the little alarm tube. Suitably armed, she returned to the intercom and picked up the receiver.

'Yes?' This time her voice was like steel. Fuck-off-and-die steel. Her thumb hovered over the rape-alarm button.

'Polly. It's me. It's Jack.'

It was Jack. There could be no doubt. There was only one Jack.

The relief! The blessed relief. But what about the Bug?

'Jack. Is there anyone else down there? A man?'

'What?'

'It's a perfectly simple question! Is there anyone else there, Jack? Thin, pale, mousy hair?'

Down in the street Jack glanced about him. He did not know what he had expected Polly to say to him, but it was not this. The reunion conversation was not shaping up the way he had expected. First he had been forced to put her on hold, now she was asking him about other men.

'There's no one in the street but me, Polly. Can I come up?'

Polly struggled to become mistress of her emotions and her thoughts. It must be coincidence. Jack and the Bug could not be connected. It just so happened that on this very strange and crowded night the two men who, in their different ways, had hijacked Polly's emotions more effectively than any other people in her life, should clash. The Bug had simply chosen this night to revert to form, the same night that Jack, Jack of all people in the world, had decided to drop by.

'What is this about, Jack?' she said into the mouth-piece.

'Can I come up?' Jack's voice replied from three floors below.

Everything seemed to be happening at a breathtaking speed. 'I'm in my nightie, Jack!'

Jack did not reply to this. He considered making some smart Alec comment but decided against it, opting to leave her protest hanging on the wire that connected them. The tactic worked. Polly realized that however inappropriate the time and the circumstances might be, she was never going to simply tell Jack to go away.

'I'm on the top floor.'

Polly pressed the buzzer and let Jack back into her life.

16

Watching from a little way along the street, in the pitch black shadows of a derelict shop doorway, Peter's inner turmoil was the equal of Polly's. He could not believe his anguished eyes. A man was entering Polly's flat, and at 2.20 in the morning! It could only be Polly he was visiting. Hers was the only light that burned in the whole building. What was worse, the man who Polly was allowing into her home at such an hour was the vicious brute who had attacked him and, what's more, attacked him with scarcely an ounce of provocation.

Peter could hardly begin to imagine what was going on. To his knowledge Polly had no current boyfriend. There had been a man a few months earlier but he didn't seem to visit any more. Perhaps it was the bricks that Peter had thrown through the man's car window on three separate occasions that had put him off. Recently Polly had always been alone. But now she wasn't. Now she was entertaining a violent American in the middle of the night.

Peter slunk further back into the shadows. He must concentrate, decide upon a course of action. He dug into the pocket of his coat for the bag of sweets he had brought with him as a comfort against the lonely boredom of the night. Sucking noisily, he tried to think.

Upstairs, behind the glowing curtain, Polly was again acutely aware of her appearance. She was still wearing nothing more than an old shirt and a pair of knickers and there was a gentleman caller upon her doorstep; it would not do. She rushed to her bed and grabbed the dress she'd chosen and also some lipstick from her handbag. Catching sight of herself in the mirror she could only groan at her pillow hair and the slight reddening around her eyes caused by her crying.

An unbiased observer might have thought that despite the strangeness of the situation and despite everything that had happened in the past, Polly still wanted to look attractive for Jack.

Knowing that she had only the time in which it takes a man to walk up three flights of stairs, Polly attempted to brush her hair, wipe her eyes and pull off her nightshirt all at the same time. She soon realized that these activities were incompatible. Particularly if one is also attempting to apply lipstick and search the unsorted clean washing bag for an unladdered pair of tights.

'Calm. Stay calm,' Polly said to herself as her stomach executed a particularly startling element of the Olympic gymnastic routine, which it had been performing ever since Polly had been awoken scarcely five minutes before.

Outside Polly's flat, in the well of the building, Jack was climbing the last flight of stairs.

So this is where she ended up, he was thinking.

There is always something rather depressing about the communal areas of multiple-household houses. The mounds of junk mail and local advertising freesheets behind the front door. The piles of letters addressed to long-since-departed occupants stacked on the rickety hall table. The bicycles obstructing the way, the unloved and unwashed stair carpet, the large and perplexing stain on the elderly wallpaper. The single framed print hanging on the wall on the first landing, the dead lightbulbs suspended pointlessly from their dusty flexes.

Such an extraordinary visit, thought Jack, and such ordinary surroundings. It was enough to quite depress a man.

Arriving at Polly's door, Jack checked the number one more time against the information in his file and knocked. Inside Polly yelped and stubbed her toe against a chair.

It was too late to get dressed. Swearing quietly, she pulled her nightshirt back down (better an old shirt than topless, she reasoned) and snatched up her dressing gown from where she had left it on the floor. One glance told her that it was not acceptable. It was as old and stained and horrid as the stairwell outside. No eyes but hers should ever look upon it. Stuffing the offending gown under the bed, she ran to the cupboard from which she had taken her selection of dresses and, scrabbling inside amongst the Chinese puzzle of wire hangers, she located and pulled out another gown. It was a tiny fluffy one, a Christmas present, slightly see-through and trimmed with fake fur. She had never worn it and she certainly could not do so now. She would rather be stained and torn than completely ludicrous and slightly pervy.

There was another knock. Polly could prevaricate no longer. In desperation she flung on a plastic rainmac. It did not look good, but it covered more of her than her nightshirt did, and it would have to do.

Polly approached her front door and peered through the spy hole. She recognized Jack instantly; even the darkness and the magnified fisheye effect of the spy hole could not disguise that handsome face and classically firm American jaw.

Jack was back.

Polly took off the chain and opened the door.

There he stood, in the shadows of the upstairs landing.

Like a spy.

He had on one of those timeless American gabardine overcoats that could as easily be worn by Humphrey Bogart or Harrison Ford. A coat that is forever stylish; like Coke and Elvis, age does not wither them. Jack wore it well, the collar turned up as with all the best men of mystery, and the belt knotted at the waist. Very little light emanated from Polly's lamplit room, and Jack was illuminated only by the streetlight orange which glowed through the bare window of the landing. Peter Lorre seemed almost to be hovering at Jack's elbow. He did not actually say, 'Here's looking at you, kid,' but he might as well have done.

'Jack? It really is you, isn't it?'

Polly was also in shadow, dimly backlit by the glow of her bedside lamp. The whole scene was classic *noir*.

'Hello, Polly. It's been a while.'

For a moment it seemed as if she would embrace him. For a moment she might have done. Then the memory of his betrayal descended upon her and turned what had begun to look like a smile into a frown.

'Yes, yes, it's been a while,' she said, stepping away from him, back into her room. 'Why change the habit of half a lifetime? What are you doing here?'

'I came to visit with you.'

He said it as if it was a reasonable thing to say. As if no further explanation was required.

'Visit?! Now?!'

'Yes.'

'Don't be bloody stupid. We don't have anything to say to each other. We have nothing to do with each other. What is this about?'

'Nothing,' he said. 'It isn't about anything, it's a social call.'

'Oh well, that's nice. Perhaps I'd better put the kettle on and crack open a packet of my finest custard creams. It's after two o'clock in the fucking morning!'

'I know what time it is. Who were you expecting?'

'What do you mean?'

Polly felt it was she who should be asking the questions.

'Who's the thin man, Polly? The guy you asked me about, the guy who was supposed to be in the street?'

Where could she start? She didn't even know Jack and now she was supposed to explain to him that she was in the process of being stalked by an obsessive. She was supposed to stand in her doorway in the small hours of the morning and talk to a virtual stranger about the worst thing that had ever happened to her.

Or perhaps the second worst thing, but then Jack knew all about that already.

'It's a man who's been bothering me, that's all. I don't think he'll call again.'

'Bothering you? What do you mean, bothering you? Like is he your husband or something? Have I walked into a domestic here?'

This was ridiculous. Suddenly it was Polly who was having to explain herself. Only a few minutes before, she'd been asleep, and now she was filling this man in on her personal details.

'No, a stranger. They call them stalkers. He's a nuisance, that's all. He thinks he loves me and rings my bell occasionally. It's not a problem or a big deal. Forget it.'

Polly always described her torment in a far lighter tone than she actually felt. Like many a victim before her, she found her pathetic vulnerability rather embarrassing. It made her feel weak and inadequate. After all, if it was her life that was being attacked rather than other people's, perhaps the problem lay with her? Perhaps it was her fault.

Jack was thinking about his recent violent encounter

at the telephone box. Thin, pale, mousy hair. The description fitted. On the other hand, it would have fitted a million men.

'Actually, there was a guy like that hanging around the callbox,' said Jack, 'but he's not out there now and I don't think he'll be back. Would it be OK to come in?'

And with that Polly realized that even in this supreme moment of strangeness, the Bug was taking over. That was the absolutely worst aspect of the Bug's crashlanding into her life. She just couldn't get the bastard off her mind. Whatever she was doing he was always there. She had not been able to fully appreciate a single thing in her life since the nightmare began. Parties, shows, work. Everything had been affected by his existence.

But this, this was different. This was bigger than the Bug, bigger than anything. Jack was back, and he wanted to come in.

'No, you can't bloody come in!'

As if she would let him in. As if she wanted anything to do with him.

'Please, Polly.'

'No! I'm not going to just—'

'Please, Polly. Let me in. If you don't I'll just keep standing here on your landing. It'll be morning in a few hours. What will you tell the other people who live in the house?'

The same voice, the same charming, sexy voice.

'Why the hell would I let you in?'

Jack suggested that old times' sake was surely a good

enough reason, and it was, of course. That and the fact that Polly absolutely longed to let him in.

'For old times' sake I ought to kick you in the balls.'

'Well, in that case you'd better do it inside. We don't want to disturb the neighbours.'

Polly looked at Jack and tried to pull herself together a little, assuming what she hoped was a cool, emotionally invulnerable expression. Interested, certainly, but detached, reserved. In control of her space and her emotions. Jack thought merely that she still had a nice smile. He smiled back at her, his old smile, still fresh as a young boy's. That smile was so familiar to Polly, so inseparable from her memories of Jack that she could almost have imagined that he had not used it since. That he had kept it carefully in some safe place so that it would remain new and sparkling until the day he brought it out again, just for her. But it wasn't true. Polly knew that Jack used that smile every day. Whenever he wanted anything.

Polly stood aside. What else could she do? Jack walked past her and into the room. She closed the door behind him, put her rape alarm back on the bedside table, and there they were. Alone together again.

They stood staring at each other, neither of them really knowing what to say or do next. Then suddenly Polly found herself enveloped in Jack's arms. She did not know how it happened, whether she had crossed the floor to him or whether he had grabbed her, or whether they had simply blended together by instant osmosis. But it happened. For a moment at least they held each other and in Polly's heart a tiny spark leapt instantly into life, a spark that had long lain hidden amongst the dead ashes of the ferocious furnace that had once burnt between them.

17

'Oh, God!' Polly shrieked.

'Oh, God. Oh, sweet Jesus! Oh, God!'

Strange how some people discover their religious side whilst orgasming. Polly never bothered God at all as a rule, in fact she was an agnostic, an atheist, even, if she was feeling brave. Yet while in the throes of carnal climax Polly could make the very heavens ring with her piety and devotion. In fact since that day, only a few weeks earlier, when Polly had discovered sex, the Almighty had scarcely had a moment's peace.

'Oh. Oh. Yes . . . yes, that's it, that's it! Oh God, Oh God, oh please, harder, longer, longer, harder . . . oh yes, oh please . . . Please . . . Yes yes yes yes!'

And then finally it was over. A quite spectacular orgasm, fuelled with love and lust and all the gay abandon of youth, had run its noisy course. Slowly the room returned to normal, the overhead light stopped swinging on its flex, the teacups on the bedside table ceased to rattle and the plaster clung less desperately to the walls and ceiling. Jack rolled off Polly's quivering body and reached for his cigarettes.

'So, did you come?'

Jack could joke at a time like that. He was older, experienced. Confident and witty. American in the way Americans are supposed to be. Sexily sardonic and capable of sparking a Zippo cigarette lighter into life using only one hand.

'Just fooling,' he said. 'I imagine that there are people in other parts of the country who know you came. Certainly the only people within this hotel who didn't know you came are either deaf or dead.'

'Sorry. Was I too noisy?'

'Not for me, I'm used to it. I used earplugs.'

Polly laughed, but she was embarrassed. Most people feel a little awkward and exposed when it comes to the noises they make during sex and it's even worse when you're only seventeen.

Jack lit two cigarettes and gave one to Polly.

'Don't worry, I'll call reception and tell them you're a Christian fundamentalist seeking enlightenment, asking God to give it to you longer and harder.'

Polly felt that Jack's joke had run its course. She might have been young, but she was a woman out of whom only so much piss could be taken.

'Look, I was enjoying myself, all right? And to do that I need to express myself. People should express themselves more. People are too uptight. If people recognized their true feelings a bit more and let them out occasionally there'd be a lot less anger and violence in the world.'

'OK, OK. Fine. I'm glad to have been a part of your personal fulfilment programme. There was me thinking we were having sex and it turns out you were making a contribution to world peace.'

Polly and Jack smoked in silence for a few moments. Polly wasn't really angry. In fact she loved fighting with Jack. She loved everything about Jack with the exception of his 'Death or Glory' tattoo. Never before in her short life had she experienced such emotions, such passion. Every atom of her physical self tingled with it. The tips of her toes were in love, the hair on her head was in love, the backs of her knees were in love. And such exciting love, dangerous and wrong. Illicit love, forbidden fruit.

Polly stretched out under the covers and felt the crisp clean hotel sheets against her body. What luxury. Only rarely did Polly experience such exotic delights as clean sheets, let alone fresh soap and towels. And a lavatory! Her own personal lavatory. With a door! Only a person who does not normally have the use of one can understand just how wonderful having a lavatory is. Polly would sit on it for half an hour and read the hotel brochures, never tiring of news of mini-breaks for two in the Cotswolds, the Peaks and the heart of England's glorious Lakeland. Jack said he sometimes felt that Polly only slept with him in order to use the toilet.

'That's not true, Jack,' Polly assured him. 'You're forgetting the little chocolate mints the maids leave on the pillows.'

Jack got out of bed, crossed the room, drew back the curtain slightly and looked out.

'Can't we have the curtains open occasionally?' Polly asked. 'It feels so claustro'.'

'No,' Jack replied. 'It makes me feel too exposed. I mean, if we were caught together . . .'

Why did he have to remind her about that? Just when she was so happy. He was always reminding her about that.

'I know. I know! You don't have to go on about it.'

'Hey, baby, I do have to go on about it because that's how I stay careful. And I have to stay careful because if my colonel ever found out about us my career would be over, you hear that? Everything I've worked at since I was seventeen would be gone. You're only seventeen right now, Polly. You don't have a life to throw away yet, but I do. They'd court-martial me, you know that? They might even throw me in the hole.'

Jack returned to bed. Some ash from Polly's cigarette fell onto the sheet. She tried to brush it off but only made it worse.

'Leave it,' said Jack irritably. 'We're paying.'

'I hate that kind of attitude,' Polly snapped. 'We've paid so we can act irresponsibly. And I hate this sneaking about too, this constant tension.'

'I do not have a choice but to sneak about. I have to be discreet, which is something, incidentally, you have made considerably more difficult by your decision to dye your hair puke colour.'

In her heart of hearts Polly had to admit that the orange and green highlight effect she had tried to create had not really worked.

'If you don't like sneaking about, baby,' Jack continued, 'go hang out with one of your own kind.'

'You don't choose who you fall in love with, Jack, and don't call me baby.'

Polly was starting to look a little teary. She didn't like it when he referred to their relationship in such a casual manner.

'Oh, come on, Polly, not the waterworks.'

All her life Polly had cried easily. It was her Achilles' heel. She wasn't a crybaby; it was just that strong emotions made her eyes water. This was actually quite debilitating in a minor sort of way. It made her look a fool. It would happen in the middle of some particularly frustrating political argument. There she would be, banging her fist on the pub table, struggling to find words to express her deeply held conviction that Mrs Thatcher was a warmongering fascist and suddenly her eyes would start getting wet. Instantly Polly would feel her image transforming itself from passionate feminist revolutionary to silly overemotional little woman.

'Well, there's no need to cry about it,' Polly's dialectical opponents would sneer.

'I am not bloody crying,' Polly would reply, tears springing from the corners of her eyes.

The tears were there now and Jack did not like emotionally charged situations. He liked to pretend that life was simple. Polly thought him repressed and out of touch with himself. Jack just felt he had better things to do with his time than get worked up about stuff. But the truth was that he was worked up, terribly worked up. Beneath his highly cool exterior he was anguished and distraught. Because Jack was in love with Polly and he knew that he would have to leave her.

'Jack,' said Polly, 'we need to talk about where we're going.'

Jack did not want to talk about this at all. He never did want to talk about it, because deep inside he knew that they were not going anywhere.

'You know why people smoke after sex?' he said, dragging at his cigarette. 'It's an etiquette thing. It means you don't have to talk.'

'What?'

'People smoke after sex to avoid conversation. I mean, in general post-coital is a socially barren zone. Particularly that difficult first time. You've known somebody five minutes and suddenly you're removing your horribly diminished dick from inside of their body. What do you say?'

Sometimes Polly found Jack's crude, abrasive style sexy and exhilarating. Other times she just found it crude and abrasive.

'We didn't say anything after our first attempt, did we? Because we were hiding in a field trying to avoid large insects and the police.'

'Yeah, well let me tell you, it saved us a lot of embarrassment. Any diversion is welcome in such a situation. Even the cops. Think about it. You're naked with a stranger. What do you say?'

'A stranger?'

'Sure, a stranger. The first time you sleep with

someone ten to one they're going to be a stranger. How many times do you have sex with someone for the first time whom you've known more than a few hours?'

'Well, there's not much point asking me, is there?'

'Yeah, well take my word for it, babe.' Jack did not like to be reminded of Polly's lack of sexual experience. It made him feel even more responsible for her than he already did.

'The first time you screw a person all you've been thinking about since you met them is screwing them. Then suddenly it's over and you don't have that agenda any more. What can a guy say? "That was fun."? "That was nice."? It's so weak, so dismissive, like the girl's body was a cupcake and you took a nibble. On the other hand, "That was awesome," is too much. She knows you're bullshitting. "Oh yeah, so awesome it lasted two whole minutes and you shouted out some other girl's name." '

Jack took another long drag on his cigarette and developed his thesis.

'So people smoke. The human psyche is so pathetically insecure that we would rather die of lung cancer than confront an uncomfortable situation. I don't know what will happen now everybody's giving up. Maybe they'll share a small tray of canapés.'

'I thought "How was it for you?" was considered the correct inquiry.'

'Nobody ever asked that. That question is a myth. How could you ever ask, "How was it for you?"? No answer would be good enough.'

'Why not?'

'Well, just now, for instance, when we made love. How was it?'

Jack had caught Polly off her guard.

'Well, it was fine . . . great, in fact, really great.'

'You see,' said Jack, as though his point were proved. 'Already I'm thinking, "fine"? "great"? Why doesn't she just come right out and say "pathetic"? That's what she means. Why doesn't she just say, "Your dick is a cocktail sausage. I get more satisfaction when I ride my bicycle over a speed hump."'

'Oh well, if we're taking puerile macho paranoia into account . . .'

'Got to, babe, it's what makes the world go around.'

Polly took another cigarette and lit it from her previous one.

'Well, I'm definitely giving up soon. Tomorrow, in fact; certainly this month or by the end of the year.'

They smoked in silence for a while. Outside, the sun was setting. When it was dark they would leave, Polly knew that. Jack rarely consented to spend a whole night with her. She got out of bed and began to search for her clothes.

Polly never ceased to be amazed at the way her clothes disappeared while she was making love. Particularly her bra and knickers. It was a side of sex that had come as a complete surprise to her. It wasn't as if she hid them or anything. She did not deliberately secrete them behind the washbasin in the bathroom or between the sheet and the mattress, or hang them from the picture rail. None the less after lengthy searching it was in such places that they would be discovered. On this particular occasion she eventually found her knickers wedged inside the Corby trouserpress.

This was Jack's favourite part of Polly's dressing process. He loved her naked, of course, he worshipped her naked, but somehow near nakedness was even more endearing. There was something he found particularly moving about Polly wearing only her knickers. Polly said that it was because like all men he was subconsciously afraid of vaginas and preferred to see them sanitized with a neat cotton cover, which Jack thought was quite literally the stupidest thing he had ever heard anybody say in his entire life.

The gathering gloom within the room was making Polly feel sombre. When the sun was shining and Jack and she were making love she could forget the circumstances of their relationship. Forget that he was a killer and she was a traitor. Forget the police and the soldiers. The razorwire and the searchlights. Forget her life in the camp. Forget the Cold War. Then night would fall and Polly would remember that it was life with Jack that was the dream. Outside was the deadly reality.

'It would be so lovely to be normal,' she said, rescuing her bra from inside the hotel kettle (the lid of which she'd have sworn had not been removed even once since they had entered the room). 'To be able to walk down a street together, go to the pub.'

'Don't even think about it.' Jack shivered at the very thought.

'I was arrested again yesterday,' said Polly. She and her comrades had been attempting to prevent the missile transporters from leaving the camp. In the event of war the strategic plan for the missiles was that they would be bussed about to various parts of the county on mobile launchers, making them less of a target for the enemy. Every now and then the army practised this deployment, using empty transporters. It was to one of these that Polly had been attached when the police arrived.

'Arrested?' said Jack casually. 'You didn't say. How'd it go?'

Jack always tried to act as if things were not important.

'Not great. You know the good cop, bad cop thing? I think there must have been an administrative cock-up. I got bad cop, bad cop. No fags, no cups of tea, just a lot of abuse.'

'That's cops.'

The police, who for a while had been friendly, had begun to tire of the Greenham women's disruption and vandalism and had started to get tough.

'I was thinking while they were both shouting at me that perhaps down the corridor someone else had got good cop, good cop. Constant tea, endless cigarettes, keep the coupons . . .'

The sun was nearly gone. Inside, the room was almost completely dark.

'Polly, are you sure you've never told anybody about us?'

'Jack, you always ask that.'

Jack got out of bed and went to the toilet. He left the bathroom door open, which Polly hated. She liked to keep a little mystery in a relationship where possible. Having a toilet door was such a luxury for her that it seemed deeply decadent not even to bother using it.

'You've told nobody?'

Jack raised his voice above the tinkling and flushing. His tone was firmer, as well it might have been, since the whole course of his life depended on Polly's discretion. He returned to the room, as always utterly unselfconscious about his jiggling, dangling, bollock-hanging nakedness. This was a side of male bedroom manners that Polly would never get used to.

'Of course I haven't told anybody,' said Polly. 'I know the rules. I love you . . .'

Polly waited, as countless women had waited before her, for the echo of that phrase, and, like the vast majority of those women, she was eventually forced to ask for it.

'Well?'

'Well what?' said Jack, lighting another two cigarettes.

'Well, do you love me too?'

Jack rolled his eyes ceilingwards. 'Of course I love you, Polly, for Christ's sake.'

'Well say it properly, then.'

'I just did!'

'No, you didn't. I made you. Say it nicely.'

'OK, OK!'

Jack assumed an expression of quiet sincerity. 'I love you Polly. I really love you.'

There was a pause.

'But really really? Do you really really love me? I mean really.'

This is, of course, the reason why so many men don't like to get into the 'I love you' conversation, because it is open-ended. Very quickly degenerating into the 'How much do you love me?' conversation, the 'I don't believe you mean it,' conversation and finally the dreaded 'Yes, and I'm sure you said the same thing to that bitch you were going out with when I first met you,' conversation.

'Yes, Polly. I really really love you,' Jack said in a tone that suggested he would have said he loved baboon shit on toast if it would keep the peace.

'Good,' said Polly. 'Because if I thought you were lying I think I'd kill myself . . .'

The room was now almost pitch black save for the glowing ends of their cigarettes.

'Or you.'

★ 18

When Jack got back to the base that night he went straight to the bar and ordered beer with a bourbon chaser. The room was empty save for Captain Schultz, who was alone as usual, playing on the space invaders machine. Poor Schultz. He hated the army as much as Jack loved it, not that he would ever have admitted it to anybody, even himself. Schultz tried not to have strong opinions about anything, in order to avoid unpleasant arguments. He had joined the army because that was what the men (and some of the women) of his family had always done. The fact that he was entirely unsuited for military command, being incapable of making a decision, was irrelevant. There had never been any choice for Schultz.

Jack had known him at West Point where Schultz had just scraped through with a combination of family connections and very hard work. Not too long afterwards, while billeted at the US base in Iceland, he had been made captain virtually by default. Schultz's superior had found the posting rather cold and had attempted to warm himself up by trying to seduce every young woman in Reykjavik. After one too many dishonourable discharges the man was dishonourably discharged and Schultz found himself achieving early command. Jack had found it an interesting circumstance that he, the most successful student in his year at military academy, and Schultz, the least successful, should be advancing at much the same pace. Jack's rise was due to his own excellence, Schultz's to the frailty of others, but they were destined to shadow each other throughout their whole careers.

That night in the bar Jack wanted someone to talk to. He was still thinking about the conversation he'd had with Polly and was in a rare communicative mood. He wished that Harry was there so that he could talk to him about the painful mixed emotions he was experiencing. But Harry was thousands of miles away in Ohio. There was only Schultz. Jack stood by the space invaders machine and watched Schultz lose all his defenders in a very short space of time.

'Jesus, Schultz,' said Jack. 'That must be the worst score anybody ever got on that machine.'

'Oh no,' Schultz replied, giving up the game. 'I've had much worse.'

'What the hell are you like with a gun?'

'As far as possible I try not to use one,' Schultz said, sipping at his soda.

'Tell me something, Schultz,' Jack enquired. 'Did you ever really really want something you couldn't have?'

Schultz considered for a moment. 'Sure I did, Kent. Why, only tonight in the refectory I absolutely set my mind on the profiteroles and then they told me they just sold the last portion. I hate that. They should cross it off the board. Why do you ask?'

'Forget it.'

Jack finished his drink and returned to his neat little army cell.

'*Dear Harry,*' he wrote. '*What the hell is wrong with me? I'm in pain here and nobody hit me. When I started this thing with Polly I thought I could handle it. You know, I thought I could have some laughs, get my rocks off and walk away when I felt like it. Except now I don't want to walk away. Even thinking about ending it makes me want to go and punch someone. This is ridiculous, Harry. I mean, what am I? Some kind of soppy dick like you that lets himself get stupid over a girl? Never in my life did I get stupid over a girl. Suddenly I'm risking my career for one! I'm sneaking out of the camp with my collar turned up and my hat pulled down just so I can be with her! I must be out of my mind. In fact, I am out of my mind, because she's in it! All day this woman is inside my head! I can't do my job, I'm a safety hazard. I'm try-ing to monitor the arrival of nuclear warheads and I'm daydreaming about being in bed with Polly! Did you feel this way about Debbie? Of course you did. You still do, you lucky fuck. You and Debbie were made for each other. You fit, like one of those horrible kissing chairs you make. You're allowed to love each other. Nobody ever said 'A furniture maker can't fall in love with a fire woman.' But me! Jesus, my colonel would probably prefer it if I told him I was sleeping with the corpse of Leonid Brezhnev.*'

19

Their embrace ended as suddenly as it had begun.

Polly broke away. 'I shouldn't be hugging you, Jack. I shouldn't be hugging you at all.'

So much of her longed to continue, but a larger part remembered the hurt that this man had caused her.

Jack stepped back too. He had not expected their embrace. It had confused him.

'Yeah, well, like I said, it's good to see you.'

Polly wanted to look at Jack properly. She turned on the lamp on her desk. The extra light further illumin-ated her dowdy room and she regretted switching it on.

'I've often wondered what your stuff would be like,' said Jack, looking around.

Things were not at their tidiest. As a matter of fact, they never were. Things had only once been at their tidiest in Polly's flat, for a single afternoon, shortly after Polly had moved in and her mother had come to inspect. In preparation for that visit Polly had tidied and cleared and cleared and tidied and polished and buffed and tidied again.

Her mother had thought the place was a mess.

She also thought that the plates should be in the pan

cupboard, the pans should be where the mugs were and the mugs should go on little hooks of which there were none, but nice ones could be got at Habitat. Polly's mother then set about effecting all of these changes with the exception of the mugs, because she did not have the hooks. The mugs she left on the draining board to await Polly's DIY efforts and there they had remained (sometimes clean, more often dirty) ever since.

Polly's little life seemed suddenly small and depressing. Poky would have been a good word for it, or dingy. She felt embarrassed, which was really rather unjust because if anyone in that room had reason to feel embarrassed it was Jack, and yet Polly knew that it was she who was going red.

Hurriedly she began to tidy up. Polly was a dropper of things and a leaver around of other things. She did not tidy up as she went along, she tidied up once every seven days on a strict routine and she was already nine days into the current cycle. There were knickers and tights on the floor, a dirty plate and various mugs by the bed, and magazines and books everywhere. Polly felt that at least the intimate clothing had to be hidden away; also anything that had mould growing on it, particularly if the two were one and the same thing.

As Jack watched Polly scurrying about, stooping to pick up her knickers and bras, he could not help but remember Polly as a young girl, searching for her underwear in hotel rooms and the backs of cars. Once she had not been able to find the elusive garment at all and they had risked going down to dinner, not only in fear of being seen together but also in the wicked knowledge that Polly was naked beneath her little denim skirt. What a wonderful meal that had been. Jack had kicked off his shoe beneath the table and as they ate his bare foot had lain between Polly's legs. In the long years since that glorious meal Jack had relived it in his memory a thousand times. He doubted that he had ever had a happier moment. Certainly not in a motel restaurant, anyway.

'Bet you didn't think things would look as shitty as this,' Polly said, stuffing dirty clothes into the clean clothes drawer.

As he watched her moving about Jack knew that it was as he had feared. That he was still in love with her.

'No, I didn't. I thought it would be much more shitty than this.'

Jack could see that virtually everything Polly owned was on view. Her furniture, her clothes, all of her stuff. It didn't seem to him that she had changed very much either. There were her souvenir mugs from the 1984 miners' strike. A poster advertising a concert at Wembley Stadium to celebrate the release of Nelson Mandela. One of those plastic flowers that dance when music comes on (but only if the battery hasn't been dead for five and a half years, which in this case it had). A poster of Daniel Ortega proclaiming 'Nicaragua must survive', a poster of Garfield the cartoon cat proclaiming that he hated mornings. A clipframed front page of the *London Evening Standard* from the day Margaret

Thatcher resigned (Jack, like many Americans, could not understand how the Brits had ever let that one happen; anyone could see that she was the best thing they had had in years – it was like after the war, when they dropped Churchill). Polly had lots of books. A couple of IKEA 'first home' easy chairs, a rape alarm, a small TV. Thirty or forty loose CDs and forty or fifty empty CD boxes.

Everything was as Jack might have imagined it. The only thing that surprised him was how little Polly owned. You would have been lucky to get two thousand dollars for the entire contents of the room. Not a lot for a woman of thirty-four. Or was it thirty-five? Not a very impressive accumulation for a whole half-lifetime.

Polly glanced up from her tidying. She knew what he was thinking. 'Not very impressive, is it?'

Polly still could not quite believe how spectacularly she had managed to screw up her life. Just how unlucky could a girl get? And why did it have to be her?

No reason, of course. Some people are fortunate in life and love, some are not, and you can never tell how the chips will fall. At school nobody would have looked at Polly and thought, she'll end up one of the lonely ones. She'll be the one who screws things up. She had been bright and attractive in every way. She might easily have made a great success of her personal life had fate favoured her, but it had not.

How cruel to reflect upon the wrong turns and unsought circumstances of an unlucky life. When Polly and her friends had sat laughing in the pub together at the age of seventeen it would not have been possible to look at them and say, 'Second from the left with the rum and Coke, she's going to have problems.' It would not have been possible to predict that Polly, who seemed so strong and assured, was very soon going to fall head over heels in love and then get devastatingly dumped. That she would then spend years drifting unsatisfactorily from brief affair to brief affair before suddenly towards the end of her twenties being seized by a sudden desperate fear of being alone. That Polly of all people would be the one to get caught up with a married man (separated, waiting for divorce) who would lie to her, cheat on her and eventually leave Polly for the ex-wife whom he had previously left for Polly.

Every golden generation, every fresh-faced group of friends, must statistically contain those who will fall prey to the sad clichés of life. The things they never thought would or could happen to them. Divorce, alcoholism, illness, failure. Those were things that happened to one's parents' generation. To adults who no longer had their whole lives before them. It comes as a shock when the truth dawns that every young person is just an older person waiting to happen, and it happens a lot sooner than anyone ever thinks.

★ 20

At the end of the summer, after Jack had left Polly, she decided to stay on at Greenham. Her parents did everything they could to persuade her to come home and go back to school but she was adamant. Her A-levels could wait, she explained, there was a planet to be saved. Polly told Mr and Mrs Slade that she had things to do, she had made great friends amongst her compatriots at the peace camp and was halfway through the construction of a ten-foot-high puppet of a She-God called Wooma, with which Polly and her friends intended to parade through Newbury. Of course, Polly did not tell her parents that she had spent the summer having a passionate fling with a man twice her age and that now he was gone her heart was utterly broken. She did not tell them that her whole being ached with sadness and that sometimes she thought she would actually go mad. She just told them about Wooma and that she was not coming home yet.

In fact Polly never did go home. Instead she moved permanently into the camp, living in a caravan with an old granny called Madge. Madge had been widowed the previous spring and had decided that she wanted to do something useful with the rest of her life, so she had bought a little caravan and moved to Greenham to save the world. Madge was a good companion and Polly loved her, but she was obsessed with bowels, particularly Polly's. She would enquire earnestly about the state of Polly's stools, reminding her always to be sure to inspect what she had produced before shovelling on the soil. Madge never tired of assuring Polly that regular, punctual movements were the secret of longevity and constantly made bran muffins of such copious fibrousness that they could have prised open the buttocks of a concrete elephant.

Polly kept in touch with her parents via postcards and the occasional photograph. It was through the latter that Mr and Mrs Slade kept up with the changes in Polly's appearance, which was drifting from rather stylish anarcho-punk to depressing 'who gives a fuck?' hippy grunge. Mrs Slade wondered how Polly washed her hair now that it was all in great shaggy dreadlocks with beads sewn into them and the terrible answer was, of course, that she didn't. Mr Slade worried that food might get stuck in Polly's new lip ring and rot there. He'd read somewhere that decaying meat was carcinogenic, then he remembered that Polly was a vegetarian and felt better. Neither of Polly's parents liked the tattoo she had had done on her shoulder, depicting the female gender symbol with a clenched fist in the centre of it. Unfortunately the tattoo had been rather inexpertly applied by a stoned ~oth at the Glastonbury festival, and the fist looked like a penis, which was hardly a feminist symbol.

The Greenham camp was a bit like the Foreign Legion for Polly, a place to nurse a lost soul. She was relatively content there, apart, of course, from her aching heart and Madge going on at her all the time about her far too infrequent evacuations. Camp life was tolerable but, then again, if you consider yourself worthless and don't care whether you live or you die, which was how Polly felt, pretty much anything is tolerable.

Some aspects of Greenham life Polly never got used to. Even in her numbed state of mind all the singing and the holding hands could get a bit wearing. The peace women were so anxious not to emulate the aggressive posturing of the male of the species that sometimes they ended up just looking a bit wet. Sometimes at night, when the women were having their lentils, the British squaddies would pile back from the pub all pissed up and chanting, 'Lesby, lesby, lesbiANS.' When that happened Polly always longed to lob a ladleful of hot roughage at them and inform them that they were a bunch of brainless no-dicks, but that sort of behaviour was not how things were done. The camp was there to stop aggression, after all, not to fuel it, so instead the huddled women would confront the baying young men with their impenetrable female energy, constructing a forcefield of love and calm through which the soldiers occasionally urinated.

Polly was not very good at this type of mystical feminism. She was more for the give as good as you get school of protest. Madge often tried to explain that this was *exactly* the type of attitude that had started the arms race in the first place, but Polly remained restive and unconvinced.

Try as she might, she never could truly welcome her periods as an old friend. She simply could not regard the monthly stomach cramps as a small price to pay for the privilege of celebrating the timeless mystery of her menstrual cycle. Being as one with the rhythms of the moon was of very little comfort to Polly when she had a hot water bottle clamped to her stomach. It turned out that she wasn't very good at puppet-making either. The She-God Wooma's head had fallen off on its first outing, nearly killing a baby outside Boots in the Newbury shopping precinct. Nor did Polly have any children's paintings to pin to the perimeter wires, or peace poems and haiku to send to the prime minister. Above all, apart from the mass protests and camp invasions in which Polly always played an enthusiastic part, life at Greenham could be very very boring. It was all right for the lesbians – they had something to do of a night – but for Polly the hours of darkness were long and lonely, and she would lie there shivering, listening to Madge snoring, trying not to think about Jack and wondering what she was doing with her life. Certainly she was saving the world, but was that enough?

After about a year Polly was ready for a break, and the miners' strike in 1984 gave her the opportunity to move on. The whole of alternative society had been ⸗alvanized by the confrontation between Mrs Thatcher and the miners. The prime minister seemed finally to have found an enemy worthy of her metal, and everybody wanted to be a part of what was confidently expected to be her defeat. Polly decided to leave Greenham for a while in order to carry a fundraising bucket for the NUM.

She went to stay with friends in Yorkshire, where she signed on the dole and offered her services at a miners' support group. There she took up with a middle-aged communist shop steward called Derek. He was a nice man but the relationship did not last long; despite both of their being politically on the far left, they were incompatible. This was, of course, inevitable, given that one of the hallmarks of the far left in those days was that almost everybody on it was politically incompatible with almost everybody else. The factionization was surreal. Groups would split and split again until individual members were in danger of being rendered schizophrenic. It made for an incredible array of radical newspapers. On the steps of every Student Union and on every picket line one could buy *The Socialist This*, *The New Left That* and *The International God Knows What* . . . Sadly, most of these papers were read exclusively by the people who printed and sold them.

And the only thing that all the disparate factions had in common was that they all hated each other. What is more they hated each other with a venom and a passion that they could never feel for the Tories. The Tories were just misguided products of an inherently corrupt system. Other Lefties were the anti-Christ.

Polly and Derek fell out over a point of sexual politics. He objected to her wishing to stand on the front line at the secondary pickets, which were becoming more and more violent as frustrations grew on both sides.

'Look, Poll,' Derek said. 'When me an't lads are stood standing at dock gates, tryin' t'stop foreign bastard scab coal comin' in, and Maggie's boot boys in blue are tryin' t'kick six types of shit out of us we do not need to be worrying about protectin' our women-folk.'

Derek, like most of the miners, still believed firmly that there was men's work and there was women's work. It was, in fact, to be the last year that men like Derek would believe such a thing, because within a very short time virtually every coalmine in Britain would be closed, the men would be out of work and the women would become the principal earners in the home.

At the time, though, Derek definitely believed that women were the gentler sex. Faced with such positively Neanderthal sexism, Polly scarcely knew where to start.

'But . . . you . . . For God's sake . . .!' Polly could feel her eyes beginning to water with frustration.

'Well, there's no need t'cry about it, love,' said Derek, and there their relationship ended.

The miners' strike finally collapsed in January 1985. Polly was alone and with no clear sense of purpose. Like Bono at about the same time, she still hadn't found what she was looking for. She thought about moving to London where yet another once mighty union, this time the print workers', was preparing to dash itself against the walls of Castle Thatcher in a futile attempt to maintain their old working practices. In the end, however, she couldn't face it. Even the peace dirges of Greenham seemed preferable to endlessly chanting, 'Maggie! Maggie! Maggie! Out! Out! Out!' and 'Here we go, here we go, here we go,' when clearly no one was going anywhere. So Polly returned to the camp to await the delivery of the cruise missiles.

That was what she told herself, anyway, but the fact that for the first month after her return she scrutinized every American face that came or left the camp suggested that Polly's heart had not yet healed. Madge could see that Polly was still troubled, but of course she thought the whole problem was lack of roughage.

But it would take more than a high-fibre diet to cure Polly's pain. Only time would do that and time moved slowly at the Greenham camp that spring for Polly. She had not told Madge about Jack, or any of the women with whom she began again to share her life. They would not have understood. Polly did not understand it herself, except to know that love is blind. Everything Jack stood for Polly truly did despise, and she despised herself for having fallen in love with such a man. What was worse, she despised herself for not having the strength to forget him.

When the missiles finally did arrive, Polly was amongst that briefly celebrated group of women who managed to breach the perimeter fence and carry their protest on to the base itself. Polly's poor, horrified parents opened their newspaper one morning to dis-cover that she and her comrades had reached the landing runway and had very nearly forced the huge US Air Force transport planes to abort their landings. It was a great propaganda triumph, which in the opinion of the USAF very nearly caused a nuclear disaster. In court Polly pleaded guilty to criminal trespass but stated that she had acted in order to prevent the greater crime of millions of people being vaporized in nuclear explosions. The magistrate declined to accept global geopolitics as mitigating circumstances and Polly was bound over to keep the peace.

'Ha!' said Polly. 'Keeping the peace is what I was doing anyway.'

Which she thought was rather a clever thing to say.

21

Polly was not the only one still grieving for the past. Jack too found himself unable to step out from under the long shadow of their relationship. With Jack, however, the effect was more positive; the memory and continuing presence of Polly in Jack's heart was to prove a considerable influence on his life and career.

After leaving Greenham Jack spent most of the rest of the eighties stationed in the lovely old German city of Wiesbaden, a part of the vast American military presence that had been camping in Europe since the end of the Second World War. Wiesbaden was the headquarters of the US Army in Europe. Over the years the local German community had grown accustomed to the presence of hordes of young foreign men in their midst and an uneasy relationship had grown up between the military and its host community. Of course, there were tensions and conflicts, but discipline was strict and scandals were rare. Rare but not unknown. One night in a bierkeller in Bad Nauheim, a town a few miles up the autobahn from Wiesbaden, there occurred an incident which the army subsequently quickly tried to forget.

Normally Jack would not have been in a bierkeller at all. He was not much of a pub man. Being extremely ambitious, he tended to reserve his spare time for study or sports. However, on this particular night Jack was ready to relax. He had been out on a week's field training, a week of camp food and camp beds, during which time he had been cold and wet for twenty-four hours a day. Jack was ready to spend an evening drinking the German winter out of his bones.

Being a little tired of Wiesbaden, he took the army bus to Bad Nauheim, where he very soon fell in with some fellow officers.

'Hey, Jack, come over here and have a beer, you enigmatic bastard,' a captain known as Dipstick shouted as Jack entered the bar. Dipstick was so called because he was a mechanical engineer and also because he liked to talk about how much sex he was getting. He shared an offbase house in Bad Nauheim with another army captain called Rod. Dipstick and Rod were a real couple of good ol' boys and were already half full of beer. Between them sat a German girl called Helga. Helga was the sort of girl who liked soldiers and in particular getting drunk and having sex with them. Had Helga been a man she would have been called a good ol' boy too, just like Dipstick and Rod, but because she was a woman it was well known that she was a scrubber.

Helga had been seeing quite a lot of Dipstick in the weeks preceding the night in question, but on one occasion she had also slept with Rod. Originally, the evening had been planned by Dipstick and Rod as a threesome. They had brought Helga to the bar in the hope of persuading her to have sex with them both. Rod and Dipstick had every reason to think that Helga would be amenable to this idea, because they had laughed about the possibility together on a number of occasions. Helga had even boasted that it would take at least two of them to handle her properly. A threesome was just the type of dangerous game that Helga was likely to get herself into because beneath her bravado she was a lonely, insecure girl and what she craved most was attention. A psychologist might have made much of Helga's exhibitionism and lack of any real sense of self-worth. Dipstick and Rod just thought that she was a crazy, horny bitch.

Also at the table when Jack arrived were Brad and Karl, two young lieutenants who had been in Germany for only three months, and Captain Schultz, Jack's characterless, ineffective acquaintance from the Greenham base. Schultz had been dropping his wife off at her bridge club and had popped into the bar for a Coke and some food. True to form, Schultz was dithering over the bar menu, unable to decide between the roast pork sandwich and the wiener schnitzel with sauerkraut.

Jack got some drinks and joined the group, which meant that there were now six men at the table and one woman.

'We're kind of guy-heavy here, babe,' Dipstick remarked to Helga. 'Could you call a friend?'

'OK, baby,' said Helga and went off to make a call.

Sure enough, in a short while a girl called Mitti turned up. It was fun for the older men to watch Karl and Brad's eyes pop out as Mitti joined their table. Her tiny waist and substantial bosom turned heads right across the bar. Mitti and Helga were both good-looking girls who were skilled at making the most of what they had, the fashions of the time being well suited to advertising one's wares. Both women wore short, ballooning ra-ra skirts and cowboy boots. Helga had on a denim jacket encrusted with glittering fake diamonds and with a picture of Los Angeles painted on the back and the words 'Hot LA Nights' picked out in twinkling studs and costume jewels. Under this she wore a pink shining spandex boobtube, from which her bosom seemed permanently in danger of escaping. Mitti wore a wetlook leather jacket, also jewel encrusted, with a collar that stood up round her ears and shoulders that jutted out about a foot and a half both ways, making it necessary for her to go through narrow doors sideways. Both Helga's and Mitti's hair was astonishing in a way that only mid-eighties hair could be; it was 'power' hair, 'me' hair, 'fuck you' hair and 'will you fuck me?' hair all rolled into one. Two great tousled blonde manes with platinum highlights. Gelled, sprayed, teased, streaked, glittered and glued and no doubt sheltering enough CFCs to bash a hole in the ozone layer the size of Germany. These were young women with lovely skin, but they had covered their faces in make-up, tan foundation, laden lashes and great bruises of purply blusher dusted across each cheekbone as if both women had been punched on the sides of their faces. They spoke through smoke-filled mouths, their glossy shining baby-pink lips edged with dark liner which made them look hard and vain.

Drinks were poured and then more drinks, and the conversation got dirtier. That old favourite, swearing in different languages, came up and caused roars of laughter as Helga regaled the soldiers with the various German words for a blowjob.

Karl and Brad were loving it. It felt great being real soldiers, hanging out with the older guys, talking dirty with the Kraut tarts. Even Jack was enjoying himself; it was all harmless enough, the girls were witty in an obscene, streetwise sort of way, and Dipstick as always knew the latest gags from the States.

'Why does Gary Hart wear underpants?' he asked. 'To keep his ankles warm!'

The Democratic primaries were underway back home and Gary Hart, a promising, charismatic politician who had at one time been frontrunner for the Democratic presidential nomination, was now in deep trouble over what were coming to be known as 'bimbo eruptions'. Hart had a reputation as a womanizer, a reputation that had been confirmed when he had been caught on a yacht canoodling with a bikini-clad girl who was in no way his wife. Most of the guys on the base were aghast that such a thing could be enough to fatally wound the man's professional aspirations.

'He'd get my vote,' Dipstick assured the company. 'What do we want in the White House? Faggots?'

The two young men roared their approval at this comment and slapped their thighs to show what regular guys they were. Schultz felt a little differently.

'Well, I don't know. I think we have a right to expect the very highest standards from those in public life,' he said. 'After all, if a man lies to his wife, how can we tell he's telling the truth to us?'

'Bullshit, Schultz,' said Dipstick. 'If a man says he doesn't lie to his wife then he's a liar anyway.'

Jack realized that Mitti was looking at him intently. He returned her stare and smiled, thinking to himself that she was probably very attractive underneath all the hair and make-up. Mitti's lips fell open slightly in the orthodox manner of the *femme fatales* of *Dynasty*. Her lips and teeth glistened, and slowly the pink, wet, pointy tip of her tongue gently journeyed from one corner of her hard-looking but soft mouth to the other. Mitti was not a subtle girl. She could not have made her intentions more clear if she had sent Jack a note asking for sex. She liked the look of Jack. She had quickly re- alized that he was a cut above the other men at the table. He roared less loudly, he leered less obviously and he was not forcing his legs against hers under the table.

Jack was surprised to find that he was interested too. It had been a long time since he had made love. He had not been entirely celibate since running out on Polly four years before, but he'd not been very active either. He still thought of Polly every day. He wanted her every day and no girl he had met since had remotely matched up to her. Certainly not this tawdry, brassy, blousey woman waggling her tongue at him across the table. She was everything that Polly had not been and vice versa. Yet there was something in Mitti's eyes, something behind the silver eyeshadow, the thick liner, the great caked mascaraed lashes, that Jack recognized. Perhaps it was honesty, or a sense of humour; it might well have been loneliness. Jack found himself returning Mitti's stare.

'This dump's getting kinda crowded,' said Dipstick, a white moustache of beer froth on his upper lip. 'How about we all go drink champagne at the American?'

The Hotel American was a favourite venue for one-night stands among the more discerning members of the Allied Armed Forces in the area. It was not sleazy, being rather well appointed and expensive, but neither did it object to partying. Its two suites boasted whirlpool baths in which three could sit comfortably and four even more so. This was a time when the almighty dollar was so strong that other currencies cowered before it; even the not unmuscular German Mark doffed its cap respectfully in the face of the purchasing power of the US buck. Americans overseas were far better off than they were at home and suites at the Hotel American were well within the budgets of discerning US officers.

Helga said she was happy to drink champagne any time, Rod was of course enthusiastic about the idea, and Brad and Karl could hardly believe their luck. Mitti just shrugged. She shrugged directly at Jack, a shrug that suggested that she would like the idea a whole lot better if he was in on it. All eyes turned to Jack. Nobody considered Schultz. Even the young officers ignored him; he was just that kind of invisible person.

Jack sucked at his beer and laughed. 'So you guys are planning a party?' he said.

'Didn't you hear?' Dipstick replied. 'Life's a party.'

It was decision time. Jack wondered what he wanted. What he wanted, of course, was Polly but he couldn't have her, so perhaps he wanted Mitti. He was drunk and she was getting more attractive by the minute. Maybe he should go along with it. Have a few laughs. He was so hard on himself most of the time; perhaps it would be fun. He looked at Mitti and her eyes were welcoming.

'Well hey, no rush,' said Dipstick. 'We'll just all sit here getting old while you think about it.'

Jack pulled himself together. He was dreaming. Orgies were not for him. It was a strange thing, but Polly, or at least the memory of Polly, had come to act as a sort of censor on Jack's life. He often found himself wondering what she would make of the things he said and the things he did. Of one thing he was sure: she would not think much of his cavorting at the Hotel American with drunken girls. It was almost as if having betrayed her utterly he was trying to make it up by not betraying her memory.

'No thanks. I'm going to get something to eat,' Jack [s]id, rising from the table.

'Hey, come on, Jack,' Dipstick protested. 'You can't break up the party.'

'You don't need me, Dip,' Jack laughed, and as he did so he caught Mitti's eye and the disappointment there. He could not help but smile at her and that was enough. Mitti got up too.

'I'm coming with you,' she said boldly.

'*Nein, Mitti*,' Helga said.

'Yeah, *nein*,' Dipstick added.

Helga and Dipstick could both see the ratio of the sexes changing from six:two to five:one and neither of them liked it.

'C'mon, Jack. You and Mitti have gotta stay.'

'Mitti can do what she likes, Dipstick, but if you think I want to see your white hairy ass in a spa bath you've been in the army too long,' Jack said, putting on his coat.

'I don't think I'll bother either, guys,' said Schultz. 'I have an early appointment at the chiropodist tomorrow and I'd hate to be all bleary for it. Thanks, anyway.'

Dipstick ignored Schultz.

'Who said anything about a spa bath, Jack?' he protested. 'We're just going to get some booze.'

'Yeah, sure, Dip. Absolutely,' Jack replied and, nodding his farewell to the table, he turned and headed for the door, but not before casting a questioning glance at Mitti. There followed a brief exchange between Mitti and Helga in German, the gist of which was Mitti asking Helga if Helga minded being left. Helga was no particularly delighted about it, but she was a grown-u girl and it was a well-established rule that in such pick-up situations it was every woman for herself. Helga told Mitti that if she wanted to go with Jack then she should do it, but she was to be sure to phone her in the morning and give her a full report.

'You too,' Mitti replied in English, 'but not too early.'

Jack was waiting at the door. Mitti grabbed her jacket and the two of them left. Outside Mitti put her arm through Jack's and they walked together through the snowy streets. She was shivering, her little ra-ra dress and wetlook leather jacket being little protection from the cold. Jack put his arm around her. Most places were shut, but after a while they found a small Moroccan restaurant in a basement called the Kasbah. The only other clientele were North Africans, economic immigrants, the subject of much resentment in the town.

That night, however, everything was smiles between the nervous black men and their unexpected guests, and Jack and Mitti sat down to couscous, lamb stew and beer.

'So you really did want to eat,' Mitti enquired.

'Sure, what else?'

They both knew what else. Mitti did not reply, but glanced coyly down at her food and then up again at Jack, which was reply enough. She did in fact have lovely eyes and without her ridiculous jacket she seemed much less hard and aggressive; even the huge hair appeared to be getting softer and less assertive.

They finished their meal and went to a small hotel

where they made love. Even as they began, Jack wished that he had not. He liked Mitti; she was a nice girl and very pretty underneath the make-up, but the truth was that she was not his type. It was partly the smell. There was no part of Mitti's person that was not scented and treated with anti-perspirant. She could have fucked for a year and not broken into a sweat. Every inch of her both reeked and tasted of chemicals, her scratchy, brittle hair, her sour-tasting neck, the soapy gloss on her lips, the all-over body spray on her breasts, even her crotch had been deodorized, her natural sexual scent bludgeoned into submission by some cloud of musky napalm. Merely undressing Mitti had given Jack a headache and a blocked-up nose. It was like trying to have sex on the cosmetic counter at Macy's. His throat hurt and he felt sick for a day afterwards, like he had swallowed a bottle of aftershave.

Jack was a gentleman and he did his best, but they both knew that his heart wasn't in it.

After a while they gave up, got dressed and Jack took Mitti home in a cab.

He kissed her goodnight and headed back to base feeling lonely and sad.

At about lunchtime the next day Mitti rang Helga to find out how her night had gone.

Helga said it had been fine, but she had sounded strange. After that Mitti did not see Helga for a week, by which time Helga had been to the police to report having been raped.

There were two stories of what happened to Helga

after Jack and Mitti had left the bar that night.

Nobody disputed that Dipstick, Rod, Brad, Karl and Helga had all left the bierkeller in Bad Nauheim together, leaving Captain Schultz to his sauerkraut. Likewise, there was general agreement that the party had removed itself to the Hotel American where Dipstick had taken the best rooms available, a suite that boasted its own bar and a whirlpool bath. After this the stories begin to diverge. Helga admitted that they had all stripped off and squeezed into the hot bath together. Also she admitted, under police questioning, that she had then voluntarily had sex in the spa with Dipstick while the other men looked on. She also conceded that she had briefly masturbated certainly one other man, Rod, she thought, and possibly one of the others, too. After this Helga claimed that Rod had suggested that she now have sex with him and then also with the two younger officers. Helga said that at this point she had become nervous, as the men were beginning to get noisy and raucous. She declined Rod's request for sex, saying that she had now had enough, and attempted to leave the spa bath. After this she claimed that Rod and Brad had raped her in turn while Karl and Dipstick sat by and continued to drink.

The men, on the other hand, all swore under oath that Helga had consented to all the sexual acts that had happened that night. They swore that there had been no difference at all between Helga's attitude to having sex with Dipstick and then having sex with the other two men. They pointed out that Helga had not cried

141

out and that afterwards she had not left the hotel until the following morning, even accepting a cup of coffee from Karl. Everyone admitted to having been very drunk.

Helga could not explain why she had not cried out, except to say that she thought she might have been too scared. She was also not entirely sure why she had remained in the hotel for some hours after the incident, apart from the fact that she had felt weak and sick and upset. When asked why it had taken her five days to report the alleged attack, she said that she had prevaricated because she knew very well how the whole incident would look. The only thing of which Helga was absolutely certain was that the last two men who had had sex with her had known that she was no longer a willing participant.

The courts decided in favour of the men. The fact that Helga had had a previous sexual relationship with both Dipstick and Rod and the fact that she had gone voluntarily for sex at the hotel told heavily against her. Besides which, in the long run it came down to the word of four people against one.

Helga moved away from Bad Nauheim almost immediately following the court case. She wrote home once or twice and Mitti heard that she was living in Hamburg, but after that she seemed to disappear.

The careers of the four soldiers never recovered. Whatever the courts may have decided, such a sordid incident was too much for the army to ignore and they were marked men. One by one they returned to civilian life in the States, angry and bitter and having learnt nothing from their experience. Quite the opposite, in fact. All four men came to believe absolutely that their treatment had been grossly unfair and that the woman Helga had set out viciously to destroy them for no better reason than feminine pique.

The case shocked and disturbed both the army and the local community. Jack, who was called as a witness to recall the course of events during the early part of the evening, found his emotions and his principles confused and divided. He engaged in a heated correspondence with his brother Harry on the issues raised by the awful affair. Harry felt that it was obvious that the four soldiers were in the wrong and that they had got off far too lightly. Jack could not see things so clearly. He remembered the sight of the young man Brad crying in the witness box, pleading that he had really thought that the sort of girl that Helga was did not care much about one man more or less.

'*And what about you, Jack?*' Harry wrote back furiously. '*Is that what you think? Does being a soldier make a guy so dumb that he can rape a woman by mistake?*'

No, Jack knew that he could never do that, but he wondered. He wondered what he would have been like as a man if he had never met Polly. Would he have been like Brad? Would he too have been capable of getting drunk and seeing a woman not as a whole and complex person, confused and in pain, but just as some kind of two-dimensional sexual animal? It was possible, of course it was possible. All men had a darker side; that was what made them capable of killing. Jack was a soldier and he knew that very well. To Jack what the Bad Nauheim case had shown was what that dark, uncivilized side of man was capable of when it gained the upper hand. It was a lesson he was not to forget.

Jack may have betrayed Polly's love but Polly's love had not betrayed him.

22

Polly finally left the peace camp with the gap that Jack had left in her heart and soul still not filled. She was unsettled and restless. She could not return to her old life, the one she had known years before; it had moved on without her. All her friends from that time were already in their second year at university. She saw them occasionally but she no longer had anything in common with them. She knew that deep down they felt sorry for her.

'But what are you going to do after all this?' they asked. 'You can't just be a protester all your life.'

'Yeah, well, maybe I can,' Polly replied, but she knew that it sounded stupid.

Still looking for something and nothing she became a traveller, a member of one of the New Age convoys that roamed the country at the time. Polly liked living on the move. It gave her the impression that she was going somewhere. She started seeing a casual dope dealer called Ziggy who owned a Volkswagen Camper. Polly was fond of Ziggy. He was thirty-six and painfully handsome with deep, piercing blue eyes. He had a Ph.D. in Ergonomics and was an extremely bright and interesting conversationalist, when he was not stoned. Unfortunately this was only for about fifteen minutes each morning. For the rest of the day Ziggy tended to merely giggle a lot.

It was fun for a while, rejecting hierarchy and property, but it couldn't last. Slowly but surely Polly began to long for a more structured life, a life where she could watch television without having to stare through the window at Dixons and go to the toilet without taking a spade. She was twenty-one, Mrs Thatcher had just won yet another election, and Polly had not been entirely clean since Duran Duran had been at the top of the charts.

She left Ziggy, which hurt him badly.

'But why, Poll?' he asked. 'I thought we had a scene going.'

'It's the giggling, Ziggy. I just can't handle the giggling.'

'I'll giggle less,' he pleaded. 'I'll start smoking hash instead of grass. It's a much mellower high.'

But it was no use. Polly left the convoy and moved to London, where she virtually became a street person, spending two months standing on the never-ending picket outside the South African Embassy. It was while on the anti-apartheid picket that Polly met an alternative comedian called Dave, whose opening line was 'Good evening, ladies and gentlemen. Would you like to see my bollocks?' Dave was nice, but he was, in his own words, 'Not into monogamy, right?' In truth, he saw his gigs as no more than a good way of pulling girls. There might have been a time when Polly would have turned a blind eye to such behaviour, but these were the great days of AIDS paranoia so Polly took one last look at Dave's bollocks and moved on again.

It was around this time that Jack also moved on, leaving his regiment in Germany and returning to the US to take up a post at the Pentagon. He, like Polly (and Bono) hadn't found what he was looking for either, but, unlike Polly, he had a good idea of what it was and where it might be found. What Jack was looking for was success and, for a soldier without a war to fight, that meant going to Washington. In Washington promotion prospects were, if not good, certainly better than on the Rhine.

It was a frustrating time for an ambitious soldier, although paradoxically the military had never been held higher in the nation's esteem. Reagan, who had never served in the forces himself, was a soldier's president. He believed in big defence budgets and plenty of parades. US prestige could not have been greater, the Soviet Union was haemorrhaging in Afghanistan and the corridors of power buzzed with news of the famed Star Wars initiative with which the Pentagon intended to militarize space. Public interest in the army was unprecedented, with gung-ho movies like *Rambo* and *Top Gun* filling the cinemas. Things had improved considerably since the dark days of twenty years before when an adolescent Jack had refused to accompany his parents and his brother Harry to see *MASH* and *Catch 22*, a terrible, demoralizing time when America had been briefly ashamed of its fighting men.

None the less, for all the celluloid mayhem, real soldiers do actually need real wars in order to be promoted. If the fellow above you does not get shot, then you have to wait twenty years for him to retire and the same goes for the fellow above him. Jack was thirty-six and getting frustrated.

'*I'm middle-fucking-aged and still a captain!*' he wrote to Harry. '*I was one of the youngest captains ever. You remember that? It was in the local paper and everything.*'

Harry did indeed remember it. Their father and mother had been furious with embarrassment.

'Not only does he have to be a soldier,' Jack Senior had lamented over his muesli and fat-free organic yogurt. 'He has to be a successful soldier. Why didn't we just bring up a fascist and be done with it! I just hope that none of my students get to hear about this. Every day I bust my ass trying to civilize young people and now my own son is the youngest damn captain in the army!'

At the time Jack had been delighted at his father's discomfort, but as the years went by and he felt himself sinking into career doldrums Jack felt less inclined to crow.

'*The youngest captain, Harry!*' Jack wrote from Washington. '*That was what I was for a couple of years, and by hell did I rub Pa's face in it? Then for a while I was a youngish captain, now I'm just a reasonable age to be a captain. It won't be long before I'm an old captain. Then like thousands of other captains I'm going to have to decide whether to retire and strike out in civilian life, fifteen years behind all the other guys (with you and Dad laughing in my face), or stay on and face the possibility of a very sad career indeed. Jesus, when Napoleon was my age he'd conquered the world once and was thinking about making a comeback! When Alexander the Great was my age he was dead! I know I'm a good soldier, Harry, but there's no way of showing it. On parade I just look the same as all the other guys. You remember Schultz? The geek nerd I told you about before? He's in Washington too and he has equal seniority with me!! Equal!! I mean, he's a decent guy and all that, but Jesus! He has the strategic instincts of a lemming!'*

Harry was in no doubt what Jack should do. He told him to cut his losses and get out.

'*Never,*' Jack wrote back. '*The army is my life and I will never give it up, no matter how badly it treats me.*'

The truth was that Jack had already cut his losses. He had given up Polly in pursuit of military glory and whether he found that glory or not, he could never get back what he had lost.

As for Polly, she was in a much worse position than Jack. As the eighties turned into the nineties she was without a proper home, without possessions, without qualifications or security of any kind, and she was lonely.

She went to live in a squat in Acton, a sad house with boarded-up windows that had been repossessed by the council because they were widening the A40 to Oxford. It was occupied mainly by the warriors of Class War, a loose collective of malcontents made up principally of Oxbridge graduates who wanted to destroy the state, probably because unlike most of their friends they had failed to get high-ranking jobs at the BBC.

At twenty-five Polly knew that her life was twisting downwards, out of control, but she did not know how to stop it. All her old friends were young professionals with incomes. Polly no longer saw them, but her mother, of course, kept her informed about their huge successes. Most of Polly's more recent friends were either stoned, in prison or chained to lumps of concrete in tunnels underneath the roadworks on Twyford Down. The new decade had also brought with it the threat of war in the Middle East, which was most depressing for Polly, since if there was one meaningful thing she had tried to do over the previous eight years it was fight for peace.

By a strange twist of fate it was because of Saddam Hussein that Polly came to see Jack again, if only for a moment and only on the television, but it was a painful shock none the less. It was in January 1991 and Polly and friends were lying around their squat on their damp mattresses watching the military build-up in the Gulf through the window of their tiny black and white portable television screen. John Major had just been speaking about the need to stand up to aggression and tinpot despots wherever they reared their heads.

'Ha!' said Polly earnestly. 'If Kuwait dug potatoes

instead of oil we wouldn't give a toss about them. We didn't mind about tinpot despots in Chile and Nicaragua, did we? And why? Because they were our tinpot despots, weren't they?'

Polly was just working herself up into a fair state of righteous anger when it happened. Suddenly, Jack was in the room. Standing in front of a tank, now a full colonel, and giving it as his opinion that Saddam's men were lions led by donkeys.

'We don't want to have to kill these soldiers,' Jack said from within the tiny TV, 'but let the butcher of Baghdad be under no illusions that we will kill them, and we will kill them quickly and efficiently.'

Polly felt like she had been kicked. It was so unexpected and over so soon. While her companions continued to argue with the talking heads on television she retreated to the kitchen, all the anger and hurt welling up inside her once again.

And the love.

He still looked beautiful to her. Achingly so. Even in one of those awful Wehrmacht-style helmets that the Americans had taken to wearing at that time. He looked so commanding and so confident, so strong, forceful and fit. All of a sudden Polly found that she did not just miss Jack, she was jealous of him. Jack knew what he wanted, he knew where he was going, he always had and he was still on the winning side. Polly wiped the silverfish off the breadboard and started to cry.

23

Jack stared at Polly and smiled.

She was still lovely. Her home might be dowdy and her possessions rather run down and few, but she lit up that room like a searchlight, like· a bright star. Jack swallowed hard. He had not expected it, he really had not expected her still to be so very beautiful. As far as Jack was concerned, the passage of time had completely failed to dull her loveliness.

'I don't think you changed, Polly,' he almost whispered. 'You didn't age a day.'

'Bollocks, Jack.'

Jack laughed. 'Now there's a word I haven't heard in a long time. But really, how did you do it? Is it some face cream made out of dead whales, or do you have a portrait in your attic of some terrible dissipated old hag?'

'This *is* my attic, Jack. I live in it.'

Now that Polly had got over the initial shock of Jack's arrival it was beginning to dawn on her how strange the situation was.

'I don't know why I've let you in. I was asleep . . . The place is a mess . . . Why have you come back?'

'Why do you think, Polly? Why do you think I've come?'

'How the hell would I know? I don't even know you.'

'You know me, Polly.'

'I know you're a bastard!'

Jack shrugged.

'It is nearly two thirty in the bloody morning, Jack!'

'I do unusual work,' said Jack, shrugging again. 'Where I come from we keep strange hours.'

He was just the same. Still arrogant, still forceful.

'Yes, well, back here on earth we tend to sleep in the middle of the night!'

'May I take off my coat? May I sit down?'

It was the small hours of the morning. He'd been gone for donkey's years and he wanted to take off his coat and sit down. Polly's mind reeled.

'No! This is absurd. I don't know why I let you in at all. I think you should go. If you want to see me you can come back in the morning.'

'I'll be gone in the morning, Polly.'

This was too much for Polly. It was hardly what might have been called a tactful thing to say, considering how they had parted the last time they'd been together.

'Yes, well, some things don't change, then, do they, you . . . You . . .'

Polly bit her lip and fell silent. Of course she was angry with him, angry with him for leaving her and angry with him for coming back in such a strange manner. But, for all that, she was so very glad that he had come back.

'It's just I'm only in Britain for a few hours, Polly. This was the only time I could come.'

'Jack, it's been, it's been . . . I don't know how long it's been . . .'

'Sixteen years.'

'I know how long it's been!'

As if she could forget. As if she didn't remember every moment of that summer and every day that had passed since.

'Sixteen years and two months, to be precise,' said Jack, who seemed also to have been carefully marking the passage of time.

'Exactly! Exactly. Sixteen years and two months, during which time it appears that you have been more than capable of getting by without seeing me, and you want to visit me now!'

'Yes.'

'And seeing as how it's only been sixteen years and two months, seeing as how it's only been the merest decade and a half since we last set eyes on each other, you have to visit immediately, not a moment to lose, at two fifteen in the morning!'

'I told you. I'm only in town for one night.'

'Well, why not drop by when you have a little more space in your diary! Heaven knows, we might even arrange a mutually convenient appointment.'

'I'm never in Britain, Polly. This is the first time I've been here since we . . . since I . . . since then,' his voice trailed off rather weakly.

They were both remembering the chill dawn when he had left.

'Why didn't you come back before?' asked Polly.

'I couldn't. I go where I'm told.'

Weak. He knew it, and so did she.

'That is pathetic.'

'Polly, I take orders.'

'That's what they said at Nuremberg.'

Jack bridled somewhat. He knew he was in the wrong but he was not the sort of person who found contrition easy and he certainly wasn't having Nuremberg thrown at him. All his life he had been deeply irritated at the way people, particularly people of a liberal persuasion, particularly his father and mother, had got into the habit of using the Nazis as some kind of ready benchmark for things of which they disapproved. If somebody wanted to cut welfare benefits they were a Nazi, if somebody wanted to raise the busfares they were a Nazi, if they objected to graffiti they were a Nazi. It was just puerile. Jack was prepared to put up his hand to the fact that he may have acted like a swine but he had not murdered six million Jews.

'Oh, please, Polly. Is everybody still a fascist? Didn't you grow out of that yet?'

'Didn't you grow out of not having a personality?' Polly's withering contempt almost singed Jack's eyebrows. ' "I take orders," ' she snarled in a mock American accent. 'What? And they ordered you never to write? Never to call? To disappear off the face of the planet and ignore every telephone in the USA for sixteen years!'

'They would not have approved.'

'And if they ordered you to stick an umbrella up your arse and open it? Would you do that?'

'Yes, I would.' Of course he would. What did she think he was? He was a soldier; did she think soldiers only did things they wanted to?

'Well, then, I hope they do. A fucking great Cinzano beach umbrella with a pointy end and a couple of twisted spokes.'

Jack glanced at his watch. It was nearly 2.30. He had to be in Brussels for a lunchtime meeting the next day. That meant flying out at 10.30 at the latest.

Polly caught his look. 'I'm sorry if I'm boring you!'

Jack hated that. Ever since Jack could remember, women had been offended with his checking his watch. As if his desire to know the time and keep his appointments was some kind of deathly insult to the power of their personalities.

'I like to know the time, that's all.'

'It's two fifteen in the fucking morning, Jack! We established that.'

It wasn't, it was already 2.30 and Jack was on a schedule.

'Polly, believe me,' he said. 'I know I should have contacted you before. There hasn't been a day when I didn't think about you. Not a single day.'

Polly did not know whether to believe him or not. It

seemed unlikely, but if it was true it was a wonderful thing. That through all those years, especially those early ones when she had hurt so much at her loss, he had been thinking about her.

'They just never sent me back to Britain before, that's all,' Jack continued.

'Even you get holidays.'

What did she know? She didn't know anything. He got time off, certainly. Time when he was not required to spend the day planning the deaths of thousands of enemy soldiers. Time when he was at liberty to go fishing or take a drive along the coast. But men in his position did not get holidays, not real holidays, holidays from who and what they were. Jack was never just Jack, not for a single moment, he was General Jack Kent, one of the most senior figures in the defence systems of the United States. Twenty-four hours a day, three hundred and sixty-five days a year.

'I'm always on duty.'

'Oh, for heaven's sake.'

'I tell it like I see it.'

'Yeah, well, so do I, and what I see is a coward and a shit.'

'Hey, Polly . . . I'm not a coward.'

He could always make her laugh. That effortlessly cool self-deprecating humour that only strong, confident people can pull off. Polly almost weakened and laughed with him. For a moment a tiny smile twitched at the corners of her mouth. He saw it, and she knew he saw it, but she wasn't giving in that easily.

'So now, after nearly seventeen years your "duty" brings you back to Britain for a night?'

'Yes. One night.'

'And you couldn't warn me? You couldn't call from the airport?'

'No. I couldn't warn you. I'm sorry, but that's the way it is. All I could do was come and I did. I got into Brize Norton tonight and I came straight here.'

It was a lie, of course, but Jack sort of felt that it was true. He had after all wanted to come straight to Polly. He had certainly come the moment his circumstances allowed him to, the moment he had made his presentation to the Cabinet and said farewell to the ambassador.

The lie worked. Polly stared into Jack's eyes. He had come straight to her. That was certainly something, something exciting she could not deny. Nor could she deny how handsome he had remained. More handsome than ever, even. She liked the grey at his temples and she preferred him without the early eighties Burt Reynolds moustache. He seemed leaner somehow, tougher. He had certainly not gone old and soft over the years.

Then she remembered that she hated him. That he had dumped her without a word, without so much as a goodbye. He was a shit.

'This is absurd, Jack. I'm bloody dreaming. What are you saying? You came straight here! Why? Why did you come straight here? I was seventeen years old. It was nearly twenty years ago—'

'Sixteen years and two—'

'I know! I know how long it was! It was another life. We are total strangers now! I ought to throw you out.'

Jack fell silent and looked at Polly. He said nothing, but his stare grew in intensity until Polly began to feel quite uncomfortable. It was as if Jack was preparing to unburden himself, to share his secrets with her. Then his spirit appeared to desert him, his shoulders sagged, his eyes dropped and he sighed.

'You're right,' he said. 'This is dumb. Completely dumb. Insane. I should go.'

Jack turned wearily towards the door, deflated and lost, a man whose poor, sad, hopeless dreams had been exposed as just that. It worked, of course.

'Don't be ridiculous! You can't just go!'

'I thought you wanted me to.'

'No! That's not fair! You can't wait sixteen years and two months, wake me up in the middle of the night, barge in and then barge out again.'

Again a pause. 'So you don't want me to go?'

'I don't know what I want.'

Polly took up a packet of slightly milder than full-strength cigarettes from the kitchen table. As she bent over the gas stove to light one, the stiff plastic mac she was wearing stood out from her thighs and revealed a little more of her bare legs. She still had wonderful legs, fabulous legs. Jack had always loved Polly's legs, but then he had always loved everything about Polly. She turned back towards him, leant against the stove and inhaled deeply. Jack almost laughed, remembering the long evenings they had spent lying together after making love, watching the glowing ends of their cigarettes in the darkness, talking, disagreeing on every single thing under the sun except their desire to be together.

24

Peter's whole being reeled with hatred. He had watched from the shop doorway as the American man entered Polly's house and had stood for five minutes or so as if in a trance. The jealousy and sense of betrayal were so all-consuming that he had found himself unable to move. She was seeing other men! Sneaking them in in the middle of the night so that he wouldn't see them! Tricking him into thinking she was being good when in fact she was nothing but a lying, cheating slag. And as for him. As for that American bastard. Peter had no vocabulary in his head with which to encompass the scope of his loathing for that man. It sat in his consciousness as a sort of red blur.

However, once Peter had come round from his state of shock he knew absolutely that he must retrieve his knife at once. If ever he needed it he needed it now. He rushed back up the road to the phonebox, back to the drain down which the hated American had kicked his knife. Peter had seen that it had lodged on a jutting brick before he had run away. The question was, would it still be there?

Of course it was. How could it not be; it was Peter's

precious knife and it would not be taken from him so easily. Kneeling in the gutter he could see it, lodged still, awaiting his retrieval. Peter went off to find a suitable tool with which to recover the knife and soon returned with an old wire coathanger picked from the rubbish in a nearby skip. Out of this he fashioned a long hook. He knew that the knife had a little hinged curve of metal attached to its innocent end by which a person might fasten the weapon to their belt. It was into this that Peter planned to place his hook. His challenge was to do this without dislodging the knife and causing it to fall further out of reach. So he knelt down in the sodden gutter and set to his task, dangling his hook into one of the numerous gaping mouths that fed and watered subterranean London with rubbish, effluence and rain.

'Bastard. Fucking bastard. I'll get you. I'll get you,' mumbled Peter under his breath, and he was not referring to the knife.

25

'You still smoke?' Jack enquired.

'I'm giving up soon,' Polly replied defensively, 'in a week or two, this month, I hope. Certainly by the end of the year. Don't tell me you quit?'

Jack hadn't wanted to give up smoking, but he'd been forced to. He worked for the government; it was either give up or become a pathetic non-person. Quite apart from anything else, smoking had got too tiring. The smoke exclusion zones around public buildings had been getting wider and wider since Clinton got in. In vain had he argued at the highest level that to make the Pentagon a no-smoking area was something of a sick joke. He and his colleagues had pointed out to their political masters that since the Pentagon was a building in which mass chemical and nuclear genocide was planned daily, it seemed almost tasteless to introduce a health code.

Polly was surprised. Jack had always been so gungho about his smoking.

'You said you'd never give up. You said you'd rather die.'

'Yeah, well I didn't know then that the greatest

country in the world would end up getting run by a bunch of killjoy liberal fucking pussies, did I?'

That was the other side of Jack, of course. Polly remembered it well. The unreconstructed reactionary. The bullying, bigoted, yobbo soldier with the sexual and political sensitivity of Ghenghis Khan's hordes on an angry and randy day. The strange thing was that she had always secretly found conservatism rather attractive. He was so honest and unashamed about being a right-wing bastard. As a deeply confused liberal herself, Polly found that kind of confidence rather compelling.

'Nice to know you haven't changed,' she said. 'The kinder, gentler America passed you by, then?'

'Oh yeah? Maybe we should start trying to be a little kinder and gentler to the guys who like to drink and smoke and read *Playboy* magazine now and again! It's the hypocrisy I can't stand. They had their fun. Fifteen years ago those same star fucking Democrat assholes that are banning smokes were taking cocaine in their coffee. Now coffee carries a health warning.'

'Yeah, well, you're lucky. I'd love to kick the fags,' Polly replied. 'Sometimes I buy one Mgs, but then I just smoke them six or seven at a time.'

Polly leant against the table, placed her fingers over the little airholes in the filter that were supposed to dilute the tar and inhaled deeply. Jack watched her chest rise as she did so and he longed to fall upon her as of old. She walked around the table to pick up an ashtray and again Jack could not help but notice how attractive her legs were. As good as ever, he thought; better, in fact. Now how could that be? He had it! They were shaved! Polly had shaved her legs, and recently, too. They were smooth and shiny, the skin bright in the light of the overhead lamp.

The old Polly, the young Polly, would on principle never have shaved her legs. She would have considered leg shaving to be a disgusting capitulation to sexist male stereotyping of the female form, a very short step from having four kilos of silicon pumped into her tits and appearing naked in *Hustler*. Not that Polly's legs had been particularly hirsute in the old days. No hairier than most girls, but then most girls actually do have quite hairy legs if they let it grow free, even seventeen-year-olds. At the time Jack had sort of liked it because he loved her. She had been so different from the plucked, waxed and sanded-down, cheerleading Barbies whom he had dated previously, but even then he had only sort of liked it. Jack was in many things a traditionalist. He liked his petrol leaded and his ladies smooth and there was no denying that Polly's shapely calf muscles were all the finer without the fuzzy edges.

Polly exhaled again. The smell of smoke had filled the room by now and Jack breathed it in greedily.

'I'd love to take up smoking again,' he said, 'but I just don't have the guts. I fought the Iraqis, but the American anti-smoking lobby scares the shit out of me. If you light up in New York some mom in California will sue you for murdering her unborn child. It's insane. Guys who operate nuclear missiles for a living are getting sacked for perpetrating secondary lung cancer.'

Polly realized that they were having a conversation. It had happened so easily she hadn't even noticed. After sixteen years and two months of pain and resentment, there they were, just having a conversation.

'Well, since you're here, Jack, you'd better give me your coat.'

Jack took off his coat and Polly gulped with surprise. Underneath the coat Jack was resplendent in the dress uniform of an American four-star general. Polly laughed. It seemed the only thing to do. Jack could not have looked more out of place if he'd been a *Baywatch* babe in a nunnery. His epaulettes glinted, his belt buckle sparkled, his buttons shone, his shoulder braid strutted grandly and his medal ribbons competed for attention upon his splendid chest. Anybody who had known Jack a decade or so earlier when he had believed his career to be grinding to a halt would have gasped to see him now. In the cabinet room at Ten Downing Street Jack had looked superb. The creaky, threadbare, down-at-heel members of Her Majesty's Government had provided a more than fitting setting for this splendid warrior from the New World. But context is everything and in Polly's bedsit he looked like the conductor in a rather tasteless brass band.

'Jesus, Jack, what are you? John Wayne? Did you come back to Britain to invade it?'

It had not occurred to Jack until that point that he was dressed in a manner that some might consider unusual. In Jack's position he was expected to wear

166

dress uniform all the time, and on the whole he rather enjoyed it. Now, however, he felt self-conscious. Like a person who has proudly put on a black tie to attend a very special function but still has to get to the event by bus. It feels great while you are attaching the bowtie and the cufflinks. It'll feel great again when you're greedily plucking the first flute of Italian sparkling from a passing tray. The period in between, however, is not so good, when one is forced by circumstance to mix with the less exalted, the ordinarily dressed. At this point, frankly, one feels a bit of a prick.

'You never did like uniforms much, did you?' he said with the tiniest hint of ill grace.

'I think they're a bit sad, that's all. If you can't express your authority without poncing about like a fascist, then you can't have had much authority in the first place.'

Again that childish fascist thing. Jack let it go.

'Yeah, well, I had to wear this stuff,' he said instead. 'It was required.'

'What, for me?'

Jack would have to be honest. 'No, not you. When I said I came straight here, what I meant was that I came straight here when I could. I had a meeting earlier, that's why I'm in Britain. Politicians like to see you in uniform. I think it makes them feel important. They're the only kind of people who ever get to play with real soldiers.'

Jack had calculated that this last comment would appeal to Polly, but if it did she ignored it.

'Politicians? What politicians?'

'Mainly your prime minister.'

Polly gulped again in astonishment. When the phone had woken her a little while ago she'd been dreaming, of what she couldn't remember, but being a dream it would no doubt have been fairly surreal, possibly containing marshmallow hippopotamuses in tutus and a great deal of falling. Since then her life had been a whirl of psycho-stalkers, old flames and ancient enemies and now casual references to visits with the highest in the land. Reality was proving far more bizarre than anything Polly's subconscious mind had been conjuring up. The pink hippos were beginning to seem rather mundane.

'The prime minister! The prime fucking minister! You've come here after seeing the prime minister!'

To Jack this wasn't such a big deal. He saw top people all the time. Certainly the prime minister of Britain was an important person, but there were any number of prime ministers dotted about the world, fifty at a minimum. They came and they went, sometimes before the newsreaders had even learnt how to pronounce their names properly. Jack had met most of them one way or another and Polly's astonished reaction rather took him aback. He was about to say, 'Yeah, the PM. So what?' but then decided it would be rude. To her, he supposed, it was as if he'd turned up at an apartment in the Bronx and casually remarked that he'd just been visiting with the president and first lady.

'It wasn't just me, you know, one on one,' he said, as

if to downplay the grandeur of the situation. 'There were the chiefs of staff ... That's the top guys in your ...'

'I know who the chiefs of staff are, Jack. Unless you'd forgotten, I once had the opportunity to study matters military at close quarters.'

'Yeah,' Jack laughed. 'I guess you were a combatant too, weren't you? A soldier of the Cold War.'

How many were there like her now? Ex-combatants of an ideological struggle that had simply faded away. All around the world were people hidden in flats and bedsits, eking out their lives, who had once been warriors. Who had once locked horns with super-powers. Soldiers, spies, resistance fighters, protesters. In her way Polly was such a one, another Cold War loser. For a time she had fought NATO with the same commitment that Jack had defended it. But it was over now and the battle that Polly had fought was fast fading in the memory of all but the people involved.

Jack remembered it, of course, and suddenly he longed with all his heart to return once again to that golden time, the summer of his and Polly's love. How he ached to see her naked once more. To be blinded afresh by her youth and beauty. A beauty that had been so pure and unencumbered by artifice. So naturally erotic, so effortlessly sexual. Jack longed to advance upon Polly then and there, as once he had, breathless and shaking with a dizzying, overwhelming passion, his entire being utterly and completely focused. No longer a whole and complex man but a desperate, straining sexual entity that knew no other time than the moment and no other purpose than to make love.

Polly caught the look in Jack's eyes as they journeyed downwards and then up again over her body, lingering for a moment on her legs, bare to just above the knee and again on the triangle of flesh visible at her open collar.

'Look, if you're staying,' she said, 'I should get dressed.'

'Why?' Jack replied.

26

Outside in the wet and empty street Peter knelt in the gutter, his fingers straining at the metal grid that covered the drain. His upper lip was crusted with blood from when the door of the telephone box had bashed his nose. The knees of his trousers were soaking up the filthy London water and the rain was falling on his head.

Peter noticed none of these things.

His whole being was concentrated on the black hilt and glinting steel blade that he could see lodged three feet or so below him. His precious knife, sitting precariously on the jutting brick within the wall of that water-bloated urban intestine. His precious weapon, teetering on the brink of the bowels of the city.

'Bastard. Bastard. Fucking bastard,' he muttered through the soggy scabs of blood and the bitter-tasting rain.

27

Polly stared at Jack. What had he just said? Don't bother getting dressed?

His eyes had been awash with sensual longing and he had told her not to bother getting dressed. Now she scarcely knew what to think. Was he asking her to bed? That would be a bold move indeed. Had he burst back into her life in order to fuck her as quickly as possible? It was, after all, how it had happened the first time, in his TR7. They had been unable to keep their hands off each other. Looking at Jack as he looked at her Polly was shocked to discover that a substantial part of her was excited at the prospect of leaping instantly into bed with this man who had betrayed her. Her sensual self wanted to surrender instantly to whatever Jack wanted. Why not? She was a grown woman, she was entitled to take a bit of comfort as and when she pleased. Unfortunately for Polly's sensual self, her intellectual and emotional self recoiled at the idea, feeling angry and abused. Her political self felt even worse about it; outraged would not be too strong a word for how her political self felt. Did Jack think that he could have it all? That he could shatter her life into tiny little bits and then pick up a piece when the fancy took him?

'What do you mean?' said Polly, defiantly drawing herself up to her full height. A gesture which served merely to raise her plastic mac higher, thus revealing rather more of her legs than was already showing.

Jack had not meant what Polly was thinking, in fact. Of course, to make love there and then would be nice, ecstatic in fact. Like Polly, a part of Jack longed to pick up where they had left off so many years before and go to bed. His sensual self would have delighted in spending the remainder of the night making the crockery rattle and furniture jump round the room. But also like Polly, Jack's intellectual self was raising objections; sex was not what he had come for, or what he had expected. There were things he wanted to discuss, things he needed to know. Sex would get in the way and Jack did not have a limitless amount of time. He tried to correct any misunderstanding.

'When I said "Why get dressed?" what I meant, of course, was why get dressed when you'd only have to get undressed again?'

Which of course did not correct any misunderstandings at all.

'What the hell do you mean by that?'

Jack tried again. 'No, I don't mean . . . What I mean is I can't stay long . . . I don't want to inconvenience you.'

'Which is why you dropped round at two in the morning.'

Polly had always had a caustic side. Jack could

remember having found it rather cute. At this point he couldn't quite remember why.

'I don't have long, that's all.'

'Well, thank you so much for giving me a whole five minutes out of your busy schedule after seventeen years without a word and at two thirty in the morning. I'm so grateful.'

'Look!' said Jack, a little more firmly than he had intended. 'I just don't have all that long. I'm sorry, but it's true. Anyway, why get dressed? You're probably better dressed now than you were when we met the first time.'

Both Polly and Jack were straddling two different times. Principally they were in the here and now and it was late and their relationship was edgy to say the least. But also, for a moment, they were back there and then and it was glorious summer and love was flowering in the very shadow of Armageddon. The first time that their paths had crossed, before their encounter at the restaurant on the A34, when they had met and did not know even that they were meeting. At the gates of the camp, when out of the valley of death had ridden a handsome soldier mounted on a jeep who had found his way obstructed by a beautiful golden maiden, a symbol of peace.

'Yes, well, sartorial considerations tended to go out of the window in those days,' Polly replied.

'Not that you had any windows,' said Jack.

'No, I didn't, that's right. You can't put windows in a woodland bender.'

Jack had not expected that he would feel things quite this violently, that his emotions would be so very much the same as they had been before.

'You were so beautiful, Polly,' said Jack. 'So wild. I can see you now as if it was only a heartbeat ago. Like some kind of . . .' He struggled for words. Jack had never been big on flowery prose, but he had a go: '. . . like some gorgeous woodland creature running along the side of the road, tanned legs in the long grass, the sun in your hair.'

'Screaming at you to fuck off and die.'

It was true. To her shame (and the embarrassment of Madge), Polly had often chosen to ignore the non-aggressive principles of the peace camp and address the soldiers in most unpeaceful terms.

'We love you! We want to understand you!' Madge would shout.

'Fuck off! Fuck off! Fuck off!' Polly would add.

And in the evening around the fire the women would all agree that it was important to try not to give mixed signals.

'You were perfect, Polly,' said Jack, his eyes half closed. 'A vision. I remember the first moment I saw you exactly. I have it fixed in my mind like some kind of idyll . . . like an Impressionist painting.'

'Jack, I was wearing a dustbin liner.'

'You still like plastic, I see.'

Polly remembered that she was wearing a rainmac and returned to the present with a bump.

'I don't have a dressing gown, I'm afraid.'

In her punkier days Polly would not have thought twice about receiving guests in a nightie and a plastic mac, but times had changed. 'I'm not used to entertaining under these circumstances. Sit down, Jack. I'd ask you to step through into the lounge, but I haven't got one.'

'Hey, you never used to have a roof.'

'Yeah, haven't I done well? I no longer sleep in the open.'

Polly was embarrassed about everything. What she was wearing, her little flat, her stuff. Why couldn't he have given her some warning of his visit? Just so she could have got herself together? She would not have needed long. Just enough time to move house and acquire some beautiful and glamorous possessions. Shift her career up ten or fifteen gears and have a little minor repair work done on the cellulite that was beginning to appear on her upper thighs.

Instead Jack was seeing her life as it really was.

'Still rejecting capitalist materialism, I see.'

Jack had never been the most tactful of people.

'No. These days capitalist materialism is rejecting me,' Polly replied. 'Getting its own back for the years I abused it. Sit down. You won't catch anything, you know.'

There were two easy chairs for Jack to choose from, both, of course, already occupied with assorted stuff. Polly's theory was that when you live in one room everything is a wardrobe. Chairs, tables, plantpots, casserole dishes. Everything is a place in or on which to put other things. In fact as far as Polly was concerned her whole flat was one big wardrobe and she was just one of the things in it. Jack could never have lived like that. Being a military man who had spent most of his life ready to pack up and leave at a moment's notice, he knew that the key to comfort was organization.

One of Polly's chairs was clearly an impossible proposition in terms of sitting down. Jack could see that there was no point in even thinking about unloading the dazzling cornucopia of things it contained. There were jumpers, books, newspapers, magazines, a partially dissected Russian doll. Stuffed toys, a guitar, an old typewriter, videocassettes, a radio, a bicycle pump attached to a deflated inner tube, coffee mugs and a roll of rush matting. Also wedged onto the chair was a Fair Trade South American string shopping bag containing three cans of baked beans and a packet of chocolate digestives. Polly was quite good about putting away groceries, but only quite. She always dealt with perishable items like milk and frozen peas the moment she got in from the shops, but dry and tinned goods she tended to leave in the shopping bag. After all, what was a South American string shopping bag if not a bag-shaped cupboard made of string?

On top of all of this was a strange, blue, plastic, tray-like object that Jack recognized immediately from the back of a thousand Sunday colour supplements. It was an abdominizer, a device for exercising the tummy. Polly had sent off for it two years previously. It had never been used, of course, and the unread instructions

177

had long since been lost. The thing just drifted gently about Polly's home from year to year, settling for a while before moving on silently and unnoticed. It had been on its current perch beside the shopping bag for about a month and was probably vaguely thinking about moving on. Perhaps to the clean clothes drawer, where there was always plenty of room. Apart from gathering dust the abdominizer's only contribution to Polly's life was to cause her the occasional pang of guilt. Not, however, a pang sufficiently strong to cause her to lie down upon the thing and gently roll her shoulders upwards by means of contracting her stomach muscles (while keeping her knees raised and her feet flat on the floor).

There was no way that Jack was ever going to be able to sit on that chair. That chair was like Doctor Who's tardis. It was bigger on the inside; there was more stuff wedged between its arms than could possibly ever logically or physically actually fit. Jack could see that if he were to empty it into the room he and Polly would have to stand outside.

On Polly's other chair was a big plastic sack of fertilizer. Jack found this item slightly surprising.

'Fertilizer, Polly?'

'I have a windowbox.'

Since the fertilizer was clearly a simpler proposition to clear than the contents of the other chair Jack lifted it to the floor. Not an easy task. This was a sack of fertilizer, not a bag but a sack.

'Jesus. Some windowbox. What are you going to d Grow a tree in it?'

'I run a tight budget. Things are cheaper in bulk.'

Jack thumped the sack down on the floor. Polly winced, thinking of the milkman below.

In the flat below, the milkman stirred in his bed. He glanced at his radio alarm clock. 2.40.

'Ha,' thought the milkman with sleepy satisfaction. The next time the upstairs woman asked him to turn down his morning radio, which he already had on so as you could barely hear it, he would be ready.

'Twatting great thumping and banging at two thirty in the morning, love,' he would say. 'Nearly jumped out of my twatting skin. Couldn't get back to sleep for an hour after . . .'

That is what he would say, the milkman thought, as he drifted back to sleep.

'Sorry,' Jack said. 'Damn thing slipped out of my hands.'

'Well, for Christ's sake be careful,' said Polly. 'I have to share this house with other people, you know.'

'Yeah, well, like I said, sorry.'

Jack looked down at the plastic sack and for some strange reason felt a momentary tremor of alarm. Something about that bag was wrong, or at least resonant of something wrong, but he couldn't imagine what. Suddenly he felt uneasy, slightly threatened as if ~e bag was a warning. He had the distinct feeling that ought to be making some kind of connection, but as eluding him. Fertilizer? What could possibly

179

be bad or sinister about that? Yet he wondered.

'Chemical, too,' Jack said, his tone betraying a slight hint of his unease.

'You have a problem with that?' Polly enquired.

'No, not at all.'

Of course he didn't. What could possibly be wrong about fertilizer?

'Except,' he added, 'it's not quite the organic pastoral utopia you and the girls used to talk about, is it? I would have thought you would have favoured natural fertilizer.'

'Yeah, well, it's tough keeping an animal in a bedsit, Jack. I used to shit out of the window, of course, but the neighbours complained.'

Jack sat down on the chair he'd cleared. As he did so his mobile phone rang. Polly jumped nearly out of her skin. For a moment she imagined that the Bug was back.

But that was just silly. He was hardly likely to have Jack's number.

28

'Excuse me,' said Jack. 'I have to take this.'

Polly's look assured him that he was not welcome.

'Yeah?' said Jack.

It was Schultz, General Kent's number two. After all the years Schultz's career was still shadowing Jack's. It was astonishing to Jack that such a man could become a general, but he seemed to have always been in the right place at the right time. And of course he never gave offence to anybody. Being incapable of making a decision, he had never ruffled any feathers and that was an important part of promotion in a peacetime army. Schultz had appeared to simply float up the ranks in the wake of better men. For the sake of the soldiers in the field Jack prayed that Schultz never floated into a combat command.

'I hope I'm not disturbing you, General,' Schultz said.

'Jesus, Schultz, of course you're fucking disturbing me. It's the middle of the night. I was asleep!' Jack snapped into his phone.

From a desk deep inside the American Embassy, General Schultz would have liked to point out that some people were lucky to be getting any sleep at all. But he didn't. He was far too scared of Jack. Instead he apologized and explained that he had been forced to call because their schedule for the following day had changed.

'It's the Brussels summit on the former Warsaw Pact nations,' Schultz explained.

This was Jack's least favourite subject. The planned expansion of NATO up to the very borders of Russia. He thought it dangerous madness. Jack had risen high in the army but he expected to rise higher and he had no wish to do so only to inherit a crippled defence alliance for which he would then be held responsible. If, a year or two down the track, NATO found itself over-stretched and unable to secure and control its own borders it would be his, not some ex-president's career, that would end in ignominy.

'It's in-fucking-sane!' Jack barked into his phone. 'We have a defence alliance that has kept Western democracy secure for over half a century and now on the whim of some fat fucking yuppie who just happens to be president we are inviting every basket case this side of the Urals to join. We can't possibly guarantee their security and we wouldn't want to even if we could. Half of them are going to end up dictator-ships anyway!'

Polly sat down on her bed. It was all too strange to take in. There appeared to be a man using her room to conduct the business of the Western nuclear alliance. She was a peace woman, for heaven's sake!

In the American Embassy General Schultz was uncomfortable too, horrified that Jack should express such robust views over an easily tappable cellular phone. Jack's opinion was so alarmingly contrary to that of the president, who was, after all, their commander in chief.

'General Kent, as you are aware, the under-secretary of state feels—'

'The under-secretary of state is a time-serving place woman. A triumph for the Pushy Ugly Women Lobby. She got her job because the president wants to show that in his America not only male assholes can achieve high office.'

Polly harrumphed loudly from the bed. Now she was being forced to listen to laddish, sexist abuse. Jack made a silent sign towards her as if to say that he was sorry and that he wouldn't be long. Polly grimaced in reply.

Schultz was grimacing too. He was only trying to do his best.

'General, as you know, the under-secretary of state has accepted your proposal that the Russians attend the summit.'

This was something. After all, it was the Russians and their worryingly unstable army whom Jack and this new NATO would be facing.

'But it seems,' Schultz explained, 'that the admiral of ̣e Russian fleet needs to get back to the Black Sea by ̣ertime. I think he's scared they won't save any food ̣m. Or that his flagship will have sunk with the rust.'

This was an attempt at a joke, but it fell flat.

'Funny, Schultz, I'm laughing here. I love to be woken up at two forty-five in the morning by comedians.'

In fact Jack did not think that the desperate plight of the ex-Soviet armed forces was remotely amusing. The fact that the world's second-largest nuclear force was now in the charge of cold, hungry and embittered guardians who had been stripped of all status and pride struck terror into Jack's heart whenever he thought about it.

'I'm sorry,' said Schultz over the phone. 'It's been a long night. Just working out the seating for this thing is a minefield. Who gets priority, the Germans or the French?'

'The Germans, of course. The French will take offence wherever you sit them, so you might as well give them something to moan about.'

'Well, anyway, the Russians want the meeting brought forward to noon Brussels time tomorrow,' said Schultz. 'That's eleven a.m. with us here in the UK.'

'Fucking Euros,' Jack grumbled. 'They think they can run a single currency; they can't even synchronize their watches.'

'Our plane needs to leave Brize Norton by ten. Can I get them to send a car for eight?'

'I'll be here at the hotel waiting.'

Jack put his phone away.

Polly was not happy. She did not like hearing her denied in such a casual manner. If Jack was asham embarrassed to be with her, then he should not have come. He had no right to sit there, on her chair, in her house, pretending that he was in a hotel. Old and bitter memories welled up inside her once more. Memories of a relationship denied, furtive and secret, conducted as if she had something of which to be ashamed. Memories of sneaking away from camp and skulking in bus shelters, waiting, sometimes for an hour, for Jack's car to appear. Memories of his making her swear over and over again that she had told no one of their affair. Of never being allowed to call Jack or even write to him directly. Of messages sent via the cold anonymity of a post office box. 'Bus shelter. Six p.m.'

For a time it had all seemed exciting and wicked, as if they were spies. But now it all looked merely deceitful and cowardly.

'Why did you pretend you were asleep, Jack? Why did you pretend you were still at your hotel?' Polly demanded. 'Still the same gutless wonder? Still keeping me a secret? Still scared what the army will think?'

Jack did not want to quarrel. He had only one night and Schultz's call had just shortened it. There was so much he wanted to say. So much he wanted to know. He pushed NATO and its business from his mind and returned to the matter in hand.

'You live alone, don't you?' he said, ignoring Polly's ʻitation and stating the obvious.

ʻ do now.'

ʻ ow?'

BEN ELTON

'I was in something for quite a long time but the relationship had problems.'

'What kind of problems?'

'Oh, nothing very much, just his wife and kids.'

Jack looked hard at Polly. Now he thought about it she did look older, of course. No less lovely but definitely older. He was a good judge of faces and he did not think that Polly's life had been a particularly easy one.

'Tell me about him,' Jack said gently.

Polly nearly did. She nearly sat down and blurted out the whole painful story of how, just when she had been getting herself back together again, she had allowed her life to be hijacked for a second time by an entirely inappropriate love affair. She nearly told him, but she didn't. Jack knew quite enough about her uncanny ability to choose the wrong men.

29

Polly left the squat in Acton in the late summer of 1991 and with a little money borrowed from her parents she took up her first entirely legal abode since leaving home eight years previously. A proper rented room in a shared house in Chiswick. From there she enrolled in a part time A-level course at the local college of further education and set about picking up her life where she had left it before the summer of Jack's love.

It was a new decade, a new prime minister (if still a Conservative one) and a new beginning for Polly, who believed that she had finally really and truly got over Jack. Seeing him on the television had helped, a shock though it had been. Until then he had remained vigorously alive in her memory as her first, her most complete and special love. His sudden devastating departure had been the watershed of her young existence, marking the point at which she had lost a grip upon her life. Then all of a sudden he was on the TV and e was a stranger. A creature from another planet. An onymous member of a hateful, sand-coloured army of a million men. He had nothing to do with her. It d extraordinary and unreal that he ever had.

The news broadcast had been repeated a number of times that evening, the same footage being shown again and again. Polly nearly told the story, she nearly pointed at the screen and stunned her friends by saying, 'See that bloke standing in front of the tank? I've had him,' but she didn't. It was all too strange. Polly no longer really believed it herself.

During her A-level year Polly worked part time as a waitress in an upmarket burger joint called New York New York (address, Chiswick High Street). The hours were unsociable but the tips were good and Polly shocked herself by discovering that with a judicious smile and a flirty manner she could make the tips even better. It did not take long for her to find out that shorter skirts meant more generous gratuities. She occasionally wondered what Madge and the girls from the camp would have made of that, but then she reasoned that if lads wanted to be wankers it seemed silly not to profit from it.

Feminism was changing anyway, at least that was what the style sections of the Sunday papers were saying. It was the year that saw the beginning of what was to become known as the new lad/new laddette trend, a period when it was pronounced all right to be a yob and behave badly. Of course in pubs and clubs up and down the country life simply went on as usual. The lads carried on drinking beer and fighting, while the girls continued to discuss male member size loudly over bucketfuls of vodka and orange. To the metropoli style media, however, the new lad trend w revelation. It appeared that boys and girls had become tired of the terrible social constrictions of political correctness and were now ready to be naughty again. With hindsight, the only lasting cultural impact of the whole business was that it became possible to have proper bra adverts again and that young women started to swear on Channel Four. At the time, though, it was all taken very seriously.

These were happy times for Polly. She liked having a proper home again, even if it was only a room plus shared everything else. The two girls Polly lived with soon became friends, despite the usual problems of communal living. It seemed to Polly that Sasha always left the bathroom reeking of horrible perfume while Dorothy appeared to require every single saucepan in the house in order to boil one egg. For their part the other girls objected to Polly's apparent need to keep all of her underwear hanging over the bath even when it was dry. Also, inevitably, each of the three was convinced that they were the only person who ever cleaned the toilet or emptied the swingbin or washed the teatowels, and there must also have been a thirsty ghost in the house because those teacups in the sink were certainly not any of theirs. The phone, of course, was also a constant problem. None of the girls had wanted to bother with a timer which would obviously be completely boring and fascistic; on the other hand, when the bills came none of them could believe that y had made a third of the calls.

ere were only occasional real rows, but when these

did happen they were proper, high-octane, full-volume, three-girl barnies which they all secretly enjoyed. Anything could set one off: the carton of milk that one person had bought and the other two had drunk, the unreplaced washing powder, the hoovering, the boyfriend who vomited on the sofa and just put a cushion on it and left.

'Right, that's it!' they would scream at each other, 'I'm sick of you bitches. I'm moving out!' But they didn't. They were having too much fun.

After A-levels Polly stayed on as a student and took a degree in sociology. Despite being rather depressingly classified as a mature student, she managed to have a pretty wild time in her first year. Illegal raves were the big thing at the time, the idea being to find somewhere vast, concrete and fantastically unpleasant and stay there for fifteen hours. This, she thought, was the reason drugs suddenly got so big again. It was the only possible way to get through such a horrible night. Polly and the other girls took ecstasy on a number of occasions, but soon got scared of it. There were so many stories going around about people who had only looked at a tab before becoming immediately paraplegic or dead.

The aftermath of a night on E was also rather painful. Polly was used to waking up with hangovers, but coming down in the cold grey light of dawn in the middle of a disused cattle market in Sussex presented new low even for her. When she took a look around at some of the dazed specimens upon whom she bestowed huge kisses and protestations of undying affection on the previous night, she decided that booze was a safer drug.

It seemed to Polly that studying and raving was all students did any more. She had been most disappointed to find how little political activism there was in the colleges. Fear of the future had long since beaten that out of the young. In the sixties and seventies it had been possible for students to rail and rant against society in the comfortable knowledge that they would shortly be joining it at a fairly elevated level. In the eighties, however, the world for graduates had become as uncertain as it was for everyone else and few students felt they had the luxury to worry about other people.

After graduating Polly managed to get elected to Camden Council, with whom she also acquired a job working in the Equal Opportunities Office. It was here that she met and fell in love with another complete disaster.

The disaster's name was Campbell. Handsome, clever, highly qualified (a doctor), Campbell was also an extremely married man. He and Polly met during a weekend conference entitled 'Race, gender, sexual preference and local government'. Until tea on the second day Polly had found the conference only slightly more interesting than being dead, but Campbell changed all that. Like her, he was a Labour Councillor, but unlike her he was a leading light in the local party, very much tipped to be selected as the parliamentary candidate to fight the next election. John Smith had died and Tony Blair's leadership had ushered in a whole new generation of slick, handsome, media-friendly professionals. Campbell was perfect for it, if a little old at forty.

Their affair was electric, one of those instant physical attractions that cannot be denied. Polly and Campbell missed the final session of the conference, 'How Many Members of Senior Management Have a Clitoris?', because they were having sex in a stationery cupboard. After that they seemed to be incapable of meeting without having sex. They took appalling risks, having it off in council offices, at Campbell's surgery, behind the speaker's chair at the town hall, in carparks, behind hedges, in front of hedges, on top of hedges and in the toilet of the Birmingham Pullman.

Polly worried about Campbell's wife, but Campbell of course assured her that he and Margaret had long since drifted apart. This, sadly, would have come as surprising news to Margaret, who had absolutely no idea that anything was wrong.

If Margaret was ignorant of what was going on, then Polly was not much wiser. Campbell was arrogant and weak and he spun a web of desperate lies around himself and both women. When he and Polly moved in together he told her that the three or four nights he spent away each week were out of obligation to his children. He explained that although he and Margaret were now separate they were still friends and had decided to maintain the family home until the kids grew up. To Margaret he explained that he had taken u part-time teaching post at the University of Manchester Medical School and hence would be away for half the week.

It could not last, of course. Campbell's lies got ever more desperate, particularly to Margaret. He told her that Telecom had still not installed a telephone line in his Manchester flat; he told her that for some reason his mobile could not get a signal where he was living. He told her not to phone the university as the cuts had so overstretched the secretarial staff that private calls were frowned upon.

And he told her, of course, he still loved her.

One Sunday morning Margaret turned up while Polly and Campbell were having breakfast together in the house they shared in Islington. Margaret had discovered the address from an electricity bill she had found in the laundry. It was probably the most excruciating encounter of Polly's life. She had stood there, a piece of toast frozen in her hand while the man who had said he loved her begged tearful forgiveness from the wife he claimed to have left.

Campbell left Polly that day. He had his kids and his political future to consider and the initial all-consuming passion between him and Polly was dying out anyway. Margaret took him back, accepting his protestations that Polly had seduced him. She didn't want to take him back, she hated the idea, but she was a middle-aged housewife. She did not know what else she could do apart from have it off with the windowcleaner in enge, which she did.

Polly could no longer afford the house on her own and moved out. After a week or two of sleeping on floors she shifted into the Stoke Newington loft where Jack was to find her. Polly was alone once more, rejected and homeless, just when things had seemed to be shaping up. Polly simply could not believe what an idiot she had been. She did not even have the energy to hate Campbell. She was too annoyed with herself.

Her next all-consuming relationship was to be with Peter the Bug.

30

Jack reached into the bag he'd brought with him.

'I brought some Bailey's and some Coke. Is that still what you drink?'

'Young girls drink stuff like that, Jack. It's like eating sweets but with alcohol. We give it up when we discover gin.'

Jack began to put his bottles away.

'Oh, all right, go on, then. I'll get some glasses.' Polly's resistance had lasted all of ten seconds. 'I haven't got anything to offer you, I'm afraid,' she said.

Polly had stopped keeping booze in the house. She only drank it. Not that she was an alcoholic, but if there was alcohol around she would certainly have it. After all, how could a girl come home from the sort of job she did and ignore a nice big treble gin and tonic if it was standing on the sideboard? And once you've had one treble gin it seems slightly absurd not to have another. If there was a halfway decent late film on the telly or she'd rented a video, Polly could do half a bottle 'n an evening. She would pay for it, of course, with a ﹏ucepan by the bed all night and a slightly spacy ﹏usea to follow, which sometimes lasted for two whole days. As Polly got older she had begun to find it safer to drink only in the pub.

Jack had also brought some bourbon for himself. Polly went into her little kitchen and rinsed out two glasses, being careful to thumb off the lipstick on the rims. A girl did, after all, have standards.

Jack poured the drinks long, alarmingly so. Polly was not sure that she could handle a quarter of a pint of Bailey's.

'But you aren't married?' Jack enquired casually. 'I mean, you've never been married?'

'No, I think marriage is an outmoded and fundamentally oppressive institution, a form of domestic fascism.'

'Still sitting on the fence, then?'

Polly laughed despite herself.

'And you live alone?' Jack added.

'Yes, Jack, I live alone in Stoke Newington, which is, incidentally, a long way from the Pentagon. How the hell did you find me after all these years?'

Polly reminded herself that it should be her setting the conversational agenda not him. Jack had no reason to be in her flat and certainly no right to be asking her about her personal life.

'Why are you here, Jack?'

'This guy, the married one. Did you ever tell him about us?'

'I said, why are you here?'

There were so many reasons why Jack was there. told you. To visit.'

'Jack, that is not a good enough answer.'

'You want me to go?'

He had her there and they both knew it. She did not want him to go, so she remained silent.

'Did you ever tell your boyfriends about us?' Jack continued.

'Why would you care?'

'I'm curious. You know . . . about what you thought of me after . . . if you thought of me at all. How you ended up describing me, to your friends and stuff . . . Did you tell them?'

'What possible business is it of yours whom I tell about any aspect of my disastrous life?'

'Well, none, I guess. I just wanted to know.'

'I'll tell you,' said Polly, 'if you tell me how you found me.'

Jack laughed. Finding people was no big deal to him. 'That's easy. I'm an army general. I can get things found out.'

'You mean you had me traced?'

'Sure I had you traced.'

Now it was Polly's turn to laugh. 'What? By secret intelligence or something? Spies?'

'Well, you know, it's not exactly James Bond. I mean nobody died or anything or used a pen that's also a flamethrower. I just had you traced. Any decent clerk can do it. You start with the last known address.'

★ 31

'A field, general?' the spook had said.

'That's right, Gottfried, that is the last address I have for her. A field in southern England called Greenham Common. We used to have a base there.'

Gottfried was a captain in military intelligence. He had a keen brain and he spotted instantly that as addresses went this one was on the vague side. He did not say so, of course, it was not his place. Gottfried had the gentle, self-deprecating air of a good butler and like a good butler he missed very little. He enquired if perhaps this field had a house on it or even a hut.

'No,' Jack replied. 'When I knew Polly she lived in a bender, although I doubt that it's still there. I guess with carbon testing you might pick up traces of the fireplace, but I doubt that would help.'

'A bender, General?' Gottfried asked.

'Yes, a bender, Gottfried. It's a shelter made of mud, sticks, leaves and reeds.'

'I understand, sir,' and something about the slight quiver of Gottfried's eyebrow made Jack fear that what Gottfried understood was that Jack was out of his mind.

'Perhaps, General,' Gottfried enquired gently, 'if you just gave me the surname of the young lady in question we could discover her address from the British tax authorities. I feel certain that they would co-operate if we made the request via the Embassy.'

'Coupla things,' said Jack firmly. 'First, do you want to make colonel?'

'Yes, General sir, I do,' Gottfried replied.

'OK, then. You don't do this thing I'm asking via the Embassy, understand? You do this yourself. You don't delegate, you don't get somebody else to do the legwork, this is just you, OK?'

'As you wish, sir,' Gottfried said.

If General Kent knew one thing about the Grosvenor Square Embassy it was that the CIA were all over it. It was their principal European station, their centre of operations. Nothing happened in that building that they did not know about and Jack did not want them knowing about Polly.

'Next thing,' said Jack. 'Her surname wouldn't help you, I'm afraid. It . . . it wasn't real.'

'Am I to understand, sir, that the young lady in question operated under a pseudonym?' Gottfried enquired.

'Yes, she did,' said Jack, reddening slightly. 'Her surname at the time I knew her was "Sacred Cycle of the Womb and Moon".'

Jack had asked Polly her real name but she had refused on principle to tell him.

'I am who I decide to be, not who society dictates,'

she used to say, and Jack had thought it simply too stupid to argue; it had not seemed important at the time.

Gottfried betrayed not an ounce of the amusement he felt.

'I see, sir,' said Gottfried. 'So that would be Polly Sacred Cycle of the Womb and Moon?'

'Yes, it would.'

The spy solemnly produced a notebook and jotted down the name, respectfully repeating it under his breath as he did so.

Jack shuddered at the memory of Polly's stupid name. Checking into hotels with a woman who insisted upon signing herself Polly Sacred Cycle of the Womb and Moon had to be one of his more excruciating memories. Eventually Jack persuaded her that it just drew attention to them and that they should pretend to be married anyway, but for a while it had been a major embarrassment for him.

At the time, Polly had been convinced that Jack was only embarrassed because he was so totally uptight and straight. She believed that if only he could centre himself and shake out his shakrahs he would see that it was a lovely name. She found it practical as well as beautiful. For a person who was arrested on a regular basis a good pseudonym was essential and having such a long one absolutely infuriated the police. They used to try to get away with just writing 'Polly Sacred,' but she would insist on her full name being noted. It drove them mad, particularly on winter mornings when their fingers were cold.

'OK, that's all I got,' said Jack. 'I'm afraid it ain't a lot.'

'I'm sure it will prove sufficient, General,' Gottfried assured him.

'Good.'

'So, then, just to recap, sir. A girl called Polly, Greenham peace lady. Seventeen years old in 1981. Find her and kill her.'

'That's right . . . *No!* For Christ's sake! Jesus, I never said anything about killing her . . .'

'I'm sorry, sir, I just assumed—'

'Yeah, well don't. Just find her, OK? Get her address, hand it over to me and then forget we ever had this conversation.'

32

'God help the American taxpayer,' Polly said with some feeling.

Jack acknowledged that it had been a questionable use of public funds, but what was the point of power if you couldn't abuse it?

'Fuck the American taxpayer. I've given them twenty-eight years of my life. Uncle Sam owes me.'

'He doesn't owe you anything. You love being a soldier.'

'Murderer, you used to say.'

'That's right.'

'It's because I'm a soldier that I lost you.'

'You didn't lose me, Jack, you discarded me and I don't think it was because you were a soldier. I think it's because you were a gutless bastard. In fact, I think you still are, since you seem to think that calling or writing to an old flame would result in a court-martial for treason.'

'I told you, Polly, I couldn't.'

Polly didn't understand and she wasn't likely to. Of course he had lost her because he was a soldier. The army would not have accepted his and Polly's relationship in a million years. Jack had been faced with a straight choice and he had chosen his career. That did not mean he liked it, it did not mean that a part of him had not regretted the decision every single day since.

'Why did you have me traced, Jack? Why are you here?'

'I thought you already had your answer. I already told you how I found you.'

'This is a subclause. Why did you find me?'

'Why do you think? To find out what I'd let go. To find out what you'd become.'

'Jack, we knew each other for one summer in a totally different decade and you dropped me. That was it, end of rather stupid story. Now you turn up out of the blue talking about us like we were a Lionel Ritchie lyric. What is this about?'

'That summer was the best summer of my life, Polly. The best anything of my life.'

'You just miss the Cold War, that's all.'

'Well, hell, who doesn't?' Jack laughed. 'And what's happening with you in the new world order, then? I noticed when I met him that you weren't the prime minister yet.'

'I never wanted to be prime minister, Jack. I wanted there not to be any prime ministers. I wanted the nation state with its hierarchies to be replaced by an organically functioning system of autonomous collectives.'

'With you as prime minister.'

'Not at all, although obviously some kind of

non-oppressive, non-authoritarian body of governance would be required.'

'And anybody who didn't like your non-oppressive, non-authoritarian governance could get shot.'

'That wouldn't happen.'

'Polly, it always happens when you fucking idealists get to defending your revolutions. You always start shooting people. By any means possible, as Lenin said. Stalin, Pol Pot, Mao. The most pious murderers in hell . . .'

Polly very nearly rose to it. Very nearly slammed her fist on the table and launched into the ancient and terminally tedious arguments of the left. Just in time, she hauled herself back from the brink.

'Jack, this is ridiculous! Are you out of your mind! I'm a completely different woman now, twice as old, for a start, and you turn up after nearly twenty years quoting Lenin and trying to continue the conversation we were having.'

Jack smiled. She was just the same. The same passion, the same beauty.

'I don't know. I just thought it might have been kinda fun, you know, for old times' sake. Like the first time we talked.'

'Fought.'

'Yeah, fought. In that hellhole on the A34.'

'Except then, of course, we ended up in . . .'

Polly did not finish the sentence. She did not need to. Her eyes gave the thought away. She did not need to say 'bed' because there it was, right there, not ten feet from either of them. Her bed, unmade and inviting, the duvet tossed aside, the deep impression of Polly's head still there upon the pillow. A bed just climbed out of. A bed ready to be climbed back into.

'I've never been in one of those restaurants since,' Polly said.

Jack fixed his stare on hers. She could feel herself going scarlet.

'That day changed me too, Polly. I'll never forget it.'

'They're just so disgusting. I mean, how do you ruin tomato soup?'

'I didn't mean the restaurant, Polly, I meant . . .' Jack's tone spoke volumes, but Polly was trying not to listen. She stuck resolutely to her topic.

'Putting a stupid hat on a sixteen-year-old school-leaver does not constitute training a chef.'

'Polly, how long can you stay angry at a bowl of soup?'

'No, but really. How do you mess up tomato soup? It was hot on the top and cold in the middle. With a skin on it! That has to be deliberate,' said Polly, once again reliving the horror of that gruesome cuisine.

'Forget the soup,' Jack pleaded. 'Walk away. It's been sixteen years, you have to let it go now. We weren't bothered about eating, anyway. We went to that little hotel. Do you remember?'

Polly looked puzzled. 'A hotel? Are you sure? I don't remember that.'

Jack could not conceal his disappointment. 'Oh, I thought you would—'

'Of course I fucking remember, you fucking idiot,' Polly said as loudly as she dared without provoking the sleeping milkman downstairs. 'I lost my fucking virginity, didn't I!'

Jack got it. 'Oh, right,' he said. 'British sarcasm.'

'Irony.'

He hated that. That was a British trick, the sarcasm and irony trick. Earlier in the evening the senior British officer had tried to make the same distinction.

'Oh, yes,' the pompous little khaki shit had said, having cracked some particularly weak sarcastic put-down or other. 'You American chaps aren't big on irony, are you?'

Jack thought it was pathetic the way the British aggrandized their penchant for paltry sarcasm by styling it 'irony'. They thought it meant they had a more sophisticated sense of humour than the rest of the world, but it didn't. It just meant that they were a bunch of pompous smartasses.

'So you do remember,' he said.

'Of course I bloody remember,' Polly replied. 'I remember every detail. The soup—'

'Forget the soup.'

'The pie—'

'Forget the pie.'

'I wrote to the restaurant, you know.'

'Christ, hadn't you made enough fuss already?'

Not that Jack had minded at the time. Usually he hated any kind of scene. Under any normal circumstances the fuss that Polly had made on the first day they met would have ended their relationship right there. The funny thing was that he had loved it then and he loved it still. He remembered every detail. Polly announcing loudly that she resented being forced to eat in a fucking charnel house, supergluing the sauce bottles to the table. Even now he laughed at the memory of that wonderful, funny, sexy, sunny lunchtime.

'You sure showed them,' he said.

'Non-violent direct action. At least we didn't pay,' Polly replied.

That was one of Polly's favourite memories of her whole life. That glorious runner. The suggestion, the decision, the execution, it had all happened in one mad moment. Suddenly the two of them, her and an American soldier, were charging for the door and out into the carpark. It had been such fun, so exciting, piling into his car and screeching out onto the A34 before anyone in the restaurant had realized what had happened.

'I just couldn't believe that you, a soldier and everything, were prepared to run out without paying.'

After sixteen years Jack decided it was time to own up.

'Actually I did pay, Polly. I left a five-pound note under my plate.'

Polly could scarcely believe it. This was astonishing, horrible news.

'You paid! That's terrible! I thought you were so cool!'

'I was cool. It got you into my car, didn't it?'

That was true enough. Jack's astute deception all those years before had certainly got her into his car, certainly made her breathless and excited and ready for anything. Who could tell? Had that little trick not occurred to him then perhaps their relationship might never have happened. After all, if Jack had simply asked Polly to go with him to a field and then to a hotel, it is most unlikely that she would have gone. It had been the drama of that single moment that had carried her into his arms and changed both their lives for ever.

'You bastard,' said Polly. 'If you hadn't—'

'Polly, life is full of ifs. If that receptionist hadn't decided to turn a blind eye to your pornographic T-shirt maybe we would have seen sense and walked away.'

'There was nothing remotely offensive about my T-shirt!' said Polly, the passage of time having done nothing to blunt the memory of that confrontation. 'That receptionist was just a stupid Nazi bitch.'

'Polly, just because somebody did not approve of what was emblazoned on your T-shirt doesn't make them a National Socialist.'

'Take the toys from the boys,' said Polly. 'What could be offensive about that?'

'Beats me,' Jack replied, 'unless it was the picture of that huge flying penis you had printed across your tits.'

Polly never failed to rise to this one.

'Well, what were those bloody missiles but big blokes' willies? Nuclear dickheads, we used to call them.'

'Yeah, we all loved that one on our side of the fence,' Jack said with heavy sarcasm (or perhaps it was irony). '"Tell us the one about missiles being penis replacements again," we used to shout. We'd laugh all day.'

'You're only taking the piss because actually you felt threatened.'

'Terrified. Couldn't sleep. You know, Polly, maybe it's kind of late in the day to say this, but the idea of dissing things because of their so-called phallic shape. It's always struck me as kind of banal.'

'Because it reveals an uncomfortable truth about yourself.'

'No, because it's dumb. Things get shaped straight and thin for reasons of aerodynamics. Missiles and skyscrapers are shaped the way they are on the soundest principles of engineering, not as monuments to the dick. In fact, so is the dick. The dick is shaped like a dick because that is the most efficient shape for a dick to be. That's why it's dick shaped. I mean a dick shaped like a table would cause all sorts of practical spatial problems. Surely you can see that?'

'Jack, it's a point of satire, not civil engineering.'

'Yes, but it's such lazy, unconvincing satire. It always annoys me so much the way you girls trot it out like you're saying something so astute and revealing. Like with cars; a guy gets a cool car and suddenly according to you and the other femmos it's his dick. Well, dicks on't look a bit like cars. No guy ever stood outside a dillac showroom and said, 'Oh, boy, I wish I had one ose. It looks exactly like my dick.' Jesus, if my dick looked like a Cadillac I'd go see a doctor. Personally, I drive a pick-up truck. You ever see a dick with a trailer?'

'Jack, I'm not interested. This is your problem. I never—'

'You might as well say a trombone is a phallic symbol, or a stick of gum! Maybe when a guy shoves a piece of gum into his face what he's really saying is that he is a subconscious homosexual and has a secret desire to be chewing on a big old Cadillac!'

'Jack—'

'Phallic symbol, for Christ's sake. When they built the World Trade Center do you think they stood around saying, "Looks great and it'll be even better when they put the purple helmet on the top"?'

Polly used to love this type of conversation with Jack. They would shout and rant and swear at each other.

Then, of course, they made love.

'Jack, don't you think you're getting a little worked up over this? Protesting too much?'

'I hate that way of arguing! That is a woman's way of arguing! Say something outrageous and when the guy gets angry act like *he's* got the problem.'

Polly wondered whether perhaps this might be the reason for Jack's visit.

'Is this some kind of therapy thing? Is that why you've come? Has some army analyst discovered you hate women and told you to go and confront your past?'

Now Jack really went off. 'Are you kidding me'

an analyst? I'd rather stick my Cadillac in a blender. Analysts and therapists have destroyed the world. They're a cancer. I'd put the lot of them against a wall and shoot them. Every one. Them, their unconscious selves, their recovered personalities, and particularly, above all, their inner fucking children.'

Polly had not expected Jack to have suddenly turned into a liberal in the years that had passed since their last meeting, but if anything he seemed to have got worse.

'You know what, Jack? It's lovely to see you and all that, but I'm rather tired, so—'

But Jack wasn't listening. He was on a subject that moved him deeply, to Polly's mind rather disturbingly so.

'Jesus, the entire twentieth century was corrupted by the theories of some Jew who thought women wanted to grow dicks and guys wanted to fuck their mothers! Where I come from that's fighting talk. We'd have killed that pervert the first day he opened his mouth. We'd have hung him from a tree, and you know what? We would have been called uncivilized.'

There was something venomous about Jack's tone that Polly didn't like. He still had all his charm but it had taken on a steely edge.

'Jack, I'm not interested in your Neolithic opinions. I have no idea why I'm even having this conversation, I have to work tomorrow. Why are you here?'

'I told you! I wanted to see you—'

'So you've seen me! What now?'

'What indeed? Jack hardly knew himself. He had

thought he knew, but that was before they got talking. Jack had rehearsed all this in his mind so many times. Yet now he was not so sure, not so sure at all. He glanced at his watch. It was gone three.

'Look, if I'm keeping you,' Polly snapped, 'you can go!'

'I'm not going, Polly. I want to be with you.'

There was something about his tone that Polly did not like. Something commanding and possessive. Polly did not like men acting as if they had the right to intrude on her own private space. She had had enough of that with the Bug.

33

Peter watched as the tail-lights of the police car disappeared around the corner at the end of the road, the spiteful red dots dragging great bloody streaks along behind them in the glistening reflection of the wet road.

Twice now Peter had been forced to retreat into the shadows as passing cars had disturbed his desperate efforts to recover his knife. Once it had been a carful of yobbos, drunken revellers shouting into the night. Their car had hurtled into the road at speed. Peter had been on all fours and had had to roll out of the gutter onto the pavement. The souped-up white Sierra had screeched past, sending up an arc of spray, further soaking Peter's retreating body. Another second, a moment's hesitation, a slower reaction, and all Polly's problems with the Bug would have been over. But he survived, wetter, dirtier and angrier. The Sierra sped on, its reckless driver unaware of how close he had been to killing a man.

Peter retrieved his coathanger and returned to his task, but no sooner had he done so than a police car appeared, not screeching and hurtling but prowling. He on the kerb and waited for it to pass. It seemed to

take for ever, slowing to a crawl as it drew parallel with
him. He put his head in his hands and ignored it. The
police officers inside the car repaid the compliment. A
few years previously they might have investigated, but
the night streets were now so full of people with
nowhere to go that if the police looked into every sad-
looking case they passed they would never get more
than two hundred yards from their station.

When the coppers had gone and he had the street to
himself again Peter knelt once more in the filthy gutter
and resumed his delicate task. It was clear to him that
if he dislodged the knife it would fall completely out of
reach. He would have only one chance to touch it with
his wire. Hook it, or knock it away for ever.

'Peter! What on earth do you think you're doing!'

He spun around, dropping his piece of wire, which
fell with a tiny clatter into the drain.

'Mum!'

'Get up out of the gutter!' Peter's mother said.
'You're filthy and you're soaking. What're you doing?
Are you drunk?'

Peter had been gone so long that his poor mother,
unable to sleep, had come out searching for him. She
had known where to look, of course. There was only
one place he would have gone at that time of night. She
felt so angry, even though she knew that he couldn't
help it. It was all starting again. Just when she had
hoped that perhaps he was getting over his madness it
was all starting again.

'I dropped my knife, Mum.'

'Good. You shouldn't have had it, anyway. You know they're illegal. What were you doing with it in the first place?'

'Just playing with it.'

'Playing with a knife? In her street? A knife, Peter! What if you were caught?'

Sometimes Peter's mother just wanted to break down and weep. She really did not know how much more of it she could bear. If that woman thought she had it hard, she should try being his mother.

Peter refused to go home. His mother tried ordering him, reasoning with him, pleading with him, but he was adamant. She stepped forward into the flowing gutter and reached out to him. Her shoe filled instantly with filthy water. Peter merely drew away.

'Come home, Peter!' His mother pleaded one more time.

'I'll come home when I've got my knife back,' was all he would say.

She gave up. There was nothing she could do. She cried all the way home, her tears mixing with rain, making her half blind.

Peter went back to the builder's skip to root out another piece of wire.

34

Jack sat back in his seat and quaffed deeply at his whiskey.

'So come on. My question. Tell me what you do now.' He had some information about Polly from the file that Gottfried had prepared, but not much. Jack had specifically asked his secret agent to confine himself to a couple of current photographs and Polly's address. He had not wanted even Gottfried to know any more about Polly than was absolutely necessary.

'I'm a councillor,' Polly replied.

Jack's face showed that he was not impressed.

'What, you mean like an analyst? A therapist? You tell fucked-up people to blame their parents?'

'Not a personal counsellor, Jack, a town councillor. I'm on the council.'

Jack laughed. 'The council! You're on the council! I thought all hierarchies were fascism.'

Yet again Polly rose to the bait. 'I was seventeen when I said that, for heaven's sake! Although they are, of course, but all structures are not necessarily hierarchical—'

Polly stopped herself. This was ridiculous. 'I do

want to discuss politics with you!'

'OK, OK. Whatever you say, Polly.'

A silence descended. Polly was getting impatient with Jack's enigmatic visit, but she did not want him to go and he did not seem anxious to explain himself, so there was very little she could do.

'So what do you do on your "council" then?' Jack asked and Polly did not like his slightly patronizing tone.

'I'm with the office of equal opportunities.'

Jack sniffed and his patronizing tone became slightly more marked.

'What? You mean it's your job to make sure there's a suitable quota of disabled black Chinese sodomites getting paid out of public funds?'

'Yes, that's exactly what I do,' Polly snapped sarcastically. 'You're incredibly intuitive, Jack. I had no idea you were such an expert on local government.'

'We have people like you in the army,' Jack said, and now it almost sounded as if he was sneering. 'Checking out that we have enough women in combat training. Homosexuals, too, that's coming. A queer quota. Can you believe that?'

Polly enquired if this offended Jack, and he replied that it damn well did offend him.

'You think that makes me a fascist, right?' he added.

The atmosphere between them, having been defi-nitely warming up, was now becoming chilly.

'Well, I certainly think it makes you a bit of a dick-d.'

Jack went over to the kitchen table and grabbed the bottles.

'Have another drink, babe,' he said, 'and let me tell you something.'

'Don't call me babe.'

Polly was still sitting on the bed. Jack marched back across the room and sloshed more Bailey's into her half-full glass before refilling his own with bourbon. He had not intended to discuss this issue but he felt too strongly about it to let it go. Besides, this night of all nights Jack wanted Polly to understand something of his point of view.

'Christ, where do you people get off! Gays in the military. What does it have to do with you, anyway? You don't care about the army, you hate it, you wish it would turn into a network of crêches for single mothers! But you still think you can tell us how to run it—'

Polly raised her hand for him to stop.

'Hang on, hang on. Hang on! Me?' she said. 'Don't lay your shit on me, mate. I'm a council worker from Camden.'

'I'm talking about your kind, Polly. It doesn't matter where you come from or what job you do. Your kind are international.'

'My kind!' Polly protested. 'What the fuck do you mean, my kind?'

'Your kind, Polly, that's what the fuck I mean. Your kind.'

Jack was sick and tired of them. These liberals, th

feminists, these gay activists. The army wasn't a laboratory for social experimentation, it was the means by which the nation defended itself. He had tried to explain this point at the congressional hearings into sexual bias in the armed forces and what a waste of time that had been. It had been like Canute trying to turn back a tidal wave of bullshit. What an impotent fool he had felt, sitting there in front of that pious pulpit of political zealots and petrified fellow travellers. It was the scared ones Jack despised most. At least the true believers believed, insane utopians though they were, but the ones who knew he was right were beneath contempt. They just did not have the guts to risk offending the current sensibilities and so they nodded and sighed and stayed silent, mindful of their thin electoral majorities back home. It was McCarthyism in reverse. The liberals had become the witch-hunters: 'Are you or have you ever been a homophobic?' There was a terrifying new orthodoxy abroad and as far as Jack was concerned whether it was happening on Capitol Hill or in Camden Council it had to be confronted.

'We take communal showers in the army, you know that, Polly,' Jack said bitterly. 'You think about that. In the field we live in the same dugouts, wash in the same puddles. I don't want no queer grunt staring at my ass instead of the soap.'

Polly did not want to discuss this, but like Jack she simply could not let it go. His attitude was just too disgusting. Every liberal instinct in her body screamed to

'Gay men are not sexual predators, Jack.'

'How the hell would you know? Straight guys are sexual predators!'

'Well, yes, you certainly showed me that!'

'Exactly,' Jack said loudly, as if this proved his point.

'Keep your voice down! There's a milkman asleep downstairs.'

On the floor below, the milkman was not asleep. Jack's voice had woken him up again and he was gleefully making a note of the time of the disturbance: *Man's voice: shouting: 3.06 a.m.*,' he wrote. It wasn't that the milkman enjoyed being disturbed, but the upstairs woman had complained so often about his radio, even threatening to involve the landlord, that the current disturbance was manna from heaven. Let her try and complain now.

Little did the milkman imagine that within a few hours his notebook would be in the hands of the police.

Jack reduced the volume but his tone remained combative.

'If you think I'm a predator, well, let me tell you, honey, I ain't the worst by a long country mile. I'm the norm.'

Jack was remembering Bad Nauheim and the night that the German girl Helga had pushed her luck too far. Not all men were of the type involved in that terrible incident, but all men were men none the less.

'If you put any of the men in any unit I

commanded in a showerful of women,' Jack continued, 'they are going to check them out for sure, and if they can they're going to try and get with them.'

'Well, then, they need to rethink their—'

Jack had just sat back down in his seat, but his frustration made him leap up again and take a step towards Polly.

'Followed by heavy footsteps: 3.07 a.m.,' the milkman wrote solemnly before rolling over and wrapping the pillow around his head.

Jack was standing over Polly now.

'I know you don't like it, Polly, but that's what young men do! They check out babes and they try to have sex with them and you can make up all the laws you like but that won't change.'

Polly rose from the bed and squared up to Jack. There was no way this man was going to win his argument with intimidating body language.

'Yes, it can, Jack, it's called civilization. It's an ongoing process.'

'Yeah well it's got a long way to ongo.'

Polly checked herself. What was she doing? She did not want to have this discussion, she had work in the morning. In fact, it very nearly was the morning.

'Look, Jack. I really don't know what we're talking out!'

'We are talking about gays in the military.'

'Well, I don't want to talk about gays in the military!'

'Well, I do! It's relevant!'

'Relevant to what?'

'Relevant to me! I want you to understand me.'

The urgency of Jack's tone subdued Polly for a moment.

'You know what straight men can be like,' he continued. 'You feel I showed you that.'

Oh yes, Polly certainly felt he had done that.

'So why not gays? What's so different about them, huh? Are you going to tell me that if you put a healthy young homosexual in a showerful of young men who are in the peak of physical condition he is not going to check out their dicks?'

Polly tried to stop herself replying. She did not wish to be having this conversation. On the other hand she had to reply. Jack simply could not be allowed to get away with this reactionary bullshit.

'Well, he might look, but—'

Jack leapt on the point. 'And when he does he's going to get himself beaten to a pulp.'

'That's not his problem—'

Jack laughed. 'Excuse me? Getting beaten to a pulp is not his problem?'

'Well, I mean, obviously it is his problem if he's being beaten up.'

'It's encouraging that you spotted that.'

His attitude was unpleasant. Polly's point was not an easy one to make. Particularly if Jack was going to take cheap shots.

'But the problem originates with the people who are doing the beating!'

'Great, next time I get shot I'll take comfort from that. Hey, this is not my problem. The guy with the gun, he has the problem, he needs to get in touch with his caring side.'

How many times in how many pubs had Polly had discussions like this one? The reactionary point of view was always so easy to put, the complex, radical argument always so easy to put down.

'Just because the world is full of Neanderthal morons doesn't mean we have to run it for their benefit and by their rules.'

Jack searched his brain for a telling argument. Somehow it was important to him that Polly understood his point of view.

'Listen, Polly, when the guy who digs up the street checks out your butt you're pretty pissed, am I right?'

'Well, yes—'

'You're furious. You'd like to knock that guy off his scaffolding and drive a dump truck into his asshole cleavage. Well, men don't like having their butts checked out either, but unlike you they're actually going to do something about it, they're going to attack the guy who is checking them out and you cannot run an army with guys either sucking each other off or beating each other up.'

Of course it sounded reasonable. Polly had spent her ʼ listening to reactionary arguments and they always ᵻded reasonable. Which was why it was all the more important to counter them. Even at nearly 3.15 in the morning. Even with a mysterious ex-lover who had turned up out of the blue after more than sixteen years' absence. Polly had a policy. It was embarrassing at times and always boring, but her view was that casual racism, sexism and homophobia always had to be confronted.

'People have to learn to restrain themselves,' she said.

Jack had a rule too. It was that he would never suffer pious liberal bullshit in silence.

'Says you, babe, and you and your people can keep on wishing!'

Polly was shocked at how bitter Jack's tone had become.

'Me and my people?' she said. 'What people, Jack? I don't have any people! What are you talking about? Why are you bringing me into this? None of this is any of my business.'

Polly was not even sure that Jack heard her. He looked strange. There was a different look in his eye; she could see real anger there.

'You know what's coming next, don't you? Pacifists.'

'What about pacifists?'

'In the fucking army! Why not? Some Congresswoman is going to announce that pacifists have a right to join the army. In fact, the army should be encouraging them! Running a programme to attract them! Because the constitutional rights of America pacifists are being denied by—'

Jack was becoming red in the face. For the first t

he looked his age. A confused, middle-aged man with a chip on his shoulder.

'I'm not interested in your paranoid ravings, Jack. I want to know why—'

But Polly might as well have been talking to herself.

'Fucking constitution! It's a sponge, it'll absorb anything anybody wants. It's like the damn Bible. Everybody can make it work for them. Well, the constitution can only take so much. One day the Supreme Court is going to rule that the constitution is unconstitutional and the United States will implode! It'll disappear up its ass.'

'Good! I'm glad.' Polly felt tired. She had to leave for work at seven forty-five.

'Jack, I can't have this conversation with you now. I have to work tomorrow. Maybe we could meet some other—'

Jack lowered his tone. He spoke quietly and firmly. 'I've told you, Polly, I only have tonight. I leave in the morning.'

He stared at Polly as if that was all he needed to say, as if Polly could like it or lump it, neither of which she was prepared to do.

'Well go, then! Go! I don't want you here. I didn't ask you to come.'

Jack did not move at all. He just stood in the middle of the room, looking at her.

'I'm staying, Polly,' he said, and for the first time ⸻ began to feel a little nervous. Something about ⸻ had changed. He was being so intense.

225

'OK, stay, stay if you want to, but . . . but you can't just drop in after sixteen years and talk about sexual politics and the constitution, and . . . It's . . . it's stupid.'

Jack looked tired too now. 'You always used to want to talk about politics, Polly. What's changed? Is there nothing of value left for you people to fuck up?'

He seemed to say it more in sorrow than in anger. None the less Polly wasn't having any of it.

'I have nothing to do with you or your hangups, Jack,' said Polly calmly. 'We knew each other briefly, years ago. We don't even live in the same country.'

'Politics is international, you always used to tell me that,' said Jack, and he smiled at the memory. 'You read it me out of that damn political cartoon book you had, *The Start-Up Guide to Being an Asshole . . .*'

'*Marxism for Beginners.*'

'That's the one.'

Polly blushed at the memory of how naïve she'd been. She had actually given Jack a copy of *Marxism for Beginners*. Not that she had ever been able to get through it herself, of course. Huge quotes from *Das Kapital* do not get clearer just because there's a little cartoon of Karl Marx in the corner of the page. It had been a gesture, a nod towards civilizing him. All Jack ever admitted to reading was the sports pages, and Polly had dreamt of politicizing him. Fantasizing about walking into the peace camp one day with Jack on her arm and saying to the girls, 'I've got one! I've converte' him.' She had imagined herself the toast of the pe movement, having persuaded a genuine baby kill' see the light. Polly had been going to make the world's first vegetarian fighter pilot.

'Wasn't I the starry-eyed little pillock?' she said.

'Well, did you ever read Churchill's *History of the Second World War*?' Jack replied. The book-giving had, after all, been a two-way thing.

'Be serious, Jack, it was about fifty volumes!'

'Oh, and Marx is easy reading, is it?'

Now they were both laughing. Neither of them had changed at all. They were still a million miles apart in every way but one.

'I wanted you to be a part of my world as much as you wanted me to be part of yours, Polly,' said Jack. 'You're not the only person who got disappointed. I believe that in my own way I loved you every bit as much as you loved me.'

Jack was terrified to discover that he still did.

'You can't have done,' said Polly quietly, avoiding Jack's eye, 'or you wouldn't have left.'

'That's not true, Polly. I had to leave. I'm a soldier. I'm not good at love, I admit that. I don't find it easy to live with. But whatever love there is inside me I felt for you, to its very limits and beyond.'

GLIMPSE FROM THE PAST

35

While Jack and Polly were wrestling with their pasts in London, back in the States another drama of betrayal was being played out. A man and a woman were sitting alone together in the faded splendour of a dining room that had been beautifully decorated twenty years before. It was dinner time in the eastern states and the couple had been sitting at their evening meal for an hour or so, but neither of them was hungry. Their food had gone cold before them. Hers remained entirely untouched; he had had a stab at his, but really all he had done was play nervously with the cold, congealed gravy.

'I'm sorry, Nibs,' he said. 'What more can I say? I don't want to do it but sometimes it just happens. I just can't help myself.'

'Nibs' was the man's private name for his wife. It was what he always called her when they were alone, their little secret, a token of his affection. These days they were alone together less and less. Their professional lives had grown so complex that dining together had become a matter for diaries, and when his work took him away she could no longer go with him. Perhaps was that, she thought. Perhaps her career had dr him into the arms of other, stupider, more available women. She wondered if he had special names for them. Perhaps he had called them Nibs also, for convenience and to avoid embarrassing mistakes. At the thought of this Nibs' eyes grew misty and briefly she took refuge in her napkin.

'I'm so sorry,' he said again, 'but it meant nothing, it was meaningless.'

'What does she do?' Nibs enquired, attempting to make her voice sound calm.

'She works at the office. She's with the travel department. She books cars and flights and stuff,' he replied.

'Fascinating,' she said bitterly. 'You must have so much to talk about.'

'The point is, Nibs . . .'

'Don't call me Nibs,' she snapped. 'I don't feel like being your Nibs right now.'

'The point is . . .'

His voice faltered. The point was that he was in trouble. That was the only reason he'd arranged the dinner, the only reason they were having the conversation. If he hadn't been in trouble he would never have told her about the girl, just as he hadn't told her about any of the other girls. Unfortunately, this current girl had not taken kindly to the brevity of their affair and had decided to hit back.

'She says she's going to accuse me of harassing her.'

'Oh, for Christ's sake. Did you?'

'Not unless taking a girl to bed a couple of times is ...sment.'

Nibs bit her lip. Why had he done it? Why did he keep doing it? He thought she didn't know about the others but she'd heard the rumours. She knew about the jokes they told at his office. She'd caught the expressions of those dumb booby women when she accompanied him to business functions. She knew what they were thinking. 'You may be a fancy lawyer, lady, but when your husband needs satisfying he comes to me.'

'I have plenty of enemies,' he said. 'If this thing gets any kind of heat under it at all it could be very bad for me at work. I could lose my job.'

'You fool!' Nibs snapped. 'You damn stupid fool.'

36

Jack swallowed half his drink down in one.

'Do you ever see any of the girls these days?'

'One or two,' Polly replied, crossing one leg over the other as she sat. She could see Jack's eyes had been caught by the movement.

'You should organize a reunion,' he said, smiling. 'You'd have a blast. Go stand in a field somewhere, paint each other's faces, make some puppets. Eat mud sandwiches and dance to the subtle rhythms of your female cycles.'

He was teasing her now. The anger had gone.

'Yes, and we could invite the American army along,' Polly replied. 'You could all drop your trousers and show us your arses. We used to love it when you did that. It was such a subtle gesture and so intellectually stimulating.'

In fact it had been the British guards who did most of the arse-showing. The Americans were mainly echnical advisers, a cut above that sort of oafishness, d were anyway on their strictest best behaviour. did not argue the point, though. He had always supported the British soldiers in their arse-showing and he would not deny them now.

'It was a clash of cultures. We were never going to get along.'

'Except us.'

'Yeah,' said Jack, trying not to stare. 'Except us.'

They were so close. He in the easy chair, she perched on the bed. Two strides and they would be in each other's arms. The room crackled with the suppressed tension.

'Let's face it,' said Polly. 'You can put up with anything if the sex is good enough.'

'Oh, yeah,' Jack replied with great enthusiasm, his voice and his wandering eyes betraying his thoughts.

Polly was torn. Should she sleep with him? She felt confident that she could if she wanted to. Of course she could. She knew what men were like, they always wanted it. Scratch a man and you find a person who fancies a fuck. Sex had to be the reason that Jack had come back. It was obvious. He felt like a little nostalgic adventure. A little blast from the past. He had been sitting in the Pentagon one night thinking, 'I wonder what happened to her?' and then he had thought, 'I know. I'm a powerful man. I'll have her traced and the next time I'm in London I'll pop round and see if I can still fuck her.' By rights Polly should be offended, she should throw him out. The feminist in her told her that if she screwed Jack she would be doing exactly what he wanted. Literally playing into his hands. But, then again, so what? She would be using him too. It was as if she'd been exactly sexually satiated of late. '

frankly, she could really do with a little passion herself. But could she trust her emotions? After what he had meant to her, after how he had behaved? Would she suddenly find herself hopelessly in love again or would she just want to kill him? Polly could not quite decide whether in the final analysis having sex with Jack would make her happier or sadder.

In her mind's eye the good memories were gaining the ascendancy.

'I nearly didn't go through with it, you know,' she said. 'That first time. When I saw that disgusting tattoo of yours. Kill everyone and everything horribly or whatever it said.'

'Death Or Glory,' Jack corrected her. 'I know you thought it was juvenile, Polly, but I'm in the army. It's our regimental motto.'

'I used to work for Tesco's but I haven't got "Great quality at prices you can afford" written across my arse.'

Jack laughed and topped up his drink. He could certainly put the booze away, but then he had always been able to do that.

'I had a tattoo done too, you know, after you left,' Polly said, pulling at the collar of her raincoat and nightie to reveal the blurred decoration that her parents had found so unpleasant. Jack inspected it.

'It's the female symbol with a penis in it,' he said.

'It's not a penis, it's a clenched fist, for Christ's sake!' y snapped. 'Why does everybody say that? It's so usly a clenched fist.'

Jack leant in a little to inspect the design more closely. 'Yeah, well, maybe.'

Except, of course, he wasn't looking at the tattoo. By now he had shifted his gaze and was using his position of advantage to drink in Polly's partially exposed breasts. Polly had been aware when she pulled down her clothing to show her tattoo that she was displaying rather more of her bosom than was decorous, and she knew that Jack was looking at it now. Polly was rather vain of her breasts. She thought them perhaps her best feature. They were not particularly large or anything, but they were very shapely, cheeky almost. Age had not yet wearied them; they were well capable of standing up for themselves, so to speak.

Polly could feel Jack's breath upon her shoulder. It was hot and damp and seemed to be coming quicker now. He wasn't exactly panting, but he wasn't breathing easily either. Polly knew that she too was breathing more quickly and that her breasts were trembling slightly beneath Jack's gaze. She also knew what would happen to her body next. Spontaneously, involuntarily, her nipples began to harden under the nightshirt. It always happened when she felt aroused, and Jack, of course, knew that.

Even through the clothes Polly was wearing Jack could see the process beginning and it brought back such memories. How he longed to pull apart Polly's shirt and press his lips once again to those glorious dark pink bud

But he didn't. He drew away and gulped again at drink.

'Yeah, well, we both had some adjusting to do in those days,' he said.

For a moment Polly did not know what he was talking about. She had lost the thread of the conversation they had been having. She readjusted her clothing, covering her shoulders, slightly confused. She knew that he had wanted to touch her, she knew that she would have let him do it too and she knew that he knew that; her body had given it away. But he hadn't touched her. Instead he was talking again. He had retreated across the room, clearly anxious to put distance between them. He was resisting his desires. Polly wondered why.

'Oh, yes, that's for sure,' Jack continued. 'We both had to make allowances in those days.'

'What allowances did you have to make, then?' Polly enquired rather sharply. 'I seem to recall that it was you who called the shots.'

'Well, for instance I cannot say I relished discovering your organic raw cotton sanitary napkins soaking in the bathroom basin.'

The years had not blunted this point of contention. Once again the ancient row bubbled to the surface.

'That's because you fear menstruation!' she retorted. 'You're scared of the ancient power and mystery of the vagina.'

'No, Polly, it's because washing your sanitary towels ן the bathroom is totally gross.'

ᴾolly still didn't understand this point of view. She ⸱d it as offensive as he had found her hygiene ᴣements.

'What? Grosser than flushing great chunks of bleached cotton into our already filthy rivers?'

That was easy. Jack could answer that. 'Yes,' he said. 'Much grosser.'

'Are you seriously saying,' said Polly, rising to the bait as she always did, 'that you find the idea of a woman disposing of her body's byproducts in a responsible manner using sustainable resources more gross than dumping used tampons into the water system? Grosser than the seas being clogged up with great reefs of them knitted together with old condoms? Grosser than fish feeding on toilet paper? Grosser than tap water being filtered through surgical dressings and colostomy bags?'

Jack had to admit that these questions were more difficult.

'Uhm . . . maybe about as gross,' he replied.

'Jesus!' Polly snapped. 'You're a soldier. I thought you were supposed to be used to the sight of blood.'

How could Jack explain that as far as he was concerned there was a big difference between proper blood, manly blood, the blood that flowed from a wound, and blood left lying about the bathroom by menstruating feminists. He knew that this was not necessarily a laudable point of view, but it was how he felt.

'Look, Polly, we see things differently, OK? We always have. I'm sorry, but that's the way it is.'

Polly smiled Jack was embarrassed, which something she had rarely seen.

'What is it they say?' she said softly. 'Opposites attract.'

And so they were back at the point at which they had been a moment before. Looking at each other, the bed beckoning. The tender tension of love in the air. Jack's knuckles whitened on his glass. Polly wondered if it would shatter. She could see that he was struggling to control his desires. She did not know why he was struggling, but she decided that she hoped he would lose.

'You look great, Polly,' said Jack, his heart thumping.

'Thanks.' Polly met his gaze. 'You too.'

Jack did not reply. He could not think what to say. He knew what he ought to say. He had business to get through, that was why he had come. There were things about his past which only Polly knew, which only Polly could help him with. What Jack needed to do was ask the questions he had come to ask. But what he wanted to do was to make love.

'I'm glad you came back,' said Polly.

37

Polly was smiling.

Polly was frowning.

She was yawning at the bus stop. Peter's mother knew those photographs almost as well as Peter did himself. Often when he was out she would find herself drawn to his room, where she would stand, surrounded by images of the woman whose existence had so infected her own. She knew what a terrible thing it was to be the mother of a child gone wrong, to be always looking back on life, searching for the moment when the change had come, when the damage had been done.

It seemed to Peter's mother that her whole life had been a preparation for this current despair. Every moment of her past had been rewritten by the present. Peter's boyhood, which had brought her such happiness, was now forever tainted by what he had become. Every smiling memory of a little boy in shorts and National Health Service glasses was the memory of a boy who had turned into a deceitful, sneaking pervert. Every innocent hour they had spent together was now revealed as an hour spent in the making of a monster. Could she have known? Could she have prevented

Surely she could and yet Peter's mother could not see how. It was true that he had never had many friends but she had thought him happy enough. After all she was lonely too and so they had always had each other. Perhaps if his father had stayed . . . but that swine had gone before Peter had even been born. She could scarcely even remember him herself.

Seeing Peter that night, her own son, the flesh of her womb, squatting in a filthy gutter like a rat, had torn at her heart. He was sinking back into madness, she could see that, and this time it would be deeper and more terrible than the last. Peter needed help, that was obvious, help that clearly she could not give him. She was the problem, she had made him in every sense. The help he needed lay outside their home, but to reach it Peter's mother knew that she would have to betray her son.

38

Once more Jack hauled himself back from the erotic adventure his whole being craved. It was not the time. He had things to do. The key to his future lay in his past and it was Polly who held it.

'Opposites may attract, Polly, but they're still opposites,' he said, hiding behind his drink. 'I guess we're lucky we didn't last too long, huh?'

This comment, rather brutal in the circumstances, brought Polly back to earth with a jolt.

'Oh yes, very lucky. You probably did us both a favour,' she said bitterly. 'When you had your final screw and then snuck off while I lay sleeping. You bastard.'

Suddenly her eyes glistened. Polly's old enemy. Her tear ducts were responding as they always did when her emotions bubbled up. Although on this occasion some of the tears were for real. Jack was surprised to see Polly become so quickly upset, surprised to discover that the wound was still so raw, even after all the years. It made him feel ashamed. She had been the last person on earth he had ever wanted to hurt.

'It was my job, Polly.'

'What? Fucking and leaving? Nice work if you can get it,' she said, dabbing at her eyes with a teatowel.

Jack studied the carpet. 'I had to leave. I get orders. It's a security thing.'

'A security thing? Not to say goodbye? Oh yeah, of course, because World War Three would probably have started if you'd said goodbye.'

What could Jack say? It had not been possible for him to say goodbye, that was all, but he knew that there was no point in saying so now.

'I mean, a note or a call to tell me our affair was over,' Polly continued bitterly. 'That might have been just the excuse the Russians had been waiting for to wipe out the free world.'

All the intimacy that had existed between them a moment before had now evaporated. Polly was suddenly cold.

'I'm sorry,' Jack pleaded, 'I couldn't.'

'You were too fucking gutless to face up to the fact that you were betraying the trust of a seventeen-year-old girl and, what's more, over sixteen years later you're still too fucking gutless to admit it. "It's my job." Pathetic!'

She was right, of course. He'd been too scared to say goodbye. Scared of seeing her hurt, scared of a scene, but most of all scared that had he woken her and seen once again that adorable, trusting, innocent love light in her eyes he would not have been able to go rough with it. He loved her too much to risk saying dbye.

Polly, of course, had known nothing of Jack's tortured emotions. To her his departure had come like a cruel thunderbolt. She had no more expected the relationship to end than she had expected it to begin. She never dreamt that Jack had in fact tried to leave her many times during the latter part of their time together. In fact, from the moment he realized that he was in love with her he had been trying to find a way out.

'*What can I do, Harry?*' Jack wrote in anguish to his brother from the camp. '*How do I find the courage to end this? How do I find a way to leave?*'

In vain did Harry advise that if the army was forcing Jack to break his own heart and also the heart of an innocent, idealistic girl then maybe it was the army that he should be leaving and not the girl. Jack screwed up Harry's letter in fury. Harry was a furniture maker, he did not understand the soul of a fighting man, he did not understand the all-encompassing power of truly vaunting ambition. Harry had never dreamt of being a leader of men.

'*What do you know, you flake? Nothing,*' Jack wrote back '*Try to understand that your weak sensibilities mean nothing to me. Try to understand that I would break the heart of every girl in the world. That I would tear out my own and feed it to a dog in the street if just once I could get the chance to lead an American army into a battle. Any army into battle. You think that's sick, I know. You think somehow Mom got inseminated by the devil, but it is what it is. I'm a soldier first, last and only.*'

'*Bullshit, Jack!*' was Harry's reply. '*You call me a flake! You're the damn flake! You want to lead an army? You want to fight the world? You can't even find the courage to hurt one seventeen-year-old girl.*' Except in the end, of course, Jack did find the courage.

39

She sat waiting for him, as she always did, hiding in the darkness afforded by the bus shelter. Her heart thumped with excitement, her ears strained at the approach of every car. She was used to waiting for an hour or more for him to appear and as autumn approached it was often chilly. Polly didn't mind. She knew that when he did arrive she would be instantly warmed by the furnace of their desire. What was more, tonight was to be a rare delight; they were actually to sleep together, sleep in the true sense of the word, be present for each other's dreams. Usually this was not possible, but occasionally Jack had a pass and those were the best times, times when they had the whole long night in each other's arms.

As Jack's car approached, Polly knew he would be moody. He always was of late, glum and preoccupied. She didn't mind that either. It was his job, no doubt. Who wouldn't be glum if they were an agent of mass murder? And he always got over it quickly. Polly soon made him smile, sometimes just a glance from h would make his face light up. She never imagined t he was glum because he was trying to say goodby

'*I couldn't do it,*' Jack wrote to Harry after one such night. '*I tried, just like I tried the other times. I told myself again that this would be the night I would leave her but again it wasn't. "Goodbye" is such a small word. Why can't I say it? Every time I try it comes out as "I love you". Because whenever I look into her eyes I just want to stay looking into them for ever.*'

When Harry read this he tried to phone, he sent a telex, he even thought about getting on a plane. He wanted to shout, 'Don't do it, you fool! Don't throw love away, it's too rare a thing. Sometimes it only comes once in a lifetime.' But it was no good. By the time Harry got Jack's letter Jack had already left Polly in the only way he felt he could. Abruptly and absolutely. Without a word.

It had been a wonderful night. Completely and exclusively passionate to the exclusion of all else, even conversation. Sometimes on their evenings together they would have some supper and talk, but on that last occasion they scarcely said a word. Jack drove them to the little country hotel he had chosen, they checked in, went straight to their room and began to make love. Time and again they made love, fervently, desperately.

Polly's joy was all in the glory of the moment, but Jack was storing up memories, trying to make love to her enough to last a lifetime. Because he knew that he had to leave her that night. He knew as he lay there beside her afterwards, listening to her gentle breathing she slowly succumbed to sleep, that this was his last ace. He was certain that his resistance could last no longer. Another day or two in the sunlight of her love and he would be lost for ever. As would his career and the life he held dear. Jack was perfectly sure then, as he had been ever since, that if he had not left her that week, that very night, he would never have left her. It was cowardly, of course, but if he had looked back even once, he would have stayed. That was something he had not been prepared to allow.

So, instead of saying goodbye Jack had waited until Polly slept and then had crept silently from their bed, gathered up his clothes and snuck out into the hotel corridor. There he had dressed in the darkness, gone downstairs, paid the bill with the night porter and left.

'*What could I have done?*' Jack replied when Harry berated him for being the cowardly shit that he was. '*I had to leave. She was a seventeen-year-old anarchist! A radical pacifist. A foul-mouthed swamp creature with a ring through one of her nipples!*'

This detail surprised even Harry, who was quite an alternative sort of person himself. This was back in the days when nipple rings were not something that nice girls had.

'*I'm a thirty-two-year-old soldier with a crewcut, Harry!*' Jack pleaded more for himself than his brother's benefit. '*Talk about starcrossed lovers! Jesus, Captain Jack Kent and Polly Sacred Cycle of the Moon and Womb make Romeo and Juliet look like an arranged marriage! Pamela Anderson and the Ayatollah Khomeir would have made a more natural-looking couple.* ' had no future, Harry, can't you see that?*'

In truth Jack did not really care if Harry saw it or not, it was Polly he hoped would somehow understand. She hadn't, of course, and she never would.

She could still remember every detail of that shocking awakening. She could still see herself, a distraught young woman standing alone in a cold, empty room clutching a piece of paper with a single word on it: 'Goodbye.'

She remembered the brown carpet, the orange coverlet, the floral pattern nylon pillowslips. She could still see the sheet of lace underneath the sheet of glass on top of the mahogany-style MFI dressing-table unit. The stained-glass-effect transfers on the windows, the ancient, scentless potpourri on the windowsill. The clock radio flashing the time at 88 past 88. Her little summer dress and leather jacket crumpled up on the floor where she had left them when she was happy. Her Doc Marten boots lying at the foot of the bed, her bra in the wastepaper basket, her knickers lodged behind a framed print of a fox hunt that hung upon the wall.

And nothing of Jack, no trace of him, remained. Polly might always have been alone in that room. Jack had even plumped his pillow before leaving. The habits of a thousand bed inspections died hard.

Polly dressed herself in a daze and went downstairs to reception.

'Excuse me,' she said, her face burning with embarrassment, 'but the man I was with . . . the American. Have you seen him?'

The woman inside the little reception hatch had had

the face of Oliver Cromwell and the same glowering air of violent righteousness.

'The gentleman's gone.' Her voice sounded as if it had been mixed with iron filings. She folded her arms menacingly, as if daring Polly to contaminate her house further. Even the woman's hair was hard and unforgiving, having been set into an impenetrable helmet of red-tinted Thatcheresque waves that would have kept their shape in a hurricane.

'He left hours ago. Didn't he say goodbye, then?'

Throughout the intervening years Polly would never forget the withering contempt of that woman's tone.

No, he had not said goodbye. Polly stood before the hatch as if bolted down, not knowing what to say or do, not able even to think. Tears started in her eyes, further blotching the black smudged make-up that surrounded them. The hotel lady misunderstood her emotions.

'Well, he paid my bill, love,' she said.

Polly knew what the woman meant immediately. The woman thought Polly was a prostitute and that her client had done a runner.

This was indeed exactly what the woman had thought. What else would she think? When a smart-looking chap with money turns up late and signs in some grubby slip of a girl as his wife? A girl with bare legs, black eyeshadow and purple lipstick? When they go straight to bed without so much as ordering a toasted sandwich or spending money at the bar. When they keep the whole house up for hours with th disgusting grunting and when the noise finally subsides, after the man's clearly had his fill, he sneaks off in the small hours leaving his 'wife' to get her breath back.

'Unless there's anything else?' the woman said, clearly anxious to rid the sanctified air of her house of Polly's noxious presence. Polly turned to leave. She could not speak to the woman; she had been struck dumb. The enormity of what was happening to her was too much to take in. Adored, then dumped, now despised. Ecstatic, then distraught, now only numb, all within a few short hours. Polly was only seventeen.

'He's paid for your breakfast, by the way,' the woman said as Polly headed for the door. 'You can have it if you want, but there's no more eggs and you'll have to be fast because I want to set lunch.'

Never had an invitation to eat been offered with less enthusiasm. The woman could not have sounded more unwelcoming if she'd said that she would be serving turds instead of sausages.

40

'I should have had it, though,' Polly told Jack, 'because when I got out of the hotel I realized I didn't even know where I was and I only had about seventy-five pence on me and I hadn't even had a cup of tea. It took an entire day of buses and hitching to get back to camp and when I did they'd finished supper. It didn't matter, of course. I couldn't have eaten anyway. You'd torn my insides out.'

Jack had no answer. There were no tears in his eyes, of course. There never had been, and Polly doubted that there ever would be such a thing, but none the less deep inside him he cried. Thinking about that unhappy morning had always been difficult for him, and at last hearing Polly's side of the story made it more difficult still.

His own day had been scarcely happier. By the time Polly had awoken he was long gone, pointing his TR7 for the coast. Jack had planned it, as he planned everything, meticulously. Everything he owned was in the car. He would not be returning to Greenham. He had arranged for his leave to begin that morning and when his leave ended he was to go to Wiesbaden in German

There he would rejoin the regiment that he had left on being posted to Britain. Jack had already done three years at the base and it had not been difficult for him to persuade his superiors that he had earned the right to return to some proper soldiering.

'I thought about leaving some money for you,' Jack said in a quiet voice. 'You know, to get back to camp and all, but you were such a feminist and all, I thought it . . . it . . .'

'Might make me look like a bit of a tart?' Polly demanded. 'Yeah, well, no need to worry about that. That was already sorted.'

They relapsed into silence for a moment before Polly continued to unburden herself.

'I rang the camp, of course,' Polly said. 'I didn't betray you even then, not that they would have believed a mad peace bitch anyway, but I was still careful for your sake. I pretended I was a cab driver who'd overcharged you. They told me not to worry about it. They said you'd gone. They said you'd left the country! Can you imagine how that felt?'

Of course he could, although he knew that she would never believe him. The truth was that he knew how she felt because he'd felt it too. As evening fell that day and he'd leant on the rail of the car ferry, watching England disappear over the horizon, Jack had felt more desolate than he had ever felt. It had been no comfort at all that he had been the architect of his own unhappiness, or that he knew that it was the only thing he could do.

'You left that day!' The bitterness of Polly's tone

wrenched Jack back from his momentary reverie. 'You left Britain the same fucking day you left me!'

'Yeah?' Jack said. For a moment he was unsure why she was dwelling on this point.

'Which must have meant that you'd already made your preparations,' Polly explained. 'That you'd known you were leaving. That when you made love to me on that last night you knew what you were going to do. Your fucking bags must have been already packed, you bastard!'

'It hurt me too!'

'Good. I wish it had killed you!'

Polly did not believe Jack. She did not think he could have felt remotely what she'd felt. He would never have done what he did. She had been so completely in love with him. She'd trusted in him so absolutely and he'd left her all alone. For weeks afterwards she had been quite literally sick with the pain. Unable to keep food down, she'd scarcely eaten for months. She lost two and a half stone, which left her dangerously under-weight, and eventually she had had to see a doctor. At seventeen Polly discovered that it is not just the heart that aches when love is lost, but the whole body. Particularly the guts; that's where a person's nervous system really makes itself felt.

'It's not pretty,' said Polly. 'It's not romantic. It wouldn't look so good on the Valentines cards. A stomach with an arrow through it.'

Jack thought about saying he was sorry again but decided against it.

'So did you stay there long?' he asked instead. 'After?'

'I stayed there until after you people delivered the missiles; three years, in fact, with a gap for the miners' strike.'

Jack was amazed. 'Three years? In that camp? In that toilet? You spent *three years* singing songs through a fence! You stayed there till you were twenty? I thought you were there for the summer. That's what you said. What about your . . . what were they called? . . . your A-levels?'

'I didn't take them, not then, and I never went to university, either.'

Jack whistled in disbelief, scarcely able to believe it. In his view, Polly had wasted the three best years of her life.

Polly knew what he was thinking. 'I was waiting for you, Jack! I loved you.'

'Three years! That's not love, that's psychosis. That's an illness.'

He was right there, it had been an illness.

'I thought I saw you a thousand times. It was pathetic. There I'd be, screaming abuse at these people, and all the time I was hoping they were you so that I could tell you I loved you.'

'Jesus, Polly, nobody takes three years to get over being dumped.'

'It took me a lot longer than that, not that I'd have admitted it at the time. I believed in what we were doing. That camp was my home. But always, at the back of my mind, especially when there were new faces, new Americans on the other side of the wire, I'd think to myself, Maybe this time he's come back? Surely not everything he said was lies.'

'You were so young, Polly. I thought you'd forget me in a week.'

'I think young people are the most vulnerable in love. They haven't learnt their lessons yet. You certainly taught me mine.'

'I'm sorry,' said Jack quietly.

'Is that why you've come back? To say sorry?'

'Sure, if it will help, if that's what you want to hear.'

The old wound was aching badly for them both.

'I don't want—' Suddenly Polly was shouting. She stopped herself. Even in this highly charged emotional moment she knew she must not forget the milkman. She dropped her voice to a harsh whisper. 'I don't want to hear anything! I don't want anything from you. I was asleep an hour ago. Why have you come back, Jack?'

Again the question he did not want to answer.

'Well . . . why not? Like you said, we never officially split up, technically you're still my girlfriend . . .' Jack laughed rather woodenly. 'You always used to say that you weren't into conventional relationships.'

'A relationship with a sixteen-year pause in it is not unconventional, it's over.'

'I thought you'd be pleased to see me.'

Why he thought that she could not imagine. Except that she was pleased to see him. Despite everything, she was very pleased. Looking at Jack it struck her that he looked tired, almost careworn.

'Are you hungry?' she asked. 'Do you want something to eat?'

'Not really, no,' Jack replied.

'That's good, because I don't have any food. Well, I do have food, sort of, just not real food. Frozen meals, serves two. That sort of thing.'

'Serves two?' Jack's interest picked up.

'No. I told you there isn't anybody.'

Jack looked hard at Polly, and for some reason she felt that some sort of explanation was required.

'They say "serves two", but they mean one, in fact not even quite one, really. You have to pad them out with toast and chocolate biscuits. They put "serves two" on it so you don't feel so pathetic when you buy them in the shop . . . So you can pretend you're not alone.'

It sounded so sad. Polly admitting that she was alone. Not positively and self-sufficiently alone, but alone because she had no one with whom to share her life. Lonely alone. The revelation hung heavily in the air between them. Polly smiled reassuringly and tried to make light of it.

'It fools the shopkeeper every time you buy one. Frozen meal for two, madam? Oh, yes, certainly. I'll be sharing this with my enormous, passionate and deeply sensitive lover. We always like to share eight and a half square inches of microwaved lasagne after an all-night hagging session.'

'How the hell does a beautiful woman like you come

to be on her own?' Jack was genuinely surprised.

'Men are nervous of single women in their thirties. They think she's either got a child already, or that halfway through the second date she's going to glance at her biological clock and say, "My God, is that the time? Quick, fertilize me before it's too late." '

'You don't have to be alone. You're just being lazy. Not making any effort.'

Who did he think he was? Her mother? He'd be telling her she had lovely hair and a super personality next.

'Not making any effort! What do you suggest I do? Stand naked on the pavement with my tongue hanging out and a large sign saying "Get it here"? I go to pubs, parties. I even joined a dating agency.'

Polly said this last defiantly. It had taken her a lot of courage to join a dating agency. It was another of those things that only a short while ago she would never in a million years have imagined happening to her. She knew what Jack would think. The same thing that everybody thought. How sad. How surprising. How pathetic. Never thought *she* would be so desperate. For months after Polly had approached 'Millennium Match' she had kept the fact as a dark and shameful secret, never telling a soul. Then one day she had decided to come out. Come out as a lonely person. A lonely person who was trying to do something about it. Since then Polly had made a point of telling people at the first chance she got.

In shops. 'Two kilos of carrots, please, a grapefrui

oh, and by the way, I've joined a dating agency.'

At work. 'Right, so before we address the issue of gender discrimination in nursery teaching, is everybody aware that I've joined a dating agency?'

The idea had been that Polly would overcome her embarrassment and shame by confronting it head on. That her proud honesty would educate people to see her decision for what it was, a legitimate effort to cope with the social challenges of an increasingly fragmented society. It hadn't worked yet, but she was persevering.

'A dating agency,' said Jack in the same tone her mother had used. 'That's insane. You're a babe.'

'You don't have to have three heads, garlic between your teeth and a season ticket to *Riverdance* to be lonely, Jack. All you need is to be alone. To have met all the people that your circumstances are likely to bring you into contact with and not be in a relationship with any of them.'

Polly knew that she wasn't unattractive, she wasn't socially inept; she was just alone. And, to her surprise, the men the agency had introduced her to were much the same. Just alone, like her. The problem was that this fact hung over every new meeting like a cloud of slightly noxious gas. Polly would sit there toying with her food thinking, not bad looking, good manners . . . but he's alone. *Why* is he alone? Finding herself unable to dismiss the unworthy suspicion that, unlike herself, this man was not merely an innocent victim of fickle fate but somebody who was alone for a reason.

Of course, Polly was sufficiently realistic to know

that the object of her doubt was almost certainly thinking the same thing about her. Even the lonely
stigmatized the lonely. The very people who knew best
that you do not need to be a psychopath or a gargoyle
to be lonely were the most wary of other lonely people.
Like outcasts everywhere, they learned to despise their
own kind.

'Polly,' said Jack. 'It's insane that you went to an
agency. The world is full of eager single guys your age.'

'I'm the same age now that you were when we were
together, Jack. You think about that. When you were an
eager single guy of my age you weren't seeking out
lonely insecure women of your age, you were seducing
a seventeen-year-old girl.'

Well, she had him there, smoking gun and all, no
doubt about that. He drained his glass and poured himself another large one.

'Jesus, Jack, I hope you're not driving.'

He was, but he was going to risk it. Jack's courage
and resolve were deserting him. The revelation that
Polly was so lonely had been a shock. For years he had
thought that he was the lonely one. He had always
imagined Polly settled and happy in some gloriously
perfect relationship. Living with a university lecturer,
perhaps, or a Labour MP. Of course, his spy had
revealed that she lived alone, but not that she was
lonely.

Oh, how he would have loved to cure her of her loneliness. To whisk her away right there and then and
make her happy for ever. He couldn't, though, for

exactly the same reasons that he had left her in the first place. He had had his chance and he had chosen his path.

'I like to drink,' he said. 'It helps with moral decisions.'

'Moral decisions? What moral decisions?'

Jack did not wish to say. 'Nothing,' he said.

'What moral decisions?' Polly insisted. Morality was a topic that Jack had never been interested in discussing in the past.

'Well, hey, every breath a person takes is a moral desicision, isn't it?'

'Is it?'

'I think it is.'

Polly could not imagine what Jack meant.

'Well, it's "to be or not to be", isn't it?' he explained. 'I mean, that has to be the question.'

'I don't really see why.'

Polly would have been surprised to know that Jack had been thinking a lot about morality of late.

'I don't see why you don't see why,' he said, 'considering what a morally minded person you always set yourself up to be.'

'I never set myself up to be anything.'

'Every moment we decide to remain alive we are making a moral choice. Because our existence has repercussions, like a pebble in a very polluted pond. Everything we eat, everything we drink, everything we wear, is in one way or another a product of exploitation.'

Polly knew that, of course, but she was most impressed that it had occurred to Jack.

'You don't have to be a sex tourist to abuse children in the Third World,' Jack continued. 'All you have to do is buy a carpet or a sports shirt. Or open a bank account. Or fill your car with gas.'

'Well, yes, of course,' said Polly, 'and it's the duty of every consumer to confront and minimize that exploitation . . .'

Jack laughed. It was a laugh with a sneer at the back of its mind. 'Confront and minimize? That's for wimps. It seems to me that the only truly moral thing a person could do in these sad circumstances is kill himself.'

41

Got it! The knife was finally hooked.

Slowly, gently, with infinite care, Peter reeled in his prize, inch by inch hoisting the wire retriever back up through the grid, watching his beloved blade ascend.

Then he had it. It was in his hand once again where it belonged. He sat on the wet kerb and studied it, carefully closing its blade and cradling it in his hands as if it were a tiny pet. Then he tried the catch. It worked perfectly; the blade sprang out of the hilt as if it were alive, snapping into place with the usual satisfying click. Peter's little pet was clearly none the worse for its time in the underworld.

Another car came round the corner, but Peter did not bother to move this time. He remained where he was, kneeling in the gutter. Now that he had his knife back he felt invulnerable.

42

In the chilly atmosphere of the formal but faded grandeur of her dining room, Nibs held her knife also. It was a cheese knife, but she was gripping it just as hard as the Bug gripped his.

The full story of her husband's most recent philandering, or as much of it as he had felt forced to tell her, had made grim listening. The dessert had been delivered and she had pushed hers away untasted; he'd eaten his, of course – he could always pig down pudding – and now the cheese had arrived. Nibs took a little English red Leicester but she couldn't eat it. They were both drinking quite hard and a third bottle of wine had been opened, but neither of them felt at all drunk.

'So I suppose you want me to stand by you,' said Nibs.

'I want you to forgive me.'

Nibs was not in a forgiving mood. Her fate was sealed. She knew that, but she was not under any obligation to be magnanimous about it. She was doomed to become one of the 'women who stand by her man'. They were a common type these days; you saw the famous ones on the television all the time. Politicians' wives, pop stars' wives – sad, trembling, red-eyed victims whom the press had hounded from their hiding places, baited onto their doorsteps and forced by circumstance to lie through their teeth before a baying mob. The clichés never varied.

'My husband and I have talked things over and decided to put this incident behind us . . . We remain very much in love . . . Miss so-and-so is no longer a part of my husband's life,' etc., etc.

All this actually meant was that the poor woman had nowhere to go, her position, her possessions, her children, her life in general, all being tied up with the mumbling apologist to whom she was married. He had taken her youth and her potential and now she had no obvious life options of her own. Nowhere to go except her doorstep, to assure the world that she was standing by her husband.

Nibs knew that she too would stand by her man. It was true that she was an accomplished professional woman in her own right. She would not be entirely lost on her own. None the less, after twenty-five years and with children still in their teens, her life was inexorably tied up with her husband's. Her career had always been just a little bit secondary to his; his business had become her business too, she'd worked hard for it. His status was hers. Like many a woman before her, Nibs was caught between a rock and hard place and the hard place was her husband's dick. She did not like being betrayed, but on the other hand she did not wish to have to rebuild her life from scratch just because she was married to a man who couldn't keep it to himself.

'I'll stand by you,' she said, 'but I'm not going to lie for you.'

'I wouldn't ask that,' he replied.

But they both knew that in the end if she had to she would.

43

It occurred to Polly that although they had been talking for nearly an hour she still knew almost nothing about Jack's life. She realized with a tinge of resentment that she seemed to have been giving most of the information.

'So how about you?' she asked 'Are you in a relationship?'

'No, I'm married.'

It was a joke, the sort of sexist little put-down in which Jack specialized. Normally Polly despised men who put their wives down behind their backs. She heard that stuff a lot. Scarcely a month went by without some married man or other telling her what a mistake he'd made with his life and how all he wanted was to be able to give his love to someone who would appreciate it. Experience had taught Polly to react to that sort of thing with nothing but feelings of sisterly solidarity.

This time, however, she scarcely noticed Jack's blokey humour. The knowledge that he was married had taken her completely by surprise. There was no reason for it to have done so, of course. Jack was an establishment man in an establishment job, he was almost bound to be married. She felt deflated. She knew she had no right to feel that way, but none the less she did. The truth was that deep deep down, without acknowledging it even to herself, Polly had been toying with the exquisitely exciting possibility that Jack might have come back for her. From the first moment she had heard his voice over the answerphone something in her most private self had hoped that he had come back to stay. It was nonsense, of course, a ridiculous notion, and she knew that now for sure. He was married, he had a life. All he had come back for was some easy sex. Perhaps not even that, perhaps he had been motivated by nothing more than curiosity.

'Oh yeah, I'm married all right,' Jack mused into his bourbon. 'But whatever we had died a long time ago.'

'I'm sorry,' Polly said, although she wasn't particularly.

Jack performed his favourite shrug. 'There's nothing to be sorry about. Literally nothing. I can't remember the last time we made love. She has a Dutch cap which ought to have been an exhibit in a museum of gynaecology. The spermicidal cream is years past its fuck-by date.'

'So why haven't you left her?'

'I don't have the guts.' Which was a silly thing to say to Polly.

'You had the guts before.'

'That was different.'

'How was it different?' Polly asked angrily.

'We were together three months, Polly! We weren't married! Did you ever try to leave someone you've been with for years? It's like trying to get off the *Time Life* mailing list. I torment myself. Would she kill herself? Who would get custody of the credit cards?'

'Oh, come on, Jack!'

Polly may not have seen Jack for a long time, but she knew him well enough not to buy this type of bullshit. If Jack wanted something he was not going to let any finer emotions or sensibilities stand in his way. He never had.

'OK, OK,' Jack conceded. 'The truth is I can't leave her because I can't risk damaging my career. I'm near the top now, Polly. I mean real near. I'm tipped to be the man. Unfortunately the army is about a hundred years behind the rest of the world on social matters. They like you to be married and they like you to stay married.'

Polly could hardly believe that it still mattered, that being a divorcé could still be a bar to promotion.

'Oh yes, it can be, Polly, in the army it can. More so now than a few years ago, the pendulum's swinging back. Can you believe it? I had to leave you for my career and now I can't leave my wife for the same reason. If I wasn't such a big success I might almost think that I'd fucked up my life.'

Jack had met Courtney shortly after his arrival in Washington to take up his posting at the Pentagon. They were introduced by Jack's bumbling old friend Schultz. The meeting took place at a Republican Party fundraiser, and it had been a rare moment of intuition on Schultz's part because Jack and Courtney became instant friends. They were as similar to each other in outlook as Jack and Polly had been opposites. Courtney, like Jack, was a sincere patriot and a conservative, but also like him she was no bubba-style redneck. The daughter of a Congressman, Courtney was accomplished, cultured and beautiful, and although still only twenty-six, she was already respected in her chosen field of company law. She and Jack made a splendid couple, he the tough, handsome soldier, she 'the gorgeous girl most likely'. Between them they looked like the stars of a Reagan campaign ad.

Harry had been suspicious from the moment Jack had introduced him to his new girlfriend. Courtney was perfectly nice and Harry could see that she certainly loved Jack, in an uptight, chilly, preppy sort of way, but Harry did not think that Jack loved Courtney. To Harry, Jack looked like a man going through the motions.

For a while Harry kept his silence, presuming that the affair would blow over, but when Jack wrote to tell him that he had asked Courtney to be his wife and that she had done him the honour of accepting, Harry could deny his fears no longer.

'This isn't a marriage proposal, Jack, it's a career move!' Harry thundered in his reply. 'It's too damn convenient to be true. If you asked the IBM mainframe to come up with the perfect bride for you it would have come up with Courtney. But real life isn't like that. You

*know that better than anyone because you loved Polly.
Love is rarely convenient. Courtney isn't for you, Jack.
You aren't in love with her, you just think you look so
good together that you ought to be in love.'*

It was combative stuff but Harry was sure that his
instincts were right. He still had Jack's letters from the
final summer that Jack had spent at the Greenham
camp. Then Jack really had been in love, with all its
attendant joy and pain. Now it seemed to Harry that
his brother was merely acquiring a lifestyle appropriate
to his status and position.

'Have you thought about Courtney?' Harry wrote. *'I
thought you officers were supposed to be gentlemen.
That girl trusts you, she loves you; don't you think she
has a right to know that you're still in love with
another woman?'*

This last point was Harry's secret weapon. He was
aware that Jack wouldn't take it lightly and he didn't.
Fortunately for the two brothers, they were half a continent apart; otherwise there might even have been
blows. Jack furiously denied Harry's accusations. He
loved Courtney, she was a terrific person. Of course he
knew that he did not feel quite the same for her as he
had once felt for Polly. His knees didn't buckle at the
thought of Courtney, his insides didn't ache, but surely
that was a good thing? His love for Polly had been stupid and obstructive, more an obsession than a proper
adult emotion. Jack certainly had no wish to go
through his married life poleaxed with love and lust
every time his wife walked into the room. It would be

far too time-consuming. He had things to do, a career to forge.

'*You think there's only one way of being in love?*' he wrote back to Harry. '*You think it always has to be like you and Debbie? Instant fucking devotion? You think I have to be some kind of wet puppydog drip like you? Jesus, I hope not. Let me tell you now. If ever me and Courtney start acting like you and Debbie did, take my gun and shoot me!*'

Jack had a point and Harry knew it. When he had first started dating his wife Debbie it certainly had been a bit gruesome. They were both very young and their powerful mutual attraction had manifested itself in a public gooeyness that should have remained private. They kissed at the dinner table, giggled together in corners and occasionally even talked babytalk in front of friends. It was inexcusable behaviour, but they just could not help themselves. There is no love like young love and theirs truly had been love at first sight. What's more, it was a love that had lasted. Harry and Debbie had become that rare thing, high-school sweethearts who seemed to have made a good and permanent marriage.

'*Yeah, well, not every marriage starts with snookey fucking ookums, pal!*' Jack wrote furiously. '*Courtney and I are adults and we love each other like adults and we're going to get married like adults, so fuck you!*'

Jack signed off, but there was a PS.

'*By the way, do you want to be the best man?*'

It was a magnificent wedding attended by senators

and congressmen, senior army and air force personnel. There was a message from President Bush and his wife Barbara, who knew Courtney's parents, and the cream of Washington society were in attendance. Even Jack's father made an effort, ditching his habitual fringed suede jacket and hiring a tuxedo for the occasion.

'Don't worry, son,' he said. 'I'll kiss ass to your Nazi pals.'

The only tiny upset on the big day was the late arrival of Jack's old pal Colonel Schultz. Almost inevitably Schultz had gone to the wrong church and had let his staff car go before realizing his mistake. He and Mrs Schultz arrived in a taxi just as the bride and her father pulled up in their limo.

At the reception Old Glory hung upon every wall, an eight-foot-high ice sculpture of the American Eagle glowered from within a sea of flowers, and impeccable waiters served Californian méthode champenoise. The band struck up Springsteen's 'Born In The USA' and Jack and Courtney led off the dancing, looking stunning, he in his dress uniform, she in a cloud of white silk, and the whole room erupted into cheers and spontaneous applause. Such a very good-looking couple, so assured, so strong, so confident. Even Harry, standing at the back of the crowd with his arm around his beloved Debbie, believed in that moment that Jack had made the right choice for his life. He still could not help wondering what the English girl whom Jack had betrayed would have made of such a scene had she witnessed it, but in the glamour and romance of the moment Harry dismissed the thought. It had all been so long ago. His brother claimed to have forgotten his first great love and she no doubt had long since forgotten Jack.

The band moved on to Huey Lewis and the News's anthem to eighties cool, 'Hip To Be Square'. Harry and Debbie joined the bejewelled and unco-ordinated mob on the dancefloor.

Jack and Courtney's marriage started off fine and for a year or so they were happy. They liked each other and found each other attractive enough to ensure a respectable if unspectacular sex life. The sad truth was, though, that Jack's heart was never truly in it. Harry had been right, and by the second anniversary that fact was becoming difficult to disguise. Jack had two loves in his life and neither of them was his wife. One was the army and the other, despite all Jack's denials, was Polly.

The breakdown of affection was hard on Courtney. She truly had believed herself in love and her wedding day had been the happiest day of her life. Unlike her husband, Courtney had not experienced real love before. Her career had always taken precedence over romantic entanglements and so inexperience fooled her into imagining that what she felt for Jack was the real thing. Therefore when Jack's attitude and manner began to grow colder she was deeply hurt. Nothing had changed as far as she was concerned, and yet it seemed that they were no longer happy.

Jack knew that he was hurting Courtney but he did not know how to stop. His cruelty to her was neither verbal nor physical, but simply that he had married her in the absence of love.

Jack wanted to write to Harry about it but he could not. Harry's life had changed too and he did not have room in it for Jack's problems. His beloved wife Debbie had left him. She had fallen for another man, a fellow firefighter, and one day she had told Harry that she was leaving. Debbie explained that even the most perfect love affairs sometimes have sell-by dates and she had reached hers. In vain did Harry protest that those sell-by dates are usually meaningless, that the food is just as good for months afterwards – years, in the case of tinned food. You just have to have the courage to not take the easy way out and throw it away but keep it until you had need of it. Debbie felt that the metaphor was overstretched. The simple fact was that she had become besotted by a big, tough, brave guy and that she no longer loved the man she had married almost as a girl, the man who spent all day making chairs and tables.

'How long has it been going on?' Harry asked.

'It doesn't matter how long,' Debbie replied, unable even to look at the man whom she had loved so well and for so long.

And Harry knew that it had been going on for some time. His love had been betrayed.

Soon Jack and Courtney's marriage was also over in everything but name. He led his life and she led hers, which, during Jack's seven months in Kuwait and briefly Iraq, began to include the occasional love affair.

There was no question of divorce. Courtney was a traditionalist, besides which Jack's career had finally begun to hit the fast track. After the Gulf War he was promoted rapidly and began to mix more in political circles. The Democrats were not going to stay in power for ever and the Republicans were on the lookout for likely lads who might help to break their hold on power, particularly handsome war veterans. Courtney was highly ambitious, and her marriage to Jack became what Harry had suspected it was all along: a mutually supportive marketing exercise.

One thing Courtney was grateful for was that, despite her occasional indiscretions, Jack appeared never to have affairs. She and he had occasional sex and that seemed to be enough for him. The only thing that Jack wanted to get inside was the uniform of the commander of the army.

'We're friends, sure enough,' Courtney confided in her mother, 'but I don't really think he has passion for anything but leadership.'

It was not true, of course. Jack still had passion for one other thing besides ambition, although he had imagined that passion was long buried. He still craved Polly and now, as Jack stood once again before her, Polly knew it. She could see it in his eyes as he stared at her across her room.

'So your wife doesn't love you and now you're here. In the middle of the night,' Polly said. 'What's the idea? Suddenly fancied a little blast from the past?'

There. She'd said it. The thing she'd been wanting to

ask from the beginning. Had he come here to try to fuck her?

Jack stared into his glass, nervously rotating it in his hand. The question was banging around his head. Had he come back to try to fuck her? The truth was, of course, that he hadn't, but by Christ he fancied it all the same.

'Well?' Polly asked again. 'You're miles from home. Your wife doesn't understand you. Did you suddenly remember me and get a little horny, Jack?'

That he could answer. 'Not suddenly, Polly. Always.'

And he meant it. Not one day had gone by since the terrible night he'd left her when Jack had not wanted to see Polly again. To taste again the delights of sex with the only girl he had ever loved.

Polly could see that he meant it, too. It was written in his eyes. Deep inside her something was laid to rest. He had loved her after all.

'Oh, Jack.' She stepped forward. She knew that she shouldn't. As a strong woman and a feminist she should spurn his selfish desires. She knew that he had only come back for a night. That he would leave again in the morning as he had done before, but she didn't care. If anyone had a right to a bit of comfort by General Jack Kent it was her. Let the devil take tomorrow; she was opting for one less lonely night.

'Do you know, I have never told my wife about us.' Jack was still fighting it, still holding back.

'I don't want to talk about your wife.'

'I thought you did.'

'Well, I don't.'

Polly shifted her weight slightly from one bare foot to the other; it was a tiny move, but sexual. A loosening of the body. Jack glanced up. She still stood that same way that she used to, relaxed, a little lazy on the hips. He felt his whole resolve dissolving.

'Yeah, well anyway, I never told her. I never told any-one.'

'As if anyone would care now?' said Polly. 'As if it matters in the slightest after all these years. Unless you're embarrassed or something. Is that it? Are you scared that one day someone else but me might find out that you're a craven shit?'

'Maybe it's just that I don't want to share you, even in my memories.'

Polly's emotions were on a knife edge. They could not have been more mixed if she'd run them through the washing machine. It is true that her desire for him had begun to overcome the anger she felt about his ancient betrayal. However, it did not take much to bring sixteen years of resentment back into focus.

'That's nice,' she said. 'Especially considering all you left either of us with is memories.'

Jack looked so crestfallen that she felt sorry for him. Something she would not have imagined possible only an hour before.

'OK, OK,' she put in quickly. 'It was a long time ago. Different decade, different world order. It happened, that's all. I suppose you're not the only guy in history who did the dirty on a girl. And anyway. You did come back . . .'

Polly's stance relaxed further and the room positively hummed with Jack's longing. Her left hip dropped a little lower, pushing the knee forward. Her mouth fell slightly open. She rested her hands upon her thighs and was reminded that she was still dressed in a rather unflattering plastic rainmac.

'Think I'll take off this raincoat,' she said. 'My nightie's probably slightly less stupid.'

Polly let the raincoat slip off as if it had been a négligé and stood before Jack dressed only in a shirt, the top couple of buttons of which were already undone. She was breathing more quickly now and her bosom was again rising and falling defiantly. Her hair, which Polly had thought a mess, might also have been described as gloriously tousled, ravishingly unkempt.

She was so beautiful, Jack could hardly bear it, yet still he hesitated.

'It's been a long time, Jack,' said Polly, which was clearly a nice way of saying, 'Come to bed.' She took a step or two towards him.

Jack could not help but catch a momentary glimpse of Polly's thighs as the movement of her legs parted her shirt at its hem. He was inches from the soft, pale splendour of Polly's most private self, and he could scarcely bear it. This had been no part of his plans.

Polly bent down and took the glass from Jack's hand. In so doing her nightshirt fell forward and Jack was almost painfully aware of her breasts as they hung before him inside the gaping shirt. He looked. How could he resist? He stared. For a moment he could actually see between her breasts and through to her stomach beyond and the top of her knickers, which were crimson against her skin.

'I've missed you too,' Polly whispered softly, her mouth not nine inches from his ear. 'I've been lonely.'

'It's an international epidemic.'

Polly put Jack's glass down on the little table beside his chair. Or rather on top of the pile of magazines, books and coffee mugs already on top of the little table by his chair. Then she took Jack's hands and drew him to his feet. Jack could now feel the warmth of Polly's breath, the warmth of her body. Her hair smelled exactly the same as it had always done. He could see that her nipples had hardened again beneath the thin cloth of her nightshirt. She had always had such responsive nipples, he remembered. They were up and down all night, leaping into life at the slightest provocation, an infallible barometer of the state of her arousal. The current provocation was scarcely slight. They were both consumed with a taut, vibrant desire and the points of Polly's breasts seemed almost to be straining to reach him.

'You're such a beautiful girl, Polly. Still just the same.'

'Nearly the same,' Polly replied. 'It's all still here, just a little closer to the ground.'

It did not seem so to Jack. She appeared to him as beautiful as the day they had first met. As the day he had left. Polly reached up to him and took his face in her hands.

'Hello, old friend,' she said and drew his lips towards hers.

And then they kissed. This time Polly did not break away as she had done when Jack first arrived. It was a kiss that spanned sixteen years, a kiss so charged and full of memory and emotion that it was a wonder that the mouths of two people could contain it all.

Now their arms were about each other, mouths working with a desperate urgency. Even through the thickness of his uniform Jack could feel the soft splendour of Polly's body against his. If he chose he knew that he could be upon it in an instant. He had only to throw off his clothes and that divine skin would be against his, those adored breasts crushed against his chest. He clasped her even tighter to him.

'Is that a gun in your pocket?' Polly whispered playfully into Jack's ear, 'or are you pleased to see me?'

Jack loosened his grip, slightly embarrassed. 'Actually it's a gun in my pocket.'

Stepping back for a moment Jack reached under his jacket and took a pistol from his trousers.

'Sorry about that,' he said and laid it down on the table beside his glass. Then he made as if to resume their embrace, but Polly raised a hand to stop him. She could hardly believe her eyes.

'A gun!' she gasped. 'You're carrying a gun! You're armed!'

'Sure,' Jack replied casually. 'I'm a soldier. It's what I take to work.'

'I'm a council worker but I don't have a file full of pointless forms and a leaky biro stuffed into my knickers! I can't believe you've brought a gun into my home.'

Where Jack came from, of course, everybody had a gun in their home. People didn't even think about it. In fact if you didn't have one you were weird. Obviously Jack knew that things were different in Britain, but it still did not seem like a big deal to him.

'I'm sorry, Polly, but I need it.'

'You need a gun in Stoke Newington in the middle of the night?'

'Yes, I do,' Jack replied. 'I'm a target.'

This was not the type of conversation that Polly would have chosen to conduct in the middle of making love, but she could not just let it go.

'You do know you're breaking the law, don't you?' she said. 'I mean, this is Britain, not Dodge City! You can't just wander around with a gun in your pocket.'

But it seemed that Jack could.

'I'm one of America's most senior soldiers. Quite a lot of people about the place would like me to be dead. It's a diplomatic thing. We have an informal understanding with Special Branch.'

Polly still could not accept it. 'You come to my house dressed like Oliver North, you have informal understandings with the Special Branch, you carry a gun! I hate people like you. I've spent my life protesting about people like you!'

Jack shrugged and smiled his smile.

'So how is it . . .' Polly continued, 'how the fuck is it . . . that you're the only man I've ever loved . . . ?'

'Bad luck, I guess,' said Jack. Then he drew her back into his arms.

For a moment Polly thought about resisting. She thought about informing Jack that she was not a tap who could be turned on and off, that she did not consort with gunmen. But then he held her and she held him. Their lips met again with even greater passion, it seemed, than they had done a minute or two before. Again Jack could feel Polly's divine form crushed against him, could feel her hands pulling at the belt of his jacket. Now he really had to see her naked once more. He stood back a little, not so far as to stop Polly from undoing his belt but far enough for him to raise his hands to the buttons of Polly's nightshirt. Whatever his original plans might or might not have been, he simply had to see her naked again. He would die if he did not. He knew that it was wrong. He had promised himself that what was about to happen was the one thing that would not happen but he didn't care. He had been mad to imagine that he could control it. He loved her and he wanted her. Nothing had changed.

Now his hands were at the middle buttons of her nightshirt, his eyes straining, waiting to feast themselves on what lay beneath. His face, usually so mature and assured, was suddenly like a boy's, eager and scared. Polly, too, could hardly restrain herself. She'd opened his jacket and her hands had stolen to the fastening of his trousers. She neither knew nor cared what had brought Jack back to her door; she was happy to give away the past and ignore the future. Her entire life was crammed into the immediate living moment. Jack's fingers brushed against her skin as her shirt fell open and he felt her shiver gently at his touch. He shivered also, and by no means gently. Polly's hands tugged at his zip. His whole body felt as if it would explode. He moved his hands from one button down to the next, allowing his fingers to explore the greater freedom that the opening of Polly's shirt now afforded. Her breasts felt smooth and firm, the skin springy and subtle. He wondered if he could ever let go now that he had them in his hands again.

'You got rid of the nipple ring, then?' he whispered.

'Yeah, everybody started wearing them.'

Polly had a hold of Jack too, her hand deep in his trousers, gripping the straining erection through his shorts. Now Jack's hands were at Polly's waist, the final button of her shirt undone, his fingers slipping under the elastic of her knickers. Another moment and all would be revealed.

Then Polly's phone rang.

44

Peter had remained in the gutter for some time, kneeling in the dirty running stream, imagining himself somehow cleansed and sanctified by the waters of the night. Water has ever had a strong hold on the spiritual side of men's minds and it was no less the case for Peter, even though his spirit was warped and his mind ill. The rain upon his face and the stream lapping at his knees seemed somehow to lend a new courage and nobility to his resolve. In his unformed fantasies he imagined himself reborn and baptized, a martyr and a saint. He spread his arms, Christ-like, as he knelt. Like Christ he was an outcast, a man alone and, like Christ, he knew a greater love.

But that love had been betrayed.

Peter had resolved upon murder. It just remained to decide who was to die. Would he kill the American? Would he kill Polly? Perhaps he would kill them both, and then himself. But if he killed himself how would his mother cope? Perhaps he would have to kill her too.

He got up, soaked to the skin but warm and happy. He had a purpose, a goal. He could see an end to his emptiness and longing.

Fumbling in his pocket for a coin, he made his way back to the phonebox.

45

Jack and Polly sprang apart. The ringing of the phone came as a shock, totally unexpected; they had been utterly lost in their mutual undressing.

'Who the hell is that?' said Jack, grabbing at his trousers to prevent them from falling down.

'How would I know? I'm not a clairvoyant,' Polly replied, closing her nightshirt. But she did know.

'It's nearly four in the morning, Polly. Who's going to ring at such an hour?'

It seemed almost as if Jack was more anxious than she was.

'You tell me. You did.'

After the sixth ring the answerphone kicked in and delivered Polly's familiar message. Of course Polly knew what was coming next. It would be the Bug. He was out there and he was trying to get in. A great wave of despair swept over her, so strong and so desolate that her knees nearly gave way and caused her to fall. Would she never have any peace from this man? This thing? Was he going to spoil every joyful moment for the rest of her life?

'You fucking whore,' said the machine. 'Is he in you

right now? Is his fat Yankee dick inside you? Yes, he is. I know he is.'

There was a pause. The line crackled. Polly and Jack did not speak. Jack was too surprised and she was too upset. Then the hated voice of the Bug began again.

'He's got AIDS, you know. He has. All Americans have, and now he's given it to you, or else you've given it to him, which is all either of you deserves, sweating and grunting like filthy pigs in your sty . . .'

Polly could no longer contain herself; it was all too much. She began to sob. Great, heartfelt, gulping sobs, dredged from the pit of her stomach. Why her? Why now? Why had she caught the Bug? Was she cursed? She made her way to the bed weeping as she went and sat down, burying her face in her hands, all the pent-up emotion of the evening spilling over into despair. For one joyful moment she had forgotten everything, both past and present pain, but it had been an illusion, she could see that now. She was just not meant for happiness. Even if she did sleep with Jack he would still be gone in the morning and she would be alone. Alone, that is, except for the Bug, who had infected her life and for which there was no cure.

Jack could only look on, his heart hurting for her in her distress. It was unbearable to see her this way. She seemed so helpless, her body shaking with her sobs, her chest, still half naked through the gaping shirt, shuddering jerkily with sorrow.

'What's he doing to you now, slag?' Peter's voice

filled the room. 'Has he come? Has he spunked his stuff into you yet? Maybe he's beating you up? You'd like that, wouldn't you, Polly? It's all tarts like you deser—'

Jack wanted very much to meet this unpleasant pest. He crossed the room and picked up the phone.

'Where are you speaking from, pal?' he asked in a friendly, matter-of-fact tone as if addressing an acquaintance. 'We could talk about all this stuff face to face.'

'I got my knife back, pal. And I'm going to kill you with it.'

'OK, that's fine. That's good. Where are we going to do this thing?' Jack could have been arranging for a couch to be delivered. 'I can meet you anywhere. We could get it over with right now if you like. Tonight. Just tell me where to go.'

Down in the box in the street Peter could see that his money was running out. He had only one more coin and he hadn't yet fixed upon his plan.

'You can go to hell, mate,' he said and slammed down the phone.

Back in Polly's flat Jack hung up.

'Pleasant fellow. I think I met him earlier,' Jack remarked casually to the top of Polly's head, her face still being lost in her hands. 'I guess he's your stalker, right?'

Polly was regaining some control. 'Yes,' she said in a snotty, teary voice. 'I'm sorry. Usually I try not to let it affect me, but it's been going on so long. He's always like that, disgusting, horrible . . .'

'Let me see if I can catch him,' said Jack, and he might have been talking about the postman.

Jack took up his coat, slipped his gun back into his pocket and hurried out of the flat, leaving Polly in a state of shock. Jack figured that there was a good chance that the man had been phoning from the callbox where Jack had seen him skulking before. It was certainly worth giving it a go, because life would be a great deal easier for Jack if he could catch the sad bastard that night.

Peter had been making his way back from the callbox on the other side of the road when he heard the door of Polly's house opening. Quickly he retreated into the shadow of a doorway. For all his bravado on the phone he realized how dangerous the American man was. Peter watched as his former assailant emerged from Polly's house and ran up the path. Peter considered leaping with his knife from the darkness as Jack ran past but the memory of their last encounter was too fresh, the taste of his own blood still in his mouth. Peter would have had to cross the road to get to the American and by the time he did that the man might have pulled out a knife of his own. Peter reasoned that he could take no chances. If he lost the fight he would never be able to take his revenge on Polly for betraying him.

Jack ran past and round the corner towards the phonebox. Peter had intended to remain in his hiding place, but then he saw something extraordinary.

Jack had left the door to Polly's house open.

46

It was too good a chance to miss. Peter had not been inside Polly's house since the very beginning of their relationship, and now the door was open and Polly was alone. Peter darted out from the shadows and scuttled across the road and up the path of her house. He hesitated for only a moment before pushing open the door and going in.

Once inside the hallway he paused and breathed deeply, taking a moment to absorb the atmosphere. This was her private place, her home, her 'sanctum', she had called it in court. He was risking a prison sentence just being there, but it was worth it. It was exquisite to be a part of her private world. He almost thought that he could smell Polly.

He began to climb the silent stairway, torn between the need to hurry and the desire to luxuriate fully in the moment. As he ascended he dragged one hand gently along the banister, imagining her hand upon the same polished wood, each morning and night.

In his other hand Peter held the knife.

A few moments later he stepped into the orange

semi-darkness of the top landing. Only one door led off it, which Peter knew to be Polly's. A light shone through the crack beneath it. She was inside, and she was alone. This, then, was it. The supreme moment. Peter did not know what would happen next. He had made no plan. His great opportunity had sprung itself upon him too quickly for that, but there was one thing he did know: if anyone was going to spend the night alone with Polly it was him.

He knocked on the door.

Inside the flat Polly stirred herself. She was grateful that Jack had returned so quickly; she had so hated being left alone. She got up from the bed, buttoned up her nightshirt and went to the door. Contrary to her usual habit she did not glance through the spyhole before beginning to undo the chain.

The phonebox had been empty. Jack had not expected anything else; hunters rarely find their quarry presented to them on a plate. There had been no point in trying to search the street either. There were so many shadowy doorways, basement stairs, gates and walls that it would have taken the rest of the night to investigate them all. Jack had longed for a set of infra-red nightsights, but of course, he reflected, you never have the right tool when you need it. He walked back to the house deep in thought. Turning the corner into Polly's road, Jack noticed suddenly that the door to her house was wide open. He broke into a breathless sprint.

Polly turned the deadlock, and before reaching for the latch dabbed at her eyes with the hem of her nightshirt. She dreaded to think what sort of state her face must be in. Her eyes stung and she wondered if they were red and puffy, but there was nothing to be done. She opened the door.

Peter had seen Polly's shadow in the crack of light beneath the door, he had even fancied that he'd heard her breathing as the door chain rattled – but he was too late. He could hear noisy footsteps bounding up the stairs behind him. His enemy had returned. Quickly he stepped back out of the gloomy light and crushed himself into the darkness of the landing, pressing himself hard against the wall.

The door of Polly's flat opened. The American reached the top of the stairs and rushed in without breaking his stride. He did not see Peter in the darkness and Peter did not leap out to attack him as he had half intended to do. It was all too quick, too confusing. Killing was not an easy business. The door closed.

Peter stood for a moment, dumbfounded, scarcely able to contain his thoughts. She had been there. The door had been open. He had missed his chance to kill the man and possess Polly, have her for his own. On the other hand, he was inside the house. He had penetrated her environment and they did not know it. They thought themselves safe. He must work out his next move. Peter retreated down the stairs and sat down on the threadbare carpet to think.

47

Inside the attic flat Polly kissed Jack, grateful to him for trying to fight the Bug and glad not to be alone. Jack returned her kisses while trying to catch his breath, tasting the salty tears around her lips. She felt so small and helpless. Jack longed to protect her, to possess her. At that moment, he and Peter were experiencing very similar emotions. Jack steeled himself against such thoughts, against Polly's magic.

'I didn't get him,' he said. 'He'd gone.'

'You'll never get him,' Polly replied. 'He's invulnerable. I've been trying for so long.'

Jack put his lips to Polly's ear. 'Did you ever think about killing him?' he whispered.

What a question. Of course she'd thought about killing him. Victims of stalkers often find themselves thinking about nothing else. Polly had wished that sick bastard dead a thousand times.

'No, I don't mean wishing him dead, Polly,' Jack said. 'I mean actually getting him dead. Killing him. For real.'

'Don't joke,' Polly replied. 'You don't know what it's like. If you knew what it was like to be a victim, how awful it is, you wouldn't joke.'

Gently Jack sat Polly down upon the bed and fetched her drink. 'I'm not joking,' he said. 'I'll kill him for you.'

'Oh, Jack, if only.' She was near to tears again.

'Polly.' Jack spoke firmly now. 'I'll kill him for you. I just need to know who he is and where he lives.'

Polly's head swam. It was such a lovely thought. Such a truly lovely thought. To have the Bug dead. Squashed. Gone for ever. Not warned off, not threatened with arrest, not made to give a solemn undertaking to stay away, but dead. Completely and utterly ceasing to exist. It was a beautiful dream. But that was what it was, a dream. You couldn't just kill people.

Jack knew what she was thinking. 'I'm a soldier,' he said. 'Killing people is what I do. It's not such a big deal.'

'When soldiers kill people it's legal?'

'Since when did you ever care about the law? Certainly not when I knew you. There is a higher law, that's what you used to say. Or maybe you think it's OK that I kill strangers whose only crime is that they come from a different country. Persecuting the weak and intimidating women is fine as long as it's legal.'

'I'm not talking about justice,' Polly said. 'I'm talking about the law, that's all. You'd get caught.'

Jack smiled that charming, confident smile. 'Hey, I'm out of here tomorrow. I'm gone. I'm on an army transport to Brussels and then home to the States. You think if I bump off some sad lowlife, nolife nut in Stoke Newington, somebody's going to say, "Hey, I bet a general in the United States army did this." Never in a trillion years.'

'Stop talking like that.'

'I was in Special Forces, Polly. Believe me, I know how to hit a guy discreetly. I can do it on my way to the airfield and still get breakfast.'

Polly was silent now. She wanted to tell him to stop again but the words would not come.

'I mean, the guy's connected to you,' Jack continued, 'but he's not connected to me, right? Of course you're connected to me, Polly, but only you and I know that, don't we? That's true, isn't it, Polly?'

By a stroke of great good fortune Jack had stumbled upon a way of finding out exactly what he most wanted to know.

'I mean, if I'm going to do this thing I need to be sure that there's nothing to connect me with you. Is there anything?'

Polly spoke as if in a trance. 'I only told the whole story once, to a guy called Ziggy, in a VW camper near Stonehenge, but he was stoned and didn't hear me.'

'Anybody else?'

'A few people, you know, over the years. Every now and then I get drunk and say that I once fucked a soldier at Greenham, but I never go into details. I don't like to remember, Jack.'

Polly was speaking, but it seemed like she was listening to someone else. She could hear herself reassuring

Jack. 'There is no way on earth anyone could connect me with you, Jack.'

They stared at each other for a moment. Jack was grinning.

'Well, there you are, then,' he said breezily. 'Where do I find him?'

He wasn't joking, she could see that. She was in a dream, but it was rapidly becoming reality. Polly drew herself back from the brink. It was time to put an end to this dangerous fantasy.

'You can't kill him. I don't want you to kill him. I don't want you even to talk about it. No matter how much I hated someone I would never ever want to kill them.'

Jack just kept grinning, his handsome eyes sparkling and his voice light. 'People die all the time. It's no big deal.'

'Shut up.'

'Just try to think of this guy as an exploiter of the planet. You remember what I was saying before? About how every breath we take we're doing damage to others? Consuming the world's resources, abusing the world's peasants. Why not let me reduce the abuse?'

'Shut up!'

'This man is an evil, useless, pointless waste of food and air. Let me take him out. We'll all breathe easier. You'll be doing the world a favour.'

Jack was still smiling; it was such a friendly smile. 'Tell me where he lives.'

'No!' said Polly, deeply shocked at the sincerity of

Jack's tone. He really did mean it. He really did believe that murdering people could be justified just because you didn't like them. She was horrified at the thought. No matter what a person's crimes, the death penalty was never justified. No one had the right to take a life. The fact that she was the victim did not change that fact.

'Shut up, Jack! I mean it. Stop talking like that, it's horrible.'

Jack shrugged and went to fix more drinks. 'OK, OK,' he said. 'If you don't have the courage to defend yourself. If your precious principles have so weakened you that you don't have the guts to make your own personal decision about what's right. Lenin knew what to do, didn't he? If you have something you believe in you defend it by any means necessary. Don't you believe in your right to happiness, Polly?'

'Of course I believe in it!'

'Then have the courage to defend it.'

Jack poured Polly another huge Bailey's and Coke and she gulped it down hungrily.

'Polly, I have to do something to help. This guy is truly a terrible thing. We can't just let him carry on abusing you.'

Even in her distress Polly thought about asking at what point Jack had suddenly become so concerned about her wellbeing, but she didn't. For the first time someone was genuinely trying to help her with the problem that had been destroying her life.

'Come on,' said Jack. 'Maybe I wouldn't even have to

kill him. I could just scare him a little. It'd be very easy to scare him.'

'It wouldn't do any good. He's too mad.'

'Polly, believe me. I know how to scare people and I know how to hurt them. When I do it they're scared and they stay hurt . . . Come on. You have a right to defend your life. Not in the law, maybe, but under any concept of natural justice. Tell me where he lives.'

Polly did not believe in violence of any sort.

She absolutely did not believe in violence.

That fact was a mainstay of her life.

On the other hand . . .

She had suffered at this man's hands for so very long. If anybody deserved to be punished it was him . . . And if it worked? If the Bug could be scared off, not killed but scared off, for ever? The prospect of liberation rose like a new dawn before Polly's eyes.

Jack could see that she was weakening. 'Where does he live, Polly?' he asked once more in his friendly, gentle tone.

Polly made her decision. She would act in her own defence. She would empower herself and defend her life. She would give Jack the Bug's address and she was glad. Why the hell should she suffer any more if she had the means to fight back? She had never done anything wrong and she did not deserve to be persecuted. That bastard deserved everything he got. Polly was fed up with being a victim. Let the other guy be the victim for a change.

The Bug's details were written on the court papers.

Papers Polly had always studiously avoided studying for fear of becoming further connected to her persecutor. She retrieved them from the file which she kept under a pile of dirty clothes, some books and a pair of running shoes and handed them over to Jack.

'Do anything you like,' she said firmly, 'but please don't kill him.'

48

The milkman's radio alarm went off, wrenching the milkman from his slumbers. He was surprised to discover that he had nodded off again after all. He had not imagined that he would do so what with all the talking and walking that was going on upstairs. However, the milkman resolved not to let the fact that he had been back to sleep diminish his righteous anger. He still had his notebook cataloguing the disturbances of the night and he decided that he would add a couple of instances more, since he was sure that the noises must have continued while he slept.

Upstairs they heard the music too.

'What the fuck?' Jack enquired.

'It's the milkman,' Polly explained. 'He gets up at four, the radio will stop at four twenty-five, then his door will bang.'

Three floors down in the stairwell Peter also heard the music. He imagined that it must come from Polly's room. Were they dancing? Or maybe they were doing 'it' to music? Either way, Peter's jealousy and resentment were amply fed. What should he do? How could he douse the fire of hatred that was burning inside him? Peter had never thought of himself as having a murderous disposition, but that American certainly deserved to die. Peter put his hand to his injured nose and nearly yelped in pain. He wondered if it was broken; it was certainly swollen. Now he had made it bleed again, a steady flow of drops falling onto his trousers. Peter spread his knees and allowed the blood to drip between his legs and stain the stair carpet. Her stair carpet; she would be walking over his blood. Then Peter positioned the blade of the knife under his bleeding nose and watched the metal turn red.

Upstairs in Polly's flat Jack was a little anxious. The milkman's alarm call, unusually early though it was, had reminded Jack that the night would not last for ever. Dawn was to be at seven fourteen that morning and Jack wanted to be away long before then. He had found out the things he needed to know. He was reasonably certain that his history with Polly was a private one, and he knew the whereabouts of Polly's stalker.

One thing Jack was certain about: this man Peter would have to die. Whether Polly liked it or not, Peter was a dead man.

'I have to leave quite soon,' Jack said, taking another slug of his drink.

It was like cold water. Somehow Polly had stopped thinking about Jack's leaving.

'I want you to stay,' she said.

'I can't, not for much longer.'

Polly felt desperate. All those familiar emotions were back, all those painful old feelings, the ones it had taken so many years to get over. Why had he returned if only to tease her and then leave her again? Now she must suffer the pain of rejection a second time and live with a newly broken heart.

'I got promoted recently,' said Jack.

Polly did not know what to say to this. It was such a non sequitur. Did he think she was still interested in making polite conversation?

'I've been promoted quite a lot over the last few years, actually. I've done very well.'

What was he talking about? Was he still fighting himself? Perhaps he really did want to stay. Perhaps he really wanted to make love. Perhaps this chattering was just a way of avoiding making a decision.

'Congratulations,' said Polly. 'You certainly never let anything stand in your way, did you?'

Everything Jack said reminded Polly of his desertion.

'You do not make four-star general just by avoiding ruinous love affairs. Nor by working hard or being talented. You have to get lucky. Very lucky.' Jack paused for a moment and then said, 'Sex.'

'What?' Polly asked.

'That's what got me where I am today.'

'I don't know what you're talking about.'

'Sex is what made me, Polly. What brought me to my current elevated status.'

'I'm not interested, Jack,' said Polly wearily.

'I need to tell you what brought me here today,' Jack insisted.

Polly sat back. It was pointless to resist. Whatever Jack wanted to do or say he would do or say in his own good time. She tried to concentrate as he spoke.

Jack began. By the end of the Gulf War, he said, he'd been a full colonel, one of the most successful soldiers of his generation, but despite this his prospects for future advancement had not looked particularly good. Traditionally, war was the way to get promoted in the army and despite Saddam's honourable efforts real wars, proper wars, were becoming less and less likely. There was, according to George Bush, a new world order. The Soviet Union had collapsed, taking with it the Warsaw Pact, thus depriving the Western allies of their best available enemy. The Chinese, who had always been next in line to fight, were embracing capitalism and waging war on the stock market. MacDonald's was opening up in Beijing, and the US was importing gangsters from Moscow. The West had won. For career soldiers like Jack it was a depressing time. All those weapons and nobody to kill. It just wasn't fair.

Of course there were the various UN, humanitarian and peacekeeping missions around the world, but that wasn't soldiering, and it certainly wasn't the way to make a four-star general. As Jack and the guys moaned to each other over bourbon in the mess, it was a very tough call to set your career alight dropping powdered milk on dead African people. Or digging up football pitches full of skulls in Bosnia.

Jack had seen the way the wind was blowing when Bush wimped out of going all the way to Baghdad.

'We should'a had Saddam's ass hanging on the Pentagon flagpole,' he and his comrades had assured each other through mouthfuls of beer and chili fries. 'But Old Man Bush listened to Pussy Powell. What kind of soldier was he? Too scared to risk his men. For Christ's sake, what is happening to the world? We have an army that thinks it has a right not to get killed! Powell was probably worried his men would sue.'

In Polly's flat Jack was pacing up and down telling his story, almost ignoring her. She wondered what on earth he could be getting at. Whatever it was, she wasn't interested.

'Pussy Powell?' she asked.

'Lots of men left the service,' Jack continued. 'But I couldn't. I didn't know any life other than soldiering. I had nowhere else to go. Besides, I'd sacrificed too much to give it up.'

They looked at each other. Polly might have spoken but Jack continued.

'Then something strange happened. Just when everybody thought they'd never get promoted again, sex came along. Sex is what saved the entire US military career structure from stagnation. Sex replaced war. Funny, huh? Kind of what you guys always wanted in a way. Make love not war and all that bullshit.'

'What are you talking about, Jack?'

Polly had resigned herself to the evening's going round in circles for ever.

'Remember Tailgate?' he continued. 'Bunch of navy flyers couldn't hold their brew and started waving their dicks at some lady sailors?'

Polly did recall it. The scandal had been big enough to be reported in the British media. There had been an appalling display of drunken brutality at a US naval conference.

'As I recall, it was all a little more serious than dick waving,' Polly remarked.

'Jesus, did the shit hit the fan. They court-martialled everybody! "Sir! Yes, sir! I waved my dick, sir!" Dishonourable discharge! "Sir. Yes, sir! I waved my dick too!" Out goes another one. A hundred and fifty thousand dollars' worth of training – gone! The brass thought they could calm things down by throwing a few minnows to the sharks. They couldn't. The shit flew upwards. "Yes, I failed to ensure that dicks were not waved." "Yes, I allowed a dick-waving culture to develop . . ." You want to know how many admirals were eventually implicated?'

Polly did not. She was not even slightly interested.

'Thirty-two, Polly! That's a historical fact. Thirty-two admirals. Our attack readiness was compromised. Navy morale was shot to ribbons. Comfort was given to our enemies. And all because we live in a world that thinks it can legislate against guys acting like assholes.'

Polly could scarcely believe it, but even at this point in the evening Jack still seemed to be anxious to compare their political points of view and yet again, despite herself, she could not help but oblige.

'You can legislate against rape and intimidation and harassment.'

'Jesus!' Jack snapped. 'These guys were sailors! The navy never should'a let those women anywhere near them. There was a time when being a disgusting fucked-up maniac was a military career requirement!'

'Change hurts sometimes,' Polly snapped back.

'Oh yes, it does, Polly, it sure does. Change hurts all right. I've seen men cry. I've seen marines cry because they've just discovered that when they pinched some secretary's ass at the Christmas party they were in fact making a career decision.'

Perhaps Jack had been right earlier when he'd spoken to Polly of 'her kind'. She could certainly empathize with this situation and her sympathies were not with the weeping marine. At her work Polly was called upon to deal with similar situations all the time and she knew all about the sort of activities that guys called 'just bum-pinching'.

'Well, perhaps your friends shouldn't go round pinching people's bums, then,' she said.

Jack threw his arms into the air in frustration, spilling his whiskey as he did so.

'Hey! We all know that now, honey! Oh, we sure do know that now! Our learning curve has been real steep! Problem was, nobody told some of these guys till they were in court! Nobody told that poor tearful marine that the way he had *always* acted, the way his daddy and his grand-daddy had acted, was suddenly criminal behaviour. Nobody ever warned that twenty-year-service marine that it wouldn't be any Soviet commando that'd take him out in the end but some little girl with a grudge.'

'Yes, well, maybe that marine should give some thought to all the little girls who've done the crying over the years.'

'Well, maybe he should,' Jack conceded, although he did so rather aggressively. 'And he's certainly going to have plenty of time to reflect on it, because suddenly there's been an awful lot of vacancies in the military. I didn't get these four stars defending democracy, I got them for keeping my dick in my pants.'

'So no female rookies raped on your watch, then?'

'I never was much of a party animal, Polly. In a way I owe that to you.'

Jack was thinking of the poor German girl, Helga, and that bleak night in Bad Nauheim in the early eighties. He knew what men were capable of when they were drunk and in packs. Particularly soldiers. He had been with the UN in Bosnia, had seen what gangs of men could do when no civilizing factor restrained them.

'You may not believe it, but you changed me,' Jack explained. 'All that stuff you told me all those years ago. It genuinely affected my outlook, made me see the other point of view. I truly believe that you influenced me for the good, Polly. I believe I've been a better soldier because of you.'

The irony of this was nearly too much for Polly.

'And over the years,' Jack continued, 'I've always asked myself what you would say about stuff. It was almost as if you were still there with me and I didn't want to make you angry.'

It was true. Jack could not be sure, but perhaps his unfinished love for that passionate, idealistic seventeen-year-old girl he had once known had refined him and caused him to avoid the mistakes made by other soldiers. He wasn't thinking about terrible incidents like the brutalization of Helga – mercifully such events were rare – but the smaller invisible pitfalls that so many of his colleagues had fallen into. The sort of thing they now called harassment. The comments, the pinchings, the endless catalogue of minor sexual impositions that men had for so long practised with impunity. Jack had avoided them all. He was recognized universally as a gentleman and, while others of his generation had found themselves demonized by the new morality, Jack had prospered.

'I've always loved you, you see, Polly,' he said. 'I still do.'

Again the circle came round. Polly could see that Jack was struggling with something inside himself but she did not know what it could be. Perhaps it was just the fact of an unhappy and unfulfilled life. Perhaps he was not so different from her, after all.

'What about your wife?' she asked gently. 'You must have loved your wife when you married her. Did you love us both?'

'I thought I loved her, Polly. God help me, I thought

I did, but now my true belief is that I married her because I was trying to get away from you.'

It was cruel, so very cruel for Polly to hear this now, after so many years of having lived under the shadow of Jack's rejection. Yet difficult though it was, her heart soared at the dawning realization that he had suffered as much as she had. That perhaps, after all, he had truly reciprocated her love.

'Jack. Oh, Jack. You tell me all this now. After all the years I've grieved for you.'

'I have to, Polly. Because . . .'

But Polly put her finger to her lips and breathed a 'shhh'. She had had enough talking now. She would put up with no more. It was her flat and she was going to take control of what went on in it. For the second time that night she crossed the room to stand over Jack, and again, as she walked, he watched the movement of her thighs, brushing against each other as she walked. Polly again took the glass out of Jack's hand and put it down.

'No more talking,' she said.

'Polly. I mustn't,' Jack replied, but his eyes were filled with a misty longing.

Polly shushed him again, this time putting a soft finger to his lips. His tongue momentarily brushed the tip. Then she cupped her hands around Jack's face and gently pulled him to his feet. Then they kissed again, long and passionately.

'No, Polly, we mustn't. That's not what I came here for.' Jack spoke almost into Polly's mouth as she continued to kiss him. Again he succumbed to her embrace. For the time being his passion for her was stronger than the guilt he felt.

Polly unbuttoned her shirt. She did it herself this time, purposefully and quickly. Having done so, she broke off their embrace and stood back, her mouth shining. Then she opened her shirt fully in order to show Jack her body. It was what he had longed for all evening, a proper sight of her, her breasts and her stomach and her neck, her navel and her legs, clear and unencumbered, with only the crimson triangle of her knickers still to be removed.

Jack felt weak with longing. 'We can't do this, Polly,' he heard himself say.

Polly did not reply. She had done with conversation. He could say what he liked, but she was now controlling the agenda. She could feel his desire even in the air between them. She knew just how much he wanted her. She took his hand. For a moment there was the faintest tug of resistance, but after a moment Jack allowed himself to be led to her bed, as Polly had known he would.

She lay down on the bed beneath Jack's gaze, and spread her shirt wide open on the sheet. Looking up into Jack's eyes, she could see that they were glistening and wet. He was crying! Not much, hardly at all, there were no actual tears, but she was sure he was crying. She had never seen him cry before. Reaching down to her hips, Polly raised her knees for a moment and slipping her thumbs under the elastic of her knickers took them off. Relaxing her legs again, she lay entirely naked save for the shirt at her arms and shoulders.

'Make love to me now,' she said firmly.

'I can't, Polly,' Jack replied, his voice cracking.

Polly reached up and took his hand. 'Jack. Stop this nonsense. I said make love to me now!'

'I ... I ... can't.' Still Jack resisted, although he could scarcely find the words to deny her.

'Yes, you can, Jack. It's why you came.'

Jack closed his eyes to shut out her beauty, to shut out the magnet of eroticism that lay inches from him. As his eyes closed tears formed at the corners.

'It's not why I came, Polly.' He said it firmly, dragging the sentence from deep within him. Then he pulled his hand from hers and returned to his chair and drink.

49

Peter's mother picked up the phone.

'Camden Police,' said a voice at the other end.

Peter's mother had anguished long and hard about informing on her son. She was absolutely loath to do it and shuddered to imagine how he would react when he found out. However, she felt that she had no choice. He had been hanging around that woman's street all night, he was wet through and not himself, and he was messing about with that dreadful knife.

She knew the terrible things her son had written to the girl after she had rejected him. They'd been read out in court. Many times he had threatened to stick a knife in her and worse; sometimes he'd been specific in his threats, talking about cutting bits off her, all sorts of horrible stuff she felt sure he'd got from videos.

He wouldn't do it, of course. She knew that, she was certain of that. On the other hand, he'd looked so very desperate. But Peter's mother would rather have her son arrested for breaking a court order than for murder, which was why she had decided to call the police.

'He's been told not to go there but he couldn't resist it, I'm afraid,' she said to the duty officer at the police station. 'He's just hanging about in her street in the rain . . . and . . . well, I know he's taken his knife with him . . . Just against yobs and muggers, you understand! I mean, he wouldn't actually harm anyone with it . . . not her, I'm sure, but perhaps you could send someone down to talk to him anyway – tell him to come home.'

The duty officer promised that they would send a car round.

'Thank you, officer. Thank you. He's a good boy, you know.'

50

For perhaps a minute afterwards Polly lay staring at the ceiling. She had pulled her shirt around her but apart from that she had not moved. The only sound in the room was the milkman's radio and a faint clatter as he made his breakfast in the room below. Polly felt foolish, angry. She had stripped herself naked in front of Jack. She had practically begged him to make love to her. He had let her do it, too. Oh, there'd been no doubting the way he'd looked at her. Jack had certainly allowed Polly to undress for him, and then he'd walked away.

She got up and put her knickers back on, buttoned up her shirt and put on the plastic mac again. Up to this point she had not looked at Jack once. When she finally did so she found that he was not looking at her but had returned to his old habit of staring into his glass.

'I think you should go now,' she said.

Jack did not move. 'I can't go,' he said.

'I don't care what you can and can't do, Jack.' Polly's voice was cold with hurt. 'I want you to leave.'

Still Jack did not face her. 'I can't leave, Polly.'

'You rejected me before, Jack. I got over it. Now you

come back and reject me again. I'm not strong enough for this.'

Jack attempted to explain, but he could not. 'It wouldn't have been right for us to—'

'Is it your wife? Is that what's stopping you?' Polly asked. She had not intended to discuss it any further, but she knew that he wanted her as much as she wanted him. She could see it in the despondent way in which he sat.

'No.'

Polly felt she had no more dignity to lose. 'I'm lonely, Jack.'

Jack did not respond.

'I'm lonely,' Polly repeated.

Again he did not respond, except perhaps for the smallest of shrugs. Polly finally decided that she really had had enough. Loneliness was better than this. The evening was over.

'I want you to leave. Now, Jack,' she said. 'And this time don't come back. Not after sixteen years, not ever.'

Polly walked over to the door and opened it.

Outside the door Peter froze. Terror and excitement in equal proportions deprived him of the means to move. He'd returned to Polly's floor and had been trying to listen, not very successfully what with that damn radio music, his ear pressed to Polly's door. Then suddenly, more quickly than he would have thought possible, he had heard her footsteps approach, her hand on the latch, and the door had opened.

BEN ELTON

He had had no time to move even had he been capable of such a thing. He stood transfixed, a knife in his hand, blood still dripping from his nose onto his mouth and chin.

'Goodbye, Jack.'

Peter heard her voice through the open door. One thin sheet of panelled wood separated them. In two steps he could be inside her flat, facing her, facing him. He held his knife. He held his breath. He could see the shadow of Polly's arm on the latch through the crack between the open door and the frame. He could see partly into her flat, the carpet, the edge of the table, a shelf with all sorts of stuff on it.

'I'm not going, Polly. Not yet.'

It was the American's voice, the despised voice of his hated rival. Peter wondered about running in then and there. He wondered whether he would have the chance to stab the man before he fought back. Peter knew that his enemy was assured, he remembered that from the confrontation at the phonebox. He did not wish to find himself beaten to his knees again, shamed and at the man's mercy in front of Polly. He decided against such a full-frontal attack. Much better to leap out of the shadows at the man later when he left. Instead Peter remained dead still, now more excited than scared, luxuriating in the exquisite tension of the moment, scarcely able to believe that he was almost inside her flat, that she was hardly a foot away from him. For sheer, tense, sensual pleasure this certainly beat swearing at her over the telephone.

'What do you mean, you're not going? You'll go when I bloody well tell you, and I'm telling you to go now,' Polly said from behind the door.

It dawned on Peter that Polly was ordering the American out. They must have had a row and now he was being told to go. Peter raised his knife. The blade was already crusted black and crimson with his own blood.

'There are things I need to tell you, Polly,' Peter heard Jack saying from within the room, 'and something I need to do. Unfinished business.'

The door closed millimetres from Peter's face. He stepped back from it, limp with the tension.

Inside the flat Polly turned on Jack.

'Hey, Jack. Look at me,' she said. 'Don't tell me what's what in my own place. This is today Polly, not yesterday Polly, not twenty-years-ago Polly. Not a little girl who you can screw and screw up. Not a vulnerable, exploitable fucking teenager. This is my place, right? It isn't much, but it's mine and while you're here you will do what the fuck you're told. And right now what I'm telling you to do is leave.'

'I'm not going, Polly.'

Polly looked at Jack and she did not like what she saw. She felt a surge of resentment. Who the hell did he think he was? She'd got by without him for sixteen years and she was happy to continue to do so.

'Yes, you are going, Jack, because I don't want you as a part of my life any more. What's more, I want you to forget about what we talked about earlier, about hurting that man. I don't want your help with that. I can fight my own battles and if anyone's going to hurt him it's going to be me.'

'Whatever,' said Jack and Polly despised his tone. He did not believe her. He did not believe she could defend herself.

'You think you're pretty tough, don't you?' Polly said.

'Tough enough,' Jack replied.

Polly took her time before replying. 'Jack, I've known a hundred men tougher than you. Men who don't need a uniform and an army to give them strength, because their strength is on the inside.'

'That's nice,' Jack replied.

Polly went back to her bed, kneeled down and dragged a bag from under it. This time Jack refrained from studying her legs as she did so. He had allowed himself to be distracted for too long. It was time to get on now.

She stood up and put the bag on the bed. 'I could kill you right now,' she said, looking Jack in the eye.

'Yes, I imagine you could,' Jack replied with the same old charming smile. 'You've certainly got cause.'

Polly could see that Jack had misunderstood her. 'No, Jack, I mean really kill you. You could be dead at any moment. I have the means.'

The smile still had charm but probably only to a person who liked being patronized. 'I doubt it, Polly.'

'You doubt it.'

'Well, you know,' said Jack. 'Killing people isn't easy, not unless you know how.'

'But I do know how.'

Jack did not believe her, of course, but there was something assured about her manner that put him on his guard none the less. He wondered what she was getting at.

'You know how to kill people?' he asked.

Before speaking Polly reached into her bag and seemed to fiddle with something or fix something up; whatever she did required both her hands to do it.

'Oh, yes, Jack. I know how to kill people. After I left the peace camp I became a traveller in a convoy. Ever hear about those? Loose wandering collectives of people who didn't fit in, people who didn't like the rules. I mentioned my friend Ziggy earlier. He was one of them. We struck fear into the heart of the British countryside a few summers back. People thought we were going to squat in their gardens.'

'Well, you know the British and their gardens,' Jack said, watching Polly closely, trying to figure out what she was getting at.

'Despite their scary reputation,' Polly went on, 'most of the travellers were entirely peaceful, more peaceful than conventional types by miles, the hippies you despise, but at the centre of it all there was a core of real anarchists.'

Jack laughed. 'Anarchists?'

'That's right. People who wanted change and were prepared to fight for it. Road protesters, animal liberationists, that sort of thing. I joined them. I'm still with them. I'm not a traveller any more, but I'm still part of the struggle.'

Jack could well believe it. Polly had always been a hellcat. He could well imagine her seeking out the crappiest people in society and joining them.

'So what do you do? Smear aniseed on hunting dogs and throw paint at doctors' cars? Chain yourself to the cosmetics counter at the chemist?'

Polly looked Jack straight in the eye. She wanted him to understand her very clearly.

'Next Tuesday we're going to blow up a veal truck. I'm the bomb maker. I got the recipe off the Internet. This is the bomb.'

Polly motioned to the bag in which she had been fiddling. Jack would have found it hard to deny that he was a little taken aback at the abruptness of Polly's statement. He smiled none the less.

'It doesn't look much like a bomb, Polly.'

'Oh, yes it does, it looks exactly like a bomb. Maybe not like the sort of bomb you boys chuck about in the army, but it does look like a bomb. Any copper in Northern Ireland would recognize it quick as anything.'

Polly peered into her bag, almost as if to check that she was not exaggerating the case. She seemed satisfied.

'Besides,' she continued, 'it will blow your head off, so it doesn't really matter what it looks like, does it? It's based on chemical fertilizer, I've bags of the stuff. I've made three bombs all in all. The first two worked perfectly – we let them off on Dartmoor. This one's my best yet, I think. All I have to do is flip the switch.'

And with that Polly reached into the bag. Despite himself Jack jumped. He glanced down at the floor where the sack of fertilizer still lay.

'Polly, if that is a bomb then you know better than to play with it.'

'I'm not playing with it, Jack,' Polly replied calmly. 'I think it's wasted on veal, don't you? I mean, now that I've got a real animal to protest about.'

She was so cool, so assured. Jack watched her face, trying to locate the lie, but he could not. He began to feel a little nervous.

'Don't be ridiculous, Polly. You're not going to blow us up.'

'Why not? I've got a chance now to really make a difference. I spent years of my life protesting against the military and suddenly here I am with the opportunity to blow up a genuine four-star general. In a split second I could rid the world for ever of an agent of mass slaughter.'

'Plus one council worker,' Jack said, leaping on a salient point.

'Yeah, well maybe I don't care about that, Jack. Didn't you say that the only true morality was to remove yourself? To end one's exploitative parasitic existence?' Polly was shaking. Jack wished she would take her hand from the bag.

'Besides,' she went on, 'I'm going nowhere. I've got nothing and I'm not going to get anything. My life went wrong when I was seventeen, but you'd know all about that, wouldn't you, Jack, you fucking bastard. Well, now's my chance to make it all right again. This bomb's big enough to trash my flat completely. When I flip this switch we'll be together again, for ever, our flesh will be as one. Entwined, mixed and blended, never to be parted, as I once dreamt it would be.'

Polly gently picked up the bag, one hand still inside it. Holding it to herself she advanced on Jack.

'You should have gone when I told you to, Jack. Now we fucking well go together.'

'Polly, please.'

'I'm sick of you and I'm sick of life. So fuck everything.'

'Polly, you can't,' Jack pleaded as she stood over him.

Her face was drawn and weary, her upper lip was quivering, the arm inside the bag was shaking. Jack wondered if he could be quick enough to grab that arm.

'No, you're right I can't,' said Polly, 'because actually this is a bag full of dirty knickers. Had you going, though, didn't I, you bastard?'

Polly laughed, rather a hard laugh, and threw the bag back onto the bed. Jack had been completely thrown.

'But . . . the fertilizer . . . ?' he said.

'I told you,' said Polly. 'It's for my windowbox. Don't you remember, Jack? I'm into peace, that's my life. I don't approve of killing people. Even people like you. People who turn up in the middle of the night and try to break a girl's heart a second time. Well, I've had enough now. It's gone four in the morning. I'm up at seven thirty and this time you really do have to go.'

Still Jack did not move. 'I'll be gone soon, Polly. Very soon. But I have to finish saying what I came to say. I have to explain.'

'Jack, it's over, gone, many years ago. I don't want to talk about it.'

'I don't mean explain what I did, Polly, but what I have to do.'

51

Outside, a police car turned into Polly's street and drove slowly towards her house. Both the officers inside the car knew the man they were looking for, having often been called out by Polly in the past to deal with him. As they searched they agreed that it was a crying shame that a nice girl like Polly should be harassed in such a way, and they resolved to give Peter the fright of his life if they found him.

They did not find Peter, but they did notice that the light was burning in Polly's flat. This struck them as strange, seeing as how it was only just after four in the morning. They concluded that either the milkman had woken her up again (they knew most things about Polly's life by now) or Peter was about and had already been pestering her.

They decided to check that Polly was all right.

From his position in the hall Peter could see the silhouettes of the police officers through the window panels of the front door. He had retreated to the bottom of the house after his shock at nearly being discovered and had been sitting on the bottom stair considering how best he could attack the American. Seeing the shadows on the window, Peter thought that the game was up. The hated peaked caps outlined clearly by the streetlights surely meant his arrest. He was, after all, inside her house, caught redhanded. For a moment Peter thought about using his knife, but there was no way he was going to stab a policeman. There were a couple of bicycles leaning against the wall. Peter leaned forward and put his knife into the saddlebag of the nearest one. If they found him with that it would be prison for sure.

Upstairs in Polly's flat the intercom buzzer went. Someone was at the front door.

Jack was on his feet in an instant. 'It's him. He's back,' he said. 'And this time he isn't going to get away.'

'What do you mean?' said Polly 'What're you going to do?'

'I'm going to deal with him.'

The buzzer went again.

'You keep him talking,' Jack continued. He was at the door now. 'I won't be long.'

'No, Jack, I don't want you to—'

The buzzer was insistent. Not for the first time that evening Polly was torn. So much of her wanted to let matters take their course. If Jack wanted to confront the Bug then why not let him? On the other hand, what if Jack got carried away? What if Jack killed him? The buzzer sounded again. Gingerly Polly picked up the receiver, half resolved to shouting a warning to her hated enemy below.

'Polly, it's Constable Dewison,' the receiver said.

Jack stopped dead, his hand on the door. 'Cops?' he hissed.

'Oh, hello, Frank,' said Polly. 'This is a surprise.'

'We had a call from your admirer's mum, Polly. She said he was hanging about. I'm sure there's nothing to worry about, but she did say that he had a knife. We just wanted to check that you were all right.'

Polly assured the officers that although the Bug had indeed been about earlier in the night she had heard nothing from him for an hour or so. Constable Dewison asked if she would like them to come up and take down the details of the harassment for an official complaint in the morning. Polly glanced at Jack. Somehow she felt that the presence of a four-star American general in dress uniform in her flat was a conversation that she did not wish to have.

'No, it's all right, officer. I think I'd rather try and get some sleep.'

Downstairs in the hall Peter watched as the silhouettes of the policemen retreated. His relief at escaping arrest was entirely overshadowed by the fury that was consuming him. Peter had heard every word that the policemen had said. He could scarcely believe it! His own mother had grassed him up! She'd even told them about his knife! Peter's blood boiled at her betrayal. Well, she'd regret it, that was for sure.

Peter would deal with his mother later.

For now, however, he was still inside the house. Inside her house. Even the police hadn't found him out! Surely this was a sign that fortune was on his side. Surely now he could do exactly as he liked.

52

Polly laughed. It seemed the only thing to do. 'I wonder who'll turn up next,' she said.

But Jack was not laughing. Quite the opposite, in fact. His face was like stone. The last thing he had expected was to find the police at the door. It reminded him as nothing else could of the vulnerability of his situation.

Polly caught the look on his face and stopped laughing. She remembered the last thing that Jack had said, before the police had called.

'Jack,' she said. 'What did you mean before, about what you have to do?'

Jack could not look at her. 'Did you ever hear about an army general named Joe Ralston?' he asked. 'He was in the news a year or two back.'

Polly did not want another endless, pointless conversation. 'Tell me what's on your mind or bugger off.'

'I *am* telling you,' Jack said quietly. 'Joe Ralston was all set to become the chairman of the US joint chiefs of staff. The most powerful soldier on earth. Employing about half a million people and spending an annual budget of trillions of dollars.'

'Which is totally obscene,' said Polly, unable to restrain herself.

'You know where he is now?' Jack continued.

'No, and I don't care.'

'Well, I don't know either, because he never stood for that top job. He withdrew his candidacy and retired from the army. Because fifteen years ago he had an affair. Fifteen years ago, while separated from his wife whom he subsequently divorced, General Joe Ralston had an affair. That is why the best soldier in America could not pursue his destiny.'

Polly remembered the case. It had indeed been on the news in Britain.

'Your people made that happen, Polly,' said Jack.

'My people? Which people would those be, then?'

'Your people, your kind. You see, around the same time that Joe Ralston was considering his application, a young lady combat flier called Kelly Flinn got caught fucking the civilian husband of an enlisted woman. She was forced to resign her commission, but not before the whole damn country had had a crisis about whether the army would have hit her so hard if she'd been a man.'

Polly recalled this case also. The British press always gleefully reported any example of America in the throes of self-torture. But she still could not see what it had to do with her.

'You know what you people have done, don't you, Polly?' Jack continued. 'You've created an ungovernable world.'

Polly had had enough of this.

'What people? Who are "my people"?'

'Your kind. Liberals. Feminists.'

'Oh, for Christ's sake, don't be so pig ignorant!'

Jack poured himself more whiskey and tried to refill Polly's glass, but she had had enough to drink. He took a gulp of bourbon and continued.

'They tried to indict the president of the United States for dropping his trousers! Are you pleased about that?'

'I don't care, Jack! I don't give two tosses! What does any of this have to do with me? What the hell are you talking about?'

Jack took a breath. He did not want to shout. He wanted her to understand what he was saying.

'The president of the United States, Polly. The most powerful man on earth. The commander in chief of the most formidable army ever known. The person responsible for weapons of destruction that could obliterate life on this planet a thousand times over. That man had put the world on hold, in order that he could prepare to be taken to court to decide whether or not one night six years ago he showed his dick to a female employee. Do you think that is a good thing or a bad thing?'

Polly shrugged. 'If the president's a nasty little shag-rat that's his problem.'

'Plenty of guys are nasty little shag-rats.'

'Yes, well maybe it's time they started facing up to the consequences.'

Despite his efforts to remain calm and reasonable Jack's frustration bubbled over and he banged his fist down on the table.

*   *   *

In the room below, the milkman looked up from his cornflakes.

Four twenty: Shouting and banging, he noted piously in his little book.

'Traditionally women have been aware of what men are like,' Jack continued, 'which is why they didn't tend to go into guys' rooms in the middle of the night!'

'A woman should be able to go where she damn well pleases!' Polly snapped back, unwilling to be lectured on gender behaviour by the likes of General Jack Kent.

'That's right!' Jack snapped back. 'And on this occasion one did and in the process she claims she got to see the then governor of Arkansas's dick! Late one night she accepted an invitation to his hotel room, he proffered his penis, she declined, retreated and there the matter rested for six years! He didn't beat her up, he didn't rape her, he showed her his dick. Then suddenly the whole world was discussing this episode, the whole world! My God, there was a time when a girl would have been proud to see a future president's dick! She would have told her grandchildren! "Hey, kids, did I ever tell you about the time the president showed me his dick?"'

'Yes, and there was a time when millions of women suffered endless abuse and harassment in silence.'

'For Christ's sake, can we get a sense of proportion here? It's like a witch hunt! Oh yeah, except we deserve it, don't we, we guys? Because every horny guy is a rapist, isn't he? I forgot that.'

Jack could still remember vividly how during the Helga trial in Bad Nauheim it had seemed as if the whole army was on trial, like they had all gone to that hotel together.

'Jesus! There are women in the States – college professors! – saying wolf whistling is rape! That seduction is rape with flowers!'

Polly pointed her finger straight at him. 'I don't know anything about that, Jack,' she said, 'but I do know that you know something about rape.'

For a moment he could not believe what she had said. It was just too surprising.

'What?' was all he could say. 'What?'

Polly's voice was suddenly quiet again. 'That last night, the night you left me. In that guesthouse. You made love to me like your life depended on it. You made love to me like a beast . . .'

Jack could scarcely believe what she was suggesting.

'You too! You wanted it! You were totally involved! What are you *saying* here? That I raped you? When you wanted it every bit as much as I did?'

Polly nodded quietly. 'Yes, of course I wanted it, Jack. I gave myself utterly and completely and happily.'

'Thank you!' said Jack.

'But do you think I would have done that if I'd known? Known that you were leaving? That your ticket was booked? If you'd taken me to your little hideaway that night, a seventeen-year-old girl, Jack, and said, "What I'm going to do now is fuck you for two hours and then walk away without a word and never see or speak to you again," do you think I'd have let you have me?'

There was silence for a moment. 'Well, no, but—'

'That's rape, Jack. Not big rape, maybe, but rape of sorts. You took me by deceit and manipulation. You took something I would never have given had I known the truth.'

For a moment it almost sounded convincing. Except that it wasn't – it couldn't be. Jack did not believe that the world could be run that way.

'Hey, Polly, people get dumped. It happens, you know. Get the fuck over it. What, you think you have a right not to be hurt? Not to be unhappy? I was a shit, I admit it, but a guy sweettalking a girl into bed is not rape. Little girls getting gangbanged in alleyways, that's rape.'

Polly smouldered for a moment and then gave it up.

'Get out, Jack. You just don't get it and you never will.'

'No! No!' Jack simply would not let the argument end. '*You* don't get it! The world is not civilized and you can't make it so.'

There was nothing Polly could do. If Jack did not want to leave she could not force him. She could call the police, of course, but she had no desire to do that. Besides which, despite herself Polly was beginning to become rather interested in Jack's obsessions. It was obvious to Polly that Jack had some deep, deep problem inside himself. A problem which for some reason he had sought her out in order to deal with. In some ways it was quite fascinating.

'They let the first women into the Citadel this year,' Jack said, producing what appeared to be a non sequitur.

'The citadel?' Polly enquired.

'It's a military training facility. They let in forty women who want to be turned into shaven-headed, desensitized grunts.'

'How depressing.'

'Is that what you wanted, Polly?' Jack snapped. 'For women to turn into men?'

'Why are you asking me this stuff? Don't you have therapists in the army?'

But Jack was not listening to Polly. 'Truth is they can't do it,' he continued, almost to himself. 'They're not up to it. Ladies can't run as fast, punch as hard or lift as much as men. At the Parris Island training centre forty-five per cent of female marines were unable to throw their grenades far enough to avoid blowing themselves up. Female trainees are twice as likely to get injured, five times as likely to be put on limited duty! These are the facts, Polly. But facts don't matter, because this is politics. Politics decides on its own reality, and if anybody objects they will be condemned as sexist Neanderthals and their careers will be over. It is a witch-hunt, Polly. Leftist McCarthyism. We're living through the fucking Crucible.'

'And you see my problem, Jack, is that I don't care,' Polly replied. 'Don't you understand? I don't care!'

Jack was pacing the room now. 'The US military manual has been changed to accommodate the equality lie. It's called "comparable effort". Women get higher marks for doing less. They do six press-ups, the guys do twenty; they only climb halfway up the rope. Assault courses are called "confidence courses" and you get to run around the walls if you can't get over them. What happens when there's a war? You think the enemy will say, "It's OK, you're a girl, we'll go easy on you"?'

Polly tried once again to get at whatever it was Jack was trying to tell her.

'Why are you projecting all this onto me, Jack? This is pathological. I'm an ordinary Englishwoman living somewhere above the poverty line in Stoke Newington. I knew you when I was seventeen! This has nothing to do with me! Yet it's almost as if you've come to me tonight to blame me for what you think is wrong with the world—'

'Well? Well! Aren't you pleased we're falling to bits? Aren't you pleased we don't know who the fuck we are any more? Gender politics is rendering the Western world ungovernable!'

Polly had been interested for a moment, but her interest was over.

'It isn't, but if it was I wouldn't care! Do you understand? I don't care about it either way, all right? What happens to your army and who you choose for president is a matter of supreme indifference to me! Because tomorrow morning I have to go to work and wade back into a sea of people who have been abused, cheated, demeaned and destroyed all for reasons of race, sex, sexuality and poverty. They don't have much hope, but if they have any I'm it, so please, Jack, leave, because I have to get some sleep.'

'OK, OK, I'm going.'

Jack got up and started to put away his bottles, and Polly sat back down on the bed feeling terribly, terribly sad.

53

The milkman had finished his breakfast and brushed his teeth. It was time to go to work. He wondered about going upstairs on his way out and speaking to the woman above. He decided against it. She still had someone with her; it would be embarrassing. He'd have a word that evening, just to let her know that two could play at the complaining game.

He turned off his radio, switched off the lights and let himself out into the hall.

At the bottom of the house, sitting in the hallway, Peter heard the door open and close and then the sound of a heavy footfall on the stair. This Peter knew was his best chance. The man above him, the man coming down the stairs, was the American. It was only minutes since Polly had ordered him to go, and now that was what he was doing. Besides which, who else would be walking out of the house at four thirty in the morning?

Silently Peter retreated into the shadow behind the stair. His enemy was on the floor above him now, the footsteps descending fast. The dark shape of a man appeared at the bottom of the stairs. Peter leapt out of the darkness and plunged his knife deep into the man's back. He heard the man try to cry out, but there was only a muffled, gurgling sound.

The milkman sank to the floor without a word and lay there gulping his last blood-sodden, strangled breaths beside the bicycle. Looking down at him, Peter noticed that one of the tyres of the bicycle was flat. He also noticed that whoever he had killed it was not the American.

54

Jack and Polly had also heard the milkman leave. Jack was relieved; he had no wish to encounter the other residents of the building. He finished putting away his bottles, then collected Polly's glass from the bedside table where she had left it and drained his own.

'I'm sorry about going on so much,' he said. 'It's just that I had to tell you all that stuff.'

'That's OK,' Polly assured him. 'Actually I'm glad. I'm glad you did.'

Jack did not ask her why, and Polly did not tell him. The truth was that the things Jack had talked about, the feelings he had displayed, had made Polly feel better about herself and, more important, better about not being, or wanting to be, any part of Jack's life. It seemed to her that he had been right in a way about linking her with the ideological struggles he found so frustrating. The world had changed a little and for the better. Big tough guys like Jack couldn't quite have it all their own way any more. Power was no longer an absolute defence against bad behaviour. Bigotry and abusive practices were not facts of nature; they could be challenged, they could be redressed. And perhaps, in her own small way, Polly had been a part of that change. She and a few million other people, but a part none the less.

Jack had stepped through into the kitchen area and was washing up the glasses.

'Jack, please, you don't have to wash up,' Polly said.

'Yes, I do, Polly. I have to wash up,' Jack replied, drying the glasses thoroughly with a teatowel.

'My God, you're a new man and you don't know it,' Polly laughed.

Having cleared up the drinks Jack took a look around the room. He seemed to be checking that everything was in order.

'So General Ralston dropped his candidacy for the chair of the joint chiefs,' he said. 'The Kelly Flinn scandal had put so much heat under the issue of sexual morality in the military that he had to withdraw rather than further provoke the liberal feminist lobby.'

Polly went and got Jack's coat. 'Goodbye, Jack.'

He put on the coat, still talking, still explaining. 'Since then they had two other tries to find the right guy. An air force guy and a marine. Both superb officers, both unacceptable. I don't know why. Probably stomped on a bug during basic training and offended the Buddhist lobby. We have a world so full of people ready to take offence it's tough to find a fighting man, any man, who never offended anybody.'

Polly was trying not to listen, but she could not ignore the significance of what Jack was saying.

'I presume what you're getting at is that they're going

to ask you to stand,' she said, impressed despite herself. 'That you are going to be chairman of the joint chiefs of staff. Is that what you came here to tell me? Am I supposed to congratulate you?'

Jack stood staring at Polly. He was gathering his thoughts. Then he stepped across the room to where Polly's answerphone was still blinking out news of the various messages of the evening. Jack pressed the erase button. The machine clunked and whirred in response, wiping clean the tape upon which Jack had announced his rearrival in Polly's life.

'What are you doing, Jack?' Polly felt a chill of fear shiver across her body, enveloping her like an icy cloak.

'Surely you know now why I'm here, Polly,' he said.

'No, Jack, I don't,' Polly replied although suddenly she was not so sure.

'People die every day.'

Polly was cold to the bone now. 'What do you mean?'

'What I say. People die every day. Famine, war, accident, design. Death is commonplace. A modern fiction has developed that life is precious, but we know it isn't so. Governments sacrifice thousands of lives every day. At least in the old times they were honest about it. There was no hypocrisy. To be a king or a conqueror you had to kill; no one ever got to the top any other way. Sometimes you even had to kill the things you loved, wives, children .. . . many kings and rulers did that. They still do.'

Polly could not credit the suspicions that were

beginning to flood into her mind. Surely this would turn out to be just another monologue, going nowhere.

'Jack—'

'You were an anarchist, Polly,' Jack continued. 'A sworn enemy of the state. When I met you your life was dedicated to the confusion of the military policies of your own country and also those of the United States. You were, to put it as I fear the press will put it, as my detractors in Congress and the Senate will put it, a foreign red. An enemy of the US.'

Jack could not be implying what it sounded like he was implying.

'I was seventeen, Jack! A teenager! It was so long ago.'

'Exactly. Seventeen, that's four years underage in my home state. An anarchist and a child to boot! Twenty years ago people would have laughed and said I was a lucky guy. These days you get burned at the stake for that stuff. If our affair ever came to light it would finish me for good and ten times over. You know it would. A soldier on active duty consorts with juvenile pacifist anarchist? I wouldn't last ten seconds in a Senate hearing.'

Polly struggled to come to terms with what Jack was saying.

'But only you and I know, Jack!'

Jack had taken his gun from his pocket and was attaching some kind of metal attachment to the end.

'That's right, Polly. Nobody else knows about us and nobody knows I came here tonight. I'm a NATO general, in Britain for a few hours, asleep in his hotel room. There is a spook called Gottfried, the guy who traced you for me, but he got promoted to our station in Kabul. Nice job for him, convenient for me – the Taliban don't tend to take the London *Evening Standard*.'

Jack levelled his gun at Polly's head.

'I love you, Polly, but I'm leaving you again. This time for good.'

'Peter!' Polly shouted.

'Who?'

'The stalker! He knows, he knows an American was here. He saw you! He could describe you!'

'That's right. He could, Polly, which is a pity for him because you told me where he lives.'

Jack's finger was taut on the trigger.

'Jack, no,' Polly whispered.

'I'm sorry, Polly, but you do see I have no choice, don't you?'

Jack meant it too. As he saw it he had no choice. In fact it was his duty. He saw himself as the best remaining candidate to lead the army he loved, and it was his responsibility to ensure that nothing compromised his ability to command. Jack had already sacrificed Polly once to the oaths he had made when he had joined the service. Now he had to find the courage to do so again. And this time he would have to do it while looking Polly in the eye.

was still sitting on the bed. Jack stood before
her, his arm outstretched, the gun levelled between
them, his target pale but somehow calm, calmer than
Jack had expected.

'We have a child,' she said.

55

Jack had been about to shoot. At the very moment that she said it he had been about to shoot.

'What?'

'When you left me I was pregnant, Jack.'

Every well-honed instinct of self-preservation within Jack's icy soul told him to shoot and shoot immediately, but somehow he could not, not yet, not for a moment.

'I don't think so, Polly.'

'Well, what the fuck would you know, you bastard!' Polly snarled. 'You left me pregnant! That was why I always waited for you ... That was why I couldn't forget you. How could I?'

If she was acting, and Jack was almost sure she was, then she was very good at it; the sudden and bitter venom of her statement was uncomfortably convincing.

It was convincing because it was true. Jack had left Polly pregnant. She realized about three weeks after he had walked out on her. It was not his fault. He could not have known; those had been in the days before AIDS, and Jack had never used condoms because Polly had been on the pill. Unfortunately, like many a young girl before her, Polly had been made careless by love and the result was that she suddenly found herself alone and carrying the child of a man who had had his way with her and then gone.

Polly stared at Jack over the vicious snout of his pointing gun, her eyes teary with angry memories.

'How could I have got over you, Jack?' she said. 'You were still there with me, growing inside me every day.'

Jack knew that this was nonsense. He tried to shoot, but still he could not. Because if it were true, although it could not be, but if it were true, it would be so . . . Jack shut the thought from his mind. He had come to kill this woman.

'It was a boy, Jack,' Polly whispered. 'We have a son.'

All Jack's life he had wanted a child, and being a soldier, of course, he had particularly wanted a son. He and Courtney had not had children; she'd been young and ambitious for her career and they'd grown apart so quickly. But to have a son with Polly! Jack had often daydreamed of exactly that, imagining what a wonderful spirited boy such a union might create. Jack struggled to regain control. He had no business to be indulging in fantasies of this sort at such a time. Imagining Polly as the mother of his child reminded him of how much he was still in love with her, but he could not afford to be in love with her. He had a higher love to answer to – his love of power, of ambition, his love of self.

Yet still he could not pull the trigger.

'What's his name?' Jack asked, allowing himself to relish the dream.

'Misty Dawn,' Polly replied instantly.

'Misty fucking Dawn? You called a boy Misty Dawn?'

'He changed it to Colin when he was at school.'

'What was wrong with Jack?'

'Everything was wrong with Jack, you bastard.'

Jack knew that he was talking too much. He knew that it was time to get on, time to do the deed. The deed that was the heavy duty of men who would be leaders of men; those who sought to command must know how to sacrifice.

Polly could see Jack's hesitation. 'You can't kill me, Jack,' Polly said slowly and clearly. 'I'm the mother of your child.'

This was madness. Jack knew it was madness. 'You were on the pill,' he said.

'I lied to you. I knew you were paranoid about anything that might damage your precious career, so I lied. I don't approve of putting chemicals into my body. I was using a natural sea sponge and it leaked.'

That sounded convincing. Polly had been just the sort of over-confident, illogical, ideological young nut who would have deployed a sponge as a barrier to a liquid. Just the sort of cocky idiot who would have considered her principles more powerful than the laws of physics. On the other hand, she had not mentioned nything before. Jack struggled to think, not an easy thing with Polly's eyes burning into him, pleading for her life, a life he held so dear.

'Fifteen years old, Polly,' Jack said. 'That's all he'd be.'

'That's right, he's fifteen.'

With a tremendous effort of concentration Jack began to get over his initial shock and doubt, and began to regain control.

'Then where is he?' Jack asked. 'Doesn't a young boy need his mom?'

'He's at his gran's!' Polly replied, perhaps a shade too quickly, too desperately. 'She spoils him. Lets him drink alcopops.'

Jack knew now. 'One photograph, Polly,' he said.

'What?'

'I don't see one photograph. Not one. Show me a photograph of our son, Polly. As a baby, as a toddler, now. One photograph, Polly.'

Polly could see that the game was up. She'd known that she could not keep up the lie for long, long enough for a course of action to present itself, long enough perhaps for her to find a way to reach across her bed and press the panic button on the wall. But it was not to be.

'I . . . I don't have any,' she replied.

Polly had not wanted the abortion. She'd loved Jack so much and suddenly she had found herself still carrying a part of him. But at the time she'd felt that she had no choice: a seventeen-year-old girl with a fatherless baby? There'd been a girl like that in the year above

Polly at school. How Polly had pitied that girl, old before her time, her whole youth sacrificed for a single moment of passion. Polly loved Jack, despite what he had done to her, and she had wanted to keep his baby, but not in exchange for her life and that was how she had seen it at the time. At seventeen she had thought that having a baby would be the end of her life. What cruel and terrible irony to know now that had she kept it, it might have saved her life.

'I'm sorry, Polly,' Jack said.

And he was sorry, so very sorry that she had no child to give him. Sorry that they had not shared their lives together, sorry that he had ever left her in order to serve a cold, ungrateful country. Most of all, sorry that despite all that, he would still have to kill her.

Polly sensed his resolve hardening, sensed her life slipping away.

'You said you still loved me,' Polly pleaded, dropping to her knees.

'I do still love you,' Jack replied and for the second time that evening there were tears in his eyes.

'Then you can't kill me,' she begged.

'Polly,' said Jack, and it was almost as if it was he who was doing the pleading. 'Try to understand. If I make chairman of the joint chiefs, do you know what the next step could be for me?' Polly had started to sob. 'President. Yes, president. Leader of the world's only superpower. There was a time when men waged war all their lives over a few square miles of mud and huts. They sacrificed their sons and grandsons to defend a paltry tribal crown. People have fought and murdered in pursuit of power since the dawn of time. Rivers of blood have flowed for it. For little power, for nothing power! I have before me the possibility of being the leader of the world! The world, Polly! Your existence severely compromises that possibility. Are you seriously suggesting that with such a destiny within my grasp I should shrink from the killing of just one single soul?'

Well, there was a foolish question. Polly could see that, even through the blind terror of her tears.

'Of course I am, you bloody fool.'

'Because I love you?' Jack asked.

'I don't care why.'

'Love is the enemy of ambition, Polly,' Jack said. 'I made that decision sixteen years ago, in the early hours of the morning in a hotel room. There's no point going back on it now.'

'Jack!'

But Polly could see in Jack's eyes that her time was up.

'Like I said,' and his voice seemed to come from somewhere else, 'people die every day.'

Jack was a stranger to Polly now. She no longer recognized him. Whatever it was that she had loved in him had simply disappeared; all that remained was pride and ambition. It was as if had shut down his heart and soul, had removed himself emotionally from the scene. He had gone over this moment in his mind a thousand times and knew that he could not trust him-

self to say goodbye, he never had been able to say goodbye to Polly.

And so in his mind at least he stood apart. It was not
his finger squeezing the trigger but some other self, a
separate personality too strong to be denied. He
watched himself as the story unfolded, knowing the
sequence of events exactly, like a series of stills from an
old movie.

The soldier shoots the girl in the forehead. The girl
falls back upon her bed, stone dead. The soldier wipes
his eyes on the sleeve of his coat (he is surprised to discover how upset he is) and takes a last look round.
Confident that there is nothing of his left in the room
save for a single bullet, he picks up his bag and without
looking again at the dead girl he lets himself out of her
flat. Ensuring that his overcoat entirely covers his uniform, the soldier descends to the front door and, having
checked that there is nobody about in the street outside,
he quietly leaves the house. He then drives himself back
to the private hotel in Kensington in which he has been
staying, parks his plain hirecar in the private car park,
and returns to his bedroom. The following morning he
is collected in an army car and begins his journey to
Brussels in order to continue with the business of
NATO.

That was what was supposed to happen, anyway.

One bullet between the eyes and leave.

But Jack did not shoot. He had meant to, he had
been about to, but he had talked too long and he had
missed his chance. Because in what was to have been

Polly's final second on earth, at the point when Jack
began to draw his finger back on the flimsy resistance
of the trigger, there was a knock at Polly's door. More
than a knock – a bang, a thud, the crash of a body
throwing itself against the solid panels.

56

The Bug had remained frozen for some time after killing the milkman. He had stood on the sodden, sticky stair carpet, gaping at the corpse that he had made, wondering what on earth he could do now. He could, in fact, do anything, because it was all up for him. He had stabbed a man to death and there was no hope of escape from the consequences. The police knew that he was about and that he had a knife; his mother had made sure of that. They would put him away now, that much was sure, not just for a month or two but for ever. His life was over and it was so unfair. All he had been trying to do was protect her. He had acted always out of love.

And now he would never have her, not even once. He would be locked away from her, never again to feast his eyes upon her beauty. Even if they ever did let him out, which he doubted, she would have long since grown old and ugly.

Then a wicked thought began to grow in Peter's mind. He would have her, he would have her that very night, before the police arrived. He would go upstairs, kill the American and make love to Polly, rape her if she resisted. Why not? He had nothing left in the world to lose now. He was a murderer already and hadn't he earned his moment with her, earned it with his love? Surely even her cold heart would not expect him to go to prison without even once knowing that for which he had sacrificed his life.

Peter turned away from the dead milkman and bounded up the stairs, all caution forgotten. He knew that the corpse could be discovered at any moment and the alarm raised. He knew that if he was to act it must be immediately. If he was to have time to force himself upon Polly and justify the life of incarceration that he faced then it must be now.

At the top of the stairs the door to Polly's flat was closed as Peter had known it would be. He hurled his body against it, hammering with the fist of his left hand. In his right hand he still held the knife, his fingers clenched around the bloody hilt, sticky with his own blood and that of the milkman. Peter was no longer afraid of the American. He had killed once, he could kill again. The moment the door opened he would stab his hated rival and then force Polly to his will.

'Let me in, you slag!' he shouted. 'You've let him do it to you! Why not let me?'

Inside the flat Jack leapt to the door. Whatever it was that was going on outside the noise would surely wake the whole house. There would soon be irate figures in the stairwell and one of them would be bound to ring the police. Jack had only moments in which to silence this new menace.

He flung open the door. Outside stood the Bug, knife in hand. Peter was caught momentarily by surprise, but then lunged forward with a shout of triumph. But the Bug was no more of a threat to Jack than if he truly had been a bug. Jack stepped neatly aside and Peter stumbled forward into the room. In some ways even this pathetic circumstance was a small triumph for Peter. He was inside Polly's home for the very first time. He glanced round, trying to take it in, store it up, memorize more of Polly's life.

But Peter had no more need of memories.

Jack raised his pistol and shot the Bug, as he intended to shoot Polly, straight between the staring, gaping eyes. Peter was dead before he hit the floor. Jack then turned back to Polly in order to complete his self-appointed mission.

But it was too late. The Bug had foiled Jack's plan, providing Polly with a tiny window of opportunity in which to defend her life. For as Jack turned back towards her Polly was already reaching up to the head of her bed; her finger was already on the panic button. Instantly as she pushed it the room was filled with the noise of jangling bells and outside the open door the stairwell began to glow a jarring intermittent red as the alarm light installed there began to flash.

Jack met Polly's eye, a surprised look upon his face.

'It's connected to the police station!' Polly shouted, having to raise her voice in order to make herself heard above the jangling of the bells. 'They'll be here in two minutes at this time of night.'

Jack stood, gun in hand, and for the first time that night he seemed at a loss.

'Go, Jack!' Polly shouted. 'Run, get out now!'

But it was too late to run. Jack had killed a man; the bloodied corpse lay at his feet and the forces of the law were almost upon him. Even now he could hear a faint siren amidst the shrieking of the bells. They would be in the street in moments. There was no escape. Yes, he had killed Peter in self-defence, but there would still have to be a police investigation. Even if Polly stood by him, and there was no reason why she should, even if she kept his terrible threat to her life to herself, the whole story of their past must eventually come out. Then would come the suspicions and the whisperings. Why had he been in her flat that night? Why had he been carrying a gun? Despite what Jack had said to Polly, it was not common practice for American soldiers to go about London armed. At the very best, Jack's career would end in pathetic and contemptible disgrace, and at worst he would be imprisoned for manslaughter. What a mess.

Downstairs, a shrill woman's voice joined the chorus of complaint now ringing round the building. The whole house had been aroused.

'Run, Jack!' Polly repeated desperately 'Get out! Get out now!'

He loved her more in that moment than he had ever loved her. He had tried to kill her and yet still she cared for him. Such was the power of love, love which he had denied all his life, love which he had tried that night to murder. But he had failed and it was love not him that would survive.

The police were at the front door now. In a moment they would be in the house.

'I love you, Polly,' said Jack, 'but I don't deserve you and I do not deserve the trust of my country. I have failed in my duty and brought disgrace and dishonour upon everything I care for.'

Then, like a Roman general of old, Jack fell upon his sword. He raised his gun to his head and pulled the trigger. As his body fell towards her Polly tried to scream but found that she had no voice. All that she could do as he came to rest on the floor before her was silently mouth his name.

57

Nibs and her husband had made an uneasy peace. She would stand by him, even lie for him, and in return he had promised that this sordid little affair would be his last. He tried to kiss her to say thank you but she was not yet ready for that.

They had just ordered coffee when a knock came at the door.

'I said we weren't to be disturbed,' Nibs' husband said as his principal private secretary entered the room.

'I'm extremely sorry, Mr President, but the State Department felt that you should know this. I'm afraid that we have bad news from London. General Jack Kent seems to have shot himself. It looks like some kind of sex thing. He was in the apartment of an Englishwoman. Another man is dead also. We have no further details at present.'

The president and the first lady were horrified. They had both known Jack quite well. Nibs in particular knew Courtney Kent and could only imagine how she was feeling.

'I'll call Courtney,' she said and left the president with his aides.

'Jack Kent of all people,' the great commander said. 'We were going to propose him for chairman of the joint chiefs.'

The president was truly sorry to hear the news, but he was a politician and already he could see that from a personal point of view there was an upside to this tragedy. Jack's suicide would be enormously newsworthy, particularly if it did turn out that there was a sexual angle to the case. Anything that diverted attention from the president's own problems was to be welcomed.

'In the meantime there are practical considerations,' the president added. 'This is going to hit the army hard. We need to fill this gap and quickly, and, for Christ's sake, can we please try to find a clean pair of hands.'

A few days later, to his utter shock and abject terror, General Schultz, Jack's blundering, indecisive colleague, whose anonymous career had shadowed Jack's for so many years, was appointed chairman of the joint chiefs. He had turned out to be the only senior officer in the armed forces who had never done anything that anybody considered suspect. The reason for this being, of course, that General Schultz had never done anything.

Two years later Schultz's name would be spoken of as a potential presidential candidate for exactly the same reason.

'It isn't a case of who's most qualified these days,' the Washington powerbrokers had wearily to admit. 'It's a case of who's least likely to be disqualified.'

58

Despite the dreadful memories of that violent night, Polly decided to stay on in her flat. At first she had intended to move. The image of the Bug's corpse bleeding on her floor was not a pleasant one, but in the end she decided that the Bug had not managed to drive her out while he was alive and she was not going to let him do so now that he was dead. Besides, there was the memory of Jack to consider. He had died in that flat, and despite the awfulness of what he had planned Polly wanted to be the keeper of that memory.

Over the weeks that followed the night of Jack's return Polly tried to come to terms with what had happened to her. It was not an easy thing to do. Three men had died, and although she knew that none of their deaths was her fault she could not help but feel in some way responsible. The milkman weighed particularly upon Polly's mind. He had died at the hands of a man who was obsessed with her. Even now Polly was the classic stalker's victim, feeling guilty, taking the blame. Polly was in truth no more connected to or responsible for Peter's madness than had been the poor milkman, but she felt that she was. She wrote to the milkman's family saying how sorry she felt for what had happened and they wrote a polite but unfriendly letter back. She also wrote to the Bug's mother, expressing her sympathy and thanking her for alerting the police when she did. Peter's mother did not reply.

Then there was Jack, for whose memory there was to be no private grieving. His death and his past with Polly were now public property. What had remained so intensely private for so many years was now worldwide news. Both the American and British media bore down upon Stoke Newington like an invading army. The British were particularly excited; it is not often that a story comes along that is front-page in the US but has a genuine British connection. Polly could have made a fortune but instead she resolutely turned down every request for an interview. It all came out anyway. The press even tracked down Ziggy, who was living in a teepee in Anglesey. He told them what little he could remember in exchange for seven pints of cider and an ounce of rolling tobacco. In the end, of course, the furore died down, and the ringing and knocking at Polly's door became less and less frequent until finally it stopped altogether and Polly was left alone.

Not surprisingly, Polly did not recover easily from the horror of that night. She often found herself weeping. Though fine at work, when she got home at night the sadness returned and she would lie on her bed and cry. Of course, she knew that in one spectacular way her life was better than it had been for years: the Bug was dead and he would never harm her again. But Jack was also dead and before he had died he had killed their love. The memory of his betrayal, which had haunted her for so long, was now made tiny by his second and more terrible rejection. He had tried to sacrifice her for his ambition and when he had failed he had sacrificed himself. Polly's love for him and his love for Polly had not been enough to save him and now she was truly alone.

She was alone on the evening when the phone rang.

Polly never picked up the phone directly. Despite the fact that she no longer felt in any danger she always let the answerphone stand as a barrier between her and callers. If nothing else it shielded her from having conversations with Telecom sales staff about their various incomprehensible discount schemes.

'Hello,' said Polly's voice. 'There's no one here to take your call at the moment, but please leave a message after the tone. Thank you.'

Then Polly heard Jack.

She had been midway through a slice of toast, but her jaw froze in horror as those soft mellow American tones emanated from the machine.

'Hullo, this is a message for Polly. Polly Slade.'

Except it wasn't Jack. It was only nearly Jack. This voice was a little deeper, sleepier, almost.

'Look, you don't know me, Polly, but I know you, a little, at least I think I do. My name's Harry, Harry Kent. I'm Jack's brother. I found your number among his effects . . .'

Harry was not in London when he called, he was in

his little home and workshop in Iowa, alone, like Polly. They talked for a very long time, and when the time came to hang up they found that they both had more that they wished to say. Harry asked if Polly felt it would be appropriate for him to come and visit her in London when he had finished the kitchen dresser on which he was currently working. Polly said that she felt it would be.

A week or so after that Polly was sitting alone in her flat, wondering why she felt so nervous, when the expected buzz came. Harry was at the door. She let him in and waited for him to climb the stairs. She was wearing her nicest dress.

Even through the little spyhole in her door Polly recognized Harry immediately. He was like Jack but different, thinner, she thought, leaner, and his hair was longer. Polly opened the door. The eyes were just the same; that same sardonic twinkle. He smiled. She knew that smile also. It was not the same as Jack's, but similar. Perhaps Polly was fooling herself, but it seemed to her that it was kinder. She stepped back into her flat and let him in.

THE END

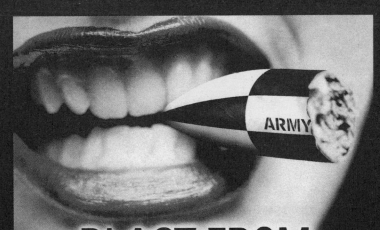

Inconceivable
Ben Elton

'EXTREMELY FUNNY, CLEVER, WELL-WRITTEN, SHARP AND
UNEXPECTEDLY MOVING . . . THIS BRILLIANT, CHAOTIC SATIRE
MERITS REREADING SEVERAL TIMES'
Nicholas Coleridge, *Mail on Sunday*

Lucy desperately wants a baby. Sam wants to write a hit movie. The
problem is that both efforts seem to be unfruitful. And given that the
average IVF cycle has about a one in five chance of going into full
production, Lucy's chances of getting what she wants are
considerably better than Sam's.

What Sam and Lucy are about to go through is absolutely
inconceivable. The question is, can their love survive?

Inconceivable confirms Ben Elton as one of Britain's most significant,
entertaining and provocative writers.

'THIS IS ELTON AT HIS BEST – MATURE, HUMANE, AND STILL
A LAUGH A MINUTE. AT LEAST'
Daily Telegraph

'A VERY FUNNY BOOK ABOUT A SENSITIVE SUBJECT . . .
BEN ELTON THE WRITER MIGHT BE EVEN FUNNIER
THAN BEN ELTON THE COMIC'
Daily Mail

'A TENDER, BEAUTIFULLY BALANCED ROMANTIC COMEDY'
Spectator

'MOVING AND THOROUGHLY ENTERTAINING'
Daily Express

Now filmed as *Maybe Baby*.

0 552 14698 6

BLACK SWAN

A SELECTED LIST OF FINE WRITING
AVAILABLE FROM CORGI AND BLACK SWAN

THE PRICES SHOWN BELOW WERE CORRECT AT THE TIME OF GOING TO PRESS. HOWEVER TRANSWORLD PUBLISHERS RESERVE THE RIGHT TO SHOW NEW RETAIL PRICES ON COVERS WHICH MAY DIFFER FROM THOSE PREVIOUSLY ADVERTISED IN THE TEXT OR ELSEWHERE.

99830 3	SINGLE WHITE E-MAIL	Jessica Adams	£6.99
99822 2	A CLASS APART	Diana Appleyard	£6.99
99842 7	EXCESS BAGGAGE	Judy Astley	£6.99
99619 X	HUMAN CROQUET	Kate Atkinson	£7.99
99786 2	NOTES FROM A BIG COUNTRY	Bill Bryson	£7.99
99824 9	THE DANDELION CLOCK	Guy Burt	£6.99
99853 2	LOVE IS A FOUR LETTER WORD	Claire Calman	£6.99
14698 6	INCONCEIVABLE	Ben Elton	£6.99
99751 X	STARCROSSED	A.A. Gill	£6.99
99759 5	DOG DAYS, GLENN MILLER NIGHTS	Laurie Graham	£6.99
99847 8	WHAT WE DID ON OUR HOLIDAY	John Harding	£6.99
99796 X	A WIDOW FOR ONE YEAR	John Irving	£7.99
99887 7	THE SECRET DREAMWORLD OF A SHOPAHOLIC	Sophie Kinsella	£6.99
99037 X	BEING THERE	Jerzy Kosinski	£5.99
99859 1	EDDIE'S BASTARD	William Kowalski	£6.99
99875 3	MAYBE THE MOON	Armistead Maupin	£6.99
99874 5	PAPER	John McCabe	£6.99
99905 9	AUTOMATED ALICE	Jeff Noon	£6.99
99803 6	THINGS CAN ONLY GET BETTER	John O'Farrell	£6.99
99718 8	IN A LAND OF PLENTY	Tim Pears	£7.99
99817 6	INK	John Preston	£6.99
99783 8	DAY OF ATONEMENT	Jay Rayner	£6.99
99846 X	THE WAR ZONE	Alexander Stuart	£6.99
99952 0	LIFE ISN'T ALL HA HA HEE HEE	Meera Syal	£6.99
99809 5	KICKING AROUND	Terry Taylor	£6.99
99819 2	WHISTLING FOR THE ELEPHANTS	Sandi Toksvig	£6.99

All Transworld titles are available by post from:

Bookpost, P.O. Box 29, Douglas, Isle of Man IM99 1BQ

Credit cards accepted. Please telephone 01624 836000,
fax 01624 837033 or Internet http://www.bookpost.co.uk.
or e-mail: bookshop@enterprise.net for details

Free postage and packing in the UK. Overseas customers: allow £1 per book (paperbacks) and £3 per book (hardbacks).